SCHOLARS IN COVID TIMES

A volume in the series

Publicly Engaged Scholars: Identities, Purposes, Practices

Edited by Anna Sims Bartel, Debra Ann Castillo, and Scott Peters

A list of titles in this series is available at cornellpress.cornell.edu.

SCHOLARS IN COVID TIMES

**Edited by Melissa Castillo Planas
and Debra A. Castillo**

CORNELL UNIVERSITY PRESS   ITHACA AND LONDON

Copyright © 2023 by Cornell University

All rights reserved. Except for brief quotations in a review, this book, or parts thereof, must not be reproduced in any form without permission in writing from the publisher. For information, address Cornell University Press, Sage House, 512 East State Street, Ithaca, New York 14850. Visit our website at cornellpress.cornell.edu.

First published 2023 by Cornell University Press

Library of Congress Cataloging-in-Publication Data

Names: Planas, Melissa Castillo, 1984– editor. | Castillo, Debra A., editor.
Title: Scholars in COVID times / edited by Melissa Castillo Planas and Debra A. Castillo.
Description: Ithaca, New York : Cornell University Press, 2023. | Series: Publicly engaged scholars: identities, purposes, practices | Includes bibliographical references and index.
Identifiers: LCCN 2022059520 (print) | LCCN 2022059521 (ebook) | ISBN 9781501771606 (hardcover) | ISBN 9781501771613 (paperback) | ISBN 9781501771620 (epub) | ISBN 9781501771637 (pdf)
Subjects: LCSH: COVID-19 Pandemic, 2020—Influence. | Learning and scholarship—History—21st century. | Social justice and education—History—21st century.
Classification: LCC AZ362 .S348 2023 (print) | LCC AZ362 (ebook) | DDC 001.209/05—dc23/eng/20230213
LC record available at https://lccn.loc.gov/2022059520
LC ebook record available at https://lccn.loc.gov/2022059521

Contents

Introduction: Considering Meaning for Scholars
During the Pandemic
Melissa Castillo Planas and Debra A. Castillo   1

Part 1   (EN)COUNTERING INTENSIFYING HOSTILITIES

1. Forming a Motherscholar Research Collaborative
*Motherscholar Collective: Helen K. Ho, Katharina A. Azim,
Summer Melody Pennell, Colleen C. Myles-Baltzly, N. A. Heller,
Maggie Campbell-Obaid, Meike Eilert, Ivanna Richardson,
Stacey H. Bender, Lucy C. Parker-Barnes, Sarah Key-DeLyria,
Stacey Lim, Jasmine L. Blanks Jones, Jennifer H. Greene-Rooks*   15

2. Timesoup, Missed Meaning, and Making a Pandemic
History
Courtney Naum Scuro   39

3. Resisting Anti-Asian Racism in Public-Facing Work
and Teaching
Joey S. Kim   59

4. Teaching German in the Settler Colonial University
Maureen O. Gallagher   74

Part 2   NEW PEDAGOGIES AND STRATEGIES

5. A Chicana Pedagogy for Digital Pen Pals
Diana Noreen Rivera and Leigh Johnson   93

6. Pandemic Community Engagement
Daniela M. Susnara, Victoria N. Shiver, and Jacob T. Peterson   119

7. Promoting Equity and Inclusion through Critical
Resilience Pedagogy
Rhian Morgan and Lisa Moody   131

8. Searching for *Ōtium* and Finding a Pedagogy of Escapism
*Alexander Lowe McAdams, with contributions by Nina Cook
and Annie Lowe*   152

vi CONTENTS

9. Performing Black Lives
Elaigwu P. Ameh   179

Part 3 **LOSSES AND DISAPPOINTMENTS**

10. Community Engaged Migration Research
Robert McKee Irwin and Juan Antonio Del Monte   205

11. Performing Connectedness across Public
and Digital Spaces
Debaroti Chakraborty   223

12. Negotiating and Rebuilding Civic Engagement
through Loss
Alicia Muñoz   243

Epilogue: Learning from Our Grief
Melissa Castillo Planas   261

Contributors   267
Index   273

SCHOLARS IN
COVID TIMES

Introduction

CONSIDERING MEANING FOR SCHOLARS DURING THE PANDEMIC

Melissa Castillo Planas and Debra A. Castillo

In December 2019 very few of us were attentive to reporting of a new virus that crossed to humans in China. When COVID-19 began to sweep around the world, our leaders, out of what they called an excess of caution, asked us all to take a two-week pause. Three years later, we pause again to look back on that time when pharmacies and liquor stores were considered equally essential businesses, when we had minipanics about incomprehensible shortages of toilet paper, masks, and hand sanitizer, and when we learned more about supply chains than we ever imagined possible. We invented new words—blursday, quarantini, podding—and, as the weeks stretched into months, we established new habits, while wondering what the "new normal" would look like. Parents experienced the chaos of working from home with their children in the background, and we academics learned novel ways of interacting with our students through the screens of newly ubiquitous technologies like Zoom and Google Meet and GoToMeeting.

We waited. Then we waited some more.

For all of us, life in 2022 includes unpredictable breaks for serious illness and for caretaking. Extended periods of time vanish into the not quite lockdown of what life looks like with continual waves of COVID-19. We struggle through, by turns, feeling anxious, suffering exhaustion, and being overwhelmed. We scramble to register fragmented events that never quite cohere into a clear narrative. In the midst of the demoralizing turmoil, the recurrent fact of illness becomes the most salient experience, and life a precarious matter of marking time between infections. To borrow from a prescient comment by Lisa Baraitser, this book is a succinct diary "underpinned by a quiet affinity to ideas of time that fails to unfold."[1] Time passes but remains the same; it is not *timely*, it never comes to an end.

Nonetheless, at the height of the pandemic, inside our homes, domestic violence reached an all-time high. Outside our windows, gun violence spiked in the United States and war broke out in Ukraine. We witnessed an attempted coup against the US government by Donald Trump and perhaps participated in protests about disregard for Black and Asian lives, women's reproductive independence, and climate change. We watched California and Europe burn in wildfires and record heat. We obsessed over the news, we binge-watched films, we reread Boccaccio, and we thought about escape, and return, and remembering. We ruminated about how to go on living and how to maintain community in isolation.

From the beginning of the SARS-CoV-2 pandemic in late 2019 to late 2022, six hundred million people have contracted the disease, and six and a half million people worldwide have died from COVID-19, vastly changing the landscape of daily life.[2] Yet the havoc wreaked by the pandemic is by no means equally distributed spatially or temporally. From the early ravages in China and Europe at the end of 2019, and the overwhelming of the health systems in Italy and New York City in early 2020, to the devastation in India a year later, then in Latin America in summer 2021, and South Africa in 2022, the implacable spread of the disease, with its uneven temporalities and morbidities, highlights both the commonalities we share as susceptible human beings as well as the many fragmentations of our societies. Alpha, Beta, Delta, Lambda, Omicron, BA-5—in 2022 we wonder which variant in the Greek alphabet of viral mutations will be the next to strike our communities. The rapid development and uneven deployment of vaccines—an unwanted excess going to waste in the United States, even as a majority of countries with little or no access to lifesaving vaccines clamor for them—further exacerbate tensions.

The ongoing challenge remains how to tell the story of the many waves of the pandemic, which continues to afflict our society in late 2022, even as some of our friends declare it over, which is an act of magical thinking. Humans think in narrative; stories help us make sense. How can we grasp underlying ideas and determine what to do next? In the United States, in the early months of the COVID-19 panic, creative writers came together in the Decameron Project, stories first published in *The New York Times Magazine* in July 2020, an homage simultaneously to escapism and unforgetting; in the brief performative monologues commissioned by the Breath of Fire Latina Theater Ensemble in August 2020 (imagined as a living altar, because "there was so much loss and nowhere to put our grief"); and in the creative documentation by novelists such as Charles Finch.[3]

While we in industrialized countries locked ourselves into our apartments with our windows onto the world framed by competing real and fake social media, essential workers were exposed to the virus on the streets and in the fields, factories, and hospitals. We had to rethink the importance of our own work when "essential" was defined by human contact or by backbreaking physical labor. "Is normalcy obsolete?" asked Frank Bruni in a December 2020 *New York Times* editorial.[4] Is that the right question to ask? Certainly, much of the world's population does not have the luxury to choose what is normal or what form their labor may take. What is normal? What is relevant? What is essential, and what is superfluous?

After decades of humanist resistance to homogenizing stories in favor of a multiplicity of diverse voices, suddenly, the background hum of the universalized narrative is absent. Thus, the economists Klaus Schwab and Thierry Maloret capture the yearning of our moment in a book whose title would be almost unthinkable in the years just before COVID-19, when culture studies scholars devoted enormous energy to tearing down the concept of their book. *The Great Narrative* is not quite as coherent as the title indicates, of course. In the book, the authors bring together in a breezy, informal concatenation the voices of fifty thinkers interviewed between January and November 2021. These were organized via a follow-up brainstorming session in Dubai, "a most propitious place to elaborate a Great Narrative as, to our knowledge, the UAE is the only country in the world to have a 'Ministry of Possibilities.'"[5]

In early 2020, the novelist and activist Arundhati Roy insightfully explored the implications of the looming catastrophe in "The Pandemic Is a Portal."[6] While much of this April 3 article is necessarily dated, Roy's clearsighted indictment of a nostalgia for normality is worth recalling:

> Whatever it is, coronavirus has made the mighty kneel and brought the world to a halt like nothing else could. Our minds are still racing back and forth, longing for a return to "normality", trying to stitch our future to our past and refusing to acknowledge the rupture. But the rupture exists. And in the midst of this terrible despair, it offers us a chance to rethink the doomsday machine we have built for ourselves. Nothing could be worse than a return to normality.
>
> Historically, pandemics have forced humans to break with the past and imagine their world anew. This one is no different. It is a portal, a gateway between one world and the next.

Roy points to a recurrent theme: the pandemic pause has given us opportunities to rethink our sense of place in the larger order of planetary existence, to consider how we can contribute to a planetary remaking. Schwab and Maloret's work, both in *The Great Narrative* and their earlier book, *COVID 19: The Great Reset*, privileges the concepts of ingenuity and foresightedness. Roy is pointing to something a bit different. Implicit in both Roy's and Bruni's work is a recognition that the ruling concept of the "normal" and the capitalist idea of success respond to an unspoken great narrative in which value is assigned to public action (the hero's quest) and very specific kinds of achievement. Only certain actions count, obviously—those of servants, slaves, essential workers, and domestic laborers throughout human history have always had to remain invisible for the heroes' actions to shine. It is this very narrative of progress and success that must be interrogated.

The pandemic, furthermore, has interrupted certain hierarchies and instated others, such as the stay-at-home orders that forced an engagement with the traditionally feminine sphere of the home and the traditionally feminine role of waiting. As Rosario Castellanos wrote in the mid-twentieth century, "*La única actitud lícita de la feminidad es la espera*" ("waiting is the only licit act of femininity").[7] Despite its imposition on much of the human race for many centuries as a proper and appropriate feminine state, the time of waiting has had little narrative value and no moral purchase.

How do we process this pandemic experience, as scholars, teachers, community activists, and human beings? Many commentators looked to the 1918 Spanish flu epidemic as our nearest correlate; others looked further back in history to the Black Death of the mid-1300s. Optimists like Scott Galloway focus on opportunity. His perspective comes from his background as a business school professor and entrepreneur. His November 2020 book, *Post Corona*, pointing to the growth of e-commerce as an example, hopefully imagines vast changes in health care, education, and food supply possibilities. "The coming of age in a worldwide crisis," he writes, "has the power to mature a generation with a renewed appreciation for community, cooperation, and sacrifice."[8] For his part, Bruno Latour begins his story of a potential opportunity for reorientation of human endeavor with a metaphor of a termite and story of metamorphosis, as if lockdown were a cocoon and we all emerge from it with wings.[9] In a similar vein, Toby Miller's manifesto, *A COVID Charter, A Better World*, written from Mexico City, cautiously imagines a better world; Schwab and Maloret's Dubai brainstorming projects a better future.[10]

Scholars come to new and humbling understandings of themselves with all their human quirks. Both Christopher Schaberg's and Kristin Ann Hass's books (*Pedagogy of the Depressed* and *Being Human during COVID*, respectively) take the form of episodic chronicles of the first year of the pandemic from the perspective of a classroom teacher who struggles to imagine effective pedagogical strategies while lives are upturned by waiting and not waiting, grieving losses, and celebrating resilience.[11] Ironically, in both cases, the obligatory turn to online formats made them more aware of social justice commitments and the need for greater community engagement. Likewise, then-MLA president Judith Butler, a philosopher known mostly for her contributions to abstract theoretical thought, made a strong argument in her column in the fall 2020 *MLA Newsletter*, "The Future of Humanities PhDs," for a shift in focus toward public scholarship and public engagement:

> By strengthening the public humanities as part of graduate training, we have a chance to make clear to nonspecialists within educational institutions and the public sphere the value of what we do and how our commitment to education can help strengthen traditions of public writing, discourse, storytelling, and critical engagement. . . . A new imagining that restructures higher education for PhDs is required to combat climate change and racism, to establish all the lives considered dispensable as indispensable and invaluable, and to build shared life that reverses the social and racial inequalities intensifying in these nearly crushing times.[12]

Still, much of the scholarship coming out of the pandemic focuses on the issue of meaningful instruction and has generated how-to books, such as the very early (July 2020) book, *Perspectives on Higher Education: Impact of the COVID-19 Pandemic*, edited by Abdulrahman O Al-Youbi, Abdulmonem Al-Hayani, and Judy McKim.[13] Unlike the optimistic turns from the economists, philosophers, and other writers briefly referenced previously, the general tenor of these studies is grim. In this respect, higher education studies reflect concerns echoed from reports in journalistic sources, in which the titles themselves become a sobering litany of seemingly unsurmountable challenges: "On the Verge of Burnout: ," "What We've Lost in a Year of Virtual Teaching," and "My College Students Are Not OK," for example. Christopher Schaberg, for instance, echoes the title of Paulo Freire's *Pedagogy of the Oppressed*, with its hope of revolutionary *conscientizacao* and societal change, but alters it to *Pedagogy of the Depressed*, the story of a bewildering slog through depression, a dread shared by students and their professors about something irremediably gone wrong.[14]

Life is now immensely different from prepandemic times. For those of us working in academia, new practices range from social distancing and masking to online schooling and remote work. We have a new vocabulary for our everyday teaching encounters and new assignment structures for our students. Consciousness of risk and contagion has thrown all expectations of regular attendance out the window. For the publicly engaged scholar, we have had to rethink the ways we conduct research and engage with community. The pandemic has taught us to question the separation that we impose on our professional and private personas as well as the hierarchization of knowledge practices such divisions also demand. In this respect, the disruption of COVID-19 to our daily lives has given us an opportunity to reflect and to reexamine how and where we live, work, and interact.

This volume documents some of these new forms of scholarship, community collaboration, and teaching in an era of contestation and crisis, detailing novel ways of thinking about what it means to be a publicly engaged scholar in the era of COVID-19. We see new forms of interaction, new spaces of creativity and exchange, and a new shape to human resilience in the face of seismic challenges.

The authors in part 1, "(En)Countering Intensifying Hostilities," grapple with the way COVID-19 heightened existing animosities toward mothers in academia and Asian American women in the United States and forced those in predominantly white studies to rethink the fields given the focus the pandemic placed on historically rooted social disparities and racial injustice. Chapter 1, "Forming a Motherscholar Research Collaborative," serves as a response by over a dozen scholars and mothers from various disciplines of a larger collective. This collective was formed to address how COVID-19 exacerbated long-standing inequities for mothers pursuing careers in academia. Through a cultivation of a philosophy of *radical feminist flexibility*, the collective advocates for the value of "motherscholars" in academic institutions while also demonstrating possibilities for collaborative scholarship and community building that support this group and could be implemented on a wider scale. For many motherscholars, a lack of time due to parenting duties as well as change in the way work time and personal time are understood are major impacting factors of the pandemic. In chapter 2, "Research, Missed Meaning, and Making a Pandemic History," Courtney Naum Scuro, a premodern scholar and mother, shares experiences from the first summer of the pandemic in 2020 to consider the misuse and potential contributions of premodern literature to considerations of how one lives and studies during this time. Through this meditation on time, Naum Scuro invites us to "consider closely how one's ideas about living become defined by experiences of time and especially, the material repercussions that these can effect."

Chapters 3 and 4 of this part ask us to consider our responses to heightened racism, xenophobia, and social injustice laid bare by the unequal effects of the pandemic from two seemingly unlikely scholarly points of view. In "Resisting Anti-Asian Racism in Public-Facing Work and Teaching," Joey S. Kim, a scholar trained in British romanticism, describes her experience as "an East Asian woman of assumed Chinese descent" who must balance the real threat of violence against her body while also navigating both demands from outside academia for public engagement and her transition onto the tenure track. While reflecting on the historical patterns of Orientalism and Asian exclusion that have given rise to anti-Asian sentiment and violence during the COVID-19 pandemic, Kim shares how this experience influenced her teaching and motivated her move into more publicly engaged scholarship. And in chapter 4, Maureen O. Gallagher shares her story as a German studies scholar hired to teach at an Australian university, remote teaching for over a year "9,000 miles and fifteen time zones away from campus." She shares the way that dislocation inspired her to think about land acknowledgements and settler colonialism in higher education. Thus in this chapter Gallagher argues for the importance of a decolonialization of universities that centers indigenous lives and thought to think critically about "the intersecting and interconnected histories of colonization that underlie modern academic work."

Like many of us who pivoted to online teaching with little notice when the pandemic reached our respective universities, the scholars in part 2, "New Pedagogies and Strategies," struggled to translate existing instructional practices and projects online. The five chapters that make up this part describe the success of digital strategies, including pen pal exchanges via e-mail, virtual community engagement programs with local youth, online Australian pathways programs as alternative entryways into higher education, and producing theater during a pandemic that also responds to urgent issues like Black Lives Matter.

Chapter 5, "A Chicana Pedagogy for Digital Pen Pals," is written by Noreen Rivera and Leigh Johnson, scholars of Mexican American/Chicanx/Latinx literature at two very different institutions: University of Texas Rio Grande Valley (UTRGV), a multicampus HSI (Hispanic-serving institution) in South Texas near the United States-Mexico border, and Marymount University, a private Catholic institution, recently granted HSI status, with a diverse international student population, in Arlington, Virginia. Rivera and Johnson detail the way they pivoted their year-long planning for study-away trips with their students to each other's campuses by focusing on one aspect of the trip preparation: digital pen pal exchanges. Adding to a robust body of literature on the benefits of pen pal writing in higher education, Rivera and Johnson highlight the possibility of digital partnerships across diverse campuses that respond to "urgent sociopolitical, public health and educational challenges" as part of their pedagogical commitment to a socially conscious study of literature. As Rivera and Johnson were honing in on the possibilities of pandemic pen pals as a way to connect students of diverse ethnic, racial, social, geographical, and other backgrounds to diverse authors, Elaigwu Ameh was also struggling with how to respond as a theater scholar and Black man working in higher education to both the pandemic and to Black Lives Matter. For Ameh, the need to respond within his college became even more urgent when a Black resident of the predominately white town where Grinnell College is located was gruesomely murdered in a very public manner. In chapter 9, "Performing Black Lives," he details his student-centered, online, and in-person process of creation, which resulted in a series of spoken word experiences that was also the college's first mainstage production with an entirely Black cast, Black director, Black playwright, and student director.

Between these two chapters in the part are three chapters that address how to continue creating accessible pathways to higher education for underserved communities. In chapter 6, "Pandemic Community Engagement," Daniela M. Susnara, Victoria N. Shiver, and Jacob T. Peterson (all at the University of Alabama) describe how they transitioned their community engagement youth summer programs, Swim to the Top (STTT) and the STEM Entrepreneurship Academy (SEA). In particular, the swimming program for youth aged four to fourteen required immense creativity and a shift in curriculum goals since swimming pools were closed over the summer of 2020. Despite the challenges, Susnara, Shiver, and Peterson outline the relevance of virtual programs and the meaningful experiences of these programs for both the youth participants and the university students who served as staff while also providing suggestions for future virtual community engagement practices.

Similarly, in chapter 7, "Promoting Equity and Inclusion through Critical Resilience Pedagogy," Rhian Morgan and Lisa Moody outline shifting pathways programs, which in Australia provide tertiary education for individuals who do not meet the traditional entry requirements for university, to an online format while also satisfying the requirements of the federal "higher education relief package." In particular, Morgan and Moody balance institutional discourse around "core skills" with their implementation of "Critical Resistance Pedagogy," which both honors student's lived experiences and forms a basis for community building in an online setting. Finally, in chapter 8, "Searching for *Ōtium* and Finding a Pedagogy of Escapism," Alexander Lowe McAdams shares her reflections on how running a civic humanities program during the pandemic shutdown developed her pedagogy. Specifically, while revising a program for urban high school students to experience college-level humanities seminars at Rice University, Adams developed what she terms a Pedagogy of Escapism. This pedagogy is based in "nonevaluative learning experiences" and borrows from the ancient Imperial Roman concept of *ōtium*, a principle of relaxed repose that is completely absent of labor. This alternative approach responds to the rigid structure of state-mandated curricula and is founded on the bedrock of accommodation via an engagement with disability studies. All three of these chapters, 6 through 8, also reflect on what was learned that continues to be useful pedagogically after the quarantine phase of the pandemic and what has been left as a relic of that experience, whether purposefully or due to institutional decisions.

INTRODUCTION 9

Part 3, "Losses and Disappointments," provides a very different space of reflection than many other volumes that address COVID-19 and higher education. While still exploring strategies for pandemic scholarship and teaching, it also provides an opportunity to grieve what was lost during extended lockdowns. In chapter 10, "Community Engaged Migration Research," Robert McKee Irwin, founder of the Humanizing Deportation digital storytelling project at University of California–Davis, and Juan Antonio Del Monte, cultural studies scholar at El Colegio de la Frontera Norte, detail the tremendous challenges and resulting frustrations of being largely unable to continue their community engaged scholarship projects with migrants due to lockdowns and travel restrictions. Accustomed to working in person on the ground in support of migrants arriving at the United States-Mexico border, Irwin and Del Monte criticize "inflexible institutional policies" that kept them from not only documenting this population during the pandemic but most importantly assisting them. Irwin and Del Monte also reflect on the lessons they learned as they returned to in-person work in 2021.

Writing from densely populated urban India, Debaroti Chakraborty ponders touch and absence as a professor at a public university and artist researcher in Chapter 11, "Performing Connectedness Across Public and Digital Spaces." Through these reflections, she describes her pedagogical shifts for virtual learning to build shared spaces of creativity and community that ultimately resulted in an immersive digital performance series titled Performing Connectedness. Finally, from Minneapolis, Minnesota, Alicia Muñoz describes her struggles to adapt her course's civic engagement component to a virtual classroom while also attempting to build a relationship with a new community partner. Contemplating the popularized pandemic term, "pivot," Muñoz writes "Yet, pivot is a facile term, obscuring the substance of loss and extraction left in its wake." Significantly, Muñoz details her experience on how to build an authentic relationship with a community partner while also recognizing what could not be accomplished.

This is a timely book by scholars from across the English-speaking world, addressing these issues from a wide range of disciplines and fields. As such, it has no pretensions to a homogeneous tone. What the contributors have in common is their flexibility and creativity in adapting and developing strategies to stay engaged in our local/national/international communities as core aspects of research and teaching. It is a volume that challenges us as scholars to think about the meaning and significance of engaged scholarship and teaching during a period that laid bare both the vast global inequities and our connectedness around the world. Together we reflect on what we overcame and what we learned. We also mourn what we lost, recognizing that "normal" is a term of the past.

NOTES

1. Baraitser, *Enduring Time*, 20.
2. Worldometer. Accessed July 20, 2022. https://www.worldometers.info/coronavirus/.
3. See http://decameronproject.org; Burbano, "Literary Manager's Note," 7.
4. Bruni, "Is Normalcy Obsolete?"
5. Schwab and Maloret, *Great Narrative*, 19.
6. Roy, "Pandemic Is a Portal."
7. Castellanos, *Mujer que sabe latin*, 14.
8. Galloway, *Post Corona*, xxi.
9. Latour, *After Lockdown*.
10. Miller, *COVID Charter*; Schwab and Maloret, *Great Narrative*.
11. Schaberg, *Pedagogy of the Depressed*; Hass, *Being Human*.
12. Butler, "Future of Humanities PhDs," 2.
13. Al-Youbi, Al-Hayani, and McKim, *Perspectives on Higher Education*.
14. "On the Verge of Burnout": Covid19's Impact on Faculty Well-Being and Career Plans," 2020, https://connect.chronicle.com/rs/931-EKA-218/images/Covid%26Faculty CareerPaths_Fidelity_ResearchBrief_v3%20%281%29.pdf; "What We've Lost in a Year of Virtual Teaching," February 17, 2021, https://www.chronicle.com/article/what-weve-lost -in-a-year-of-virtual-teaching; Malesic, "My College Students Are Not OK"; Freire, *Pedagogy*; Schaberg, *Pedagogy*.

BIBLIOGRAPHY

Al-Youbi, Abdulrahman O, Abdulmonem Al-Hayani, and Judy McKim, eds. "Perspectives on Higher Education: Impact of the COVID-19 Pandemic" (McKimm Consulting, 2020).

Baraitser, Lisa. *Enduring Time*. London: Bloomsbury, 2017.

Bruni, Frank. "Is Normalcy Obsolete?" *New York Times*, December 27, 2020.

Burbano, Diana, ed. *The COVID Monologues: 54 Writers Respond to the Pandemic*. Santa Ana, CA: Breath of Fire Latina Theater Ensemble, 2020.

Butler, Judith. "The Future of Humanities PhDs." *MLA Commons*. November 18, 2020. https://president.mla.hcommons.org/2020/11/18/the-future-of-humanities-phds/

Castellanos, Rosario. *Mujer que sabe latin*. Ciudad de México: Fondo de cultura económica, 1973.

Chan, Roy Y., Krishna Bista, and Ryan M. Allen, eds. *Online Teaching and Learning in Higher Education during COVID-19*. New York: Routledge, 2022.

"The Decameron Project." *New York Times Magazine*, July 12, 2020.

Finch, Charles. *What Just Happened: Notes on a Long Year*. New York: Knopf, 2021.

Freire, Paulo. *Pedagogy of the Oppressed*. Trans. Mayra Bergman Ramos. New York: Continuum, 2005.

Galloway, Scott. *Post Corona: From Crisis to Opportunity*. New York: Penguin, 2020.

Hass, Kristin Ann. *Being Human during COVID*. Ann Arbor: University of Michigan Press, 2021.

Kumar, C. Raj, Mousumi Mukherjee, Tatiana Belousova, and Nisha Nair. *Global Higher Education During and Beyond COVID-19*. Singapore: Springer, 2022.

Latour, Bruno. *After Lockdown: A Metamorphosis*. Translated by Julie Rose. Cambridge: Polity, 2021.

Malesic, Jonathan. "My College Students Are Not OK." *New York Times*, May 13, 2022, https://www.nytimes.com/2022/05/13/opinion/college-university-remote -pandemic.html.

INTRODUCTION 11

Miller, Toby. *A COVID Charter, A Better World.* New Brunswick: Rutgers University Press, 2021.

Roy, Arundhati. "The Pandemic Is a Portal." *Financial Times*, April 3, 2020.

Schaberg, Christopher. *Pedagogy of the Depressed.* New York: Bloomsbury Academic, 2022.

Schwab, Klaus, and Thierry Maloret, *COVID-19: The Great Reset.* Cologny, Switzerland: Forum Publishing, 2020.

Schwab, Klaus, and Thierry Maloret, *The Great Narrative: For a Better Future.* Cologny, Switzerland: Forum Publishing, 2022.

Part 1

(EN)COUNTERING INTENSIFYING HOSTILITIES

1

FORMING A MOTHERSCHOLAR RESEARCH COLLABORATIVE

*Motherscholar Collective: Helen K. Ho, Katharina A. Azim,
Summer Melody Pennell, Colleen C. Myles-Baltzly,
N. A. Heller, Maggie Campbell-Obaid, Meike Eilert,
Ivanna Richardson, Stacey H. Bender,
Lucy C. Parker-Barnes, Sarah Key-DeLyria,
Stacey Lim, Jasmine L. Blanks Jones,
Jennifer H. Greene-Rooks*

Before the pandemic I basically suffered in silence. . . . Now that the pandemic has hit, all of the stuff that we [motherscholars] do constantly to try to juggle all of our lives and our responsibilities as parents . . . has just been completely exposed. So, the struggle that we've gone through is now completely out in the open for everyone to see.

—Francis, motherscholar

I'm in a situation . . . where I'm working fully remotely and all [three] of my young kids are also home with me. And I just feel like I'm being torn in a million directions all at once and [have] no time to think or focus or reflect on anything.

—Sara, motherscholar

The challenges of being a mother in academia were well documented even prior to the COVID-19 pandemic, especially vis-á-vis difficulties associated with establishing an adequate work-life balance. The demands of parenting, paired with the extra service responsibilities absorbed by women at colleges and universities, have been shown to detract from women's available time for research and scholarship, which can hinder career advancement.[1] For these women, who we term motherscholars, these professional challenges coexist alongside the emotional and psychological challenges of new parenthood.

New parenthood, and new motherhood in particular, can be isolating. New mothers have found support through social networking sites; they reported their participation in these groups helped reduce some of the stress surrounding new motherhood.[2] Similarly, research has demonstrated that educators have used social networking sites as sources for professional development,[3] to seek early career support, to further pedagogical skills,[4] or to garner advice and support in navigating hostile work environments.[5] As the COVID-19 pandemic further isolated mothers of infants with work closures and stay-at-home orders, social networking proved an important source of support for people in private and professional spaces.[6]

For academic mothers of young children, virtual mutual-support groups serve as a sounding board for discussing personal and professional challenges. This was especially helpful during the pandemic. Through online conversations, mothers discovered that the pandemic struggles of parents of young children were presented by institutions as individual problems, when in fact these ongoing barriers are systemic rather than circumstantial.[7] The neoliberal framing of collective struggles as personal failures results in an overarching narrative of motherhood-as-liability and families-as-complications to overcome, rather than a true discussion of historic oppression, exclusion, and sexism in academic and policy spaces.

Examples of systemic disparities include greater household and childcare responsibilities compared to male academics, differences in teaching and service or mentoring loads, and less protected research time,[8] among others. During the COVID-19 pandemic, systemically problematic policies exacerbated inequities for academics with young children. Limited cultural and social support in academic departments and programs were heightened, and new parents surrounded by older colleagues or those with older children found themselves faced with impossible expectations. These were often accompanied by administrators' failure to acknowledge the increased burdens of working and parenting during a pandemic, along with the denial of essential accommodations for those managing full-time parenting and scholarship.[9] Because academic culture obscures the realities of parenting among faculty and students, virtual spaces came to constitute a protected space for having those conversations.

Challenges associated with parenting and working full-time during the pandemic compounded existing inequities for women in the workforce.[10] Women left the workforce at faster rates than men, and one in four women reported plans to leave their jobs or slow their careers due to COVID-19.[11] These trends extended to academia as well: eighty-six percent of female tenured professors reported increased workloads,[12] and women with children reported having less research time each day compared to their colleagues without children.[13] Minello and colleagues stress scholars' needs for "time, silence, and concentration" to succeed in the academy,[14] and young children during the pandemic made all three practically impossible to find. Pivoting to remote or virtual instruction required an increase in time devoted to teaching, and, as a result, research time was replaced by teaching preparations and course management. These time constraints resulted in even more disparities regarding typical measures of scholars' success, as evidenced by a reduction in peer-reviewed articles from female authors[15] and, in particular, Black female authors.[16]

This gap widens the professional divide between academic women with children and their male and childless colleagues, negatively impacting mothers' professional advancement with tenure and promotion. Another gap revolves around the representation of, and equity for, mothers of color.[17] Mothers of color already face many systemic barriers, including systemic racism, classism, sexism, and other negative mental and physical health outcomes regardless of a pandemic; additionally, they were and continue to be exposed to increased academic and societal triggers related to postpartum depression and anxiety. Mothers of color also experience challenges related to hiring, promotion, and tenure due to the intersectional "-isms" they experience (including but not limited to racism, sexism, classism).[18] During the COVID-19 crisis and afterward, mothers of color were (and still are) expected to compartmentalize the reality that members of Black and Latinx communities die disproportionately due to structural health and social inequities.[19] For example, many mothers of color are deprived of medical and mental health care due to macroscale gentrification and displacement of resources and experience infertility and poorer birth outcomes regardless of socioeconomic status.[20] Mothers of color also thus contend with repeated race-related stressors and less social network support than their white counterparts and men.[21] In addition, motherscholars of color receive less workplace and career support.[22] While some undoubtedly succeed in academic and occupational worlds, for example, by successfully achieving raises, promotions, and tenure, motherscholars of color continue to face incredible social and professional pressures such as increased service work and tokenism.[23]

In this way, the COVID-19 pandemic has highlighted the complex ways that intersecting social and professional identities are impacted by systemic oppression. Already gathering online for support as parents in academia, the group discussed in this chapter found urgency in seeking new ways to support each other as mothers* and scholars, and adopting radical flexibility to account for diverse needs and demands at every stage of parenting and professional life. Specifically, members approached the founding of the Motherscholar Collective, and the ongoing work within it, as aligned with the spirit of "alliance and resistance" among academic mothers. This is described by Low and Damian, who recommend collaboration over competition and suggest that the perspectives of mothers in the academy, including struggles that may come with the dual role of being a motherscholar, be welcomed.[24] Lapayese defines the term mother-scholar as a woman who holds academic positions in higher education institutions and navigates the gendered space of academia.[25] The term encompasses the intersectional identities of mother and scholar and the negotiation of the various personal and professional roles attached to these identities.

Members of the Motherscholar Collective are scholars who understand and empathize with the dynamic and compounding challenges of parenting and scholarship and support practices that enable the dual roles of motherscholars (e.g., chestfeeding or pumping during meetings, leaving meetings to care for children, welcoming babies and other children in the meetings). As highlighted by Matias, and as reflected in the Collective's work since the start of the pandemic, the identities of mother and scholar do not merely exist parallel to each other but are entangled and enmeshed.[26] The group practices radical inclusivity, allowing and acknowledging each individual to be both a mother* and scholar in tandem. In describing the shared experiences as motherscholars, the Collective seeks to be both radically flexible as well as radically inclusive—leading us to use an asterisk with the term *mother** as a way of highlighting and acknowledging the complex identities of the Collective members. Not all members of the Collective are cisgender women, and some may use a different parental name that (better) suits their gender identity. In addition, the Collective welcomes and supports motherscholars with intersecting identities related to disability, graduate student status, race/ethnicity, and LGTBQ+ status.[27] While we use mother* to describe the motherscholar members of the collective, mother (without asterisk) references general conversations around the topic.

This chapter documents the formation of the Motherscholar Collective, a working group centered around a philosophy of *radical feminist flexibility*; the impetus for establishing the Collective; and the ways this model might inform the work/life of academic mothers* and the broader research community. The Collective hopefully serves as inspiration for future collaborative research as well as a call to the research community that the dual identity of motherscholar is valuable to the advancement of knowledge and should be better supported by academic institutions.

The difference between the norms and standards prepandemic and, importantly, outside of a radically flexible and inclusive group like the Motherscholar Collective (referred to hereafter as the Collective), is that those who differ from the academic norm (i.e., white, cisgender, heterosexual, and male) get left behind. In contrast, implicit and explicit shared norms that allow for flexibility and that nurture research innovations challenge normative expectations and expand scholarly opportunities. The work of the Collective has revealed that the research process can be different from the status quo, allowing for flexibility and more inclusive pathways to success and making space for another way forward.

Social Media Community Networks and How to Leverage Them as Motherscholars

> Somehow in a pandemic, I figured out how to do a pipeline of research in a way that I never did before, and the Collective is part of that. . . . I feel like I'm a researcher. I'm a real researcher, I'm doing research! But then also I have such support with a collective and larger mamas group that I also kind of know how to "mom"—if I can use it as a verb—I'm not as clueless as I thought. . . . I'm doing well at both and that feels good. . . . I'm more capable than I realized. . . . I read all this work before I had a baby that said, "Don't have a baby on the tenure track. That's a terrible idea. It's the worst time," and we're freaking doing it, we're surviving, and in a pandemic! . . . I feel more capable than I realized. . . . My personal identity is a mom and . . . a scholar.
>
> —Jamie, motherscholar

While there is a paucity of research on social networking sites specifically related to academic mothers, there has been research on social networking communities (such as on Facebook) for academics/educators and, separately, for mothers/parents. Educators use social networking to identify professional development opportunities,[28] to seek support from fellow colleagues who have more experience in the field, or to gather advice for navigating hostile work environments.[29] Similarly, social networking sites like Facebook have been used by mothers seeking support in parenting their children. In their study, Holtz and colleagues noted that mothers and mothers-to-be found their Facebook group to be more convenient than other online groups and that the social and parenting support it generated reduced their levels of stress; higher levels of social support have been associated with a higher sense of well-being and better sleep patterns.[30] Social network groups provide not only information but also advice and support in an environment that feels safe to their members.[31]

Social distancing during the COVID-19 pandemic severely restricted opportunities for in-person interactions, compounding anxieties around work and new motherhood.[32] The American Psychological Association recommended that maintaining social relationships via technological means would aid in building a sense of normalcy and alleviating anxiety.[33] As the COVID-19 pandemic plunged motherscholars into a space where the lines between parenting, teaching, and research blurred, online social networks became an important resource not only for socioemotional support but also for advice in navigating challenges in pedagogy, work responsibilities, and family duties.

A unique benefit of a social networking group for motherscholars is that it allows its members to integrate the dual identities of mother and scholar. Mothers may be less visible in academia, with some academic mothers choosing not to talk about their children at work because of the negative perceptions of motherhood as a liability.[34] Moreover, mothers in academia face systemic gender inequities (e.g., higher teaching and service expectations) while still being expected to be productive researchers.[35] On top of these challenges, motherscholars are often the primary caregivers at home.[36]

Motherscholars cope with competing demands in myriad ways. Some meet high professional expectations by working during their infants' rest times, sacrificing personal well-being to maintain their identity as a researcher. They ask, "Could I not allow myself to rest and recover? While negotiating a myriad of emotions as a new mother, I still think that my very own project, my beloved research, gave my vulnerable and recovering body much-needed strength and confidence."[37] Some mothers adjust their own expectations of research productivity (e.g., publishing fewer articles, attending fewer conferences, stopping the tenure clock) to also meet their own, and others', expectations of being a "good" mother. Others adjust their own responsibilities at home, reducing their housekeeping standards or hiring caregivers.[38] Others change career paths, including leaving tenured or tenure-track positions.[39]

The Collective emerged from conversations in a Facebook group consisting of mothers* facing all the challenges noted previously. It became apparent that the issues group members faced were not just personal struggles but were rather shared among motherscholars across all types of career stages and academic institutions. The challenges of the pandemic put motherscholars at a distinct disadvantage in various aspects of their work, wherein benchmarks for success in the academic environment were more attainable for some groups (e.g., white, male, cisgender, childless) than others.[40] In other words, when one group is systematically at a disadvantage in relation to another group, it becomes difficult for the disadvantaged group to reach benchmarks for success.[41] Moreover, the lives of academic mothers should be viewed holistically, given the intersections of work and home.[42] To this end, the Collective offers personal and professional support to academic mothers* of young children in order to make space to work together, noncompetitively, to publish during a time when conducting research is particularly challenging yet still a key indicator of scholarly success.

The Motherscholar Collective: Formation

> I was like trying to be . . . a full-time parent and also do my job. . . . At some point, [you] don't even like it, you're just like, trying to get through it and like bat down all these . . . whack-a-mole . . . situation[s].
>
> —Joy, motherscholar

The Collective was created in the summer of 2020 to engage in personally and professionally meaningful research by collecting data on the experiences of academic mothers* parenting young children. In a Facebook group for academic mothers* of children born in 2019–2020, many realized their struggles to maintain any semblance of ordered, functional routines of work and private life were common to other mothers*, regardless of academic institution, professional rank, position, or department. Across the board, mothers* posted on ways their lives shifted due to COVID-19–related restrictions and lockdowns, closures of daycares and schools, remote teaching and advising, and the insurmountable double burden of "doing it all" in scholarship and childcare.[43] Simultaneously, these stories were relatable and validating, and they highlight the fact that these were not individual struggles but indeed a collective experience.

As pandemic-related calls for proposals appeared, members of the Collective expressed concern that motherscholar voices would be left out of that research due to work and home demands. In the vein of "no research on us without us," the Collective embraced feminist collaboration and turned to participatory action research. To accomplish collectively what could not be accomplished individually, the Motherscholar Collective transforms personal experiences into a research agenda.[44] Specifically, the Collective works together toward several interrelated ends:

- to offer unique social support to academic mothers* of young children with shared experiences of being parents and scholars navigating work and motherhood during a global pandemic
- to offer career support as members work together, noncompetitively, to publish during a time when conducting research is particularly challenging
- to make space for the tandem task(s) of scholarship and mothering during a time when, by necessity, both come together

During the pandemic, the Collective developed research questions, questionnaires, and journaling prompts to capture the individualized experiences as well as broader structural discourses that informed academic mothers'* lives during COVID-19. Hesse-Biber et al. note that honoring women's experiential knowledge and centering their lived experiences in scholarship are crucial aspects in feminist research. The Collective seeks to deliberately and reflexively underscore the structural barriers that academic mothers encounter by using a feminist research approach (and "making good use of our experience[s]," by systematically recording them). [45] In this way, members can see their own personal or professional struggles reflected in others' stories while simultaneously acknowledging the intersectionality of motherscholar experiences and the plurality of members' voices. These factors are continuously encouraged and highlighted in the research process and underscore the Collective's feminist stance.

Coming from varied lenses and backgrounds in diverse fields (see the appendix), motherscholars work as participant researchers to create a flexible and reciprocal methodology valuing the needs of each motherscholar. To determine steps for data collection, members brainstormed areas of research interest in shared documents. Additionally, the group members—which grew from fifty at the start to ninety-one members at time of writing—met virtually through live videoconferencing to categorize interests into research subfields and concrete projects. During these and subsequent meetings, members encouraged each other to engage in reflexivity as feminist practice, to interrogate the ways in which the individual experiences of motherscholars in higher education institutions exhibit broader social structures that may transfer to and resound with academic mothers* outside the Collective.[46]

Because members have a wide range of experience with quantitative and qualitative methodologies, empirical surveys and open-ended journaling prompts were primarily chosen for data collection. Survey questionnaires helped to record an overall snapshot of motherscholars' demographics and mental wellness throughout the fall of 2020, and the reflexive nature of the journaling prompts collected stories and other forms of experiential knowledge on community, connection, sharing, and emotion.[47] Journaling prompts asked motherscholars about the complexity of their identities, job navigation and transitions, and parenting during the pandemic. As self-identified motherscholars collecting data *on* motherscholars, members of the Collective were mindful to employ inclusive and intersectional language and to ensure the voices particularly of minority motherscholars were represented when capturing the data, which Miner and Jayaratne describe as essential feminist principles.[48] As a problematic but real reflection of the general academic landscape, the participation of motherscholars of color and motherscholars with disabilities was particularly low at the beginning of the Collective's work and required deliberate recruitment. Due to the double pandemic of COVID-19 and racism experienced by communities of color, barriers to participation may have been especially high for motherscholars of color parenting young children.[49] Additionally, given ableist pandemic protocols within already exclusionary higher education structures, motherscholars with disabilities faced additional obstacles to engage in this research work.[50]

Collective members still are encouraged to provide detailed feedback on methodology, survey content, flow, and timing of each project. Throughout this process and all aspects of the Collective's work, feedback is considered with equal weight, with no hierarchy or power structure in place. At its conception, the Collective drew up an agreement on data ownership and usage, establishing that all group members own the data but must use the data transparently and collaboratively. Any motherscholar wanting to use data for publication proposes a manuscript idea to the Collective and actively seeks out at least two additional coauthors from the Collective for collaboration. In direct opposition to the competitiveness of academic publishing, the Collective supports members professionally through collaborative authorship and acknowledging and leveraging individual strengths and expertise. Authorship decisions are made based on who benefits most from the opportunity rather than on seniority, prestige, and so forth. The Collective acknowledges that the structure of institutional rewards based on authorship is arguably antithetical to feminist values and deliberately supports Collective members to help them meet their current professional needs.[51] This is driven by an implicit understanding and valuation of the fact that Collective efforts are decentralized and ultimately shared. For example, a first author position may be designated to someone who is seeking promotion at their institution or on the job market rather than to a senior scholar who already has several first-authored publications. In some cases, a random sequence generator is used to determine the order of authors. As research projects evolve and membership grows, the Collective will face various dilemmas in its feminist practice and will continue to engage in collaborative, reflective, and inclusive discussions to determine its path forward.[52]

The Motherscholar Collective: Philosophy

> I feel that this is the only space . . . where I don't have to apologize constantly for either not being prepared enough, or on time enough, or having my children be silent enough, or having my husband take over for me. [When] I advise my students I say, "Don't be apologetic. There's no need for you to apologize for part of your—for part of your identity." . . . And yet all the time, I feel the need to say, "I'm so sorry. You know, I'm so sorry, I couldn't make it to this meeting because I couldn't find childcare." And then, of course, you get the eye rolling and you get the silence. [Now] I don't feel the need and I feel that this is preparing me to be much less apologetic.
>
> —Jane, motherscholar

> What we've seen with this group is that we're actually working better when we don't have to divorce ourselves from our actual lived experience. When we don't have to say, "Okay, I have to set that aside now, then just focus—just focus on this." That, when we're accepted for saying, "Well, look, I'm dealing with this right now, um, and I, you know, I don't have any choice about it," that it takes so much pressure off our work.
>
> —Francis, motherscholar

Veletsianos and Houlden discuss the need for radical flexibility in education during the pandemic, defining the practice as "taking seriously the nature and purpose of learning itself at the fundamental level of human life, where human life is understood to be enmeshed relationally with all that goes on around, with, and through."[53] The Collective takes this same approach to research and collaboration, in a practice members term *radical feminist flexibility*.

The Collective's motherscholars choose their own level of participation and engagement, depending on professional and personal needs. Each project has a small core group that structures the manuscript and sets meetings and deadlines. However, as working mothers*, project members understand the importance of flexibility. For instance, it always remains acceptable to communicate to the group a need for more time or even to abandon a project, perhaps due to lack of childcare or to professional or family demands. With ninety-one members, there is always someone to pick up the work if needed. While this rotating door of scholars may seem chaotic, the looser process works well as motherscholars' immediate needs and priorities are constantly in flux.

The Collective's approach also allows motherscholars to work in a way that emphasizes the training and skill sets in the technical areas of data analysis and writing, rather than specific academic fields. Members have skills with different methodologies: some are talented at conducting literature reviews; others excel at synthesizing conversations into cohesive narratives. Similar to the interdisciplinary knowledge and skills needed as mothers*, the Collective uses interdisciplinary knowledge and interprofessional collaboration to increase the quality of its work.

As the pandemic made long-term planning impossible for most, the radical feminist flexibility of the Collective helped to ensure that projects continued while members juggled work/life demands. Conversations consistently reiterated that members were all academic mothers* living through a pandemic, and it helped to develop trust among motherscholars contending with shifting circumstances. Particularly because of shared experiences and struggles as academic mothers* with young children, members continue to find the empathy of others validating and a motivational factor in remaining engaged in and passionate about the Collective's research. Being open about current situations and challenges creates a network of reciprocity and trust; there is no pressure or demand to justify any individual's level of involvement throughout a project.

Meetings and online group conversations are influenced by radical feminist flexibility to create a supportive climate. It is the norm for Collective members to work meetings around childcare and nap times or to be caring for children during a meeting. In these meetings, being a mother* is not a liability but rather an inherent aspect of being a scholar. Multitasking is often a necessity for academic mothers*. Because the pandemic generally meant a lack of outside support for childcare, mothers* met while chestfeeding, pumping, or moving in and out of meetings to take care of children. As a geographically dispersed group, virtual meetings remain a necessity but also provide an advantage: they allow motherscholars to remain involved in research while taking care of needs at home. Sessions are recorded, with videos and transcripts archived in shared folders for members to view. For many academic mothers*, work time often occurs outside of standard business hours, and this archive of communication allows members to stay connected to projects of interest.

Group communication occurs primarily through a private Facebook group, with events for meetings, suggestions for manuscript proposals, reminders about data collection, and questions about the research process. Moving to an online project management platform has allowed for project-specific messaging and can increase lines of communication, particularly for Collective members who have stepped away from or limited Facebook use. Because the Collective was formed from a more general Facebook group for academic mothers* of young children, some members already know each other in some capacity and, due to the social nature of the platform, are able to engage with each other in casual and informal ways. The use of a social networking site also allows for members to have flexible schedules and locations, enabling group engagement as interest and availability shift, and for participation from mobile devices as needed—essential for scholars juggling parenting and other responsibilities. While Facebook promotes a certain amount of inclusivity and flexibility in these ways, the Collective also acknowledges that it might be simultaneously limiting as not all motherscholars use the platform. In other words, because the Collective (co)operates mainly via Facebook, some self-selection is inevitable. However, any research collective will be inherently and ultimately limited in terms of its membership based on who is recruited and how, as well as in terms of the number of participants needed to remain functional. Facebook does, though, allow for a large pool of potential participants and helps the Collective stay connected, facilitating the group's dispersed and decentralized philosophy for, and approach to, scholarship.

The Motherscholar Collective: Innovation and Implications for (Publicly Engaged) Scholarship

> You know, we all benefit from [using] a more robust research model, especially as parents. . . . We have this flexibility and yet we're able to do all of these things right by going multidisciplinary [and working together]. . . . We're all parents, we all have constraints.
>
> —Britney, motherscholar

> That flexibility is important, and it's really shown me that if the work is important or enough people believe in it, it gets done. And it gets done still with people being flexible and being accommodating . . . like, it's okay to incorporate those things. . . . I think a lot of times before it was like, "Well, if we don't have these hard deadlines and these firm boundaries and these firm parameters for who can participate, and how and when, and in what capacity," then . . . the project will just never happen.
>
> —JMC, motherscholar

Participation is a perpetual dilemma for publicly engaged, community-based, or otherwise participatory scholarship; figuring out who shows up, who does not, and how to bridge the gap between them is a challenge that scholars continually face.[54] Acknowledging that a consideration of engaging with particular publics is a worthy pursuit, the Collective—with its focus on a public of motherscholars— considers how its successes can be captured and leveraged for use with other hard-to-reach, or marginalized, publics.

As has been explored elsewhere, the shifts people have experienced across socioeconomic spectra in response to COVID-19 have produced both "goods" and "bads," and it is worth considering which of the "goods" should be kept even as we resolve the "bads."[55] Similarly, changes to how research is conducted—both in terms of researchers' expectations and practices as well as norms and approaches for working with target populations—can help to foster more flexible, cooperative, and positive working experiences in the future. For example, while conducting research via videoconference is suboptimal on many levels, the increased reliance on, familiarity with, and openness to virtual modes of interaction are sure to have long-lasting benefits in terms of improving access to some communities that historically have been more difficult to reach within participatory or publicly engaged scholarship (e.g., parents, people who work nontraditional hours, those with limited transportation). Determining a viable methodology for working within and among (sub)groups of people in asynchronous, virtual, and yet still inherently collaborative ways could be a boon to those trying to create community, develop a sense of solidarity, and to coproduce knowledge.

While the digital divide is both real and persistent, access to telecommunication technology has drastically increased, and people's willingness to engage with others via those means has likely increased as well. The success of the scholarly collaborations within the Collective suggests that one way researchers may be able to better reach specific publics is by engaging with and in familiar social media platforms—Facebook, Twitter, Discord, and so on—since they are widely used and are relatively easy to collectively manage.

The work of the Collective provides a multitude of benefits for research, including empowering motherscholars to make change in their institutions and in their own communities; creating a community for professional and social support; innovating in collaborative, multidisciplinary research; and actively pursuing research in an empowered and paradigm-changing way (i.e., walking the walk, not just talking the talk). With its scholarship, the Collective represents and respects motherscholars' contributions and thus seeks to make their voices heard while moving toward actionable change.

Beyond methodological approaches, the Collective offers insight into how reconfiguring identities and boundaries promotes a more human approach to scholarship. The increasingly detrimental separation of private/professional life has been well documented, and figuring—and supporting—how to bridge that arbitrarily imposed boundary in the academy can be incredibly valuable for feminist research(ers) and beyond. Such "bridging" is essential for motherscholars, where separating these identities has been difficult—if not impossible—and contributed to demonstrable professional setbacks before, during and, potentially, after the pandemic.

Overall, the formation of the Collective provides examples of how scholarship has changed during COVID-19 and can continue to change, in ways that acknowledge, welcome, and value the intersectional experiences of motherscholars. A radical feminist flexibility allows for a constantly shifting, diverse, and asynchronous collaborative to develop a strong community with rich social capital: one that is motivated to turn research into action, builds broader professional identities, and supports members' lives beyond scholarship.

In its embrace of radical feminist flexibility, the Collective also finds value in participatory action research—which has, as Massey and Barreras write, "the potential to play an effective role in some form of social and political change, or is useful as a tool for advocacy and activism."[56] Participation in the Collective's survey and journal research has been empowering for those who feel unheard or are without support; data analysis and publication have given motherscholars the language and literature to acknowledge—and challenge/change—issues of inequity in the workplace and the home. By foregrounding the experiences of motherscholars, the Collective highlights systemic inequities along the academic career trajectory, from doctoral studies to professorships, including difficulty completing degree requirements, inequitable work expectations, lower base pay, and the lack of parental leaves and family-friendly policies, not to mention the micro- and macroaggressions from professors, supervisors, colleagues, and students. The research produced by the Collective empowers participant-researchers to bring evidence-driven change to the very institutions that have marginalized, stigmatized, or invalidated them.

Disruptions can trigger innovation; as Eatman et al. note, "Many scholars have responded to changing demographics within higher education as well as the contemporary demands of societies to address challenging issues of inequality, environmental degradation, and democratic exclusion, among others, by developing less hierarchical and more cooperative forms of scholarship."[57] The emergence of the Motherscholar Collective is a prime example of such innovation, as it addresses challenges and inequities that were foregrounded and exacerbated by the COVID-19 pandemic. As such, there are several takeaways that other institutions might find useful in promoting and supporting collaborative research aimed at mitigating inequality and exclusion, and not just in higher education.

The Collective is located in a space not confined by academic institutions. Often organizational norms and resources determine whether and how researchers collaborate with each other, within and across institutions. However, social media transcends institutions and, in a time of urgency, motherscholars were successfully able to define their ideal workspace, irrespective of the norms and resources of their institutions. The asynchronous, disentrained nature of social media works hand-in-hand with the multidisciplinary, radically flexible collaborations of the Collective.

The radical coproduction demonstrated by the Collective's successful collaborative work can offer best practices for how to bring together and motivate a diverse and dynamic group. By bringing differently situated, differently trained scholars together, such that varying levels of expertise are available on a project, researchers are able to learn from each other and contribute in a nonhierarchical, decentralized way. The Collective's approach suggests that academic institutions might encourage innovations in collaboration among marginalized researchers as a viable way to create opportunities and space for productivity, professional development, and formative mentoring. Less-experienced scholars can observe research in action, which is valuable for scholars of all ranks but may be especially so for graduate students and early-career scholars; close-knit, noncompetitive, mutually supportive collaborations present opportunities that marginalized scholars would not have at their institution. As everyone is treated as experts (namely, as mothers* and scholars), Collective members can trade off tasks and/or replace each other as necessary, with the intent that such labor-sharing is supportive rather than competitive or punitive.

The philosophy and practices of the Collective offer a means for unifying two crucial aspects of motherscholars' identities: scholar and mother*. Traditional institutions may find these innovations break from their norms and expectations, but it is nevertheless essential to provide creative spaces for motherscholars to flourish. Prepandemic norms and standards contributed to the marginalization and erasure of those who simply cannot adhere to the arbitrary bifurcation of private and professional life; the Collective offers an alternative.

Figuring the means and methods for inclusive collaboration is an essential task for scholarship. While it seems obvious that some elements of pandemic-modified life will disappear as fast as they appeared, others may persist in the long term. Flexibility in terms of form(at) of participation, amount of time committed (and the time of day that time is committed), and improved recognition of and support for the concept of collaboration are all integral to the Collective and are crucial to the success of motherscholars. As people have shifted their work lives in a variety of ways, the value of collaboration and flexibility has become increasingly evident. In the case of the Collective, shared experiences and constraints create communicative and work-related norms that ensure collaborations are respectful, trusting, and flexible. Regardless of career stage, professional status, discipline, or career trajectory, each motherscholar works toward the same goals in the shared work of the Collective.

The Future of the Motherscholar Collective

> A lot of these issues that people are facing aren't going to go away once things, you know, quote unquote, go back to normal whenever that is and whatever that looks like. So it's an opportunity, right, to continue evaluating or reevaluating the institutional responses to things the way people with children are treated, you know, parenting, academia, all of it.
>
> —JMC, motherscholar

> All of us have constraints and we're all working this full-time job, yet we're all able to work on this additional research on the side. And we've been successful, so . . . you know it can be done and it can be done in a positive way. . . . Why would we not continue this after the pandemic? To me, that just seems kind of like a no-brainer.
>
> —Britney, motherscholar

While the Collective initially formed to meet an immediate need of working together to research the experiences of managing parenting and scholarship during the pandemic, it became clear early on that many members hoped the Collective would outlast the COVID-19 pandemic. As outlined in this paper and other work by the Collective, the challenges exacerbated by the pandemic are not unique to it, and the Collective can continue to be a support structure for academic mothers*—both pragmatically and emotionally. The Collective continues to be a safe and supportive space to work and is also highly productive. The group has published extensively on related topics, from individual experiences during the pandemic to lessons learned from different teaching settings, to exploring the experiences of motherscholars both during the pandemic and during motherhood.[58] Membership in the Collective has grown from an initial group of fifty members to ninety-one. The group has evolved to focus on how it can harness a productive working philosophy of radical feminist flexibility to both support members' individual research goals and elevate voices of color within the group through collective scholarship. As a group, the Collective has already begun to extend work to topics beyond those related strictly to the pandemic, bringing collective expertise and unique perspectives together to address topics such as antiracist teaching practices and perspectives on climate change–related attitudes and behaviors. The Collective's embrace of radical feminist flexibility has alleviated burdens of time and organization for more motherscholars of color to guide and be heard on these projects and to lend expertise where their voices have historically not been heard.

The challenges and systemic inequalities that motherscholars face in academia persist. There has been no ease in the differential burden of service that women in academia bear, nor a rebalancing of the often unequal workload mothers take on at home. The approach of the Collective improves the scholarly productivity of its members, but it does not—and cannot—change the inequitable and biased systems of academia in which motherscholars work. While the Collective innovates through collaboration and multidisciplinary scholarship, it also seeks to create a community for professional and personal support and to embolden motherscholars to approach structural change in their institutions and communities.[59]

The Collective has done the important work of creating a space for mothers* to examine their own experiences and to experience radical feminist flexibility in action. It has enabled interdisciplinary collaborations in a nonhierarchical, cooperative environment that allows members to thrive mentally and emotionally while allowing them to express their authentic selves. This does not negate the necessity of advocating for systemic change within the systems that created the need for this group, but the collaborative structure and philosophy of the Collective could, and perhaps should, be a model for how to develop collaborative, healthy, productive scholarship.

Finally, the publicly engaged scholarship of the Collective can benefit all motherscholars; the successes and struggles of the Collective reveal what is required to (better) support mothers* in academia or engaged in other research-related work. Future scholarship from The Collective will work to counteract the viewpoint that being a mother* is a liability in terms of being a scholar or vice versa. In the meantime, the framework underpinning the Collective can be used not only to champion motherscholars engaged in interdisciplinary and cross-institutional collaborative work but also to serve as an impetus to advocate for change within the inequitable systems that made such a collaboration necessary for so many mothers* in academic careers.

Appendix

TABLE 1. Academic fields of motherscholars

MOTHERSCHOLAR	ACADEMIC FIELD(S)
Katharina A. Azim	Educational Psychology, Women's Reproductive Health
Stacey H. Bender	Education, Kinesiology
Jasmine L. Blanks Jones	Education, Africana Studies
Maggie Campbell-Obaid	Social Psychology, Political Psychology
Meike Eilert	Marketing
Jennifer Greene-Rooks	Counselor Education
N. A. Heller	Developmental Psychology
Helen K. Ho	Communication Studies
Sarah Key-DeLyria	Speech and Hearing Sciences
Stacey Lim	Audiology
Colleen C. Myles-Baltzly	Geography and Environmental Studies
Lucy Parker-Barnes	Counselor Education
Summer Melody Pennell	English Education, Queer Studies in Education
Ivanna Richardson	Linguistics

NOTES

Epigraphs: Pseudonyms.

1. Armenti, "Gender as a Barrier."
2. See Haslam, Tee, and Baker, "Use of Social Media"; Holtz, Smock, and Reyes-Gastulum, "Connected Motherhood"; McDaniel, Coyne, and Holmes, "New Mothers."
3. Goodyear, Parker, and Casey, "Social Media."
4. Alberth et al., "Social Media as a Conduit."
5. Mercieca and Kelly, "Early Career."
6. Ollivier et al., "Mental Health."
7. Doherty, "Quiet Crisis"; Morgan et al., "Unequal Impact."
8. Augustus, "Impact of the COVID-19"; Hermann et al., "COVID-19"; Morgan et al., "Unequal Impact."
9. Doherty, "Quiet Crisis."
10. Allen and Piercy, "Feminist Autoethnography"; Heggeness, "Estimating"; Kramer, "Virus Moved."
11. U.S. Bureau of Labor and Statistics, "Employment Situation"; McKinsey & Company, *Women in the Workplace.*
12. "Faculty Well-Being."
13. CohenMiller and Izekenova, "Motherhood in Academia"; Deryugina, Shurchkov, and Stearns, "COVID-19 Disruptions"; Pettit, "Covid-19 Has Robbed."
14. Minello, "The Pandemic," 2.
15. Frederickson, "COVID-19's Gendered Impact"; Gabster et al., "Challenges."
16. Staniscuaski et al., "Gender, Race."
17. Njoroge et al., "Association of COVID-19."
18. Sattar, "Academic Motherhood"; Durham, "Unmasking."
19. Murch, "Black Women"; Simien & Wallace, "Disproportionate Service."
20. Patterson, Beckre, and Baluran, "Gendered Racism."
21. Staniscuaski et al., "Gender, Race"; Miller, "Too Much."
22. Ohito, "Some of Us Die."
23. Collins, et al., 2021. "COVID-19 and the Gender Gap"; Evans-Winters and Esposito, "Researching the Bridge."
24. Low and Damian Martin, "Surviving," 1.
25. Lapayese, *Mother-Scholar.*
26. Matias, "Cheryl Matias."
27. Blanks Jones et al., "All You Can Say"; Blanks Jones et al., "Coping through Kinship"; Lim et al. "Motherscholars with Disabilities"; Pennell, Greene-Rooks, and Wagner, "Pandemic Academic Parenting."
28. Goodyear, Parker, and Casey, "Social Media."
29. Mercieca and Kelly, "Early Career Teacher."
30. Holtz, "Connected Motherhood"; Grey et al., "Role of Perceived Social Support."
31. Haslam, Tee, and Baker, "Use of Social Media."
32. Aydin, "Becoming a Mother"; Montgomery et al., "Navigating Uncertainty."
33. Wiederhold, "Using Social Media."
34. Fothergill and Feltey, "I've Worked Very Hard."
35. Ashencaen Crabtree and Shiel, "Playing Mother."
36. Rafnsdóttir and Heijstra, "Balancing Work-Family Life."
37. Huopalainen and Satama, "Mothers and Researchers," 112.
38. Fothergill and Feltey, "I've Worked Very Hard."
39. McKenzie, "Unequal Expressions."

40. Fothergill and Feltey, "I've Worked Very Hard"; Leonard and Malina, "Caught between Two Worlds."

41. Bailyn, "Academic Careers."

42. Bailyn, "Academic Careers."

43. Collins et al., "COVID-19"; Güney-Frahm, "Neoliberal Motherhood."

44. Fine and Torre, "Critical Participatory Action," 435.

45. Ettorre, *Autoethnography*; Allen and Piercy, "Feminist Autoethnography," 156.

46. Jaggar, "Feminist Ethics."

47. Jaggar, "Feminist Ethics."

48. Miner et al., "Using Survey Research."

49. Blanks Jones et al., "Coping through Kinship"; Starks, "Double Pandemic."

50. Davenport et al., "Moms Are Not OK"; Saunders, Jackson, and Visram, "Impacts of Face Coverings."; Lim et al., "Motherscholars with Disabilities."

51. Monk, Manning, and Denman, "Working Together."

52. Schultz, "Working the Ruins."

53. Veletsianos and Houlden, "Radical Flexibility," 852.

54. Monk, Manning, and Denman, "Working Together."

55. Myles, "Lemonade."

56. As cited in Sandwick et al., "Promise and Provocation," 480.

57. Eatman et al., "Co-Constructing Knowledge," 534.

58. Blanks-Jones et al., "All You Can Say"; Blanks-Jones et al. "Coping through Kinship"; Lim et al., "Motherscholars with Disabilities"; Pennel, Greene-Rooks, and Wagner, "Pandemic Academic Parenting"; Wagner, Eilert, and Lim, "Academic Mothers"; Motherscholar Collective et al., "Pandemic Challenges"; Motherscholar Collective et al., "Transformative Collaborations."

59. For discussion, see Cardel, Dean, and Montoya-Williams, "Preventing a Secondary Epidemic"; Fulweiler et al., "Rebuild the Academy"; Shah et al., "Turning the Tide."

BIBLIOGRAPHY

Alberth, Mursalim, Siam, I Ketut Suardika, and La Ino. "Social Media as a Conduit for Teacher Professional Development in the Digital Era: Myths, Promises or Realities?" *Teflin Journal* 29, no. 2 (2018): 293–306.

Allen, Katherine R., and Fred P. Piercy. "Feminist Autoethnography." In *Research Methods in Family Therapy 2*, edited by Douglas H. Sprenkle and Fred P. Piercy, 155–169. New York: The Guilford Press, 2005.

Allen, Kelly-Ann, Kerryn Butler-Henderson, Andrea Reupert, Fiona Longmuir, Ilana Finefter-Rosenbluh, Emily Berger, Christine Grove, et al. "Work Like a Girl: Redressing Gender Inequity in Academia through Systemic Solutions." *Journal of University Teaching & Learning Practice* 18, no. 3 (2021): 3.

Armenti, Carmen. "Gender as a Barrier for Women with Children in Academe." *Canadian Journal of Higher Education* 34, no. 1 (2004): 1–26, 2004.

Ashencaen Crabtree, Sara, and Chris Shiel. ""Playing Mother": Channeled Careers and the Construction of Gender in Academia." *SAGE Open* 9, no. 3 (2019): 1–14.

Augustus, Jo. "The Impact of the COVID-19 Pandemic on Women Working in Higher Education." *Frontiers in Education* 6 (2021): 648365.

Aydin, Ruveyde. "Becoming a Mother in the Shadow of COVID-19: A Grounded Theory Study." *Journal of Psychosocial Nursing and Mental Health* 60, no. 6 (2022): 43–51.

Bailyn, Lotte. "Academic Careers and Gender Equity: Lessons Learned from MIT." *Gender, Work & Organization* 10, no. 2 (2003): 137–53.

Blanks Jones, Jasmine L., Ivanna Richardson, Jordan Conley, J. L. A. Donohue, and Caroline Loomis. "'All You Can Say Is That You Plan On Being Finished Soon': Doctoral Student Mothers During the COVID-19 Pandemic," in "Snapshots of History: Portraits of the 21st Century Pandemic," edited by S. Marie McCarther, special issue, *American Educational History Journal* (2022): 233–40.

Blanks-Jones, Jasmine L., Jessica P. Cerdeña, Chonika Coleman-King, and Mahauganee D. Shaw Bonds. "Coping through Kinship during COVID-19: Lessons from Women of Color," in "Snapshots of History: Portraits of the 21st Century Pandemic," edited by S. Marie McCarther, special issue, *American Educational History Journal* (2022): 51–58.

Cardel, Michelle I., Natalie Dean, and Diana Montoya-Williams. "Preventing a Secondary Epidemic of Lost Early Career Scientists." *Annals of the American Thoracic Society* 17, no. 11 (2020): 1366–70.

CohenMiller, Anna, and Zhanna Izekenova. "Motherhood in Academia during the COVID-19 Pandemic: An International Online Photovoice Study Addressing Issues of Equity and Inclusion in Higher Education." *Innovations in Higher Education* 47, no. 5 (2022): 813–35.

Collins, Caitlyn, Liana Christin Landivar, Leah Ruppanner, and William J. Scarborough. "COVID-19 and the Gender Gap in Work Hours." *Gender, Work & Organization* 28 (2021): 549–60.

Davenport, Margie H., Sarah Meyer, Victoria L. Meah, Morgan C. Strynadka, and Rshmi Khurana. "Moms Are Not OK: COVID-19 and Maternal Mental Health." *Frontiers in Global Women's Health* 1 (2020): 1–6.

Deryugina, Tatyana, Olga Shurchkov, and Jenna Stearns. "COVID-19 Disruptions Disproportionately Affect Female Academics." *American Economic Association Papers and Proceedings* 11 (2021): 164–68.

Doherty, Maggie. "The Quiet Crisis of Parents on the Tenure Track." *The Chronicle of Higher Education* (2021). https://www.chronicle.com/article/the-quiet-crisis-of -parents-on-the-tenure-track.

Durham, Aisha. "Unmasking the Strongblackwoman in Mentoring." *Communication, Culture and Critique* 14, no. 4 (2021): 682–86.

Eatman, Timothy K., Gaelle Ivory, John Saltmarsh, Michael Middleton, Amanda Wittman, and Corey Dolgon. "Co-Constructing Knowledge Spheres in the Academy: Developing Frameworks and Tools for Advancing Publicly Engaged Scholarship." *Urban Education* 53, no. 4 (2018): 532–61.

Ettore, Elizabeth. *Autoethnography as Feminist Method: Sensitising the Feminist "I."* London: Routledge, 2016.

Evans-Winters, Venus, and Jennifer Esposito. "Researching the Bridge Called our Backs: The Invisibility of 'Us' in Qualitative Communities." *International Journal of Qualitative Studies in Education* 31, no. 9 (2018): 863–76.

"Faculty Well-Being and Career Paths: What Campus Leaders Need to Know." *The Chronicle of Higher Education* (November 2020). https://www.chronicle.com /page/faculty-career-paths-a-conversation-for-presidents.

Fine, Michelle, and María Elena Torre. "Critical Participatory Action Research: A Feminist Project for Validity and Solidarity." *Psychology of Women Quarterly* 43, no. 4 (2019): 433–44.

Fothergill, Alice, and Kathryn Feltey. "'I've Worked Very Hard and Slept Very Little': Mothers on Tenure Track in Academia." *Journal of the Association for Research on Mothering* 5, no. 2 (2003): 7–19.

Frederickson, Megan. "COVID-19's Gendered Impact on Academic Productivity." 2020. https://github.com/drfreder/pandemic-pub-bias.

Fulweiler, Robinson, Sarah W. Davies, Jennifer F. Biddle, Amy J. Burgin, Emily H. G. Cooperdock, Torrance C. Hanley, Carly D. Kenkel, et al. "Rebuild the Academy: Supporting Academic Mothers during COVID-19 and Beyond." *PLOS Biology* 9, no. 13 (2021): e3001100.

Gabster, Brooke Peterson, Kim van Daalen, Roopa Dhatt, and Michele Barry. "Challenges for the Female Academic During the Covid-19 Pandemic." *The Lancet* 395, no. 10242 (2020): 1968–70.

Goodyear, Victoria A., Melissa Parker, and Ashley Casey. "Social Media and Teacher Professional Learning Communities." *Physical Education and Sport Pedagogy* 24, no. 5 (2019): 421–33.

Grey, Ian, Teresa Arora, Justin Thomas, Ahmad Saneh, Pia Tohme, and Rudy Abi-Habib. "The Role of Perceived Social Support on Depression and Sleep during the Covid-19 Pandemic." *Psychiatry Research* 293 (2020): 113452.

Güney-Frahm, Irem. "Neoliberal Motherhood During the Pandemic: Some Reflections." *Gender, Work & Organization* 27, no. 5 (2020): 847–56.

Haslam, Divna M., Amelia Tee, and Sabine Baker. "The Use of Social Media as a Mechanism of Social Support in Parents." *Journal of Child and Family Studies* 26, no. 7 (2017): 2026–37.

Haskins, Natoya H., Jolie Ziomek-Daigle, Cheryl Sewell, Lonika Crumb, Brandee Appling, and Heather Trepal. "The Intersectionality of African American Mothers in Counselor Education: A Phenomenological Examination." *Counselor Education and Supervision* 55, no. 1 (2016): 60–75.

Heggeness, Misty L. "Estimating the Immediate Impact of the COVID-19 Shock on Parental Attachment to the Labor Market and the Double Bind of Mothers." *Review of Economics of the Household* 18 (2020): 1053–78.

Hermann, Mary A., and Cheryl Neale-McFall. "COVID-19, Academic Mothers, and Opportunities for the Academy." *American Association of University Professors.* 2020. https://www.aaup.org/article/covid-19-academic-mothers-and-opportunities-academy#.YubJruzMI-Q.

Hesse-Biber, Sharlene Nagy, Patricia Leavy, and Michelle L. Yaiser. "Feminist Approaches to Research as a Process: Reconceptualizing Epistemology, Methodology, and Method." In *Feminist Perspectives on Social Research,* edited by Sharlene Nagy Hesse-Biber and Michelle L. Yaiser, 3–26. New York: Oxford University Press, 2004.

Holtz, Bree, Andrew Smock, and David Reyes-Gastelum. "Connected Motherhood: Social Support for Moms and Moms-to-Be on Facebook." *Telemedicine Journal and E-Health: The Official Journal of the American Telemedicine Association* 21, no. 5 (2015): 415–21.

Huopalainen, Astrid S., and Suvi T. Satama. "Mothers and Researchers in the Making: Negotiating 'New' Motherhood Within the 'New' Academia." *Human Relations* 72, no. 1 (2019): 98–121.

Jaggar, Alison. "Feminist Ethics." In *The Blackwell Guide to Ethical Theory,* edited by Hugh LaFollette and Ingmar Persson, 433–60. Malden, MA: Blackwell, 2013.

Kramer, Jillian. "The Virus Moved Female Faculty to the Brink. Will Universities Help?" *New York Times,* October 6, 2020. https://www.nytimes.com/2020/10/06/science/covid-universities-women.html.

Lapayese, Yvette V. *Mother-Scholar: (Re)imagining K-12 Education.* Rotterdam, Netherlands: Sense Publishers, 2012.

Leonard, Pauline, and Danusia Malina. "Caught Between Two Worlds: Mothers as Academics." In *Changing the Subject: Women In Higher Education,* edited by Jocey Quinn, Sue Davies, and Cathy Lubelska, 29–41. London: Taylor & Francis, 2017.

Lim, Stacey R., Jessica P. Cerdeña, Katharina A. Azim, and Kathryn Wagner. "Motherscholars with Disabilities: Surmounting Structural Adversity Suring COVID-19," in "Snapshots of History: Portraits of the 21st Century Pandemic," edited by S. Marie McCarther, special issue, *American Educational History Journal* (2022): 133.

Low, Katharine, and Diana Damian Martin. "Surviving, But Not Thriving: The Politics of Care and the Experience of Motherhood in Academia." *Research in Drama Education: The Journal of Applied Theatre and Performance* 24, no. 3 (2019): 426–32.

Matias, Cheryl. "'Cheryl Matias, PhD and Mother of Twins': Counter Storytelling to Critically Analyze How I Navigated The Academic Application, Negotiation, and Relocation Process." Division G-Social Context of Education/Section 2, American Educational Research Association (AERA), Louisiana, 2011.

McDaniel, Brandon T., Sarah M. Coyne, and Erin K. Holmes. "New Mothers and Media Use: Associations Between Blogging, Social Networking, and Maternal Well-Being." *Maternal and Child Health Journal* 16, no. 7 (2012): 1509–17.

McKenzie, Lara. "Unequal Expressions: Emotions and Narratives of Leaving and Remaining in Precarious Academia." *Social Anthropology* 29, no. 2 (2021): 527–42.

McKinsey & Company. "Women in the Workplace." October 18, 2022. https://www.mckinsey.com/~/media/mckinsey/featured%20insights/diversity%20and%20inclusion/women%20in%20the%20workplace%202021/women-in-the-workplace-2021.pdf

Mercieca, Bernadette, and Nick Kelly. "Early Career Teacher Peer Support through Private Groups in Social Media." *Asia-Pacific Journal of Teacher Education* 46, no. 1 (2018): 61–77.

Miller, Chantelle. "Too Much for a Heart to Bear: A Systematic Review and Mini Meta-Analysis on The Role of Skin-Deep Resilience in the Weathering of Black People in America." 2022. DePaul University Library, College of Science and Health Theses and Dissertations.

Minello, Alessandra, Sara Martucci, and Lidia K. C. Manzo. "The Pandemic and the Academic Mothers: Present Hardships and Future Perspectives." *European Societies* 23, no. 1 (2021): S82–S94.

Miner, Kathi N., Toby E. Jayaratne, Amanda D. Pesonen, and Lauren Zurbr. "Using Survey Research as a Quantitative Method for Feminist Social Change." In *Handbook of Feminist Research: Theory and Praxis*, 2nd ed., edited by Sharlene Nagy Hesse-Biber, 237–63. Thousand Oaks, CA: SAGE, 2012.

Monk, Janice, Patricia Manning, and Catalina Denman. "Working Together: Feminist Perspectives on Collaborative Research and Action." *ACME: An International Journal for Critical Geographies* 2, no. 1 (2003): 91–106.

Montgomery, Elsa, Kaat de Backer, Abigail Easter, Laura A. Magee, Jane Sandall, and Sergio A. Silverio. "Navigating Uncertainty Alone: A Grounded Theory Analysis of Women's Psycho-social Experiences of Pregnancy and Childbirth during the COVID-19 Pandemic in London." *Women and Birth* (2022): S1871–5192.

Morgan, Allison C., Samuel F. Way, Michael J. D. Hoefer, Daniel B. Larremore, Mirta Galesic, and Aaron Clauset. "The Unequal Impact of Parenthood in Academia." *Science Advance* 7, no. 9 (February 24, 2021). https://www.science.org/doi/10.1126/sciadv.abd1996.

Motherscholar Collective, Lynn Bielski, Jasmine L. Blanks Jones, Tiffany P. Brooks, Jennifer H. Greene-Rooks, Stacey R. Lim, and Summer M. Pennell. "Pandemic Challenges during Field Experiences: Responding with Creativity and Flexibility," in "Breakthrough: From Pandemic Panic to Promising Practice," edited by

Shirley Marie McCarther and Donna M. Davis, special issue, *American Educational History Journal*, forthcoming.

Motherscholar Collective, Alexandra K. Frazer, Kathryn E. Frazier, Amanda Harmon, Chonika Coleman-King, Colleen C. Myles-Baltzly, Emily T. Cripe, et al. "Pushing Boundaries and Balance: Finding Humanity in Pandemic Pedagogy," in "Breakthrough: From Pandemic Panic to Promising Practice," edited by Shirley Marie McCarther and Donna M. Davis, special issue, *American Educational History Journal*, forthcoming.

Motherscholar Collective, Jasmine L. Blanks Jones, Lynn M. Bielski, Jessica P. Cerdeña, Ivanna Richardson, Chonika Coleman-King, Colleen C. Myles-Baltzly, et al. "Building a Virtual Village: Academic Mothers'* Online Social Networking During COVID-19." In *It Takes a Village: Academic Mothers Building Online Communities*, edited by Sarah Trocchio, Lisa Hanasono, Rachael Dwyer, Jessica Jorgenson Borchert and Jeanette Yih Harvie. Forthcoming.

Motherscholar Collective, Myles-Baltzly, Colleen C., Helen K. Ho, Ivanna Richardson, Jennifer Greene-Rooks, Katharina A. Azim, Kathryn E. Frazier, et al. "Transformative Collaborations: How a Motherscholar Research Collective Survived and Thrived during Covid-19." *International Perspectives in Psychology* 10, no. 4 (2021): 225–42.

Murch, Donna. "Black Women, Mutual Aid, and Union Organizing in the Time of COVID-19." American Association of University Professors. 2020. https://www .aaup.org/article/black-women-mutual-aid-and-union-organizing-time-covid -19#.Yrr-b3bMI2w.

Myles, Colleen. "Lemonade." *Medium*. 2021. https://medium.com/@fermentedlands /lemonade-aea98c628454.

Njoroge, Wanjikũ F. M., Lauren K. White, Rebecca Waller, Markolline Forkpa, Megan M. Himes, Kadina Morgan, Jakob Seidlitz, et al. "Association of COVID-19 and Endemic Systemic Racism with Postpartum Anxiety and Depression among Black Birthing Individuals." *JAMA Psychiatry* 79, no. 6 (2022): 600–609.

Ohito, Esther O. "Some of Us Die: A Black Feminist Researcher's Survival Method for Creatively Refusing Death and Decay in the Neoliberal Academy." *International Journal of Qualitative Studies in Education* 34, no. 6 (2021): 515–33.

Ollivier, Rachel, Megan Aston, Sheri Price, Meaghan Sim, Britney Benoit, Phillip Joy, Damilola Iduye, and Neda Akbari Nassaji. "Mental Health & Parental Concerns during COVID-19: The Experiences of New Mothers Amidst Social Isolation." *Midwifery* 94 (2021): 102092.

Patterson, Evelyn J., Andrea Beckre, and Darwin A. Baluran. "Gendered Racism on the Body: An Intersectional Approach to Maternal Mortality in the United States." *Population Research and Policy Review* 41, no. 3 (2022): 1261–94.

Pennell, Summer, Jennifer Greene-Rooks, and Kathryn Wagner. "Pandemic Academic Parenting: Finding the Radically Queer within Our Mundane, Monotonous, and Sometimes Homonormative Experiences," in "Snapshots of History: Portraits of the 21st Century Pandemic," special issue, edited by S. Marie McCarther, *American Educational History Journal* (2022): 183–90.

Pettit, Emma. "Covid-19 Has Robbed Faculty Parents of Time for Research. Especially Mothers." *The Chronicle of Higher Education*. 2021. https://www.chronicle.com /article/covid-19-has-robbed-faculty-parents-of-time-for-research-especially -mothers.

Rafnsdóttir, Gudbjörg Linda, and Thamar M. Heijstra. "Balancing Work-Family Life in Academia: The Power of Time. *Gender, Work & Organization* 20, no. 3 (2013): 283–96.

Sandwick, Talia, Michelle Fine, Andrew Cory Greene, Brett G. Stoudt, María Elena Torre, and Leigh Patel. "Promise and Provocation: Humble Reflections on Critical Participatory Action Research for Social Policy." *Urban Education* 53, no. 4 (2018): 473–502.

Sattar, Atia. "Academic Motherhood and the Unrecognized Labors of Non-Tenure Track Faculty Women of Color: What the Invisibility of the Most Marginalized Reveals." American Association of University Professors. 2022. https://www.aaup.org/article/academic-motherhood-and-unrecognized-labors-non-tenure-track-faculty-women-color#.Ysdn4XbMKUm

Saunders, Gabrielle H., Iain R. Jackson, and Anisa S. Visram. "Impacts of Face Coverings on Communication: An Indirect Impact of COVID-19." *International Journal of Audiology* 60, no. 7 (2020): 495–506.

Schultz, Callie Spencer. "'Working the Ruins' of Collaborative Feminist Research." *International Journal of Qualitative Studies in Education* 30, no. 6 (2017): 505–18.

Shah, Anuj, Isabella Lopez, Bapurao Surnar, Shrita Sarkar, Lunthita M. Duthely, Asha Pillai, Tina T. Salguero, and Shanta Dar. "Turning the Tide for Academic Women in STEM: A Postpandemic Vision for Supporting Female Scientists." *ACS Nano* 15, no. 12 (2021): 18647–52.

Simien, Evelyn M., and Sophia Jordan Wallace. "Disproportionate Service: Considering the Impacts of George Floyd's Death and the Coronavirus Pandemic for Women Academics and Faculty of Color." *PS: Political Science & Politics* (2022): 1–5.

Staniscuaski, Fernanda, Livia Kmetzsch, Rossana C. Soletti, Fernanda Reichert, Eugenia Zandonà, Zelia M. C. Ludwig, Eliade F. Lima, et al. "Gender, Race and Parenthood Impact Academic Productivity during the Covid-19 Pandemic: From Survey to Action." *Frontiers in Psychology* 12 (2021): 1–14.

Starks, Briana. "The Double Pandemic: COVID-19 and White Supremacy." *Qualitative Social Work* 20, no. 1–2 (2021): 222–4.

U.S. Bureau of Labor Statistics. "The Employment Situation—September 2020." 2020. https://www.bls.gov/news.release/archives/empsit_10022020.pdf.

Veletsianos, George, and Shandell Houlden. "Radical Flexibility and Relationality as Responses to Education in Times of Crisis." *Postdigital Science and Education* 2 (2020): 849–62.

Wagner, Kathryn, Meike Eilert, and Stacey R. Lim. "Academic Mothers with Disabilities: Navigating Academia and Parenthood during Covid-19." *Gender, Work and Organization* 29, no. 1 (2022): 342–52.

Wiederhold, Brenda K. "Using Social Media to Our Advantage: Alleviating Anxiety During a Pandemic." *Cyberpsychology, Behavior, and Social Networking* 23, no. 4 (2020): 197–98.

2

TIMESOUP, MISSED MEANING, AND MAKING A PANDEMIC HISTORY

Courtney Naum Scuro

Times of crisis can place every aspect of our lives into sharp relief. Or they can seem to bleed them of their meaning. Or they can do both . . . even simultaneously. Central to my experience of this pandemic has been the disorienting feeling that time's passage somehow lost its significance—that I drown in an undifferentiated deluge of moments that I like to call timesoup. In this chapter, I explore the difficulty in making sense of this pandemic's strange early days and finding relevance in scholarly work during them. For some, what follows may seem like an unsuitably personal and narrative account for an academic project.[1] I beg your indulgence. If this experience has taught us anything, I believe it is to question the separation that we impose upon our professional and personal personas and the hierarchization of knowledge practices such divisions also demand.[2]

One of the key issues taken up in this volume is, what does it mean to be an engaged scholar? And, more specifically, what does it mean in light of COVID-19? To the many answers offered, I add this: engaged scholarship is an embodying scholarship. Or, put another way, it is scholarship that sees the messy, fleshy, visceral dimensions of being as sources of knowledge too. Bodies vary, along with experiences of being in one, as scholars of race and disability studies in particular teach us.[3] An engaged-embodying scholarship should be attuned to variations in bodily experiences (past as well as present, with an alertness to cultural and historical contingencies), it should promote self-reflection on embodiment's effects, and it should explore how these factors can and do shape knowledge-practices (like it or not). It starts with self-examination. Engaging in such scholarship means first questioning how one personally lives in the world and how to do so more conscientiously and justly, while also actively working to open pathways to more aware living for others.[4] As the pandemic eases, people continue to struggle to make sense out of the bewildering experience of being in the world since spring 2020. Humanities scholars could have an important role to play in that process, but only if we can find ways to make our knowledge-producing work feel more relatable, accessible, and collaborative to the public-at-large. An engaged-embodying approach can help us to do just that, I argue, and thus may also help us to reassert the relevance of the humanities to public life writ large.

For premodern scholars like myself, this work is especially crucial because of the ways subjects from this field are appropriated in troubling and even dangerous ways.[5] In a February 10, 2021, Fox News interview, Senator Ted Cruz called the impeachment trial of former President Donald Trump "reminiscent of Shakespeare, that it is full of sound and fury and yet signifying nothing" in an overt attempt to leverage Shakespeare's cultural capital to delegitimize those proceedings.[6] Then, on April 17, 2021, Marjorie Taylor Greene and Paul Gosar's plans surfaced for an "America First Caucus" that would "promote uniquely Anglo-Saxon political traditions."[7] Immediately I flashed to *Beowulf*'s opening lines and that Anglo-Saxon poem's claim that "a wrecker of mead-benches . . . one good king makes."[8] I envisioned a pack of paunchy, pasty men in Brooks Brothers suits smashing heavily lacquered, expensive wooden chairs on the House floor while a scant smattering of well-heeled women in conservatively slitted wool pencil skirts hovered nearby, offering libations. The sheer absurdity of Greene and Gosar's attempt to extol "Anglo-Saxon political traditions" might have been amusing if it were not for the deeply disturbing way alt-right, white nationalist discourses were being invoked with that brand of medievalism (along with images of the January 6, 2021, siege on Capitol Hill).[9] As with Cruz, here one sees elected officials trying to leverage historical subjects in order to authenticate problematic political positions in front of an American public ill-prepared to appreciate how such manipulations work. Flash forward to June 2022, when the first Select Committee hearing on the January 6 Capitol attack aired. Ed Pilkington of Guardian US reported: "Caroline Edwards, the Capitol police officer, described slipping in people's blood—not the first time in the evening that *Shakespearean* imagery was invoked" (my emphasis).[10] Edwards' testimony described chaos, carnage, and a war zone that day. So, why "Shakespearean," Pilkington? What's Will got to do with it?

The issue is, these allusions essentially all make the same problematic move: they attempt to use some glorified emblem of past cultural greatness in order to assert the significance, insightfulness, and/or timeless-and-therefore-unquestionable truth of whatever is being said right now. Regardless of what politics that rhetorical move serves, these uncritical allusions unavoidably reassert forms of intellectual elitism, white exceptionalism, and exclusionary historiographies because those ideologies are all tied up in how something like Shakespeare and many types of medievalism gained and maintain their iconic statuses.

Instead, actively thinking with something like Shakespeare can and should be used to help dismantle the sorts of troubling, subjugating ideologies that Bardolatry in particular (i.e., the excessive worship of the man and his work as some universal and timeless fountain of truth) has too often served over the last four hundred years. For example, in my spring 2020 Intro to Shakespeare course, students were invited to creatively explore how Shakespeare (mis)represents them. In response, Mackenzie wrote a scene in which depictions of desire in Shakespeare's sonnets both engaged and misaligned with her character's experience of queer sexual discovery. The piece came about because she "craved representation of LGBT relationships" and to "write a piece that [she] could more closely relate to" than his sonnets; ultimately, her intervention de-privileged Shakespeare by exposing his text's limitations and leveraged his critique to enact a self-affirming examination of her lived experience. Let me be clear, the class may have provided occasion and encouragement to critique Shakespeare's cultural capital, but students like Mackenzie are who make that work really happen.[11] Is it work that a wider public could be encouraged to undertake? I would like to think so. But to figure out how, scholars like me must first find ways to embrace the kinds of engaged-embodying pathways to knowing like Mackenzie locates in desire. That is where this chapter comes into play.

Through a series of episodes taken from summer 2020, I ask you to explore along with me how alternative ways of knowing can reveal the need to reassess how one lives in, studies, and understands this contemporary moment. These episodes center what would typically be pushed to the margins in scholarly work, if not occluded altogether: my personal life, affectiveness, and lived bodily experiences. Taking this approach to the making of a pandemic history, I begin to unravel the complex interconnectedness of temporal attitudes, identity, and social responsibility impacting individuals' varying responses to the early days of this pandemic. And in doing so, I hone in one of the biggest lessons to be taken from COVID-19: the need to keep time better.

Critical theory I relegate to the endnotes. Why? Generally speaking, I believe the radically disorienting nature of the last several years demands equally disorienting intellectual experimentation in response. More specifically, I see these endnotes as a way to make legible a divide between living life and thinking life that I have often felt.[12] By materially manifesting that split through the forthcoming pages, I hope to highlight the need to plot a course to more whole-person or self-affirming forms of scholarship, ones that might simultaneously embrace the different ways of knowing given space on these pages. This framework results, I freely confess, in something of an overcorrection: theory should not—cannot—simply exist in sidelined isolation from one's actual engagement in the world.[13] There I place it for now, however, in order to emphasize the contingent and suspect significance that many scholarly traditions take on within the alien contexts of the last several years.

Finally, here I also try to embrace the intelligence offered by <u>not</u> knowing and by the unknowable[14]—an effort legible in the faults, omissions, and silences that will surface throughout this project.[15] These points are best approached by asking oneself, what does this part of the text <u>not</u> mean or fail to legitimize? And then, what kinds of relating and meaning does it leave room for in the process? Such holes subtly invite you to make a pandemic history of your own alongside mine by bringing your personal experiences into the conversation; the *Reflections* found at the end of each episode explicitly make that appeal. It is still too soon to know what these pandemic times might come to mean, but I hope reflecting together at this point will prove useful even as pieces may later seem obvious, out of place, or even wrong.[16]

Mine will prove an imperfect history, surely, but it is one I write to serve the living, not the past.[17,18]

Episode 1: *Nothing to Say Here*

"So, with everything going on, you must have a lot to say about time right now."

A chasmal silence fills the phone line facilitating this safely socially distanced meeting with my mentor. Her assumption is a fair one but also widely inaccurate, as it happens. I wrack the far reaches of my memory for a thought, any thought, on this topic that I have had since the start of the pandemic. Nothing. No idea has graced my brain since April. Or was it March? It may have been February. It is now nearly June. Luckily, she is a generous enough soul that I can simply be honest.

"Actually, I haven't really thought about time now. I think I have been too busy living in it."

It is an unpremeditated but all too telling confession, thanks to that adversarial relationship between living and thinking at its core. Present circumstances have exposed deeply unsatisfying fault lines in how time, work, and life come together in my day-to-day existence. Healing these fissures—and figuring out what to say about time now—will mean seeking new connections.

Who's with me?

Reflection

How have living and thinking related for you during the pandemic? Did the pandemic leave you feeling less than fully present and connected? What does finding more self-affirming ways forward mean for you?

Episode 2: *Desperate Times, Desperate Matters*

I think back to July 2020—California's stay-at-home order just four months old, a vaccine a distant hope, and death tolls rising. How new, how uncertain the risk of this virus still is in this moment. And yet, already resolve is crumbling. I remember watching as people increasingly ignore calls for caution and communal duty for the sake of familiar, but quite frankly unnecessary, forms of self-gratification: bar-hopping, birthday parties, dine-in restaurants, and pedicures. "I just need to go on living" or "I can't just keep staying home" or "Life *has* to go on," they say again and again. "No, it doesn't," I recall grumbling to any available listener: the dog, a houseplant, an ear of corn (audiences are hard to come by "safer-at-home"). This virus keeps its own schedule and it does not give a damn about anyone's social calendar.[19]

Summer 2020 precedes the intense exhaustion, mounting politicization, and increasingly relative perceptions of risk that will develop as this pandemic drags on. These early days can therefore show us things that later become harder to see—like how fairly mundane and material ways of relating to time can shape individual reactions. For many, the initial spread of COVID-19 forced changes to daily ways of living that rendered impossible the performances of temporal differentiation by which the passage of time gains meaning. What these performances are exactly can be as different as the subjects performing them: going to work, planning a trip, or partaking in a social event requiring real pants. That disturbance also happened suddenly and on a large, collective scale. So, even for those whose lives continue to feel fundamentally unchanged, an unsettling sense of suspension can still settle in. My brother falls into this category. "My work/life routine really hasn't changed much," he admitted to me in late 2020, and yet, he still felt suddenly stuck on pause.[20] In other words, broader social contexts matter and can have a rippling effect.

Some form of patterning and repetition-with-variation still likely structures day-to-day experience for most even during a lockdown. However, for those whose lives suddenly feel put on hold, existence occurs in the absence of what makes life feel meaningful. What are those meaning-activating elements? Again, answers vary. But I find myself particularly drawn to reflecting on what seemingly insignificant social interactions may only reveal their true value in absentia: that serendipitous exchange with the stranger next in line, immersing in a crowded coffee shop's hums and rumbles, or greetings with the grocery clerk sans masks. By summer 2020, these were all suddenly gone. However, this problem notably reflects an affliction of the privileged: those whose health, economic, food, housing, employment stability, and general ability to carry out lives free from threat of violence or persecution prevented these same times from instead feeling extraordinary.

On May 26, 2020, George Floyd was murdered by police and large-scale protest followed. **Black Lives Matter**. There are many, very different experiences from this same summer than those described in this account. These are critical histories to remember. They are also better served by other voices than mine.[21]

Instead, this chapter's conversation is about monotony.[22] As time's passage lost its meaning, many lost an ability to identify with it.[23] This loss in time's significance has also been occurring alongside events compelling us to acknowledge human mortality in new and frightening ways.[24] For some, what has resulted is not simple longing for a return to normalcy, as I at first mistakenly took it, but a desperate need to rectify the void of nonmeaning suddenly shaping life. What is striking is how significant longings, emotions, urges—not thoughts, per se!—are when we begin to trace out how our motivations connect to our individual perceptions of temporality.[25] Reading on reopenings happening in the midst of California's climbing infection rates in July 2020, there is this particularly captivating description:

> On Friday afternoon, hundreds of people wandered around Downtown Disney, a strip of restaurants and shops that ends at the gates to Disneyland. . . . It had reopened the day before to such demand that security had to close the adjacent Simba parking lot to keep people away.
>
> "We just wanted to get out and start living again," said Kimberly Poff, an annual pass holder who proudly held up her newest purchase: a navy blue 65th anniversary long-sleeve shirt that sparkled in the sunlight. She was equipped with hand sanitizer and disinfectants."[26]

Poff's assorted germ-killing agents admit her to be neither unaware nor unconcerned about the contagion likely lurking in the crowd. Nevertheless, here the focus is definitely *not* on the virus, nor guarding against it, but on "her newest purchase: a navy blue 65th anniversary long-sleeve shirt that sparkled in the sunlight." That single word "newest" betrays the seriality that is as intrinsic to this scene as its splash of novelty.[27] For the subject operating within the strictures of our capitalist system, a gratifying return to consumerism affords the opportunity to turn the moment exceptional.[28] This temporalizing happens on two fronts, at least. First, the shirt becomes a material marker of time's distinctiveness; there is the-time-before-possessing-this-shirt and the time after. Powerfully, the ability to differentiate time in this fashion especially belongs to the object's owner for whom the very act of purchasing may be a ritualized or fetishized event, as scholars have extensively explored.[29] Depicted as a source of pride as it "sparkled in the sun," the shirt exudes special sensorial allure. There is something, dare I say, almost magical about this moment, as the shirt works to make time feel differently for those in its presence and, especially, its possessor. Second, there is the commemorative function of the shirt. Marking the "65th anniversary" of Disneyland earns this shirt special affordances as a timekeeper while it also offers its owner her own small purchase in the unfolding timescape that this shirt helps to materially construct and turn legible. And voila, if only just for a moment, time matters once again.

"We just wanted to get out and start living again," Poff insists. But what does that really mean? Really, it is a desire to "get out" of an enervating state of temporal bleed, in which one day begins to feel nearly indecipherable from the next, and the next, and the next—a state antithetical, it seems, to contemporary ideas about "living." Put in those terms, Poff's impulse begins to feel more familiar. Arguably, I followed a not-so-different yearning just a few weeks earlier, on Father's Day. The outer space–themed celebration that I planned for my little family had its own fetishist materialist angle. From craft paper star garlands, to matching space ensembles, and rocket-shaped breakfast food, that event had revolved around a carefully curated set of objects meant to prop up the meaningfulness of the day—to give it a bit of sparkle, if you will. What were these festivities, really? They were my desperate attempt to try to make the day feel "special-new-and-different," as my daughter would say. In summer 2020 it suddenly became her highest form of praise, reserved for anything managing to break through her near persistent case of toddler-sized ennui. She is too young to understand why we are safer-at-home, but she certainly grasps how bored to her bones she is there.[30]

Prolonged periods of homebound isolation also have many consuming media at higher rates than ever before.[31] And what is its overwhelming message? These are exceptional times. These are the moments that define a generation, a century, an era, and so on. So, how can time mean both too little and too much all at once? The vertiginous nature of that paradox leaves me a little ill.

Reflection

How has time mattered to you during this pandemic? What seemingly insignificant, mundane activities do you recall missing (or still miss)? What sorts of rituals have you replaced them with? What do your desires betray about how you value time's passage?

Episode 3: *Face Value*

One of my great pandemic struggles has been acclimating an extremely strong-willed two-and-a-half-year old to wearing a mask. I sew her one that matches Mommy's. It doesn't help. When her face mirrors my furrowed brow, I see written in those folds my own urge to resist this strange reality. Maybe a mask for her beloved stuffed bunny, Flops, might help? It seems worth a try. My work begins in the post-bedtime silence. Later that night, I will break a needle and cry alone in the quiet (figure 1).

It isn't about the needle.

Reflection

What moments from these pandemic times feel important to you to record, but without ready rationale? Are such experiences, nevertheless, important? Or do I exceed the bounds of an engaged-embodying scholarship by making space for such a moment?

Episode 4: *Hey, Watch It Now*

It is August 2020 and suddenly I realize that I haven't worn a watch in over a month. That confession probably feels less than extraordinary until I admit to having been a faithful, daily watch-wearer for over twenty years. Why, yes, I *am* one of those people with that tan line.

Point being, for me to stop wearing a watch—to no longer feel the necessity of it in some fundamentally visceral way—represents a fairly significant shift in how I experience and engage with time on a day-to-day basis. Perhaps part of my less-than-conscious resistance to wearing a watch suddenly has something to do

FIGURE 1. Photo by the author, 2020.

with my gut-deep discomfort over the strangeness of these times and my need for them to keep feeling strange as a way to repel their normalization. That is probably part of it. But even in the likely case that my sudden shift in watch-wearing behavior has a deeply personal, emotionally reactive dimension to it, I also think it speaks to a wider-spread disorientation in temporal values that is worth pondering for a minute—or for ten, or three, or I don't know how long. I'm not wearing a watch, remember?

There is a question that must be asked—to what extent is the relationship to a watch, or a calendar, or any other device aimed at objectivizing and measuring time really, in fact, about trying to turn time's passage into some sort of easily discernible matter (in both senses of the word)? Was my wearing a watch about containment: about restricting my quotidian engagements with time inside the steady and reliable sweep of three rotating hands? Time might be mysterious still, sure, but only further out at a distance. Right here and right now, the kind of time sitting closest to my skin is the one that I mark, that I manage: in essence, the one that can make me feel in control. Not all watch-wearing necessarily feels this way, but I believe it did for me. What I do not believe, however, is that I am alone in having had certain devices and routines afford me a sense of power over how time's passage came to gain meaning in my day-to-day life. And the problem wrought by this pandemic is that experiences of time's passage have fallen widely out of sync with our familiar systems for it (that are at the same time, systems of value). So, what happens? Well, apparently, many of us start to say that time is meaningless (figure 2).

Instead, perhaps we need to consider whether the issue is not that time suddenly means too little, but that its significance weighs on us too much. Time has somehow become more: more stifling, more subjugating, more affecting. My watch just can't handle the weight of it all. Clock, calendar, days of the week: ways in which I may not have even realized that I wanted and needed time to matter made no sense . . . and maybe they still don't (or at least, not the way they once did). Affect overrules reason; that point feels important to make. And again, because it cannot be said often enough, it is a privileged perspective that I speak of: a temporal experience for those safe and secure enough at home to suddenly feel quite differently time's strange creeping.

In 2016 a company named The Matters first released their design for a watch whose face simply and continuously proclaims the time to be NOW. For the (frankly, absurd) price of ninety-nine dollars, you too can possess one of these "time-less-pieces": a watch purposefully designed to frustrate any attempt to actually know what time it is.[32] Had I seen this product pre-COVID-19, I would have called it the height of pretentious hipster absurdity. Within the very different contexts of today, however, this intention to suspend clock-time isn't without its appeal. "For if we live life like it matters—it will," The Matters' website contends, by reorienting what we invest with meaning, energy, and attention. It sounds good, sure, but I am highly skeptical of what help, if any, this brand of vaguely philosophical sentimentality can truly bring. In fact, I suspect that this

TIMESOUP, MISSED MEANING, AND MAKING A PANDEMIC HISTORY

FIGURE 2. My favorite meme in 2020. I only wish that scrambled bit feels like it did end by December 2020 (creator unknown).

demanded divestment in familiar ways that time immediately and tangibly means would only heighten senses of loss and devaluation for quite a few people. That said, many of the usual methods for relating to and valuing time suffered a profound breakdown in 2020. It is time to lean into pandemic-induced uncertainties and take a hard look at the different ways time's meaning materializes in our individual lives—whether through a watch, or Disney shirt, or any other seemingly essential matter. Only then, might one begin to discover how to keep time better. NOW.[33]

Reflection

How do you watch time pass (pun intended)? How do you make a moment stand out? Are there ways in which your relationship to time changed or even just felt differently during lockdown? What might these shifts reveal about how time unconsciously matters to you? And do you want it to change?

Episode 5: *Difference-Wise*

It is August 2020 and I decide to take a walk downtown in the summer's heat . . . and in my mask. It is uncomfortable and disconcerting to feel my own hot breath bouncing back against my skin. And yet, the sensation is also surprisingly soothing. It is as if in so much absence of the familiar, I find myself more able to live in this moment and in this tense, uncertain body that I presently occupy, if everything would just mutually agree to misalign with how things were before. None of it is logical, I realize. And yet, in a deeply embodied way, one that supersedes my attempts to rationalize or theorize these circumstances, I begin to sense that managing not just to live in but also to learn from this pandemic life may mean embracing the radical alterity of it. It may mean being willing to really feel myself within the contours of this crisis. And so, I sink into the sweaty spaces where fabric melds to flesh, and the boundary between where my mask ends and skin begins becomes unclear. I inhale these once busy but now eerily empty streets. Such a moment offers a different kind of knowing.

Reflection

Are there different kinds of knowing that you want your work and life to value? What experiences of yours embody these? What do they tell you?

Coming to Conclusions

To conclude implies a kind of finality that, at present, feels particularly problematic. It is now summer 2022 as I revise this chapter for one final time. The virus carries on. Life does, too. Much has changed. Much stays the same. But public sentiments, broadly speaking, seem more fractious than ever. Nevertheless, I remain as convinced as I was when starting this project nearly two years ago that the key to finding better ways forward will be to dig into the messy bits of this pandemic experience and to learn from what that look back betrays. And so, here are where things stand in making this pandemic history . . . for now.

In the summer of 2020 many struggled with what meaning, if any, the passage of time continued to hold. Neologisms like *#whatdayisit*, *quaran-time*, and *blursday* proliferated social media and late-night TV soundbites to testify to the incipient sense of monotony suddenly coloring the American experience. Twitter user @drewfoundland summed up this new strain of temporal malaise nicely in a single tweet when he wrote, "It's finally friday. You know what that means folks: absolutely nothing because time is fake now."[34] To be home, bored, and unsure of the day of the week during the early days of COVID-19 was a privilege, let us remember. Yet the enervating effects of ennui did not belong only to those safer-at-home. Instead, a sense of prolonged dread increasingly qualified many experiences of time—and that feeling lingers on even as the worst of the pandemic appears past here in the United States.

This pandemic has demonstrated how tenuous the meaning of time's passage can be. And this issue with time matters because of the ways in which one's sense of missing relevance can manifest. An innate need to just go on living turned many of those in the position to stay safer at home into potential virus vectors willing to risk not only their own health but that of the community at large. I cannot hazard a guess as to what impact such attitudes could continue to have through the later phases of this pandemic. Responses are increasingly politicized all while a virus that we still do not fully understand continues to morph and linger. I can say that I started out extremely critical of decisions made in early days not to forgo birthday parties, crowded gyms, or indoor dinners with assorted friends as infection rates climbed. Now, without condoning it, I nevertheless see the gravity that can accompany such a decision if it feels like the difference between still having a life worth living or losing it. Point being, the unconsidered ways in which many individuals relate to time can have real, material consequences. It is therefore imperative that each of us consider closely how one's ideas about living become defined by experiences of time and especially, the material repercussions that these can effect.

In other words, it is time to keep time better. That, in the first, means interrogating what time means and how perceptions of time might impact individual and collective ideas about living. However, I begin to suspect that the problem lies less in what time means and more in the quite unconscious and uninterrogated ways in which most of us allow those meanings to materialize in our day-to-day lives. Take a step back from familiar methods for rationalizing and quantifying time (like clock or calendar), and time quickly becomes less a thought than it is a sense or a feeling, especially when something seems wrong with it. Because of this quality, embracing the messy, fleshy, visceral ways in which one knows time—in other words, pursuing an engaged-embodying study of it—will be crucial to better understanding how perceptions of time's passage can drive priorities and decision making. It also will be crucial to fostering the kinds of scholarship necessary to bring these concerns into the public sphere. We need accessible, relatable forms of critique capable of affirming individual experiences of crisis during COVID-19 while encouraging more incisive orientations toward perceptions of time and living, in particular. By the time this book goes to print, perhaps COVID-19's pandemic phase will actually be over, but the related issues with time will continue.

As I draw to a close, I am struck by how much there is still to do. This essay helps to unveil some of the monotony-inducing dynamics of quaran-time, surely, but what it does not do is delve into how issues of class, race, age, ability, or gender shape time-senses. Mine is just one voice, one perspective; many are needed in this conversation (hence the importance of frankly asking you to step in, too, as you read).

In the prologue, I argued that premodern scholars like me urgently need more engaged-embodying forms of public scholarship in order to foster more widespread, public cultures of critique that would be capable of pushing back against attempts to politically leverage subjects from these fields (with Ted Cruz and Marjorie Taylor Greene providing alarming examples). Manipulative historicizing happens all the time, but often goes unrecognized. It is just one way mainstream American culture demonstrates a lack of awareness about how relationships to time can influence how one feels about, thinks about, and decides what is most important in day-to-day life. Historical subjectivity is, thus, intimately linked to the troubles with time today (but trying to unravel that whole issue will have to wait for another space and time). Point being, I see more engaged-embodying scholarship as a possible pathway to empowering a broad audience to apprehend their unacknowledged attachments to history and its subjects in surprising new ways. But just as importantly, I also see this form of scholarly experimentation as a way we scholars can surprise ourselves. Amidst the wildly defamiliarizing effects of this pandemic, taking up an engaged-embodying exploration of our subjects just might allow us to discover new, unexpected kinds of relevance for our work. That has certainly been the case for me.[35]

Life today seems to have animated some things strangely akin to Shakespeare and his peers' own uncertain relations to time. Time hurts to the very bones (Hamlet: "The time is out of joint").[36] Its passage marked in passions (Lady Macbeth: "I feel now the future in the instant").[37] And time can suddenly seem to defy the metronomic reliability promised by clock-time (Rosalind/Ganymede, *As You Like It*: "Time travels in divers paces with divers persons").[38] To our shock and disbelief, today's lived experiences of time seem suddenly incapable of being explained and quantified by clock or calendar. But at the turn of the seventeenth century, folks were yet to believe they could be defined by these measures. Yet to be enveloped in the objectivizing illusions of clock-time, early modern writers prove highly suspicious of how one might keep time, why, and what these practices could mean for a community at large. Keeping time is continually marked by uncertainty, discovery, and debate. So while the daily social dynamics of Shakespeare and his contemporaries sharply differ from those today, they might still help us to consider what it can mean—or not mean—to "carve out dials quaintly, point by point" and "[t]hereby to see the minutes how they run" in an attempt to make "the hour" of life "full complete."[39] The aim is not to valorize the past, mind you, but to utilize it as a productive counterpoint to expose the seemingly innate, yet arbitrary relationships one can form to fairly mundane phenomena—like, well, the daily passage of time—and how these impact lived experiences. The strangeness of the past can serve to defamiliarize the present and, in the process, help to open up the possibility to imagine other kinds of futures—including futures filled with more deliberate and just ways of being in the world. Even if one does not explicitly bring the distant past into conversation with the present (as I do not through most of this project), the kind of critical agility fostered by studying the past can bring with it another perspective (as this essay aims to show), thus giving premodern scholars an important part to play in debates on life today.

"When things get back to normal . . ." I hear this phrase more and more. But such nostalgia promotes a false kind of hope. While there is so much that has been lost to this pandemic, and so much that each of us yearns to "get back" if possible, one cannot go back. And "normal" (whatever that means) is just not good enough. It never was. There is a better kind of future out there. Let's go make it, NOW.

NOTES

Many thanks to Heidi Brayman for unwittingly inspiring me to write this piece and for her continuing support of it. Thanks also to its early readers and responders, Chelsea Silva and Colleen Rosenfeld, and to this volume's editors, Debra Ann Castillo and Melissa Castillo Planas, for their invaluable feedback.

1. Queer theory scholars, however, have powerfully demonstrated the efficacy of models of inquiry drawing on personal history and experience. Reading their writing made this little experiment feel possible. I especially owe debts to Eve Kosofsky Sedwick, José Esteban Muñoz, and Karen Barad.

2. It is not a new question, but in this present crisis, a newly urgent one. Feelings of distress, fracturing, and denial can seem a nearly inescapable part of academic identity formation and can intensify based on gender, sexuality, race, class, ability, and even parenthood. Notable calls to radically reframe our ideas about knowledge, scholarship, and the university (that also demonstrate the range of critical responses) include Stefano Harney and Fred Moten, *The Undercommons*; Róisín Ryan-Flood and Rosalind Gill, *Secrecy and Silence in the Research Process*; Irit Rogoff, "What is a Theorist?"; Maggie Berg and Barbara K. Seeber, *The Slow Professor*.

3. As a premodern scholar, I am especially indebted to the following scholars for recent, thought-provoking presentations: on critical race theory, David Sterling Brown, Jennifer L. Stoever, and the Folger for their *Critical Race Conversation* series, Ian Smith, Ayanna Thompson and the ongoing work of the RaceB4Race symposium; on disability studies, Allison Hobgood, Amy Kenny, and Elizabeth B. Bearden.

4. "We should be asking ourselves the same sorts of questions when we write our texts, when we put things together, as we do in living our lives. . . . If not, we are not," Sarah Ahmed, *Living a Feminist Life*, 14–15.

5. "Just as we count on our colleagues in climate science to speak up against the voices that deny global warming, we humanists must counter the forces that denigrate knowledge-based discourses, threaten human values, and whitewash historical events. Those of us who teach Renaissance literature specifically must refuse the appropriation of canonical figures or cultural formations to bolster nefarious ends," Hyman and Eklund, "Introduction," 2. Also see Ruiter, ed., *Shakespeare and Social Justice*; O'Dair and Francisco, *Shakespeare and the 99%*; Shapiro, *Shakespeare in a Divided America*.

6. Cruz, "America's Newsroom."

7. Diaz et al., "Marjorie Taylor Greene."

8. Heaney, trans., *Beowulf*, 2, 11.

9. "Fascism thrives on false narratives, particularly those that involve misleading origin myths and manipulation of terminology and symbols to reinforce hate. That makes it essential that we get the past right, especially when false narratives are used to justify so much anti-democratic politics in today's world," Gabriele and Rambaran-Olm, "Middle Ages."

10. Pilkington, "Primetime January 6 Hearing Shows."

11. In a May 2021 talk, Shelley Haley offers a brilliant examination of Audre Lorde's assertion that "the master's tools will never dismantle the master's house," which highlights the inescapable limitations of the kind of approach that I propose. But what it can still accomplish—as just a first step of many—is a crucial demystifying of Shakespeare that exposes the house of Bardolatry as a destructible thing . . . so grab an ax; Haley, "Reimagining the Classics."

12. "With a few notable exceptions, time has been doomed to the vast realm of that which is unthought, perhaps because it at once seems so obvious . . . and on closer examination seems impossible," Cohen, *Medieval Identity Machines*, 1.

13. "I found a place of sanctuary in 'theorizing,' in making sense out of what was happening. I found a place where I could imagine possible futures, a place where life could be lived differently." However, "theory is not inherently healing, liberatory, or revolutionary. It fulfills this function only when we ask that it do so and direct our theorizing towards this end," bell hooks, "Theory as Liberatory Practice," 1. Here hooks articulates the possibility—and the difficulty—of pursuing a critical practice animate with living relevance. To reach this "theorizing" end, first we must question the relevance of our theoretical inheritances for *now*—work these endnotes will serve.

14. "I confess to you . . . that I still do not know what time is, and I further confess to you . . . that as I say this I know myself to be conditioned by time" and I would add, the more I try to know time, the truer these words become; Saint Augustine, *Confessions*, trans. Henry Chadwick, 239.

15. In this provocation, I find endless inspiration: "If we bracket the assumption that knowledge is the logical end (implicit purpose, developmental telos, final terminus) to ignorance, we are emboldened to ask not only *why* we do not know what we do not know, but what we might make with and of such a 'lack,'" Traub, *Thinking Sex*, 311.

16. The key word there is might. "In an enigmatic sense, which will clarify itself *perhaps* (perhaps, because nothing should be sure here, for essential reasons), the question

of the archive is not, we repeat, a question of the past. It is a question of the future, the question of the future itself, the question of a response, a promise and of a responsibility for tomorrow. *The archive: if we want to know what that will have meant, we will only know in times to come. Perhaps,*" Derrida, *Archive Fever*, 36 (added emphasis). Derrida likely had a more complex system in mind than my little history here, but his point still stands. I cannot know what this account might mean in the future, if anything, but out "of a response . . . and of a responsibility for tomorrow," I offer it. Derrida's observations on the inescapable enigma of archivization are easy to take in the negative. One would like to know one's efforts will matter (not might). However, lurking in the uncertainty of Derrida's "perhaps"— or, in the power of not knowing—is an invitation to imagine what futures may be. Such efforts might ultimately prove ineffectual, perhaps, but they are not meaningless.

17. "The difficulty with the notion of a truth of past experience is that it can no longer be experienced, and this throws a specifically historical knowledge open to the charge that it is a construction as much of imagination as of thought and that its authority is no greater than the power of the historian to persuade his reader that his account is true. This puts historical discourse on the same level as any rhetorical performance and consigns it to the status of a textualization neither more nor less authoritative than literature itself can lay claim to," White, *Content*, 147.

18. "To be sure, we need history. But we need it in a manner different from the way in which the spoilt idler in the garden of knowledge uses it. . . . That is, we need it for life and action. . . . We wish to use history only insofar as it serves living," Nietzsche, "Use and Abuse of History," 57–142. Or at least, this must be the aim, even if one cannot know yet what our present efforts might come to mean (thank you, Derrida).

19. "A relation of cruel optimism exists when something you desire is actually an obstacle to your flourishing . . . when the object that draws your attachment actively impedes the aim that brought you to it initially," Berlant, *Cruel Optimism*, 1. How truer could these words be than when a purported desire to live compels someone to risk their life? As this virus has evolved, so has our understanding of it and the risk it poses, but early in this pandemic, especially, many seemed unconsciously caught up in a kind of cruel optimistic conundrum driven by presumptions about what it means to truly live.

20. "Differences in the pace of life turn out . . . to have far-reaching consequences. This shouldn't be surprising. After all, the pace of our lives governs our experience of the passage of time. And how we move through time is, ultimately, the way we live our lives," Levine, *Geography of Time*, XIX. Levine puts a lot of stock in personal pace/tempo, perhaps too much. Consider my brother, whose daily tempo underwent very little actual alteration through the early days of the pandemic and yet he still suffered from time's slow slide into seeming senselessness. In other words, the mechanisms by which time's most ordinary motions take on meaning may have a deeply communal element, one few of us appreciate or understand.

21. For a poignant example, one that incisively critiques Shakespeare's political relevance, see Allen, *#ToBeBlack*.

22. "Unless we develop concepts of time and duration which welcome and privilege the future, which openly accept the rich virtualities and divergent resonances of the present, we will remain closed to understanding the complex processes of becoming that engender and constitute both life and becoming" and that "a concept of new provokes," Elizabeth Grosz, "Thinking the New," 38. When I first read it in February 2020, Grosz's call to embrace "temporality and futurity . . . as modalities of difference" seemed like it might offer a way to harness an American obsession with narratives of progress so that these might actually serve traditionally marginalized groups by instilling ideas of difference with fresh value and significance, and in doing so, disrupt continuing discourses of diminution. But what happens when the future feels put on hold? Reading Grosz again

in July 2020 (a mere five months later, let's make note), I began to wonder if our attachment to a future defined by pursuits of the new may, in fact, be an issue. Were it not for contemporary attachments to defining and valuing time based on its perceptible forms of desirable distinctiveness, would monotony feel like such a burden?

23. "The implication might be that if time loses meaning, and we're in this perpetual present, it may be more difficult to do things for the long run. . . . I'm not sure that time itself has actually lost meaning. But I am worried that people are losing meaning within these stretches of time because we aren't quite sure what to do with ourselves," Hal Hershfeld, quoted in Shayla Love, "Time Is Meaningless Now." Acts, passage, meaning: they intertwine to impact our experiences of time in no small way, but Hershfield seems to struggle to capture in exactly *what* way. I can relate.

24. And on the day that I go back to edit this section, this headline dominates the news waves: "Coronavirus Far Deadlier than Flu, on Track to Become 2nd Leading Cause of Death in LA County."

25. "We are talking about . . . not feeling against thought, but thought as felt and feeling as thought: practical consciousness of a present kind." In other words, emotion is not just "private, idiosyncratic" but is a deeply (in)formative dimension of the social experience, Williams, *Marxism and Literature*, 132.

26. Arellano, Sheridan, and Lai. "Coronavirus Rages in Orange County."

27. In her coda, Lauren Goodlad addresses "seriality's special illusion," namely, of a phenomenal repetitiveness that is without end, but still filled with *fresh* feelings of familiarity." While Goodlad's focus is fiction, I find her concept of seriality equally applicable to the stories we tell ourselves about actual lived experience, Goodlad, *Victorian Geopolitical Aesthetic*, 268.

28. "Whatever the *experience* of optimism is in particular . . . the *affective structure* of an optimistic attachment involves a sustaining inclination to return to the scene of fantasy that enables you to expect that *this* time, nearness to this thing will help you or a world to become different in just the right way," Berlant, *Cruel Optimism*, 2.

29. See Marx, *Capital*, trans. Ben Fowkes. See also: Rook, " Ritual Dimension," 251–26; Belk, Ger, and Askegaard, "Fire of Desire."

30. Boredom: an experience variably defined by philosophers as a mood, a state, and an affect, boredom happens when one's experience of being (in time) fails to feel significant or fulfilling and so suspends one in a stew of inconsequentiality. Then comes the question, if this moment does not really seem to matter, do I matter while living in it? On scholars' increasing interest in boredom as "a critical concept that centres [sic] on issues and problems of experiencing meaning," see Julian Haladyn and Michael Gardiner, eds., *Boredom Studies Reader*, 1.

31. "Covid Impact on Consumer Media Usage."

32. *The Matters.*

33. "An awareness of temporality and the time taken to live requires—and presupposes—an investment in the meaning-making practices of everyday life" and might lead to more attentive, invested, careful practices of relating, engaging, and consuming as part of "living in the global everyday," Parkins and Craig, *Slow Living*, 8. Parkins and Craig say that at their best, slow living movements embody a kind of quotidian ethicality that Michael Gardiner describes as "a longing for a different, and better way of living, a reconciliation of thought and life, desire and the real, in a manner that critiques the status quo without projecting a full-blown image of what a future society should look like" (quoted in Parkins and Craig, *Slow Living*, 51). The purported glory and pleasure of stalling life's pace, which slow-life proposes certainly felt ironic, circa 2020 (especially for someone naturally quick paced, like myself). However, I increasingly begin to see this movement's call for more critical yet affectively intoned orientations to time as staging an important intervention.

34. Love, "Time is Meaningless."

35. "The possibilities of extending our understanding depend not just on what we already understand, but also on what sorts of people we have become," Collini, *English Pasts*, 237.

36. Shakespeare, *Hamlet* in *The Riverside Shakespeare*, edited by G. Blakemore Evans and J.J.M. Tobias, 1.5.188.

37. Shakespeare, *Macbeth*, 1.5.57–58.

38. Shakespeare, *As You Like It*, 3.2.308–309.

39. Shakespeare, *3 Henry VI*, 2.5.24–26.

BIBLIOGRAPHY

Ahmed, Sara. *Living a Feminist Life*. Durham, NC: Duke University Press, 2017.

Allen, Lewis. *#ToBeBlack*, performed by The Public Theater, June 19, 2020. https://www.youtube.com/watch?v=LbEvpe9suGg.

Arellano, Gustavo, Jake Sheridan, and Stephanie Lai. "Coronavirus Rages in Orange County, but Don't Tell That to Disney Fans." *Los Angeles Times*, July 10, 2020. https://www.latimes.com/california/story/2020-07-10/coronavirus-disneyland-orange-county-downtown-disney-reopening.

Augustine. *Confessions*. Translated by Henry Chadwick. Oxford: Oxford University Press, 1991.

Belk, Russell W., Güliz Ger, Søren Askegaard. "The Fire of Desire: A Multisited Inquiry into Consumer Passion." *Journal of Consumer Research* 30, no. 3 (2003): 326–51. https://doi.org/10.1086/378613.

Berg, Maggie, and Barbara K. Seeber. *The Slow Professor: Challenging the Culture of Speed in the Academy*. Toronto: University of Toronto Press, 2016.

Berlant, Lauren. *Cruel Optimism*. Durham, NC: Duke University Press, 2011.

Cohen, Jeffrey Jerome. *Medieval Identity Machines*. Minneapolis: University of Minnesota Press, 2003.

Collini, Stefan. *English Pasts: Essays on Culture and History*. Oxford: Oxford University Press, 1999.

"Coronavirus Far Deadlier than Flu, on Track to Become 2nd Leading Cause of Death in LA County." *NBC4* (Los Angeles). July 22, 2020. https://www.nbclosangeles.com/news/coronavirus/coronavirus-is-far-deadlier-than-flu-on-track-to-become-2nd-leading-cause-of-death-in-la-county/2400767/.

"Covid Impact on Consumer Media Usage: March and April 2020." *Interactive Advertising Bureau (IAB)*. May 28, 2020. https://www.iab.com/wp-content/uploads/2020/05/ Consumer-Media-Usage-2019-through-April-2020.pdf.

Cruz, Ted. "America's Newsroom." Bill Hemmer and Dana Perino. *Fox News*. Aired February 10, 2021.

Derrida, Jacques. *Archive Fever: A Freudian Impression*. Translated by Eric Prenowitz. University of Chicago Press, 1996.

Diaz, Daniella, Annie Grayer, Ryan Nobles and Paul LeBlanc. "Marjorie Taylor Greene launching 'America First' caucus pushing for 'Anglo-Saxon political tradition.'" *CNN*. April 17, 2021. https://www.cnn.com/2021/04/16/politics/marjorie-taylor-greene-america-first-caucus/index.

Gabriele, Matthew, and Mary Rambaran-Olm. "The Middle Ages Have Been Misused by the Far Right. Here's Why It's So Important to Get Medieval History Right." *Time*, 21, November 2019. https://time.com/5734697/middle-ages-mistakes/.

Goodlad, Lauren. *The Victorian Geopolitical Aesthetic*. Oxford: Oxford University Press, 2015.

Grosz, Elizabeth. "Thinking the New: Of Futures Yet Unthought." *symplokē* 6, no. 1/2 (1998): 38–55, https://www.jstor.org/stable/40550421.

Haladyn, Julian, and Michael Gardiner, eds. *Boredom Studies Reader*. New York: Routledge, 2017.

Haley, Shelley P. "Re-imagining the Classics: Audre Lorde was Right" (RaceB4Race: Politics Conference, May 4, 2021, virtual).

Harney, Stefano, and Fred Moten. *The Undercommons: Fugitive Planning and Black Study*. London: Minor Compositions, 2013.

Heaney, Seamus, trans. *Beowulf*. New York: Norton, 2000.

hooks, bell. Theory as Liberatory Practice." *Yale Journal of Law and Feminism* 4, no. 1 (1991): 1–12.

Hyman, Wendy Beth, and Hillary Eklund. "Introduction: Making Meaning and Doing Justice with Early Modern Texts." In *Teaching Social Justice Through Shakespeare*, edited by Hillary Eklund and Wendy Beth Hyman, 1–26. Edinburgh: Edinburgh University Press, 2019.

Levine, Robert. *A Geography of Time*. New York: Basic Books, 1997.

Love, Shayla. "Time Is Meaningless Now." *Vice*, April 10, 2020. https://www.vice.com/en/article/m7qyev/time-is-meaningless-now.

Marx, Karl Marx. *Capital*. Translated by Ben Fowkes. New Orleans: Pelican, 1976.

The Matters. Accessed July 20, 2020. https:www.matters.com.

Nietzsche, Friedrich. "On the Use and Abuse of History for Life." *Untimely Meditations*, Translated by R. J. Hollingdale, 57–142. Cambridge: Cambridge UP, 1997.

O'Dair, Sharon, and Timothy Francisco, eds. *Shakespeare and the 99%*. London: Palgrave MacMillan, 2019.

Otnes, Cele C., and Linda Tuncay Zayer. *Gender, Culture, and Consumer Behavior*. New York: Routledge, 2012.

Parkins, Wendy, and Geoffrey Craig. *Slow Living*. Providence, RI: Berg, 2006.

Pilkington, Ed. "Primetime January 6 Hearing Shows Set-piece TV Can Still Pack a Punch." *Guardian US Edition*, June 10, 2022.

Rogoff, Irit. "What Is a Theorist?" Reprinted in *The State of Art Criticism*, edited by James Elkins and Michael Newman, 97–109. New York: Routledge, 2008.

Rook, Dennis W. "The Ritual Dimension of Consumer Behavior." *Journal of Consumer Research* 12 (1985): 251–26. https://doi.org/10.1086/208514.

Ruiter, David, ed. *Shakespeare and Social Justice*. New York: Bloomsbury, 2020.

Ryan-Flood, Róisín, and Rosalind Gill. *Secrecy and Silence in the Research Process: Feminist Reflections*. New York: Routledge, 2010.

Shakespeare, William. *As You Like It*. In *The Riverside Shakespeare*, edited by G. Blakemore Evans and J. J. M. Tobias. Boston: Houghton Mifflin, 1997.

Shakespeare, William. *Hamlet*. In *The Riverside Shakespeare*, edited by G. Blakemore Evans and J. J. M. Tobias. Boston: Houghton Mifflin, 1997.

Shakespeare, William. *Henry IV*. In *The Riverside Shakespeare*, edited by G. Blakemore Evans and J. J. M. Tobias. Boston: Houghton Mifflin, 1997.

Shakespeare, William. *Macbeth*. In *The Riverside Shakespeare*, edited by G. Blakemore Evans and J. J. M. Tobias. Boston: Houghton Mifflin, 1997.

Shapiro, James. *Shakespeare in a Divided America*. New York: Penguin, 2021.

"Theory as Liberatory Practice." *Yale Journal of Law and Feminism* 4, no. 1 (1991): 1–12.

Traub, Valerie. *Thinking Sex with the Early Moderns*. Philadelphia: University of Pennsylvania Press, 2016.

White, Hayden. *The Content of the Form*. Baltimore: The John Hopkins University Press, 1987.

Williams, Raymond. *Marxism and Literature*. Oxford: Oxford University Press, 1985.

3

RESISTING ANTI-ASIAN RACISM IN PUBLIC-FACING WORK AND TEACHING

Joey S. Kim

It has been a remarkably unpredictable and unprecedented time to be a scholar, professor, and public-facing intellectual in the time of COVID-19. The COVID-19 era has given me new challenges and opportunities that have forced me to create and adapt to new modes of research, teaching, and public-facing humanities. In addition to being an academic, however, my physical embodiment as an East Asian woman of assumed Chinese descent has put me in a distressed place of psychological turmoil with an emotional toll. Anti-Asian, xenophobic, and "Yellow-Peril" rhetoric rose in the wake of the virus's signification as the "China virus," "Kung-flu," the "Wuhan virus." These names place blame and hypervisibility on a type of Asian and Asian-presenting body saddled with the compounded weight of historical and present danger.[1] In this chapter, I consider the signification of my East Asian embodiment in the wake of the global COVID-19 pandemic and its resultant surge in anti-Asian, xenophobic, and "Yellow-Peril"– like rhetoric. I share my personal experience of publicly engaged scholarship and teaching as an Asian American woman during this heightened time of Asian visibility and precarity.

Since the first reports of COVID-19 released in December 2019, there have been increases in racist and xenophobic hate speech, actions, and violence across the world, particularly aimed at Asian people and people of presumed Chinese descent. Some of the earliest recorded incidents include the London attack on Singaporean student Jonathan Mok as well as Vietnamese curator An Nguyen's experience of being barred from London's Affordable Art Fair due to Asians being seen as "carriers of the virus."[2] One year later, eighty-four-year-old Vicha

Ratanapakdee was killed in a random attack on the street in San Francisco.[3] Two years later, in February 2022 the gruesome murder of Christina Yuna Lee demonstrated that the crisis continued. In its first two weeks of reporting, the online reporting council Stop AAPI Hate received 1,135 reports of anti-Asian discrimination, assault, and violence, blocked from entering establishments, vandalism, online threats, and so on. Since then, Stop AAPI Hate has compiled yearly national reports, which show a continued rise in these events. Between March 2020 and December 2021, "10,905 hate incidents against Asian American and Pacific Islander (AAPI) persons were reported to Stop AAPI Hate. Of the hate incidents reflected in this report, 4,632 occurred in 2020 (42.5%) and 6,273 occurred in 2021 (57.5%)."[4] Organizers say the rate of reporting is likely a severe undercount of the actual incidents taking place every day across the country. The victims are people are of various ages, ethnicities, gender identities, and geographical locations. In this ongoing COVID-19 moment, the Asian body is under public scrutiny, suspicion, attack, and exhibition.

While hate crimes in the country's largest cities declined overall by 7 percent in 2020, those targeting people of Asian descent rose by nearly 150 percent, according to a report by the Center for the Study of Hate and Extremism at California State University, San Bernardino.[5] The report shows that more than two million Asian American adults have experienced a hate crime, harassment, or discrimination since the beginning of the pandemic. This rise in hate crimes is compounded by rampant social media coverage, viral videos, and the shift in national coverage to anti-Asian racism as a more mainstream issue.[6] While nationally covered, these incidents and crimes are often not viewed as fundamentally "American" issues for various reasons, including the inability for medial venues to understand this country's rampant history of Asian exclusion, xenophobia, and racism. The sustained lack of knowledge of Asian diasporas and Asian Americans in the United States has been remediated by the rise of Asian American Studies programs in the past fifty years. However, only in the years just before publication of this book have Asian American Studies scholars been able to actively shape the public understanding of events such as the rise in anti-Asian hate crimes: the 2021 Atlanta spa shooting, where six Asian women were killed, and the FedEx Indianapolis shooting, where four Sikh Americans were killed and many others injured. These are just a couple in a series of high-profile incidents involving the murders of Asian and Asian American people.

The word "Asian American" is primarily a rights-based and political category that was created to build coalitions of antiracist and anti-imperialist activism. In contrast, however, the historical patterns of Orientalism that undergird today's anti-Asian racism contradict the activist roots of the Asian American movement that thrived in the 1960s and 1970s. "Asian American" was a term of self-determination and can be traced back to 1968 when UC-Berkeley students Yuji Ichioka, Emma Gee, Floyd Huen, Richard Aoki, Victor Ichioka, and Vicci Wong cofounded the Asian American Political Alliance as way to unite Japanese, Chinese, and Filipino American students on campus in alliance with the Black Power Movement, the American Indian Movement (AIM), and the protests against the Vietnam War. Now, the term "Asian American" has expanded to be under the umbrella of Asian American Pacific Islander (AAPI), Asian Pacific American (APA), Asian American and Native Hawaiian/Pacific Islander (AANHPI), and other politicized acronyms, and it is informed by questions of race, colorism, and the heterogeneity of the Asian diaspora when thinking of South Asian, East Asian, Central Asian, and Pacific Rim countries. Due to interlocking systems of racial capitalism and identity tokenism, however, "Asian American" persists as a racial and ethnic wedge of exclusion, white adjacency, and perpetual foreignness that has never been subsumed into the "American" catchall.

This new Asian American reality of public and private discrimination, exclusion, and violence is part of the longer story of the Westernized production of the Oriental subject. I use "Oriental" and "Orientalism" to describe a public-facing discourse of East/West binary thinking that pivots between imaginative idea and historical and political reality. The ever-shifting figure of the Orient is intensified during moments of crisis or conflict affecting the European and Western world. Global powers have, in histories of conquest and plunder, been rooted in European imperialism and a hegemonic West delinked from clear borders or limits. This asymmetrical relationship between East and West continues in the present-day COVID-19 moment, with the East becoming a trope of racialized contagion and reactivated Orientalism. In the process, geographical referents such as Wuhan, China, and Asia become metonyms for a certain type of homogenized body in space, including my own.

From the moment China appeared in the global lexicon of COVID-19 discourse, the virus was racialized and Orientalized. The current level of anti-Asian and xenophobic psychocultural turmoil recalls previous eras of Japanese internment camps and legal actions like the Chinese Exclusion Act of 1882. In particular, the idea of the Asian body of presumed Chinese descent has, for many people around the world, turned into a hypervisible signifier of virus, infection, and contagion. This stereotyping has created a human target for reacting to the threat of infection and death. Due to this racialization, the Asian-presenting body is under constant threat of not only blame but violence and death. Orientalism and its expressions of otherness propagate misinformed conceptions that are now finding expression in the Asian and Asian-presenting body as viral signifier.

Erica Lee, director of the Immigration History Research Center at the University of Minnesota, argues that "[f]uture historians will look upon this period as the absolute high point of xenophobia in our history."[7] Xenophobia is a question of belonging, and for Asian and Asian American people, our belonging became critically distorted with the misinformation about COVID-19's origins. Across the world, the ethnic and racial assumptions behind COVID-19 showed how, as Hortense Spillers notes, "race is both concentrated and dispersed in its locations."[8] This varying density of race and racial signification creates barriers to rights and representation from which publicly engaged scholarship must consciously build an antiracist framework of democratic and inclusive education. Edward Said discusses the role of the public intellectual, linking the intellectual's task with a universal identification of suffering: "In dark times an intellectual is very often looked to by members of his or her nationality to represent, speak out for, and testify to the sufferings of that nationality. . . . For the intellectual the task, I believe, is explicitly to universalize the crisis, to give greater human scope to what a particular race or nation suffered, to associate that experience with the suffering of others."[9]

Said's link between identity representation and larger, multinational networks of coalition building is the nexus from which I have produced differing research, teaching, and public-facing projects because of the pandemic. To universalize is not to limit or exclude but to build the common ground from which many of us feel othered, dispossessed, and/or silenced.

The recent surge in anti-Asian hate and violence repeats historical and long-standing patterns of oppression. The China virus, Kung-flu, and the Wuhan virus signify more than a place of presumed origin. They deploy Orientalist rhetoric that is historically bound to empire, colonization, slavery, and genocide.[10] This rhetoric hearkens back to the end of the nineteenth century when European imperialist powers were expanding into vast expanses of interior Africa and Asia for the first time. When Russian sociologist Yakov Novikov (1849–1912), writing in French, popularized the term "Yellow Peril" in his 1897 essay, "Le Péril Jaune," he activated a color metaphor that persists in racializing Asian bodies today. The phrase quickly became de facto grounds to distrust, objectify, and dispossess the Asian body of individual human qualities.[11] In the past half century, decolonization and globalization may have unseeded the primacy of the West in the world's political order, but the discourse of polarized East vs. West worldviews persists, as well as the implicit threat of the Asian other. In this era of COVID-19 with geographical links to China, Yellow-Peril rhetoric has been adapted and manipulated to serve multiple purposes that continually dispossess the rights of the visibly "Asian" body and body politic. This feeling of dispossession is what I encountered in the post–COVID-19 moment, and I responded to

The Identity-Building Work of Publicly Engaged Scholarship

While adapting my scholarship and teaching for COVID-19 times, I also have managed an intense personal need to better process the mainstream coverage of anti-Asian racism and attacks. I was seeing the news coverage across the country, and I could not find the words to process the weight of what I was seeing. This led me to write multiple public-facing articles on the historical linkages between histories of Orientalism and COVID-19 anti-Asian racism. As a result, I have been positioned in a place of fielding public speaking and media requests, community outreach inquiries, and institutional service requests to discuss the rise in anti-Asian hate crimes and help craft statements condemning anti-Asian racism. As a scholar trained in nineteenth-century British literature who wrote a dissertation on British Romantic poetry and Orientalism, I was unprepared to discuss anti-Asian hate crimes and Asian American civil rights issues, but my embodiment told the world otherwise.

Like many scholars, my ability to work, research, teach, and participate in academic life was hampered by the pandemic and the new rules, restrictions, and confusion it produced. I started a new visiting teaching position and moved to a new state during the height of the pandemic. My first year in this position consisted of virtual meetings and classrooms and almost no in-person communication with new colleagues or students. This isolation did afford me time to research and produce new work, including my first book of poems, *Body Facts*, and it also kept me safe from having to commute or be in public at risk of attack. This isolation, however, also heightened my sense of apartness and stoked a desire in me to connect with like-minded individuals and supportive communities.

My heightened sense of isolation and unbelonging pushed me to find other ways to immerse myself in the world. I published multiple public-facing pieces for national venues, including the *Truthout*, the National Center for Institutional Diversity, the *Los Angeles Review of Books*, and *Shondaland*. For *Shondaland*, I wrote about the paradox of being Asian American while witnessing both the rising reporting on anti-Asian hate crimes and rising coverage of Asian American and Asian films and music including *Parasite*, *Minari*, and K-pop groups like BTS. My piece for *Shondaland* starts by noting how the day before the Atlanta spa shootings, *Minari* garnered six Oscar nominations and Steven Yeun became the first Asian American Oscar nominee for Best Actor. *Minari* has been celebrated both domestically and globally for its nuanced and poetic portrayal of the Korean American Yi family. It is set in rural Arkansas and details the Yi family's multigenerational experiences in the United States. Still, and to much debate, it was deemed a "foreign-language film" by the Hollywood Foreign Press Association and barred from the best motion picture categories in the 2021 Golden Globe awards. I remember watching the film with my parents, Korean immigrants who came to the country in the early 1980s and feeling a sense of both pride and confusion at the state of Asian American representation in American pop culture.

The story of being Asian and Asian American in the United States during the pandemic is not just a question of our lack of complexity or humanity in the nation's cultural imaginary but also a question of how we have been taught to perceive ourselves. I grew up watching and internalizing the racist and stereotypical representations of people who looked like me on television and movie screens. Now as a scholar of Asian American studies, I study a US-centric cultural imaginary of generalizations, stereotypes, and images, including the model minority, the perpetual foreigner, the hypersexuality and submissiveness of East Asian women, the "Dragon Lady" trope, the "Tiger Mother," and other normalized ways of representing Asian and Asian American cultures. This cultural realm of flattened and compressed representation leads not only to fetishization of the Asian other, but violence and death, as witnessed in the Atlanta spa shootings on March 16, 2021, a little over a year after the World Health Organization declared the COVID-19 outbreak a global pandemic.[12] These targeted murders of six Asian women in Atlanta exemplify how women and gender nonconforming people of color, in particular, are more likely to experience the consequences of white supremacy in exacerbated ways. Structural factors, including intersecting racism and misogyny, have rendered many women and gender nonconforming people vulnerable and contributed to their violent deaths.

These compounded factors of vulnerability must not be sidelined for the one celebrity or exceptional example of Asian or Asian American acclaim. While *Parasite*, *Minari*, K-pop bands (BTS, BLACKPINK), streaming Asian dramas, and other Asian-authored works are gaining national coverage and fame, Asians and Asian Americans are being scapegoated and attacked because of COVID-19 concerns and frustrations. This contradiction between cultural representation and lived experience influenced the piece I wrote for the *LA Review of Books* on the perpetuity of the "model minority" stereotype in the face of constant Asian otherness in Western cultures. Why was it that the same ethnic and racial groups scapegoated for bringing COVID-19 to the United States were also the ones historically essentialized as the "model minority" and "good" citizens in stark contrast to other minority groups?[13] The paradox of being both model minority and enemy Other dislodged my sense of identity and perception in public spaces. With the killing of some of our most vulnerable, including the elderly and the undocumented, I wrote about how Asian bodies were being treated as tools and objects of human rage. The rage was caused by economic hard times, indignation at a government that has not served its people, low communal morale, mental health crises, and a litany of unprecedented catastrophes. The ability to write to a global community with open and free access to my words was empowering and liberating in the face of feeling disempowered of bodily safety and autonomy.

In my article on the Netflix show *The Chair*, I was able to merge questions of anti-Asian racism with teaching at a predominantly white institution (PWI). The show stars Sandra Oh, herself Korean Canadian, and Oh plays Ji-Yoon Kim, the first woman to chair the English department at the fictitious Pembroke University. Ji-Yoon is a Korean American woman taking the helm at a failing department, where there are few staff members of color. Like Ji-Yoon tells her college's dean, the faculty at Pembroke is "87 percent white." I started my tenure-track position when the show first aired, so the specificity with which the show depicted both Ji-Yoon's personal and public lives in terms of ethnic Korean identity and the ins and outs of straddling multiple cultures at once made it easy at first to feel connected to Ji-Yoon. Like many women of color in academia and beyond, Ji-Yoon's embodiment does not match the long-standing, persistent stereotypes of who gets to not only teach but lead departments. What Ji-Yoon experiences is not new to me or many women of color, because like many of us, she is working in a system that sets expectations for her that do not match the reality of what it takes to get the job done.

In one key scene, Ji-Yoon tells Yaz, the only other faculty person of color in the department, "I don't feel like I inherited an English department; I feel like someone handed me a ticking time bomb because they wanted to make sure a woman was holding it when it exploded." As Nancy Wang Yuen notes, "This is a documented phenomenon called 'the glass cliff,' in which institutions elevate women and BIPOC to positions of power during crises that puts them at risk of 'falling off' and failing."[14] Ji-Yoon is ultimately disempowered by this system, which is truthful of what happens to many of us. By the show's end, the cyclical nature of the model-minority trope is clear: no matter how hard we work or how much we go "running around playing nice," as Yaz reminds Ji-Yoon, the entrenched systems of white privilege that we enter continue to function and, in fact, function better with model minorities firmly in place as so-called proof that meritocracy works.

Cathy Park Hong reminds us that if Asian Americans do not speak out, "we will disappear into this country's amnesiac fog. We will not be the power but become absorbed by power, not share the power of whites but be stooges to a white ideology that exploited our ancestors."[15] This white ideology is a psychocultural structure that has never been fully exposed, and thus, never effaced. In pursuing more publicly engaged scholarship and service to the community during the pandemic, I exposed myself to criticism and attacks but also hoped to garner visibility for the problems many of us Asians and Asian Americans were experiencing. With the rise of anti-Asian racism, hate crimes, and the mainstream reporting on these attacks, the responsibility and burden to explain them to a ravenous public fell on those of us who looked like the victims, including me.

I received a barrage of requests from local and national news outlets to discuss the rise in anti-Asian attacks while navigating my new visiting faculty position and being on the tenure-track job market. Due to the pandemic and nationwide higher education budgetary issues, I saw the smallest number of tenure-track jobs in my field. I understood the risk of doing illegible or undervalued publicly engaged work, and I asked myself what doing these interviews and media requests could do for career advancement or perhaps tenure-track consideration at my current institution. I could not determine a conclusive answer. In Imagining America's (IA) 2008 Tenure Team Initiative Report, Julie Ellison and Timothy Eatman use a number of terms to describe public-facing faculty work. These include "publicly engaged academic work, public scholarship, public engagement, public scholarly and creative work, community partnerships, publicly engaged humanists, civically engaged scholars, civic agency, civic professionals, and community engagement."[16] While these terms show an interest in diversifying and deepening the language of public-facing work, they also propagate a host of meanings and rhetoric that make it hard to effectively document and evaluate one's work for job and performance review.

The IA report defines publicly engaged academic work as "scholarly or creative activity *integral to a faculty member's academic area*."[17] What qualifies as activity "integral to a faculty member's academic area" becomes murky especially for faculty of color, as the report shows. Ellison and Eatman write, "Disturbingly, our interviews revealed a strong sense that pursuing academic public engagement is viewed as an unorthodox and risky early career option for faculty of color."[18] I knew that my public articles, interviews, podcasts, panels, and roundtables were not directly related to my "academic area" of British Romanticism and global Anglophone literature of the nineteenth century, but I also knew we were all living through a fraught time of crisis and change. Preserving culture in times of crisis has and continues to be a larger goal of public humanities and public scholarship more broadly, so representing Asian American voices during this time of ethnic and racial trauma became increasingly vital to my praxis and sense of scholarly identity.

To keep myself accountable, I did a personal assessment of the work I had done so far in my career and what types of scholarship and pedagogy had sustained my sense of identity, integrity, and belonging. I grew up feeling and knowing that the historical and long-standing issues of cultural stereotyping and generalizations of Asians and Asian Americans were so enmeshed in everyday, casual interactions. With public work, I had the rare opportunity to be the protagonist of my story and lead the conversation. This internal review of my work and its purpose helped me plan my media requests, public events, and community engagement in a way that seemed sustainable to me and not detrimental to my institutional advancement or intellectual agenda. The public interviews and events I did also gave me the opportunity to talk to genuinely interested people who wanted to process and understand the anti-Asian racism and attacks in a generative and committed way. I was no longer alone in my quarantined bubble watching the anti-Asian attacks happen without an ally or supportive community. I was able to talk with fellow Asian American scholars, activists, and our allies to better understand the collective moment and better process what was happening through historical and theoretical frames. This is not to say all went well or the work was pleasurable. I switched my register for differing audiences and was put under constant pressure to answer hard, often biased questions and endured a litany of microaggressions. The newfound visibility of my public-facing work raised the stakes and purpose of my research and teaching in unpredictable yet sometimes empowering ways.

Teaching during COVID-19

My publicly engaged work in the community afforded me a sense of intellectual agency from which to combat my rampant sense of Asian and Asian American disempowerment. Alongside public scholarship, teaching during the pandemic shifted my positionality and sense of authority to caring for my students in this time of distress. I knew I was teaching English literature at a time when the idea of an Asian and Asian American person was under new scrutiny due to the pressures of paradoxical representations of us as A-list celebrity, model minority, COVID-19 carrier, and perpetual foreigner.

When the pandemic first started and I was teaching in person, my students and I were all struggling with how to discuss it in the classroom as a topic of conversation. I knew as an Asian woman in front of the classroom at a PWI, my body could signify something different in the context of the pandemic. I remember the first time I coughed in front of class after choking on some water. A usually respectful and conscientious student exclaimed, "It's COVID!," loud enough so the entire class could hear. I was filled with a sense of anger and dread at the future of how teaching could be in the face of COVID-19 stereotyping. In response to the student's comment, I do not remember exactly what I said in front of the class to get back to the day's lesson. I remember telling him something like his comment being "inappropriate" or another passive-aggressive phrase for his racism. I felt defeated and caught my bearings in the bathroom after class. Classes soon went fully online after that incident, and my anxiety about being in front of the classroom and a target of intended and unintended racist speech lessened.

The fall of 2020 in particular was an unprecedented semester for pedagogical advancement and adaptation. It brought with it challenges to conducting group work or peer review, class discussions, and student engagement in ways many of us had never seen. Yet these challenges also presented me with unique opportunities to develop more effective pedagogical tools for fostering intellectual curiosity, growth, and student access to online learning methods. For my courses, I created Blackboard shells that include interactive modules for every week of the semester. In each module, students accessed their daily assignments and the readings. For me, access extends to students being able to afford the course materials, especially during a global financial crisis. This means students having access to most course readings free of charge. Among the three courses I taught in fall 2020, I scanned and uploaded readings so that students were only required to purchase one book, which was less than ten dollars.

Most of my students showed technological preparedness and an ability to adapt to constantly shifting academic rules and expectations after they were forced to switch from in-person to online learning models. In addition, I responded on a more case-by-case basis to student needs and concerns, as the problems they were encountering were broad, diverse, and many times intensely personal or a direct result of COVID-19 exposure, recovery, or the loss of a loved one to COVID-19. I met students where they were at individually, adapted assignments and modalities depending on their personal technological literacy and access, and tried to maintain a "culturally sustaining" pedagogy online.[19] As Django Paris suggests, the educator's goal should be to "perpetuate and foster— to sustain—linguistic, literate, and cultural pluralism as part of the democratic project of education."[20] In particular, cultural pluralism and technological access were central to my teaching, as I knew some of my students did not have daily access to a private space and personal computer from which to fully attend every synchronous class session. A majority of my students have outside jobs and are on financial aid, so in addition to lowering textbook costs, I incorporated new texts by first-generation and minority college students and maintained a less rigid policy of excused absences to care for them in a time of death, sickness, and overwhelming precarity.

Wanting to be a supportive ally to my students in this moment of trauma and often grief, I realized the role of teaching as a first-responder role in many cases. My students were focusing on academic performance and grades while having to navigate the unpredictable and precarious world of COVID-19 rules and restrictions, so I kept this in mind with each individual student e-mail, meeting, or phone call. I became in many cases a liaison between students and institutional support networks or offices so that students knew whom or where they could reach out to with their myriad of concerns, questions, and calls for help. As a result of this mediating role, I have learned skills and tools to better respond to individual student needs and to sustain a pedagogy of adaptation and empathy. What teaching online during the pandemic also gave me was a regular social activity to look forward to from the confines of my home. The pandemic has caused so much isolation and loss of family time and friendship, and being able to have a regular group of students to talk to kept me connected to social networks.

After teaching solely online at the beginning of the pandemic, I taught the 2021–2022 academic year fully in person. It was also my first year transitioning to the tenure track, bringing with it a host of lessons, discoveries, and anxieties. Like many other universities, there was a mask mandate and a vaccine requirement for all students, faculty, and staff. These rules gave me a sense of safety, but I was still very concerned with how to transition my online classes to face-to-face while remaining supportive of students at the whims of COVID-19. With the motivation from all my public-facing work on Asian American representation, I also designed and taught the first Asian American literature course for the university. As an introductory course with mostly non-English majors, I was surprised at how receptive my students were to the texts and authors. Grounded in honest, seminar-based discussions, some students told me they did not realize Asians experienced racism or that Asian Americans were people of color. I knew that my course was more than a literary studies course; it engendered an entire perspectival shift in the students' very understanding of race in the United States.

Having taught both online and in person during the COVID-19 pandemic, I have learned the benefits of spontaneity, adaptability, and patience. Particularly with my Asian American literature courses, I have found a way to funnel my public-facing work toward teaching courses that also raise awareness about Asian American topics and issues. This has bridged my public and pedagogical identities in generative ways. I have improved my technological literacy and ability to teach multimodally, especially for students who respond better to different modes than in-person classes only. Crisis forces adaptation, and the lessons and skills of teaching during a pandemic have been a growth opportunity for my larger pedagogical goals of access, inclusivity, and cultural pluralism.

Continuing the Work beyond COVID-19

Producing publicly engaged scholarship and teaching during the pandemic was a challenge for all of us. As an Asian American woman researching and teaching during the height of anti-Asian and anti-Chinese sentiment, my susceptibility to racist violence was elevated, but I also knew I could not live in fear or constant uncertainty of my embodiment. What living through the pandemic has taught me is that the histories of Orientalism and Asian exclusion that underpin the COVID-19 narrative may be reactivated but they do not have to be fixed. As a public-facing scholar, it is important to trace the evolution and mutation of racism and to respond to it accurately and objectively. Due to COVID-19 fears, the Asian-presenting body finds itself in a precarity of unclear futurity for how we are perceived in public. Anti-Asian sentiment and racism are not new American issues, but the rise in global coverage of these attacks and changing public opinion of these attacks as an "American" issue shows a shift in national consciousness toward understanding anti-Asian racism as an important issue.

Anti-Asian racism is part of the larger history of a country founded on the racial and racist logics of white supremacy. The challenge of representing myself and my communities is not a challenge of positioning my suffering in comparison to other groups but a challenge of differentiation, specificity, and attention to the unique facets of each minority struggle against this onslaught of white supremacy that is still at the foundation of US political consciousness. This challenge requires me to recognize the complex and interlocking nature of hate crimes, anti-Asian racism, and racial discrimination and to situate these within the daily and unrelenting assaults of white supremacy. It means refusing white supremacy's divide-and-conquer tactics of identity politics and racially divisive lines of innocence, guilt, or blame—presumptions that too often pit Asian lives against Black, Brown, Latinx, and Indigenous ones. The representation of not only Asian American voices but the historically marginalized, disenfranchised, and silenced groups of our collective antiracist struggles is an urgent global public health issue that all of us must face. The time is now to speak up and stand in solidarity with each other.

While the COVID-19 crisis is fundamentally epidemiological, the phenomenology of the human is more uncertain than ever. Maurice Merleau-Ponty argues that "[t]he problem of the world—and to begin with, the problem of one's own body—consists in the fact that *everything resides within the world*."[21] The situatedness of our bodies in a capricious world—a world of ever-shifting laws, social restrictions, cultural norms—shows us the possibility that the amplified level of today's anti-Asian racism can be transient. By building coalitions of antiracist scholarship, pedagogy, and publicly engaged work, we can disrupt the grip of white supremacist ideology and its insidiousness within the status quo. For me, this is empowering work and comprises a collective enterprise with and for the public.

NOTES

1. The "Yellow Peril" level of psychocultural turmoil against the body of presumed Asian descent has materialized into physical violence and death.

2. Busby, "Vietnamese Curator."

3. Lim, "84-Year-Old Killed."

4. Jeung, Yellow Horse, and Matriano, "Stop AAPI Hate National Report (3/19/20–12/31/21)."

5. "FACT SHEET: Anti-Asian Prejudice March 2021."

6. The common stereotypes many Asians and Asian Americans are encountering on a face-to-face basis are now exacerbated by virtual forms of anti-Asian racism and hate speech. Thus, Orientalist and racist rhetoric in response to the pandemic is online as well as physical. This disembodied mode of anti-Asian targeting bridges the physical and mental disorientation of Asian self-identity and identity formation.

7. Loffman, "Asian Americans Describe 'Gut Punch.'"

8. Spillers, *Black, White, and in Color*, 380.

9. Said, *Representations of the Intellectual*, 43–44.

10. For more on the interlaced continental histories and "imperial projects of conquest, slavery, labor, and government" across the past three centuries, see Lowe, *Intimacies*, 17. For more on US American racism during outbreaks, see Lanham, "American Racism in the Time of Plagues."

11. For example, political leaders including the last German emperor Kaiser Wilhelm II used the term "Yellow Peril" in the late nineteenth and early twentieth centuries to justify European colonialism in China.

12. White supremacist ideologies are often hidden or coded when describing crimes against people of color, such as the discourse of shooter Robert Aaron Long's "sexual addiction" as the explanation for his targeting of the Atlanta spas he frequented, to "take out that temptation."

13. The roots of the American model minority stereotype can be traced to sociologist William Petersen's *New York Times* article, "Success Story, Japanese-American Style." Petersen argues for the idea that Japanese-Americans were "good" citizens "better than any other group in our society, including native-born whites. They have established this remarkable record, moreover, by their own almost totally unaided effort."

14. Wang Yuen, "I'm an Asian American Woman."

15. Park Hong, *Minor Feelings*, 35.

16. Quotation by Ellison and Eatman as cited by Diane M. Doberneck, et al. "From Rhetoric to Reality," 5.

17. Ellison and Eatman, "Scholarship in Public," 1.
18. Ellison and Eatman, iv.
19. Paris, "Culturally Sustaining Pedagogy," 93.
20. Paris, "Culturally Sustaining Pedagogy," 93.
21. Merleau-Ponty, *Phenomenology of Perception*, 204.

BIBLIOGRAPHY

"Asian Lineage Avian Influenza A(H7N9) Virus." *Centers for Disease Control and Prevention*, Centers for Disease Control and Prevention, December 7, 2018. https://www.cdc.gov/flu/avianflu/h7n9-virus.htm?web=1&wdLOR=cA096DD52-0C5B-4E4D-923F-E1FB72BC01F2.

Busby, Mattha. "Vietnamese Curator Dropped Because of 'Coronavirus Prejudice,'" March 5, 2020. https://www.theguardian.com/world/2020/mar/05/vietnamese-curator-dropped-because-of-coronavirus-prejudice.

Doberneck, Diane M., Chris R. Glass, and John Schweitzer. "From Rhetoric to Reality: A Typology of Publically Engaged Scholarship." *Journal of Higher Education Outreach and Engagement*, 14, no. 4 (December 2010): 5–35.

Ellison, J., and T. K. Eatman. "Scholarship in Public: Knowledge Creation and Tenure Policy in the Engaged University." *Imagining America*. 16, 2008. https://surface.syr.edu/ia/16/. May 1, 2021.

"FACT SHEET: Anti-Asian Prejudice March 2021." *Center for the Study of Hate & Extremism*, California State University, San Bernadino. March 2021. https://www.csusb.edu/sites/default/files/FACT%20SHEET-%20Anti-Asian%20Hate%202020%20rev%203.21.21.pdf.

"Figure 18. Percentage of All Active Physicians by Race/Ethnicity, 2018." *AAMC*. https://www.aamc.org/data-reports/workforce/interactive-data/figure-18-percentage-all-active-physicians-race/ethnicity-2018.

Jeung, Russell, Aggie J. Yellow Horse, and Ronae Matriano. *Stop AAPI Hate National Report* (3/19/20–12/31/21. Asian Pacific Policy and Planning Council. May 4, 2022. https://stopaapihate.org/wp-content/uploads/2022/03/22-SAH-NationalReport-3.1.22-v9.pdf.

Kim, Joey S. "As a Korean American Professor, Here Is What I Think "The Chair" Gets Right." *Truthout* (September 19, 2021). https://truthout.org/articles/as-a-korean-american-professor-here-is-what-i-think-the-chair-gets-right/.

Kim, Joey S. "'Model Minority,' Still 'Other.'" *LA Review of Books*, February 26, 2021.

Kim, Joey S. "Orientalism in the Age of COVID-19." *LA Review of Books*, March 24, 2020.

Kim, Joey S. "The Paradox at the Heart of the Atlanta Spa Shootings and the Rise in Anti-Asian Hate." *Shondaland*, April 1, 2021. https://www.shondaland.com/act/a35995814/paradox-at-the-heart-of-the-atlanta-spa-shootings/.

Lanham, Andrew. "American Racism in the Time of Plagues." *Boston Review*, March 30, 2020. https://www.bostonreview.net/articles/andrew-lanham-american-racism-plague-times/.

Lim, Dion. "84-Year-Old Killed after Horrific Daytime Attack Caught on Video in San Francisco." February 1, 2021. https://abc7news.com/san-francisco-senior-attacked-sf-man-pushed-on-video-day-time-attack-caught-anza-vista-crime/10205928/.

Loffman, Matt. "Asian Americans Describe 'Gut Punch' of Racist Attacks during Coronavirus Pandemic." *PBS*, Public Broadcasting Service (April 7, 2020). https://www.pbs.org/newshour/nation/asian-americans-describe-gut-punch-of-racist-attacks-during-coronavirus-pandemic.

Lowe, Lisa. *The Intimacies of Four Continents*. Durham, NC: Duke University Press, 2015.

Merleau-Ponty, Maurice. *Phenomenology of Perception*. Translated by Donald A. Landes. New York: Routledge, 2014.

Paris, Django. "Culturally Sustaining Pedagogy: A Needed Change in Stance, Terminology, and Practice." *Educational Researcher*, 41, no. 3 (2012): 93–97. https://doi.org/10.3102/0013189X12441244.

Park Hong, Cathy. *Minor Feelings: An Asian American Reckoning*. New York: Penguin Random House, 2020.

Petersen, William. "Success Story, Japanese-American Style." *The New York Times* (January 9, 1966). https://www.nytimes.com/1966/01/09/archives/success-story-japaneseamerican-style-success-story-japaneseamerican.html.

Said, Edward. *Representations of the Intellectual*. New York: Penguin Random House, 1994.

Spillers, Hortense. *Black, White, and in Color: Essays on American Literature and Culture*. Chicago: University of Chicago Press, 2003.

Wang Yuen, Nancy. "I'm an Asian American Woman in Academia. Here's What 'The Chair' Gets Right." *Los Angeles Times*, August 20, 2021. https://www.latimes.com/entertainment-arts/tv/story/2021-08-20/the-chair-netflix-sandra-oh-amanda-peet.

4

TEACHING GERMAN IN THE SETTLER COLONIAL UNIVERSITY

Maureen O. Gallagher

In October 2020 the Coalition of Women in German, a scholarly society devoted to feminist approaches to the field of German studies, met for its annual conference. COVID-19 meant that we were unable to gather in person for panels, papers, meals, and discussion; instead, we Zoomed from our homes and offices distributed throughout North America, Europe, and Australia. The conference opened with a land acknowledgement, a statement recognizing the traditional Indigenous custodians of a particular place, read by a representative from the host institution, Sewanee, the University of the South. However, in this virtual gathering, the land acknowledgement did not remain singular and finite but echoed throughout the conference, as panel organizers and panelists located across North America acknowledged the traditional owners of the lands on which they lived and worked. The exercise revealed in stunning clarity the breadth of stolen lands on which much of modern higher education is built. The pandemic's disruption to normal scholarly mobility revealed the spatial dimension of colonization and the interconnected histories of colonialism that enable higher education in North America and elsewhere.

While institutional land acknowledgements now commonly open meetings, conferences, and other events at higher educational institutions in the United States, Canada, Australia, and New Zealand, they are not without criticism. Hayden King, who wrote Ryerson University's territorial acknowledgement, expressed regret about it in January 2019 in an interview with the Canadian Broadcasting Corporation, noting that it has the potential to offer listeners "an alibi for doing the hard work of learning about their neighbors and learning about the treaties of the territory and learning about those nations that should have jurisdiction."[1] Acknowledging the traditional owners of the land without any further commitment is inadequate and can become a "settler move to innocence," Eve Tuck and K. Wayne Yang's term—building upon the work of Janet Mawhinney—for the strategies that assuage the guilt of settlers without requiring the surrender of power and privilege.[2]

Listening to the multiple land acknowledgements throughout the Women in German conference clarified for me a personal discomfort I felt with my own institution's land acknowledgement during the COVID-19 pandemic. On the first day of the term, I read my university's acknowledgement of country: "We acknowledge and celebrate the First Australians on whose traditional lands we meet, and pay our respect to the elders past and present."[3] While it is important to acknowledge the traditional owners of the land on which my university campus is built, the words felt inadequate to convey the complexity of the situation of teaching remotely during the COVID-19 pandemic. In July 2020 I began a new academic position at Australian National University. COVID-19 and the resulting strict closure of the Australian border left me with no way to enter the country to start my job. When I first drafted this chapter in May 2021, I was one year into remote teaching from nine thousand miles and fifteen time zones away from campus. To acknowledge solely where I worked without acknowledging where I lived failed to capture the whole story. I had at that point never set foot on the territories of the Ngunnawal and Ngambri peoples, and at that moment, not all of my students were there either, with many having returned to their family homes due to the pandemic. Throughout my first year in the job, I experimented with different ways to acknowledge this tension and ambiguity, by, for example, stating that my German and Irish ancestors settled on the traditional lands of the Pawnee in the late nineteenth century or that I was currently located on lands that have been or are the home to the Kaw, Kickapoo, Sioux, and Osage peoples. Both statements are accurate, but neither felt like it captured the whole story in its intricacy and complexity.

The growing discussions of diversity and decolonization across scholarly spaces influence my thinking on this issue. COVID-19, as a major force of disruption that altered where and how we do our work and interact with each other in drastic ways, offers an opportunity to think through these conversations, paying particular attention to dimensions of space and place. Though my case might be an extreme example, I am not the only person who works remotely, whether it is from another city, state, country, or even hemisphere. For many, COVID-19 meant that university work—lecturing, teaching, research, meetings—moved home. Reading an institutional land acknowledgement can obscure the intersecting and interconnected histories of colonization that underlie modern academic work. COVID-19 might allow us to think about decolonization and the work of universities as, on the one hand, rooted in specific places and histories of displacement and, on the other hand, rootless, implicated in competing and intersecting histories of colonization, particularly as they expand their reach beyond campus through digital outreach and infrastructure.

In this chapter I reflect on these issues from several perspectives, including discussions of decolonizing the curriculum, particularly in relation to my own field of German studies, diverging understandings of decolonization across international and institutional contexts, particularly in the specific context of university work in settler states, and the impact of COVID-19 on understandings of the place and nature of university work through the lens of decolonization. I approach this topic as a white scholar with a family history of settlement in North America whose academic career is enabled by settler colonialism. As a non-Indigenous scholar in a predominantly white field, I seek to respectfully and responsibly engage with discourses of decolonization as they come to occupy a larger role in scholarly societies and university strategies.

Defining Decolonization

Decolonization is a term with competing and overlapping meanings. While initially referring to the "global-scale political change" of the end of European colonization, it has come to refer to the "intellectual effort to reconfigure the world" or even be "the rallying cry for those trying to undo the racist legacies of the past."[4] Influential in these later, broader understandings of decolonization is Ngũgĩ wa Thiong'o's concept of decolonizing the mind.[5] Elizabeth Mackinlay and Katelyn Barney summarize these competing discourses: "Decolonisation is a concept that takes on different meanings across different contexts—it simultaneously evokes a historical narrative of the end of empire, a particular version of postcolonial political theory, a way of knowing that resists the Eurocentricism of the West, a moral imperative for righting the wrongs of colonial domination, and an ethical stance in relation to self-determination, social justice, and human rights for Indigenous peoples enslaved and disempowered by imperialism."[6]

As the discourse of decolonization has become more mainstream, some scholars, particularly Indigenous scholars, have resisted some of these broadened definitions. In their seminal article in *Decolonization: Indigeneity, Education, & Society*, Tuck and Yang write against the metaphorization of decolonization:

> When metaphor invades decolonization, it kills the very possibility of decolonization; it recenters whiteness, it resettles theory, it extends in-

nocence to the settler, it entertains a settler future. Decolonize (a verb) and decolonization (a noun) cannot easily be grafted onto pre-existing discourses/frameworks, even if they are critical, even if they are antiracist, even if they are justice frameworks. The easy absorption, adoption, and transposing of decolonization is yet another form of settler appropriation. When we write about decolonization, we are not offering it as a metaphor; it is not an approximation of other experiences of oppression. Decolonization is not a swappable term for other things we want to do to improve our societies and schools. Decolonization doesn't have a synonym.[7]

Tuck and Yang argue that decolonization refers to the "repatriation of Indigenous land and life," and the word cannot be substituted for other antiracist or social justice projects or curricular reform efforts.[8]

As sites for the "creation and legitimation of knowledge," universities are deeply implicated in questions of colonization and decolonization.[9] Discussions about decolonizing the curriculum, particularly at colleges and universities, reflect similar overlapping and contradictory discourses that depend on particular local contexts and relationships to colonial histories. Compare, for example, Keele University's definition of decolonizing the curriculum with that of Karlee Fellner of the University of Calgary in the *American Journal of Community Psychology*, which represent general academic definitions of decolonization from nonsettler (England) and settler (Canada) academic contexts:

> Decolonizing the curriculum means creating spaces and resources for a dialogue among all members of the university on how to imagine and envision all cultures and knowledge systems in the curriculum, and with respect to what is being taught and how it frames the world.[10]
>
> Decolonizing curriculum may be conceptualized through the interconnected processes of deconstructing colonial ideologies and their manifestations, and reconstructing colonial discourse through Indigenous counter-narratives.[11]

While Keele University's definition centers the epistemic dimensions of decolonization—the dominance of whiteness and Eurocentric perspectives to the exclusion of Black, Asian, and minority ethnic (BAME) perspectives and the privileging of certain knowledge systems over others in the curriculum—nowhere in their manifesto do you find mention of Indigenous perspectives or land repatriation that are central to questions of decolonizing in settler colonial states as thematized by Tuck and Yang and reflected in Fellner's definition. As Marie Battiste, Lynne Bell, and L. M. Findlay note, there are "important distinctions between, on the one hand, national entities and populations that have achieved political independence, and on the other, Indigenous peoples who remain in large measures colonized, even or especially in sovereign states that lay claim to all the qualities of mature nationhood."[12] The understanding of decolonization is therefore context dependent, and what it means to decolonize varies from the place of a formerly colonizing country, a formerly colonized country, or a site of ongoing settler occupation.

Decolonization and German Studies

In settler colonial contexts, German studies—and European area studies more broadly—is situated at the intersection of these competing definitions. German studies scholars have variously framed decolonization as dismantling Eurocentrism and moving beyond diversity and inclusion paradigms to challenge master narratives.[13] At the same time, the study and practice of German studies in settler states "means to navigate the colonial pasts of two nations" and "attend to two colonial histories," both of which have been comparatively understudied in a German studies context.[14] Decolonizing German studies in a settler context thus requires navigating colonial pasts and presents simultaneously in order to challenge Eurocentric epistemologies. Beverly Weber notes the need for pedagogies that disrupt German studies as a colonial project in two ways:

1. enabling students to create (geo)politics of knowledge that decenter Europe as a sort of originary location of knowledge, modernity, and progress. This includes challenging the ways in which German intellectual traditions have participated in racist thought and ideas;
2. working to construct a politics of place that can challenge the violence of settler colonialism.[15]

Enacting structural change related to issues of decolonization and diversity in the field of German studies has thus far proven challenging. German is the whitest modern language discipline in the United States, with 84.6 percent of BA degrees granted to non-Hispanic white students between 2010 and 2014.[16] While there are no recent data about the racial background of German teachers, a 1994 survey found that 98 percent were white.[17] In spite of early attention to the issue of diversity in, for example, a 1992 special issue of the journal *Die Unterrichtspraxis/Teaching German* with the topic "Focus on Diversity," the "future in which Scholars of Color, women, LGBT people, Jewish people, refugees, immigrants, non-native speakers, and low income learners would meaningfully count . . . as core makers of the consciousness of German Studies . . . remains announced, but not enacted."[18] There persists a racial and socioeconomic gap in access to language education in the United States.[19] Further, German textbooks still portray Germany as overwhelmingly white, demonstrating what Silja Weber terms a "whiteness bias."[20] In the face of a majority-white profession and majority-white student body, immediate efforts at diversification have focused largely on course content, which Regine Criser and Suzuko Knott call the "first steps" in decolonizing German studies: "by recognizing and centering the full range of diverse lived experiences in a German-language context, we help our students understand a diverse German-speaking world and in turn uncover the global within our discipline."[21]

Immigration is often (but not always) at the heart of these efforts to offer a more diverse representation of the German-speaking world, with post-WWII migration and immigrant writers like Emine Sevgi Özdamar, Yoko Tawada, or Sharon Dodua Otoo featuring prominently. However, the question of immigration shows the "diverging perspectives on immigration in these two critical frameworks" of diversity and decolonization.[22] A German curriculum that centers immigration stories can help naturalize immigration as a universal force for good, neglecting the unique context and meaning of immigration in settler colonial states where "the colonizer comes to stay."[23] As Tuck and Yang write, "Settlers are not immigrants. Immigrants are beholden to the Indigenous laws and epistemologies of the lands they migrate to. Settlers become the law, supplanting Indigenous laws and epistemologies. Therefore, settler nations are not immigrant nations."[24] A German curriculum that centers immigration without making this distinction or sufficiently problematizing how the role of immigration differs in diversity and decolonization frameworks can serve to further normalize settler colonialism.

Questions of the ongoing impact and structure of settler colonialism are tied to questions of the nation, which is a topic that has in recent years been debated in the field of German studies. Jakob Norberg argued in a 2018 article that not only was the field of German literary studies—*Germanistik*—indebted to the national paradigm but that it "must remain so if it is to continue to exist."[25] Norberg's assertion of the importance of the nation to the history and shape of the discipline is uncontroversial, but the second part of his claim, that it "must remain so," has been the subject of much discussion.[26] The editors of a special issue of the journal *Seminar* devoted to Indigenous studies and German studies note the importance of taking seriously the role of the nation in the formation of German studies for its connection to colonialism: "if we centre the concept of the national in our considerations of *German* Studies, then we also must recognize the role that German Studies played in the Western project of settler colonialism."[27] Emina Mušanović and Ashwin Manthripragada similarly note,

"German Studies holds a position in the global education curriculum because of German-speaking Europe's political and economic global power, which is indebted to colonialism."[28] German studies as a field is thus indebted to the German nation's role in these histories of colonial oppression and settler colonialism and their ongoing material effects.

The Federal Republic of Germany continues to exert a material impact on where and how German is studied around the world, including in higher education contexts. Arguments for the study of German from professional organizations like the American Association of Teachers of German tend to rely on neoliberal claims for the usefulness of the language due to Germany's economic strength and EU leadership.[29] The Goethe Institute, the German government's international language and culture institute, offers German classes and events, often partnering with local universities.[30] The German Academic Exchange Service (DAAD) administers five hundred visiting academic positions in German studies in higher education institutions around the globe with funding from Germany's Foreign Office.[31] In the United States, the German Embassy provides funding directly to colleges and universities for cultural programming and outreach events as part of its "Campus Weeks" program.

These kinds of cultural activities have formed a core pillar of Germany's foreign policy since the 1970s, as discussed in a recent report for the Institute for Foreign Relations (Institut für Auslandsbeziehungen) by Sigrid Weigel. According to this report on Germany's foreign cultural and educational policy, the kinds of programming offered by the German government's sponsored language and cultural institutes can be seen as an exercise in soft power and nation branding, marketing an image of Germany abroad as "enlightener and gentle educator, as cultural development helper," in service of the overall foreign policy goals of the German government, as Jörg Häntzschel for *Süddeutsche Zeitung* paraphrases the report.[32] Weigel calls for a rethink of this approach to instead emphasize relations among equals and the promotion of values such as democracy, the rule of law and freedom of speech at home as well as abroad.

German programs thus not only benefit from or capitalize on this nation-branding in how they market and sell the benefits of learning German to students, but they also actively participate in it. In focusing on the nation-state of Germany at the expense of other German-speaking countries or regions, partnering with the Goethe Institute, and accepting money from the German government for cocurricular programming, German programs participate in the German government's foreign cultural and education policy. As Mušanović and Manthripragada write, "In effect, German Studies departments and researchers are also partially but directly financially sustained through colonial wealth accumulation, through funding streams established, for example, by the German government."[33] In these times of academic precarity—evidenced by declining language enrollments and accelerating language program eliminations—the reliance on these funding sources is understandable but should still be critically assessed as part of any diversification or decolonization projects.[34]

German Studies in the Settler Colonial University

Patrick Wolfe calls for understanding settler colonialism as a structure, not an event: it is not a singular happening in the past that is over and done, but an ongoing means of shaping political and social relationships.[35] This structure impacts all university teaching in settler states, regardless of the discipline. Higher education in the United States is built on the dispossession of Indigenous land in unique ways due to the 1862 Land-Grant College Act, also known as the Morrill Act after the bill's sponsor. According to a report by Robert Lee and Tristan Ahtone for *High Country News*, the United States paid approximately four hundred thousand dollars for the title to eleven million acres of Indigenous land—though for more than a quarter of the land nothing at all was paid—which were sold or leased to establish endowments at fifty-two United States universities. The "Land-grab universities" report estimates these land grants are worth half a billion of today's dollars. The report quotes Sharon Stein of the University of British Columbia: "There would be no higher education as we know it in the United States without the original and ongoing colonization of Indigenous peoples and lands, just like there would be no United States. . . . There is no moment or time or place or institution that is not deeply entangled with the violence of colonialism."[36] Or as the report succinctly phrases it, US higher education was not only built "on Indigenous land, but with Indigenous land."[37]

The university is thus embedded in the eliminationist project of settler colonialism, which operates on a logic of replacement.[38] Tuck and Yang use Natty Bumppo of James Fenimore Cooper's *Leatherstocking Tales* to illustrate this refashioning of the settler as Indigenous, embodying the "settler fantasies of adoption," which "alleviate the anxiety of settler un-belonging."[39] Tuck and Rubén A. Gaztambide-Fernández connect this idea to "the settler colonial curricula project of *replacement*, which aims to vanish Indigenous peoples and replace them with settlers, who see themselves as the rightful claimants, indeed, as indigenous."[40] The widely known figure of Old Shatterhand, from Karl May's *Winnetou* novels of the 1890s and their subsequent popular film adaptations, can be seen as a German counterpart to Natty Bumppo.

German is implicated in this curricular project of replacement as part of the displacement of Indigenous languages by European languages. As an illustration, though there were an estimated three hundred Indigenous languages in Australia before European colonization, today only seven of them can be studied at Australian universities. By contrast, Australian universities teach twice as many modern and classical European languages, in addition to many Asian languages.[41] Playing into these discourses of replacement are efforts to secure a future for German studies in the face of declining language enrollments and accelerating closure of language programs. These efforts position German as a useful, relevant, and economically advantageous language to learn with a long history in settler states like the United States and Australia.

A German studies focused on the German nation state, even a German studies critical of the German colonial past and its ongoing legacies of racism, Eurocentrism, and xenophobia, can also participate in this curricular project of replacement by appealing to settler sensibilities. Avery Smith, Hine Funaki, and Liana MacDonald define these sensibilities as "imagined social narratives that omit colonial violence towards Indigenous communities, to promote harmonious settler-Indigenous relations that direct settlers towards a feeling of home and belonging on 'empty' and 'untouched' territories."[42] Emphasizing the special relationship between Germany and the United States and the large numbers of US-Americans with German heritage—over forty million Americans, or nearly 15 percent of the population, have German roots, according to the US Census Bureau—elides German participation in and benefit from the dispossession of Indigenous land.[43] Mušanović and Manthripragada analyze materials from the German Studies Association and the German-American Fulbright Commission to show how these organizations "predominantly present German settlement in the United States as a meritorious step towards securing the American dream."[44] Presenting German-American relations as a valorous story of immigration and multiculturalism is to cater to settler sensibilities and obscure how this special relationship is predicated on the eradication, erasure, and replacement of Indigenous people.

COVID-19, Hospitality, and Hospicing the University

My impetus for writing this chapter was to go beyond the land acknowledgement to think through the connections between place, COVID-19, and decolonization. I wished to connect the scholarship and conversations occurring in German studies scholarly spaces to my own personal story, particularly my frustration with my own immobility during COVID-19 times, privileged as it might be.[45] German studies, like all academic disciplines, is implicated in the settler colonial project, and spending the first year of the pandemic thinking, reading, and writing about decolonization in its overlapping, contradictory, and contested meanings allowed me to see how my own academic career is also implicated in the question of settler colonialism. I am now drawn to a different scholarly definition of decolonization: "To decolonize in the broadest sense, therefore, is not just to learn about the ravages of colonialism, but perhaps primarily to learn to live an examined life in relation to place."[46] My personal situation of spending COVID-19 working from home in the United States for a university in Australia has meant the boundaries between these spaces of home and work are both distant and blurred, yet it has also given me an opportunity to think through these relationships to place.

The disruption of COVID-19 to our daily lives gives an opportunity to reexamine how and where we live, work, and interact. It has shown the vulnerability of humans to nature and the danger of unchecked encroachment without proper stewardship of land and resources.[47] It has also revealed systemic inequities, the gaps between those who have the socioeconomic privilege to stay home and isolate and those who do not. COVID-19 has had a disproportionate impact on people of color, particularly Indigenous communities.[48] At the same time, COVID-19 brought new forms of outreach and accessibility. Online and virtual classes, conferences, talks, and panels meant that academic work was accessible to a broader audience. Freed from the constraints of campuses— crowded classrooms, limited space, parking restrictions, and finite travel and event budgets—university activities moved online and found new publics.

I am drawn to viewing this as a kind of hospitality—we invited our colleagues, students, and the public into our homes, sometimes disguised with virtual backgrounds, other times with pets, children, and household chaos on full display. We found new ways to connect and communicate. Remote work and online venues offered new possibilities for how and where university work can occur, resulting in many cases in the convergence of public and domestic spheres in potentially problematic ways. In moving university work home, as Julie Smith and Fiona Jenkins write for *The Conversation*, "employers have in effect requisitioned parts of our homes—rent free and without paying utility costs."[49] This raises questions about the distribution of resources and equity, particularly with the disproportionate burden of extra house and unpaid care work being shouldered by women, as well as questions about whether it was right of employers to ask us to show this kind of hospitality.

In connecting this notion of hospitality to the university as an institution, it is important to think through the question of who has the right or responsibility to issue an invitation and show hospitality. In an article on hospitality and Indigenous epistemologies in the academy, Rauna Kuokkanen notes the dual nature of hospitality: "both parties, the guest and the host, have their responsibilities to build a lasting, reciprocating relationship."[50] Kuokkanen refers to the academy as the assumed host and the "host-guest" to show how the boundaries between host and guest are blurred in the settler colonial university.[51] COVID-19 has further blurred these boundaries. What does it mean to tell my students I "acknowledge and celebrate the First Australians on whose traditional lands we meet" from my home in Kansas City? Universities moved their work from the land on which they reside, acknowledged with an institutional land statement, to the land on which we all live, which might be hundreds or thousands of miles away from campus, all without an invitation. Throughout the pandemic, I heard some officials at my university begin to acknowledge the "lands *and airwaves* on which we meet" as a nod to the distributed and remote nature of university work in the time of COVID-19. It begs the question of whose airwaves we are meeting on and who has access to the spaces of campus, be they virtual or physical. COVID-19 heralded new forms of public outreach and engagement thanks to the embrace of digital technologies that enabled greater accessibility and openness.[52] Will these new publics be invited into the physical spaces of a university campus as COVID-19 allows for a return there?

After a pandemic year marked by death and loss, the way forward, perhaps, is not in the concept of hospitality but the etymologically related concept of hospice, which is at the core of the work of the collective Gesturing Towards Decolonial Futures. As they explain, "It is about hospicing worlds that are dying within and around us with care and integrity, as well as attention to the lessons these deaths offer, while also assisting with the birth of new, potentially wiser possibilities, without suffocating them with projections."[53] Their use of the term "hospice" refers to a kind of end-of-life care for harmful or outdated institutions or practices to see them through the end of their natural lives. One can "hospice" the university "by learning from past mistakes and preparing for the transition into different decolonial futures."[54] It is not about destroying but about acknowledging institutions or ways of life that are unsustainable or no longer supportable. In this way hospicing can be seen as a type of harm-reduction strategy.[55]

When I wrote the first draft of this chapter in the summer of 2021, it felt like we were at a collective turning point. Vaccinations were becoming available, COVID-19 case numbers were dropping, and many universities were cautiously eyeing a return to something almost like normality in fall 2021. I initially saw it as an opportunity to mourn what has been lost and let go of what should not return to allow for different futures. Now more than one year after first writing those words, I question what lessons we have learned from COVID-19. We have dealt with successive waves of infections and new, immunity-evading variants, all the while rolling back public health measures and reducing or removing remote accessibility options. These changes have meant that I was finally able to travel to Australia once international travel restrictions were lifted, return to in-person teaching, check out books from the campus library, work from my campus office, and get to know my new home, but this has come at a cost to others. The return to in-person teaching, conferences, and events has led to the exclusion of those for whom these spaces remain inaccessible, while COVID-19 continues to have a disproportionate impact on the elderly, the disabled, the marginalized, and the less privileged. In our third pandemic year, it is more important than ever to think critically about the uneven access to spaces and the other material resources that universities control. We must urgently think through the ways that campus infrastructures—physical and digital—acknowledge traditional owners rather than settlers and accommodate the interlinked histories of colonization, racialization, and oppression that connect the modern world and all the physical spaces at which members of a university community work and study. It is both more complicated and more important than ever to "live an examined life in relation to place" in COVID-19 times for universities and individuals committed to projects of decolonization, indigenization, or reconciliation.

NOTES

My sincerest thanks to Dr. Carol Anne Costabile-Heming and the members of the Diversity, Decolonization, and the German Curriculum virtual writing support group, in particular to Dr. Kathryn Sederberg and Dr. Holly Yanacek, who both read and provided valuable feedback on an earlier draft of this essay.

1. King, "'I Regret It.'"
2. Tuck and Yang, "Decolonization Is Not a Metaphor," 9.
3. While in North America these statements are generally known as land acknowledgements, in Australia they are more commonly referred to as an Acknowledgement of Country in reference to the particular meaning of Country within Aboriginal and Torres Strait Islander cultures as signifying the interdependent relationships between peoples and their ancestral lands.
4. Betts, "Decolonization," 32.
5. Ngũgĩ wa Thiong'o, *Decolonising the Mind*.
6. Mackinlay and Barney, "Unknown and Unknowing Possibilities," 55.
7. Tuck and Yang, "Decolonization is not a Metaphor," 3.
8. Tuck and Yang, "Decolonization is not a Metaphor," 21.
9. Stein and Andreotti, "Decolonization and Higher Education."
10. Quoted in Elizabeth Charles, "Decolonizing the Curriculum," 1.
11. Fellner, "Embodying Decoloniality," 284.
12. Battiste, Bell, and Findlay, "Decolonizing Education," 89.
13. Malakaj, "State of Diversity," 94; Criser and Malakaj, "Introduction," 5.
14. Criser and Knott, "Decolonizing the Curriculum," 151; Criser and Malakaj, "Diversity and Decolonization in German Studies," 3. Germany's colonial history is often omitted from comparative histories of empire. In spite of German Chancellor Otto von

Bismarck's initial reluctance to acquire overseas territories, Germany nonetheless did engage in colonial efforts abroad in the 1880s, prompting the Berlin Conference in the winter of 1884, which is now often seen as the start of the so-called Scramble for Africa. Germany's colonial empire was noticeably smaller than that of European neighbors like France and England, eventually encompassing approximately one million square miles (three million square kilometers) and twelve million inhabitants throughout Africa, Asia, and the South Pacific in the territories of German East Africa (present-day Tanganyika, Rwanda, and Burundi), German Southwest Africa (present-day Namibia), Cameroon, Togo, Kiaochow (on China's Shandong Peninsula), and parts of New Guinea, Samoa, and other Pacific islands (the Bismarck Archipelago, the Solomon Islands, and the Marshall, Mariana, and Caroline Islands). Many of these colonial projects stemmed from initially private settlement and economic projects, while others built on missionary work that had begun in the early to mid-nineteenth century. After suffering generally quick military defeats in WWI, Germany's colonies were redistributed among the Entente Powers under the terms of the Treaty of Versailles. Though smaller in scale and shorter in scope than many other European empires, the impact of Germany's colonial rule was neither small nor meaningless to the colonized, including the almost one hundred thousand Herero and Nama people who died between 1904 and 1907, victims of the first genocide of the twentieth century. Only very recently has Germany begun to make tentative steps toward apologizing for this genocide and other colonial atrocities and negotiating reparations to Namibia and its people.

15. Qtd. in Malakaj, "State of Diversity," 99.

16. Murphy and Young Lee, "Gender and Race," 56.

17. Malakaj, "State of Diversity and Decolonization," 93.

18. Diversity, Decolonization, and the German Curriculum Collective, "Open Letter," See also the discussion of this open letter in Bryant et al., "Announced But Not Enacted," 347–54, as well as George Peters, ed. "Focus on Diversity." Special issue, *Die Unterrichtspraxis / Teaching German* 25, no. 2 (1992).

19. Anya and Randolph, "Diversifying Language Educators," 24.

20. Weber, "Visual Representation," 8.

21. Criser and Knott, "Decolonizing the Curriculum," 151.

22. Manthripragada and Mušanović, "Accounting for our Settler Colonialism," 27–28.

23. Tuck and Yang, "Decolonization Is Not a Metaphor," 5.

24. Tuck and Yang, "Decolonization Is Not a Metaphor," 6–7.

25. Norberg, "German Literary Studies," 1.

26. In response, the journal *German Quarterly* devoted a special issue to the question, "Does German Cultural Studies Need the Nation-State Model?" Ed. Carl Niekerk. Special Issue, *The German Quarterly* 92, no. 4 (2019).

27. Watchman, Smith, and Stock, "Building Transdisciplinary Relationships," 321.

28. Mušanović and Manthripragada, "Unsettling Futurity," 400.

29. Malakaj "State of Diversity and Decolonization," 89.

30. The Goethe Institute is also instrumental to Germany's punishing visa regimes, with applicants for family reunification visas for migrants or refugees required to complete German language classes at a Goethe Institute before migrating. For applicants from Afghanistan, this meant traveling to India, Pakistan, or Uzbekistan, as the last Goethe Institute in Afghanistan closed in 2017. With the fall of Afghanistan to the Taliban in 2021, restrictions were loosened to allow alternate means of demonstrating German proficiency without attending a Goethe Institute course. Meisner, "Familiennachzug aus Afghanistan."

31. These "Lektor" positions are offered at a variety of ranks and in a variety of disciplines but primarily in the fields of German literature and German language.

32. Weigel, *Transnational Foreign Cultural Policy*, 23, 26; Häntzschel, "Deutsche Nationalkultur?" 8. The translation from the German is my own.

33. Mušanović and Manthripragada, "Unsettling Futurity," 400.

34. According to data from the Modern Language Association, enrollments in languages other than English at US higher educational institutions declined 9.2 percent between 2103 and 2016. In the same time period, more than 650 college-level language programs were closed, Johnson, "Colleges Lose."

35. Wolfe, *Settler Colonialism*, 2.

36. Lee and Ahtone, "Land-Grab Universities."

37. Lee and Ahtone, "Land-Grab Universities."

38. Tuck and Gaztambide-Fernández, "Curriculum, Replacement," 72–89; Wolfe, "Settler Colonialism," 387–409.

39. Tuck and Yang, "Decolonization," 15–16.

40. Tuck and Gaztambide-Fernández, "Curriculum, Replacement," 73.

41. University Languages Portal Australia.

42. Smith, Funaki, and MacDonald, "Living, Breathing Settler-Colonialism: The Reification of Settler Norms in a Common University Space," 133.

43. United States Census Bureau, "People Reporting Ancestry 2018."

44. Mušanović and Manthripragada, "Unsettling Futurity," 401.

45. The concept of privileged immobility comes from Robin Cohen's writings on how the pandemic illustrated the class dimensions of mobility and immobility, Cohen, "Coronavirus Puts Class Dimension." See also Jennifer Hosek's contribution to *Digital Feminist Collective* on this topic: Hosek, "Hollow Privilege."

46. Greenwood, "Place, Land," 370.

47. An editorial in the medical journal *The Lancet*, for example, refers to the climate emergency and COVID-19 as "converging crises," noting that both are "borne of human activity that has led to environmental degradation." "Climate and COVID-19," 71.

48. A study by the US Centers for Disease Control and Prevention found that incidences of COVID-19 were 3.5 times higher among Indigenous Americans than among the non-Hispanic white population and that these groups are at higher risk for severe illness, complications, and hospitalization, Centers for Disease Control, "CDC Data Show." A report by Indigenous Navigator has also documented the impact of COVID-19 on Indigenous communities in eleven countries, highlighting how it has exacerbated already existing gaps in access to healthcare, education, food security and other human rights: Indigenous Navigator, "The Impact of COVID-19 on Indigenous Communities."

49. Smith and Jenkins, "About That Spare Room."

50. Kuokkanen, "Toward a New Relation," 280.

51. Kuokkanen, "Toward a New Relation," 282.

52. Here I think of the title of a decolonization manual produced by the British Columbia Federation of Post-Secondary Educators: *Whose Land is it Anyway?* Edited by Peter McFarlane and Nicole Schabus.

53. *Gesturing Towards Decolonial Futures*.

54. Stein and Andreotti, "Decolonization and Higher Education."

55. Tuck and Yang, "Decolonization Is Not a Metaphor," 21.

BIBLIOGRAPHY

Anya, Uju, and L. J. Randolph. "Diversifying Language Educators and Learners." *The Language Educator* (October/November 2019): 23–27.

Battiste, Marie, Lynne Bell, and L. M. Findlay. "Decolonizing Education in Canadian Universities: An Interdisciplinary, International, Indigenous Research Project." *Canadian Journal of Native Education* 26, no. 2 (2002): 82–95.

Betts, Raymond F. "Decolonization: A Brief History of the Word." In *Beyond Empire and Nation: The Decolonization of African and Asian Societies, 1930s–1970s*, edited by Els Bogaerts and Remco Raben, 23–38. Leiden: Brill, 2012.

Bryant, Andrea Dawn, Nichole M. Neuman, David Gramling, and Ervin Malakaj. "Announced But Not Enacted: Anti-Racist German Studies as Process." *Applied Linguistics* 42, no. 2 (2021): 347–54.

Centers for Disease Control. "CDC Data Show Disproportionate COVID-19 Impact in American Indian/Alaska Native Populations." Press Release, August 19, 2020. https://www.cdc.gov/media/releases/2020/p0819-covid-19-impact-american -indian-alaska-native.html.

Charles, Elizabeth. "Decolonizing the Curriculum." *Insights* 32, no. 1 (2019): 1–7.

"Climate and COVID-19: Converging Crises." *The Lancet* 397, no. 10269 (2020): 71.

Cohen, Robin. "Coronavirus Puts Class Dimension of Mobility into Sharp Focus." *The Conversation* (April 14, 2020). https://theconversation.com/coronavirus-puts -class-dimension-of-mobility-into-sharp-focus-135896.

Criser, Regine, and Suzuko Knott. "Decolonizing the Curriculum." *Die Unterrichtspraxis/ Teaching German* 52, no. 2 (2019): 151–60.

Criser, Regine, and Ervin Malakaj, "Introduction: Diversity and Decolonization in German Studies." In *Diversity and Decolonization in German Studies*, edited by Criser and Malakaj, 1–22. Cham: Palgrave, 2020.

Diversity, Decolonization, and the German Curriculum Collective. "Open Letter to the AATG: A Ten-Point Program of the Diversity, Decolonization, and the German Curriculum Collective," *DDGC Blog* (April 16, 2019). https://diversityingermancurriculum .weebly.com/ddgc-blog/open-letter-to-the-aatg-a-ten-point-program-of-the -diversity-decolonization-and-the-german-curriculum-ddgc-collective.

Fellner, Karlee D. "Embodying Decoloniality: Indigenizing Curriculum and Pedagogy." *American Journal of Community Psychology* 62, no. 3–4 (2018): 283–93.

Gesturing Towards Decolonial Futures. Accessed July 2, 2020. https://decolonialfutures.net.

Greenwood, David Addington. "Place, Land, and the Decolonization of the Settler Soul." *The Journal of Environmental Education* 50, no. 4–6 (2019): 358–77.

Häntzschel, Jörg. "Deutsche Nationalkultur? Die Kulturwissenschaftlerin Sigrid Weigel fordert in einem Gutachten einen Kurswechsel in der Kulturpolitik." [German National Culture? Cultural Studies Scholar Sigrid Weigel Calls for a Change of Direction in Cultural Politics in a Report.] *Süddeutsche Zeitung*, August 26, 2019. https://www.sueddeutsche.de/kultur/auswaertige-kulturpolitik-deutsche -nationalkultur-1.4576458.

Hosek, Jennifer Ruth. "The Hollow Privilege of Immobility in the Time of Covid-19." *Digital Feminist Collective* (July 2, 2020). https://digitalfeministcollective.net/index .php/2020/07/02/the-hollow-privilege-of-immobility-in-the-time-of-covid-19/.

"The Impact of COVID-19 on Indigenous Communities: Insights from Indigenous Navigator." *Indigenous Navigator* (December 14, 2020). https://indigenousnavigator.org /publication/the-impact-of-covid-19-on-indigenous-communities.

Johnson, Steven. "Colleges Lose a 'Stunning' 651 Foreign-Language Programs in 3 Years." *Chronicle of Higher Education* (January 22, 2019). https://www.chronicle.com /article/colleges-lose-a-stunning-651-foreign-language-programs-in-3-years/.

King, Hayden. "'I Regret It': Hayden King on Writing Ryerson University's Territorial Acknowledgement." Interview by Rosanna Deerchild. *CBC Radio* (January 18, 2019). https://www.cbc.ca/amp/1.4973371.

Kuokkanen, Rauna. "Toward a New Relation of Hospitality in the Academy." *American Indian Quarterly* 27, no. 1–2 (2003): 267–95.

Lee, Robert, and Tristan Ahtone. "Land-Grab Universities: Expropriated Indigenous Land Is the Foundation of the Land-Grant University System." *High Country News* (March 30, 2020). https://www.hcn.org/issues/52.4/indigenous-affairs-education-land-grab-universities.

Mackinlay, Elizabeth, and Katelyn Barney. "Unknown and Unknowing Possibilities: Transformative Learning, Social Justice, and Decolonising Pedagogy in Indigenous Australian Studies." *Journal of Transformative Education* 12, no. 1 (2014): 54–73.

Malakaj, Ervin. "The State of Diversity and Decolonization in North American German Studies." In *Transnational German Education and Comparative Education Systems*, edited by Benjamin Nickl, Stefan Popenici, and Deane Blackler, 85–101. Cham: Springer, 2020.

Manthripragada, Ashwin, and Emina Mušanović. "Accounting for Our Settler Colonialism: Toward an Unsettled German Studies in the United States." In *Diversity, Decolonization, and German Studies*, edited by Regine Criser and Ervin Malakaj, 23–40. Cham: Palgrave, 2020.

Mbembe, Achille Joseph. "Decolonizing the University: New Directions." *Arts & Humanities in Higher Education* 15, no. 1 (2016): 29–45.

McFarlane, Peter, and Nicole Schabus, eds. *Whose Land is it Anyway? A Manual for Decolonization*. British Columbia: Federation of Post-Secondary Educators of BC, 2017.

Meisner, Matthias. "Familiennachzug aus Afghanistan: Deutschpflicht bleibt" (Family migration from Afghanistan: German requirement remains), *TAZ* (September 5, 2021). https://taz.de/Familiennachzug-aus-Afghanistan/!5798688/.

Murphy, Dianna, and Seo Young Lee. "The Gender and Race or Ethnicity of Majors in Languages and Literatures Other Than English in the United States, 2010–14." *ADFL Bulletin* 45, no. 2 (2019): 43–89.

Mušanović, Emina, and Ashwin Manthripragada. "Unsettling Futurity." *Seminar* 55, no. 4 (2019): 398–414.

Ngũgĩ wa Thiong'o. *Decolonising the Mind: The Politics of Language in African Literature*. Portsmouth: Heinemann, 1986.

Niekerk, Carl, ed. "Does German Cultural Studies Need the Nation-State Model?" Special issue, *The German Quarterly* 92, no. 4 (2019).

Norberg, Jakob. "German Literary Studies and the Nation." *The German Quarterly* 91, no. 1 (2018): 1–17.

Peters, George, ed. "Focus on Diversity." Special issue, *Die Unterrichtspraxis/Teaching German* 25, no. 2 (1992).

Smith, Avery, Hine Funaki, and Liana MacDonald. "Living, Breathing Settler-Colonialism: The Reification of Settler Norms in a Common University Space." *Higher Education Research & Development* 40, no. 1 (2020): 132–45.

Smith, Julie P., and Fiona Jenkins. "About That Spare Room: Employers Requisitioned Our Homes and Our Time." *The Conversation* (June 11, 2020). https://theconversation.com/about-that-spare-room-employers-requisitioned-our-homes-and-our-time-139854.

Stein, Sharon, and Vanessa de Oliveira Andreotti. "Decolonization and Higher Education." In *Encyclopedia of Educational Philosophy and Theory*, edited by Michael A. Peters. Singapore: Springer, 2016. https://www.researchgate.net/publication/309419202_Decolonization_and_Higher_Education.

Tuck, Eve, and K. Wayne Yang. "Decolonization Is Not a Metaphor." *Decolonization: Indigeneity, Education & Society* 1, no. 1 (2012): 1–40.

Tuck, Eve, and Rubén A. Gaztambide-Fernández. "Curriculum, Replacement, and Settler Futurity." *Journal of Curriculum Theorizing* 29, no. 1 (2013): 72–89.

United States Census Bureau. "People Reporting Ancestry 2018: American Community Survey 5-Year Estimates Detailed Tables." https://data.census.gov/cedsci/table?q=ancestry&tid=ACSDT5Y2018.

University Languages Portal Australia. Accessed July 2, 2020. https://ulpa.edu.au.

Watchman, Renae, Carrie Smith, and Markus Stock. "Building Transdisciplinary Relationships: Indigenous and German Studies." *Seminar* 55, no. 4 (2019): 309–27.

Weber, Silja. "Visual Representation of Whiteness in Beginning Level German Textbooks." *International Journal of Bias, Identity and Diversities in Education* 2, no. 2 (2017): 1–12.

Weigel, Sigrid. *Transnational Foreign Cultural Policy—Beyond National Culture: Prerequisites and Perspectives for the Intersection of Domestic and Foreign Policy.* ifa Edition Culture and Foreign Policy, 2019. https://nbn-resolving.org/urn:nbn:de:0168-ssoar-62984-6.

Wolfe, Patrick. *Settler Colonialism and the Transformation of Anthropology: The Politics and Poetics of an Ethnographic Event.* London: Cassell, 1999.

Wolfe, Patrick. "Settler colonialism and the elimination of the native." *Journal of Genocide Research* 8, no. 4 (2006): 387–409.

Part 2

NEW PEDAGOGIES AND STRATEGIES

5

A CHICANA PEDAGOGY FOR DIGITAL PEN PALS

Diana Noreen Rivera and Leigh Johnson

> **Movidas are also—as they were for the generations before us—about creating an analytic from which to understand power and build a theory that centers subjects who experience multiple and intersecting oppressions, in order to better understand, and more importantly undo, relations of domination and subordination.**
>
> —Dionne Espinoza, María Eugenia Cotera, and Maylei Blackwell,
> *Chicana Movidas*, 30

As scholars of Mexican American/Chicanx/Latinx literature and educators who centralize community learning and public humanities as part of our respective teaching, we formed a partnership to provide students enrolled in our spring 2020 Mexican American/Borderlands literature courses with an expanded curriculum. We aimed to broaden our students' literary and cultural perspectives with experiential learning based on travel, collaboration, reflection, and multicultural public observation at a time of heightened racial tension in our national history, where fearmongering and racism, which compounded since the start of the COVID-19 pandemic, have intensified violence against Black and Brown people of color along with other ethnic minorities who are citizens, refugees, and working-class immigrants alike. Leigh Johnson is an associate professor of literature at Marymount University (MU), a private Catholic institution and recently designated Hispanic-serving institution (HSI) with a diverse international student population, in Arlington, Virginia. Noreen Rivera is an associate professor of literature and cultural studies at the University of Texas Rio Grande Valley (UTRGV), a multicampus HSI in South Texas near the United States-Mexico border.

For us, the disruption to higher education caused by COVID-19's spread across the United States in spring 2020 entailed the loss of not only traditional teaching modalities in the material classroom but also a year's worth of planning and anticipation leading to what would have been a climactic point in our partnership: one-week study away trips that would physically bring together UTRGV and MU students as collaborative learners and ambassadors of their regions and cultures. MU students were to visit the UTRGV Brownsville campus and tour the South Texas borderlands, then UTRGV students were to visit their counterparts at MU in a joint class session and tour Washington, DC. To facilitate camaraderie, collaboration and cultural exchange among our students, before travel, we created a series of graded, digital pen pal exchanges, in which UTRGV and MU students corresponded via e-mail to introduce themselves, share their literary learning, and reflect on the ways in which the course content related to their lives and current events.

The cancellation of our joint study away trips, however, did not mean forfeiting our fundamental educational, collaborative, and democratic aims. Our students, like the majority of students enrolled at institutions of higher education and K–12, were thrust into online, remote learning situations in March 2020 as states mandated stay-at-home orders to curb transmission and death during the initial months of viral spread. We immediately recognized the valuable discursive conversations continued by our students in their digital pen pal partnerships. Many of our students collaboratively engaged in what is best described as learning networks of care, as pen pals motivated each other to persevere as their personal concerns and pandemic hardships came through in their literary evaluations. For example, we noticed students expressed their fears of COVID-19 and wished each other safety and caution before turning to observations and dialogues on the analysis of structures of racism and poverty in literary works like the play *blu* by Virginia Grise or the novel *George Washington Gomez* by Américo Paredes. Soon, letters reflected that some students and their parents lost retail, service, and factory jobs or continued to work in conditions that fueled anxiety of contracting COVID-19. As a result, the success of our pen pal maneuver placed us on a notable journey that extended our instructional partnership, digitally connecting students from the south Texas-Mexico borderlands and the Washington D.C. metro area of the national Capitol into the academic year of 2020–2021. We both fortunately ended the spring 2021 semester healthy, but we were exhausted. We reflected on three semesters of digital connection that united our students and helped us establish a network of care between ourselves as mothers, scholars, and teachers, juggling our roles during a historic year for educational activity in which aborted full-campus openings and mass "crisis-response migration methods" in higher education drove faculty and students into emergency remote teaching and learning situations.[1]

The benefits of integrating pen pal models for face-to-face and online learning, across disciplines, at the level of higher education through elementary in the era of pre-COVID-19 instruction, are well documented. Researchers and instructors of STEM, literacy studies, preservice teacher education, and Collaborative Online International Learning (COIL) consistently describe meaningful collaborations in which students participating in pen pal projects experience positive cultural exchanges, connections, and cross-curricular learning through peer support.[2]

In this chapter, we add to the body of pen pal pedagogy by considering our digital partnership in ways that directly take into account the urgent sociopolitical, public health, and educational challenges during COVID-19, rather than by formulating our experience as an apolitical teaching method repurposed for pandemic times. Given our mutual commitment for instilling a democratic and humanitarian consciousness in our students via the study of literature and in hindsight of where we started to where we have sojourned, we align our digital pen pal collaboration as an extension of the historical and conceptual pedagogy found in Dionne Espinoza, María E. Cotera, and Maylei Blackwell's groundbreaking anthology *Chicana Movidas: New Narratives of Activism and Feminism in the Movement Era*. Like Chicana education scholars and pedagogues of various disciplines, we, as literary and cultural scholars, believe in building on the important work of Chicana feminists such as Gloria Anzaldúa, whose activist works have inspired educational practices and studies by Dolores Delgado Bernal, Ines Hernandez-Avila, Aida Hurtado, Norma E. Cantú, Debra A. Castillo, and many more. Just as Anzaldúa has offered Chicana feminist epistemologies for educators to rethink Western/patriarchal educational practices and develop transformative pedagogies for the traditional classroom, we credit Espinoza, Cotera, and Blackwell's historical anthology *Chicana Movidas* for providing us critical epistemological tools to articulate the linked digital learning activities our students from UTRGV and MU completed during our pandemicera partnership, across remote, online, and hybrid classrooms.

In *Chicana Movidas*, Espinoza, Cotera, and Blackwell present a collection of scholarly essays and *testimonios* (testimonies) centering Chicana feminist organization, activism, and leadership in the late 1960s and 1970s. As Espinoza, Cotera, and Blackwell elaborate in their editorial introduction, Chicana activists in this historical period were far from being dissuaded by their marginalized positions in the Chicano and (white) feminist movements. Rather, they "enact[ed] a new kind of *polítca* [politics] at the intersection of race, class, gender and sexuality" and they "developed methodologies and technologies of resistance" that in turn generated new theories, art forms, organizational spaces, and strategies of alliance.[3] These essential maneuvers undertaken by Chicana activists like Martha Cotera, Francisca Flores, Olga Villa, Esther Hernández, and the scores of *mujeres* (women) in the anthology are termed *movidas*. The word movidas has its sociopolitical origins in the Hispanic/Latin American cultural movements of the late twentieth century. However, the types of movidas in which the editors are invested in spotlighting concern the overlooked day-to-day tactics by Chicana activists during movement history. They forgo emphasizing major figures or events in order to bring critical awareness to the "minor strategies and tactics rarely included in conventional histories."[4] Movidas, in the context of Chicana activism, are "acts of everyday labor and support as well as strategic and sometimes subversive interventions."[5] Espinoza, Cotera, and Blackwell build on the work of Gloria Anzaldúa and Chela Sandoval to expand the concept of movidas by providing a rich lexicon for articulating the small but meaningful ways Chicanas named oppressions; challenged the marginalization of their communities; and "opened up spaces for different approaches to organiz[e] with other women . . . to imagine and enact social change."[6] More important for the editors is the fact that the collection stands as a "pedagogical commitment" to the continuation of movidas beyond the movement era, which they and the contributors partake when writing on the Chicana movidas of the past and critically think about "what those lessons teach us about the present."[7]

Inspired by Espinosa, Cotera, and Blackwell's anthology and the ways in which the editors unite their contemporary educational/research praxis with the activism of movement era Chicana foremothers, we respectfully position the collaborative, digital instruction we as educators and publicly engaged scholars made during the first year of the COVID-19 pandemic as pedagogical movidas. In the spirit of Chicana foremothers' collective maneuvers for democratic activism and social change, we view our cross-national, digital pen pal student partnerships as a small but meaningful action for educational transformation in the time of this novel pandemic. As such, this chapter narrates our linked instruction in the time of COVID-19 as pedagogical movidas, in which we desired to provide for our students from the federal metropole of the DMV and the RGV borderlands of south Texas/Tamaulipas the following:

1. collective learning experiences that offset educational isolation from the sudden shift to remote learning and promoted networks of care
2. cross-cultural/cross-racial discursive connections during contentious political times intersecting with the pandemic
3. digital spaces of testimonio (testimony) affirming student and public epistemologies of lived experience during COVID-19
4. a pedagogical praxis that resists traditional, Western instructional methods that, still, too often circulate and are promoted by corporate-driven institutions of higher learning in pre-pandemic and pandemic-accelerated times

Social Politics of Our Field

Our digital pen pal collaboration is rooted in our friendship, which began in graduate school at the University of New Mexico in Albuquerque. Our studies overlapped from 2007 to 2011 as we honed our specialization in Chicanx literature and theory from the historical trajectory of nineteenth-century Mexican American writers to the contemporary period. Equally important, we were taught to recognize the politics of teaching our research specialization meant challenging a Eurocentric American literary canon that erases Mexican American/Chicanx subjects on two temporal fronts—the contemporary and the past. Our respective course syllabi prior to the COVID-19 pandemic and afterward during our collaboration includes nineteenth- and early twentieth-century works by authors of Mexican descent that have been reintroduced to literary studies largely by scholars of the international program Recovering the US Hispanic Literary Heritage.[8] As academics who have conferenced and published with Recovery, we each embrace the program's aims to preserve and disseminate Hispanic culture in its earlier literary formations. In particular, people of Mexican heritage are a subgroup that makes up over 60 percent of the US Latinx population and 11 percent of the total counted population of the United States.[9] Teaching students to recognize the historic longevity of Mexican Americans in our nation via literary study helps situate into the narrative of our country a sizeable ethnic body displaced from our nation's history since the outcome of the US-Mexico War in 1848. In our respective teaching of earlier Mexican American literature, we each have our students question the mythologies of manifest destiny, rugged individualism, and the frontier myth of the American West that too often reinforces conservative, white male perspectives on the history and culture of the US nation-state. Our syllabi in the spring 2020, fall 2020, and spring 2021 semesters also included contemporary Mexican American works written after 1980. Writings by Gloria Anzaldúa and Sandra Cisneros informed both our syllabi. In addition, Leigh independently taught works by Lucha Corpi, Alicia Gaspar de Alba, and Ana Castillo. Noreen taught a novel by Oscar Casares and twenty-first century oral literatures directly responding to the COVID-19 pandemic in the form of corridos (Mexican folk ballads) and first-person narratives collected as part of the Voces of a Pandemic Oral History Project, which launched in 2020 under the directorship of Maggie Rivas-Rodriguez, founder of the Voces Oral History Center at the University of Texas at Austin, to document and preserve Latinx pandemic stories and included a nation-wide collective of institutional and community partners. Teaching contemporary Mexican American literature in conjunction with earlier works means giving students the opportunity for literary and cultural analysis that can replace harmful stereotypes of

Mexican American culture with complex representations of a diverse body politic navigating modern systems of economy, education, military, public health, and immigration directed by cultural, racial, and gendered hierarchies.

Institutional Geographies and Demographics

The digital pen pal partnership gave us the opportunity as instructors to make unified, pedagogical movidas aligned with our politics for teaching Mexican American literature and other multicultural works by Latinx writers at a critical time when many students who identify as Latino/a/x continue to find themselves in predominantly white educational settings where there has been little or no attention given to Latinx history, literature, or cultural differences. It goes without saying this also remains a critical time when non-Latino/a/x students are largely uneducated about Latinx lived experiences. Therefore, one of the things Leigh hoped to accomplish with the pen pal experience was to expose MU students to place-based identities of the United States-Mexico border so that her students could start to see how borders shape identities in the geopolitical borderlands as well as identities far from the literal border between nations. Moreover, Leigh recognized for most Marymount students, including those who are international students or immigrants, the United States-Mexico border is a place to be imagined from rhetoric presented in film, news, or photograph.

In the 2020–2021 academic year, MU's diverse body of nearly thirty-nine hundred students included approximately 14 percent international students and an ethnic undergraduate population of 25 percent Hispanic, 16 percent Black/African American, 7 percent Asian, 31 percent white, and 5 percent multiracial.[10] UTRGV is the third-largest HSI in the United States with an enrollment of 90.5 percent Hispanic students out of 32,441 students registered in fall 2020.[11] Over 92 percent of UTRGV students live in the four-county region (Starr, Hidalgo, Cameron, and Willacy) of the South Texas borderlands that make up the Rio Grande Valley.[12] Many of these students, however, lead transborder lives with connections to family and friends across the Rio Grande in Matamoros, Tamaulipas, the city of Reynosa, or other towns dotting the Mexican border. In terms of first-generation students, in 2019, UTRGV had 54 percent first-generation students and MU had 28 percent.[13]

Born and raised in the Rio Grande Valley like the majority of her students, Noreen recognized a dual advantage for her students' participation in literary and cultural pen pal exchanges with MU students that centered on the simultaneous sharing and studying of their borderlands culture and identity. As US-

Mexico borderlands denizens and cultural insiders who practice, to varying degrees of assimilation, Mexican customs in their daily lives, Noreen understood her students could largely dispel the fabricated south Texas "war-zone" imaginary promoted by conservative media and right-wing politicians. Indeed, the Rio Grande Valley's large population of approximately 1.4 million people and its geography as a transnational thoroughfare for narcotics and human smuggling render it a space of violent activities. However, Texas Department of Public Safety records show border cities like Brownsville, Edinburg, and McAllen consistently have less violent crime than other Texas cities of similar population away from the United States-Mexico border, such as Beaumont, Amarillo, Midland, and Corpus Christi.[14]

By contrast, if poverty and chronic illness were considered systemic crimes, the Rio Grande Valley would be at the top of the charts with over 30 percent of the population below the federal poverty rate and one of nation's unhealthiest areas for chronic illnesses like diabetes, obesity, and cervical cancer.[15] Moreover, Noreen knew, because the state of Texas excludes from its K–12 curriculum and standardized testing the vast majority of Mexican American history and literature spotlighting social inequalities and the historic struggle for democratic rights, her students, while cultural insiders, would not be academic insiders on their culture. Noreen hoped UTRGV students' digital pen pal partnerships with MU students would have a positive and self-empowering effect reflective of studies noting the benefits of Chicanx/Mexican American Studies for first-gen Latinx students, as her students exchanged learning with students over a thousand miles away, from different racial heritages, who also learned and were interested in Mexican American culture.[16] Additionally, Noreen hoped all her students would increase their aptitude for communicating and empathizing with students from different cultural heritages to prepare students for interactions with ethnically diverse publics after college.

Digital Pen Pal Methodology

The cross-cultural partnering of our students that occurred organically in our mostly randomized parings, which will be narrated further in the theoretical application of our pen pal activity as pedagogical "movidas of crossing," resulted in a spectrum of ethnically diverse partnerships. Ethnic pairings of our students across three semesters included Pan-Latinx collaborations between students of Mexican and Afro-Dominican, Puerto Rican, and Salvadoran descent; Black American, African (Ghanaian, Ethiopian, Egyptian), and Mexican American collaborations; Mexican American and white American collaborations; Native

American/Polynesian and Mexican American collaborations; and the partnering of Arab American/Muslim students and students of Mexican descent.

Current events driving the urgency of our instructional collaboration included, in early months of 2020, conservative media stoking fears of a migrant caravan from Central America, horrifying images of child separation from parents at the southern United States-Mexico border, the continuation of the Remain in Mexico policy that forced families of mostly women and young children seeking asylum to live in deplorable conditions along the southern banks of the Rio Grande in Matamoros, and debates hardened about building more "wall" along the United States-Mexico border. Initial exchanges in early 2020, in our paired Mexican American and borderlands literature courses, composed of upper-division undergraduates and graduate students, focused on border politics, both those on the ground in Texas and those wending their way through the political apparatus. We evaluated twenty-three student partnerships between UTRGV and MU in spring 2020. We also organized an end-of-semester Zoom videoconference the week before final exams at our institutions, which is a practice we continued the following academic year to conclude e-mail exchanges. With almost 100 percent participation, our students logged on, joined breakout rooms with their pen pals, and discussed four questions we jointly wrote to facilitate their conversations. When our students came back to the main room, they said that they had not even needed the questions—they already felt like they knew each other and were continuing a conversation begun tentatively in January of 2020, foraged gracefully through the hardships of March and April, and celebrated for its resilience in May. Our students' feedback reinforced the effectiveness of our collaborative, instructional "movida" was not reliant on a communicative method of synchronous videoconferencing but in the paced, epistolary conversation of reliable, low-bandwidth e-mail.

In fall 2020 we expanded the pen pal exchange to include two sets of collaboration between our undergraduate students enrolled in Noreen's asynchronous "Introduction to Mexican American Literature" and "Survey of American Literature" courses and Leigh's synchronous and hybrid "American Voices" and "Ethnic Literary Traditions" courses. We scheduled five exchanges that composed 15 percent of our students' overall grade. Students were directed to copy both instructors on all e-mail exchanges. We each created grading rubrics to independently evaluate our respective students and to communicate instructor expectations for the use of a respectful tone, discussion of academic, cultural, and socially relevant content. Further, in today's social media universe of textspeak, we reminded students about the etiquette of e-mail writing. Black Lives Matter protests, the killing of George Floyd, and discussions of race, policing, and microaggressions were on students' minds as we introduced literature of social justice, including "The Hammon and the Beans" by Américo Paredes and *The Hate U Give* by Angie Thomas, in our respective American literature courses, each taught with a multicultural framework. In class, we turned a critical eye to the social and historical circumstances that shaped the literature, and the students wrote reflectively to each other, finding moments of movida and resistance in their exchanges.

As aforementioned, Noreen also collaborated in fall 2020 with Maggie Rivas-Rodriguez's, Voces of a Pandemic Oral History Project, to engage her students in public humanities scholarship that digitally preserves the Latinx stories of struggle and resilience during the COVID-19 pandemic. We will address this facet of our pen pal partnership in the section Memory Movidas. By the end of this unprecedented semester, nearly fifty student partnerships successfully fulfilled all five exchanges.

Spring 2021 brought more hope to our campuses and students as they and their families began to be eligible for vaccines, and campus life started to look toward an in-person graduation by March. This semester we scaled our pen pal activity to one course each—Noreen's asynchronous Survey of American Literature and Leigh's hybrid Major Authors. This helped to streamline our collective management of student partnerships, which entailed fielding student questions if their partner was late with an e-mail or repartnering students if their pen pal dropped the course. Our students continued on a literary and cultural trajectory similar to the fall 2020 semester, but with added hardship for UTRGV students: the February winter storm gripped South Texas and decades of energy privatization affected students' internet connections, shelter, and finances. Students in Northern Virginia and the Rio Grande Valley alike struggled with family members' deaths from COVID-19, and many continued isolation and social distancing to stave off outbreaks on campus and in their communities.

In total, our pen pal collaboration across three semesters created eighty-four student partnerships and over six hundred e-mails. It brought together our diverse students from the DMV and South Texas-Tamaulipas borderlands in ways that created digital dialogues of camaraderie, care, and critical thinking in a time of remote/isolated learning, intense social vitriol, and public health crisis. As specific pedagogical movidas articulated in our subsequent narrations, digital pen pals were small but meaningful acts of curricular labor, performed by our students and us as their evaluating instructors. These acts functioned as a technology of resistance for challenging isolation and marginalization of students and their communities in pandemic times.

Hallway Movidas

The pen pal exchange created the opportunity for what we see as "hallway movidas." According to the editors' introduction in *Chicana Movidas*, the spatial metaphor of the "hallway" locates movidas undertaken in interstitial spaces where Chicanas trafficked ideas, discourses, and experiences from one movement to another to generate a more complex revolutionary praxis. In our remote teaching experience during COVID-19, these hallway movidas became digital places where students found consciousness, discussed issues, and deployed their interventions into the spaces. We trace this to the ways that Chicanas participating in Chicano movement consciousness-raising groups "frequently formed counterstudy groups to directly address Chicana experiences or break patriarchal forms of female competition . . . that stood in the way of solidarity, community, and radical consciousness raising."[17] While we created these counterspaces in our remote classrooms, our students are the ones who grasped this digital space, often using it for their own purposes, devoid of the competition that comes from a classroom interaction with students in the same class. In this way, the hallway movida rendered a rigorous academic analysis more accessible for students as they puzzled out their ideas with a pen pal peer outside their institution and offset the educational isolation of virtual learning during COVID-19.

Leigh's Narrative

For both of us, and I suspect many other professors who have experienced the isolation of teaching online in 2020, our mostly deserted campuses starkly showed how much I rely on "campus life" to create energy and intellectual enthusiasm. I missed seeing students joking around with others, eating in the cafeteria, and reading in the grass. In class, I missed watching them interact with peers before and after class and during group work. Their letters gave insight into how they communicated with each other and the issues and events of the day that resonated with them. For instance, there was joy in making a small connection with another person in an icebreaker activity, reflected in this comment from a first e-mail introduction: "I feel your pain on not being able to work out due to COVID-19. Just when I was getting ready to hit the weights hard again the lockdown happened. So yeah, it's been a lot of long days indoors racking up hours playing Call of Duty. Haha, we may have even played each other once or twice without knowing."[18] As Luke Winkie notes in the *New York Times*, "[Small talk] proves that we are willing and capable of being friendly with one another and that the parameters of our exchange will be limited to things we can agree on. No matter where you are in the world, it's rude to express an existential uneasiness upon first impression. The pandemic has broken that golden rule."[19] As the previously mentioned interaction illustrates, the student attempts pleasant small talk, but the experience of living through a pandemic is so overwhelming that it pervades even banal conversations about working out and gaming, conversations that students rely on to make friends.

In a time when I could not walk around our classrooms listening to groups working on literary analysis tasks (and I tried sneaking into breakout rooms a few times, until the horror of feeling like I was ambushing students took over, and I waited for them in the main room), I *could* overhear how students were linking texts to their lives in these e-mails. The letters enabled me to hear their voices and senses of humor outside of strict academic writing; the letters became a testing ground for ideas they would more formally develop in classroom spaces, a hallway movida. For one student, reading Anzaldúa for the first time brought on mixed understanding and emotions they tried to share with their pen pal partner:

> As bilingual, I was fascinated with her writing method. Unfortunately, not all of my classmates experience the same. They explained feeling confused at moments and anguished to know what she meant. Since our professor encouraged us not to use google translator, you can imagine the darkness they had to confront. I felt exactly the same when I arrived in the United States without knowing how to write or speak English. It was a torment that I had to go through. I am still learning but I am more confident about my linguistic skills than before.

This student extended empathy to their classmates while reflecting on how Anzaldúa's project revolutionizes border theory. In another instance, I was privy to a little bit of shade thrown on me for the demands of the class, as a student remarked to her pen pal: "I hope you are doing well. I just finished reading *The Hate U Give* by Angie Thomas. Before I go into detail about how I feel about the book, I just want to say that I have never read a book with almost 500 pages in less than 2 weeks. It amazes me how little time we had to read this book but I am glad that I enjoyed it and it made me read on even more." These were things I sometimes overheard as students negotiated the workload of the class.

Taking the pulse of the hallway helps instructors correct for exhaustion, midterm fatigue, and other stressors for students. Sometimes this manifested as more serious issues. Some students expressed sensitive information to their peers about feeling overwhelmed with coursework, family situations, and general feelings of wellness or languishing. We were able to reach out to these students to help them get institutional support. One student, when their pen pal commented on financial hardship from the pandemic, responded by commiserating and sharing that their relative had passed from COVID-19 immediately before the semester began. The student was able to connect with campus support services to help them address their grief and financial difficulties. The ability to alert campus resources is always a challenge for instructors; as mandated reporters, we have a responsibility to the health and safety of the student and community. In these instances, I am grateful for my role as a writing instructor who can seek resources for students who need them.

Noreen's Narrative

In the 2020–2021academic year, I taught 100 percent asynchronous courses, returning to a modality I had not practiced in ten years. Studies since the early years of the twenty-first century illustrate the importance of social presence and interaction in distance learning, but in this era of pandemic, my urgency for sustaining the pen pal partnership with Leigh intensified after a summer swell in COVID-19 cases and deaths in the Rio Grande Valley.[20] The region became a national hotspot in July and August 2020 with local and national news outlets covering the arrival of refrigerated trailers for bodies, hospitals at capacity, and around-the-clock running crematoriums. I anticipated my students, especially those from the Rio Grande Valley's most vulnerable populations impacted by COVID-19, could benefit from a pedagogical "hallway movida" that creates community and reinforces learning. Like many educators across K–16, I remain concerned about COVID-19's impact on students of color and students from low-income households in terms of learning retention and dropout rates, some of which are now presented by the US Department of Education's Office for Civil Rights.[21] Teaching asynchronous courses heightened my concerns, which is why this pen pal activity was a small maneuver for transforming students' solitary learning experiences during this pandemic into ones of educational solidarity.

UTRGV and MU students largely formed learning networks of care in their pen pal partnerships that merged socialization with academic sharing that exceeded my expectations. As I measured the pulse of these "cyber hallways" across three semesters, I noticed students trafficked ideas in ways that academic writing genres like reports and research papers do not account. By shifting the rhetorical situation and changing the primary audience or recipient of the writing product from the professor to their pen pal, students' writing about subject matter was more expressive and cogent as they engaged in socialized learning with their MU pen pal in this digital format. As one example out of many, this excerpt is by a UTRGV student to their MU pen pal in their icebreaker exchange:

> I really appreciated learning about you from your first letter! I love that you are finding that you are able to relate to the ideas in your own way already, and to me, that makes perfect sense. . . . I am excited to continue to hear about your thoughts on what you learn about Mexican American culture and what kind of effects it has on the understanding you have about your own mixed Hawaiian heritage! . . .
>
> During the first week of class we read a poetry piece written by Chicana scholar Gloria Anzaldúa and a Journalistic article about the COVID-19 crisis in our region. Anzaldua was born and raised in the RGV and advanced important ideas concerning Mexican-American identity, sometimes ethnically conceived of as a "Mestizaje," that originated from the miscegenation between Native Americans and Spanish colonizers. The "New Mestiza" consciousness, a term coined by Anzaldua, represents her ideas about embracing the duality of this identity in the borderlands.

This icebreaker e-mail evidences the exclamatory joy of a student "excited" at the prospect of future intellectual exchanges with their partner. The student expresses empathy and interest in how their partner's learning in Leigh's Mexican American literature course relates to their Hawaiian ethnic experience before transitioning to a summation of learning in my course. As an asynchronous instructor, instead of relying solely on asocial assessments, like multiple-choice quizzes, to measure students' retention of course material, I gauged students' individual learning and identified problems relevant to course outcomes that I could reinforce in a short e-mail to the student or, if widespread, on my next video lecture.

Moreover, UTRGV students trafficked their love of region to educate their MU pen pals with narratives that resist the continuing saga of criminally violent stereotypes articulated by conservative media and politicians, as this UTRGV student eloquently wrote:

> I wish I could give you a piece of home so you could get the experience of feeling the RGV. It has its own charm and sometimes it doesn't get enough attention. The land is rich in culture, stories and life. . . . The palm trees always greet me when I come home from a trip. The dogs that lay together under the mesquite trees trying the stay cool during their naps. The ranchero music on a Saturday morning announcing its

time to clean. You need to try our food one day, straight from the hands of the local food vendors. The *paletero* honking his bicycle horn and getting an *arroz con leche La Brisa paleta* (ice-cream, rice-sugar-and milk, ice-cream popsicle). I'm not sure what the translation is! HA-HA

The editors of *Chicana Movidas* write that hallway movidas for Chicanas during the movement era enabled the expansion of ideas that moved Chicanas toward alliance building that bridged difference in the interest of collective social change.[22] This young Chicana student does not express an overt political rationale for her narration of home. However, she seizes this exchange in the cyber hallway to provide a multisensorial illustration of her geography as she has experienced it for the purpose of stimulating positive affect. She desires to "give" to her MU pen pal unfamiliar with the United States-Mexico borderlands "the experience of feeling the RGV" in ways that expand ideas of her home region and build a cultural perspective about the RGV that "doesn't get enough attention."

Movidas of Crossing

Movidas of crossing create discursive space for interracial and intercultural connections and collaboration during a time of racial division. Espinoza, Cotera, and Blackwell describe movidas of crossing as "understanding the strategic importance of difference in successful organizing work, learning to shift the center in order to illuminate the ways in which oppressions impact communities differently, working through the delicate negotiations between self and other, [and] understanding the self *in* the other."[23] The murder of George Floyd and subsequent protests throughout the summer of 2020 raised students' awareness of themselves as change agents and heightened their ability to link their personal experiences with racism to institutionalized oppression. Because of persistent resistance to change nationally, including insular ideas and anti-Critical Race Theory legislation, we found that movidas of crossing in pen pal exchanges were particularly powerful when they linked students from different backgrounds who then found common ground. Students reflected upon their experiences to seek understanding with their peers as they asked questions of a person who, until the moment of digital exchange, was "other" to them.

Leigh's Narrative

Because our student bodies are diverse in many ways, it was inevitable to create partnerships that crossed cultural, racial, age, gender, nationality, and economic lines. Student analysis revealed the commonalities in the ways they positioned themselves. Consider the following excerpt from a student's letter:

> I found your point about the "nopal en la frente" to be so interesting. It's an idea that I've been thinking a lot about lately. I know black people who were supporting Trump were called "Uncle Toms" and the black community was going to "take their black card." While I do feel like I have to question anyone who voted/supported Trump and his craziness, I also think it's unfair to make people feel like their ethnic identity is contingent on their political associations, etc. No one Mexican American thinks exactly the same way as another Mexican American. No one Black American thinks exactly the same way as another Black American. I do believe that people have the right to feel the way they feel and not fear their ethnic identities be at stake because of it. But at the same time, people who support a known racist should be taken to task for it. It's a really fine line that I'm still trying to wrap my mind around.

This kind of direct discussion and comparison is a clear example of how students expressed their subject position in relation to their peers—both seeking commonality and drawing distinctions between community perceptions. As Alejandra Marchevsky notes in her article, "Forging a Brown-Black Movement," "[t]hough experienced through different cultural lenses, black and Chicana activists shared similar commitments to racial self-pride and conceptions of freedom that included women of color's sexual and economic autonomy."[24] Discussions of collaboration between Black and Latina women have been subsumed under the urgently needed discussion of the invisibility of Afro-Latinx representation in media and film. However, multiethnic collaborations are necessary to make progress in many civil rights efforts.

The cross-cultural pen pal partnerships showed a trajectory of introduction, education, difference, collaboration, and camaraderie within difference. For instance, a partnership between a Mexican American student and a Palestinian American student resulted in cautious welcoming introductions, progressed to the sharing of TikTok videos explaining cultural references, and culminated in deep analysis of how white, insular communities force people of color to pass or keep silent for white comfort. As they eloquently concluded:

> Growing up Middle Eastern and Muslim in an area in which there was neither, I was trained to accommodate to the white people of the town because they were the ones that feared me most. . . . So people ask what the problem is with white savior books and films. It is not simply because it shows white people doing good things, white people are always shown

doing good things. It is that they depict only an emphasis on their goodness. That they are the healers, they are the just, they are our heroes. Taking away the spotlight from the people of color that had to step on their own backs, bite their own tongues, just to make the white person feel comfortable enough to see the truth of them; maybe even enough to fight for them one time.

To this their peer responded:

> "How to Tame a Wild Tongue" made me feel incredibly *seen*. It's as if she were writing that chapter for me. I also cried while reading it because I had never seen someone write about my culture and make me feel like my feelings about it were valid. I'll stop right here because I really don't want to ramble on too much, but these two writings just got me thinking a lot about all the things I've put up with in order to do right by my culture. I've had a lot of those experiences where I try to hide myself so that people don't notice that I am not white and if they do I want them to know I am a good Mexican.

These moments of connection and collaboration create a pedagogical movida of crossing, as students understand how oppression impacts communities differently and begin to see how they can see themselves in others' struggle.

Noreen's Narrative

Positioning our pen pal activity as a pedagogical movida of crossing means highlighting Espinoza, Cotera, and Blackwell's emphasis on Chicana activists of the movement era "learning to shift the center in order to illuminate the ways in which oppressions impact communities differently, working through the delicate negotiations between self and other, [and] understanding the self *in* the other."[25] Leigh and I, like scholars across disciplines who teach from multicultural or ethnic studies frameworks, "shift the center" in our field to spotlight nonwhite ethnic literary voices. Our curricular movida of crossing provided a critical entry point for our racially diverse students to make their own movidas of crossing as pen pals discussing literature and their lives through the lens of race. Specifically, I noticed how several student partnerships of Mexican American/Hispanic and African American descent, as historically oppressed communities on our nation, negotiated their identities via literary study to form understandings of "self *in* the other" across difference and similarity.

For example, in fall 2020, near the end of the semester, Leigh and I taught *The Hate U Give*, the young adult novel inspired by the Black Lives Matter movement that follows Black female protagonist Starr Carter, who witnessed the fatal shooting of her friend by a white policeman. With pen pal exchanges at their penultimate stage, and many students at ease with the discursive relations and friendships, one UTRGV student wrote to their African American pen pal about the novel:

> I feel so close to Big Mav (Starr's dad). I see my own papa in him which makes me reflect and connect with him the most. Mi papa struggled to survive in Mexico City. . . . When his family moved here, papa didn't want to lose where he came from and feared being seen as a quitter or a weak man. That meant dropping out of middle school and working in the fields. Like my papa, Big Mav struggles with his inner struggles with race, egoism, and family. Getting past that, for la familia is what keeps them moving and that is what gets me sentimental when I read how good of a father he is, even if he seems too intense.

In addition to expressing cross-racial connections on paternal masculinity, some students at this later stage made movidas of crossing into revealing experiences with racism. A Black MU student wrote about Leigh's course, "Each and every story opened my eyes to different obstacles and stereotypes different minorities face and attempt to overcome every day, which to me was extremely interesting. As a person who has experienced racial profiling first-hand to read about it from other peoples' perspectives was very eye opening."

Their UTRGV pen pal replied in the following excerpt: "I have experienced racial profiling as well. . . . An Immigration officer asked to see my documentation, green card, but I told him I didn't need one because I was an American born citizen. . . . Our class just concluded reading Angie Thomas's *The Hate U Give* . . . a beautiful young adult/Social protest novel and reading Starr's story allowed me to recognize to watch my privilege." In this instance the UTRGV student relates to their pen pal's shared experience of racial profiling; however, as a sign of understanding how oppressions impact communities differently, after reading Thomas's novel, this UTRGV student recognizes their privileges in the face of Black America's historic struggles.

Angela Valenzuela is an accomplished professor of educational leadership and policy at University of Texas-Austin and publicly engaged scholar who is a leader in the fight for integrating ethnic studies in Texas public school curriculum. Valenzuela argues the need for "learning based on real-world problems that realistically prepare students for productive, civically engaged lives as members of moral communities."[26] With anti-Critical Race Theory state legislation being used to shut down discussions of present-day racism in the United States in K–12 schools, the need to foster civil discussions of race for the purpose of expanding democracy largely falls on publicly engaged scholars in the college classroom.[27] This pen pal model, to borrow the language in this chapter's opening quote from *Chicana Movidas*, "creat[ed] an analytic" for students "to understand power" through the centering of "subjects who experience multiple and intersecting oppressions, in order to better understand, and more importantly *undo*, relations of domination and subordination."[28] Concerning undoing relations of domination, I give the final word for this section to a UTRGV student who shared with their pen pal in a final e-mail: "It is sad to see the events that are happening in our country with this pandemic due to the virus but also with this racial pandemic like the death of George Floyd and the international protests calling for justice. . . . I think being able to get all those different perspectives through different forms of literature will help us become better informed writers and more importantly better people for our community."

Memory Movidas

We also situate our pen pal activity as a pedagogical "memory movida," providing our students a digital, discursive space to testify, without separation, the intersections of their personal lives and the lives of their communities alongside their collegiate studies. Espinosa, Cotera, and Blackwell created the term memory movida to describe how Chicanas during the movement era as well as contemporary scholars deploy technologies available to recover or rework histories and complex identity perspectives of Mexican American women, which have been submerged, distorted, or discounted from mainstream history and historical record.[29] In addition to writing histories, creating archives, and producing visual art forms, the editors cite storytelling as a central memory movida, since storytelling is more than a simple narration of what happened; rather it is an intentionally constructed act that fuses personal narrative with collective experience.[30] Testimonios, in particular, are types of memory movidas because, like the editors and other Chicana feminist epistemology (CFE) scholars have asserted, giving one's testimony allows a storyteller to speak truth to power by bearing witness to social struggles/injustice, giving voice to silences, and affirming the agency of their lived epistemologies in the form of what Cherríe Moraga terms a "theory in the flesh."[31] Students grasped our instructional support for expressing their learning in ways that merged mind, body, and even spirit to testify to their personal hardships and resilience as well as those of their community members during the COVID-19 pandemic.

Noreen's Narrative

Speaking as a Chicana scholar, I see myself as part of a long genealogy and current collective of Chicana scholars/educational activists who aim to give voice to Chicanx/Latinx communities. So, for me, opening a digital space for students to testify to life and learning during this pandemic was one of the most important and permeating pedagogical movidas to emerge from our digital pen pal activity. In this section, I address how digital pen pals as memory movidas of testimonio helped me, once more, as an asynchronous instructor, as well as allowed me to reinforce a second publicly engaged scholarly activity I had my students complete as part of their literary studies in pandemic times—contributing to Voces of a Pandemic.

First, I must emphasize that fostering a digital pen pal environment welcoming students' e-mail exchanges as testimonios involves having a like-minded instructional partner who supports CFE pedagogies that, in decolonial fashion, "bring together critical consciousness and the will to take action to connect with others with love and compassion."[32] If Leigh or I were to have discouraged our respective students from freely integrating their lived experiences, past or present, this would have shut down the meaningful, student conversations that merged their literary studies with their lives. Many of the pen pal excerpts we provided as pedagogical hallway movidas and movidas of crossing, in my view, double as memory movidas because our students shared their lived epistemologies, the knowledges they know best, to relate to one another and make meaning of the literature together. As an asynchronous instructor, having a digital learning space where students could speak their total selves, their bodymind-spirit, was transformative for me because students expressed their whole personhood in ways that may have gone unspoken, especially in an asynchronous modality of teaching.[33] For instance, nearing semester exams, a UTRGV student wrote to their pen pal: "You have absolutely no idea how glad i am to hear from you! I wanted to start off my letter by telling you that you have nothing to be ashamed of. We are college students trying to survive during a pandemic not only financially or health related but as well as academically and mentally. . . . It has been insanely difficult especially since I have been working double shifts and trying to juggle double the labor, schoolwork, and spending time with my family. I really hope you don't give up and reach the goals you are trying to accomplish."

Effective remote teaching and learning in the era of COVID-19 mean acute listening across multiple relational dyads in higher education (student-instructor; student-student; instructor-student). As a publicly engaged scholar, this also involves students taking measure of their community. Another memory movida I made as part of my educational and scholarly praxis was accepting Maggie

Rivas-Rodriguez's invitation to higher education institutions and civic organizations to partner with her national oral history project, Voces of a Pandemic. Rivas-Rodriguez, founder of the Voces Oral History Center at University of Texas-Austin, is exemplary as a Chicana, publicly engaged scholar who, for decades, has utilized evolving technologies to preserve Latinx oral histories by conducting interviews. When COVID-19 spread across the United States in the summer of 2020, she established Voces of a Pandemic to document Latinx stories, via Zoom interview procedures, to help researchers, journalists, and the broader public better understand Latinx pandemic experiences.[34]

Using training materials and protocols Rivas-Rodriguez and her team provided institutional collaborators, I integrated Voces of a Pandemic into my undergraduate courses to extend my classes' study of oral literary genres into the public realm and train UTRGV students to conduct interviews that would effectively archive regional stories. To help students value their role as agents of community preservation during this historic time, in my asynchronous teachings, I stressed the importance of testimonio as a subgenre of oral literature and its democratic power for vocalizing stories of marginalized peoples without the time, tools, or skills to write the "great American novel." My training as a Recovery scholar also sensitizes me to how swiftly historical amnesia can occur, and the stories of others, even in one's own backyard, so to speak, are forgotten and rendered invisible. For example, while the Rio Grande Valley has been disproportionately impacted by COVID-19, community members' hardships vary, and students who experience greater socioeconomic stability can be shielded from more devastating pandemic outcomes affecting the working-class, undocumented, or unfortunate.

Students in my classes contributed to the growing institutional archive I coordinate and, equally important, students testified to their pen pals their experiences as publicly engaged scholars and agents for preserving stories of their community.[35] One student wrote: "I was determined and excited in covering her story and making sure she got her testimony out so others one day can reflect back and get a better understanding how much COVID-19 affected the Latino/Latina community especially here in south Texas. I learned that . . . our stories matter, how COVID-19 has affected my community and my home matters, and the better we understand our stories and our experiences of how my community has been affected the better we can avoid a pandemic like the one we are encountering now in present day."

Another student stated, "My interview for the Voces of a Pandemic project went great! . . . I learned that having lived here my whole life, I often forget that I'm part of the statistically poorest and most uneducated part of the country, and this project helped me put into perspective just how important it is that we help make underrepresented voices heard by those that have power to help."

I am grateful Leigh shared with her students the work UTRGV students completed for Voces of a Pandemic. Pedagogical memory movidas resist historical erasure and succeed when others listen.

Leigh's Narrative

The memory movida that enables students to offer their own and hear their peers' testimonios creates powerful connections to the mindbodyspirit that recognizes the importance of holistic approaches to teaching and learning. In this vein, many students shared what was deeply important to them with their peers. One student explained why she came to wear the hijab, even though it was not traditional in her family, whereas another discussed her relationship to hair politics in the Black community. Students chose to share memories of childhood and connections between the literature and their lives. These communications work to break down assumptions about other people that are woven deeply into the American social fabric.

The act of testimonio depends on reception as well as expression. Students in my spring 2021 American Voices class did not participate in a pen pal exchange, yet they still engaged with projects created by Noreen's students. As UTRGV students polished their interviews for Voces of a Pandemic and published them, my students listened to the recordings and identified themes they saw in the literature that were reflected in the interviews. Students noted that the testimonios showed how people adapted to situations in which they had little control over the origin or outcome, noted how external conflict shaped both narratives and events in a community, and how different opinions or perspectives on a global issue might cause strife or grief among family members. A long history of American literature showed students the ways in which defining identity is both personal and political, and the testimonios revealed that this tension is still present in people's stories.

Reflections and Moving Forward

Advantages of the pen pal exchange to students were numerous, as we found when we collected data from course evaluations. Student comments about the pen pal exchange were overwhelmingly positive, pointing to concrete advantages in meeting someone from a different area of the country: "I also very much enjoyed the pen-pal experience and getting a personal connection to individuals living in la frontera"; "The pen pal writings were important to help understand other people's cultures;" and "Having someone from another school to discuss the material outside of class made a great impact to keep me motivated."

Tensions to negotiate were minimum but did include a few white students' resistance to centering narratives by writers of color. This resistance to multicultural learning would have existed whether or not we used pen pal pedagogy. In fact, the exchanges made it clear to us which students felt entitled to their definitions of literary value as a white, male canon, and we were able to clarify the canonical debates of our field and situate expressive culture as the basis for literary production. One student also noted their skepticism, stating, "Writing the pen pals can be an awkward experience, maybe ask the class if this is something they feel comfortable with first or have people within the class be pen pals with each other." We worked to make it clear that students need not share personal information beyond the required rubric.

Looking forward, the COVID-19 pandemic has undoubtedly affected higher education business models. The *Harvard Business Review* describes this shifting landscape as a "critical turning point between the 'time before,' when analog on-campus degree-focused learning was the default, to the 'time after,' when digital, online, career-focused learning became the fulcrum of competition between institutions."[36] While remote learning was already seeing steady growth in the decade prior to COVID-19, the acceleration caused by this pandemic gives rise to concerns of whether meaningful publicly engaged learning can occur in remote corporatized classrooms. We feel the pedagogical movidas we made that put our students from diverse communities in digital conversation mediate, if not help to offset, current directions. Furthermore, in our field, if we teach Literature (with a capital L), as publicly engaged scholars and educators, then we will get to the questions of race, class, and social justice, but if the explanation of this falls only on those working in ethnic literature studies, then we lose the opportunity to deeply engage students with these issues in a timely way. Attention to these issues needs to happen at the department and university levels, with faculty colleagues pushing other colleagues who believe this does not have anything to do with their work. It was clear to us that insisting to our colleagues that the pen pal experience was rigorous academic discourse was a way to dislodge the structures that keep conversations about race apart from those of literary production and value.

Outside our field, we believe that this model of pen pal pedagogy as pedagogical movidas extends to other disciplines, especially those in which a subject-informed positionality imbues analysis and critique, which exists in almost all disciplines, including STEM, whether practitioners of those disciplines value the subject identity or not.

Since 2020–2021 we have continued our pen pal partnership and plan to sustain it into the future, to understand better how the pedagogical movidas we make as instructors lead our students to make movidas themselves. In their conversations about literature and culture with their peers and families, Noreen's students in online learning environments and Leigh's students in the traditional classroom have, on the whole, found surprising connections, which add a digital dynamic of extended community. While we live in an era of greater uncertainty than in pre-COVID-19 times, we remain hopeful and eagerly look forward to connecting our students through a 2025 study away program to Washington, DC, and the Rio Grande Valley of South Texas.

NOTES

1. For more on university "crisis response migration methods," see Adedoyin and Soykan, "COVID-19 Pandemic and Online Learning."

2. Studies discussing pen pal models for STEM instruction reviewed include Norton-Meier, Drake, and Tidwell, "Writing Mathematics Community," 245–56; Wiener and Matsumoto, "Ecosystem Pen Pals," 41–48. Literacy studies reviewed include Larrotta and Serrano, "Pen Pal Writing," 8–18. Preservice teacher education pen pal studies consulted are Hughes and Mahalingappa, "Experiences and Perceived Benefits," 253–71; Moore and Ritter, "Oh Yeah, I'm Mexican?" 505–514; Walker-Dalhouse, Sanders, and Dalhouse, "University and Middle-School Partnerships," 337–49; Wilfong and Oberhauser, "Pen Pal Project," 40–50. A study reviewed for COIL (collaborative online international learning) is Minei, Razuvaeva, and Dyshko, "Modern Day Digital Pen Pals," 336–44. Studies emphasizing positive cultural exchanges and cross-curricular learning through peer support reviewed include Barksdale, Watson and Park, "Pen Pal Letter Exchanges," 58–68; McMillon, "Pen Pals Without Borders," 119–35, and Lemkuhl, "Pen Pal Letters," 720–22.

3. Espinoza, Cotera, and Blackwell, "Introduction," 2, 21.

4. Espinoza, Cotera, and Blackwell, "Introduction," 3.

5. Espinoza, Cotera, and Blackwell, "Introduction," 2.

6. Espinoza, Cotera, and Blackwell, "Introduction," 3.

7. Espinoza, Cotera, and Blackwell, "Introduction," 30.

8. See "Recovery Program," *Recovering the US Hispanic Literary Heritage.*

9. "DP05, ACS Demographic and Housing Estimates," 2020: ACS 5-Year Estimates Data Profiles, American Community Survey, United States Census Bureau. Additionally, on the important subject of ethnic signifiers, to account for the fluid and diverse identities of our students and their communities, we use a variety of terms (Latino/a/x, Mexican American, Hispanic, etc.) in this essay.

10. See "Most International Students, Regional Universities South," *U.S. News & World Report.* Also see Marymount University, "Demographic Profile." Additionally, it is important to note this data does not clearly account for the Afro-Latinx population at Marymount University.

11. "UTRGV Institutional Summary."

12. "UTRGV Institutional Summary."

13. "Washington Monthly 2019 Best Bang for the Buck Rankings: South" and "Washington Monthly 2019 Best Bang for the Buck Rankings: Southeast."

14. Texas Department of Public Safety, "The Texas Crime Report for 2020."

15. "Rio Grande Valley."

16. See Nuñez, "Counterspaces and Connections," 639–55.

17. Espinoza, Cotera, and Blackwell, "Introduction," 16.

18. Quotes from students reflect the spelling, colloquialisms, and mechanics of the original e-mail.

19. Winkie, "Coronavirus Has Killed Small Talk."

20. For studies demonstrating the importance of social presence and interaction in online distance learning see Swan, "Virtual Interaction," and Chih-Hsuing Tu and McIsaac, "Relationship of Social Presence," 31–150.

21. "Education in a Pandemic," 2021.

22. Espinoza, Cotera, and Blackwell, "Introduction," 15.

23. Espinoza, Cotera, and Blackwell, "Introduction," 21.

24. Alejandra Marchevsky, "Forging a Brown-Black Movement," 227–44, 230.

25. Espinoza, Cotera, and Blackwell, "Introduction," 21.

26. Valenzuela, *Lead the Change Series*, 1–6.

27. Hernández and Griff Witte, "Texas Bill."

28. Espinoza, Cotera, and Blackwell, "Introduction," 30.

29. Espinoza, Cotera, and Blackwell, "Introduction," 23–24.

30. Espinoza, Cotera, and Blackwell, "Introduction," 24.

31. Moraga, "Entering the Lives," 19.

32. Rendón, *Sentipensante*. Quoted in Dolores Delgado Bernal, Rebeca Buricaga and Judith Flores Carmona. "Chicana/Latina *Testimonios*," 363–72.

33. Lara, "Healing Sueños for Academia," 436.

34. *Voces of a Pandemic*.

35. UTRGV, "Scholarworks @ UTRGV, Voces of a Pandemic."

36. Gallagher and Palmer, "Pandemic Pushed Universities Online."

BIBLIOGRAPHY

Adedoyin, Olasile Babatunde, and Emrah Soykan. "COVID-19 Pandemic and Online Learning: The Challenges and Opportunities." *Interactive Learning Environments*, Taylor & Francis Online (2020). doi:10.1080/10494820.2020.1813180.

Barksdale, Mary Alice, Carol Watson, and Eun Soo Park. "Pen Pal Letter Exchanges: Taking First Steps Toward Developing Cultural Understandings." *The Reading Teacher* 61, no.1 (September 2007): 58–68. Wiley Online Library. doi.org/10.1598/RT.61.1.6.

Chih-Hsiung, Tu, and Marina McIsaac. "The Relationship of Social Presence and Interaction in Online Classes," *American Journal of Distance Education* 16, no. 3 (2002): 131–50. Taylor & Francis Online. doi:10.1207/S15389286AJDE1603_2.

Delgado Bernal, Dolores, Rebeca Buricaga, and Judith Flores Carmona. "Chicana/Latina *Testimonios*: Mapping the Methodological, Pedagogical, and Political." *Equity & Excellence in Education* 45, no. 3 (2012): 363–72. Taylor & Francis Online. doi:10.1080/10665684.2012.698149.

DHR Health Institute for Research and Development. "Rio Grande Valley Is Among the Unhealthiest Areas in America." Accessed July 5, 2021. https://dhrresearch.org/rio-grande-valley-is-among-the-unhealthiest-areas-in-america/.

"Education in a Pandemic: The Disparate Impacts of COVID-19 on America's Students." U.S. Department of Education, Office for Civil Rights (June 9, 2021). https://www2.ed.gov/about/offices/list/ocr/docs/20210608-impacts-of-COVID-1919.pdf.

Espinoza, Dionne, María Eugenia Cotera, and Maylei Blackwell. "Introduction." In *Chicana Movidas: New Narratives of Activism and Feminism in the Movement*

Era, edited by Dionne Espinoza, María Eugenia Cotera, and Maylei Blackwell, 1–30. Austin: University of Texas Press, 2018.

Gallagher, Sean, and Jason Palmer. "The Pandemic Pushed Universities Online. The Change Was Long Overdue." *Harvard Business Review* (September 29, 2020). https://hbr.org.

Hernández, Arelis R., and Griff Witte. "Texas Bill to Ban Teaching of Critical Race Theory." *The Washington Post*, June 2, 2021. https://www.washingtonpost.com /national/texas-critical-race-theory-bill-teachers/2021/06/02/4a72afda-bee9 -11eb-9bae-5a86187646fe_story.html.

Hughes, Elizabeth M., and Laura Mahalingappa. "Experiences and Perceived Benefits of a Digital Pen Pal Experience on Preservice Teachers' Preparation for Working with English Learners." *Action in Teacher Education* 40, no. 3 (2018): 253–71. Taylor & Francis Online. doi:10.1080/01626620.2018.1486750.

Lara, Irene. "Healing Sueños for Academia." In *This Bridge We Call Home: Radical Visions for Transformation*, edited by Gloria Anzaldúa and AnaLouise Keating, 433–38. New York: Routledge, 2002.

Larrotta, Clarena, and Arlene F. Serrano. "Pen Pal Writing: A Holistic and Socio-Cultural Approach to Adult English Literacy." *Journal of Adult Education* 41, no. 1 (2012): 8–18. ERIC. eric.ed.gov/?id=EJ991453.

Lemkuhl, Michelle. "Pen-Pal Letters: The Cross-Curricular Experience." *The Reading Teacher* 55, no. 8 (2002): 720–22. https://www.jstor.org/stable/20205127.

Marchevsky, Alejandra. "Forging a Brown-Black Movement: Chicana and African American Women Organizing for Welfare Rights in Los Angeles." In *Chicana Movidas: New Narratives of Activism and Feminism in the Movement Era*, edited by Dionne Espinoza, María Eugenia Cotera, and Maylei Blackwell, 227–44. Austin: University of Texas Press, 2018.

Marymount University. "Demographic Profile: Student Gender and Race/Ethnicity Percentages by Program." "Fall 2020, Undergraduate Programs." "20FA-Demographic-Enrollment-Tables_UG." https://marymount.edu/wp-content/uploads/2021/03 /20FA-Demographic-Enrollment-Tables_UG.pdf.

McMillon, Gwendolyn M. T. "Pen Pals Without Borders: A Cultural Exchange of Teaching and Learning." *Education and Urban Society* 42, no. 1 (2009): 119–35. SAGE. doi:10.1177/0013124509336066.

Minei, Elizabeth M., Tanya Razuvaeva, and Denis Dyshko. "Modern Day Digital Pen Pals: A Semester-Long Collaborative Online International Learning (COIL) Project." *Communication Teacher* 25, no. 4 (2021): 336–44. Taylor & Francis Online. doi:10.1080/17404622.2021.1887906.

Moore, Rita A., and Scott Ritter. "'Oh Yeah, I'm Mexican. What Type Are You?'" Changing the Way Preservice Teachers Interpret and Respond to Literate Identities of Children." *Early Childhood Education Journal* 35 (2008): 505–14. Springer. doi.org/10.1007/s10643-007-0226-z.

Moraga, Cherríe. "Entering the Lives of Others: Theory in the Flesh." In *This Bridge Called My Back: Writings by Radical Women of Color*, 4th ed., edited by Cherríe Moraga and Gloria Anzaldúa, 19. Albany: SUNY Press, 2015.

"Most International Students, Regional Universities South." *U.S. News & World Report*. Accessed July 25, 2022. https://www.usnews.com/best-colleges/rankings/regional -universities-south/most-international.

Norton-Meier, Lori, Corey Drake, and Mary Tidwell. "Writing Mathematics Community: A Pen Pal Inquiry Project." *Language Arts* 86, no. 4 (2009): 245–46. https:// www.jstor.org/stable/41483535.

Nuñez, Anne-Marie. "Counterspaces and Connections in College Transitions: First-Generation Latino Students' Perspectives on Chicano Studies." *Journal of College Student Development* 52, no. 6 (2011): 639–55. ProjectMUSE. doi:10.1353/csd.2011.0077.

"Recovery Program." *Recovering the US Hispanic Literary Heritage.* Arte Público Press, University of Houston, 2020.

Rendón, Laura I. *Sentipensante (Sensing/thinking) Pedagogy: Educating for Wholeness, Social Justice and Liberation.* Sterling, VA: Stylus, 2009.

"Rio Grande Valley Is Among the Unhealthiest Areas in America." DHR Health Institute for Research and Development., https://dhrresearch.org/rio-grande-valley-is-among-the-unhealthiest-areas-in-america/.

Swan, Karen. "Virtual Interaction: Design Factors Affecting Student Satisfaction and Perceived Learning in Asynchronous Online Courses," *Distance Education* 22, no. 2 (2001): 306–31. Taylor & Francis Online. doi:10.1080/0158791010220208.

Texas Department of Public Safety. "The Texas Crime Report for 2020." Crime in Texas. Accessed July 25, 2022. https://www.dps.texas.gov/section/crime-records/crime-texas.

University of Houston. Arte Público Press. "Recovery Program." Accessed December 19, 2022. https://artepublicopress.com/recovery-program/.

University of Texas at Austin. "Voces of a Pandemic." Accessed December 19, 2022. https://voces.lib.utexas.edu/voces-pandemic.

UTRGV. "Scholarworks @ UTRGV, Voces of a Pandemic." Accessed December 19, 2022. https://scholarworks.utrgv.edu/voces/.

"UTRGV Institutional Summary 2020–2021." Office of Strategic Analysis & Institutional Reporting, University of Texas Rio Grande Valley. https://www.utrgv.edu/sair/_files/documents/instsummary2020.pdf.

Valenzuela, Angela. *Lead the Change Series: Q&A with Angela Valenzuela.* AERA Educational Change Special Interest Group 42 (September 2014): 1–6. http://www.aera.net/Portals/38/docs/SIGs/SIG155/42_Angela%20Valenzuela.pdf.

Voces of a Pandemic. The U of Texas at Austin, Voces Oral History Center, Moody College of Communication, 2021. https://voces.lib.utexas.edu/voces-pandemic.

Walker-Dalhouse, Doris, Vonnie Sanders, and A. Derick Dalhouse. "A University and Middle-School Partnership: Preservice Teachers' Attitudes Toward ELL Students." *Literacy Research and Instruction* 48, no. 4 (2009): 337–49. Taylor & Francis Online. doi:10.1080/19388070802422423.

"Washington Monthly 2019 Best Bang for the Buck Rankings: South." *Washington Monthly.* Accessed July 5, 2021. https://washingtonmonthly.com/2019college-guide/best-bang-south.

"Washington Monthly 2019 Best Bang for the Buck Rankings: Southeast." *Washington Monthly.* Accessed July 5, 2021. https://washingtonmonthly.com/2019college-guide/best-bang-southeast.

Wiener, Carlie S., and Karen Matsumoto. "Ecosystem Pen Pals: Using Place-Based Marine Science and Culture to Connect Students." *Journal of Geoscience Education* 62, no.1 (2014): 41–48. ProQuest. doi:10.5408/12-401.1.

Wilfong, Lori G., and Casey Oberhauser. "A Pen Pal Project Connects Preservice Teachers and Urban Youth: Preservice Teachers Experience Rewards of Working with Urban Youth through a Pen Pal Project." *Middle School Journal* 43, no. 5 (2012): 40–50. https://www.jstor.org/stable/23119440.

Winkie, Luke. "The Coronavirus Has Killed Small Talk." *New York Times*, May 27, 2020.

6

PANDEMIC COMMUNITY ENGAGEMENT

Daniela M. Susnara, Victoria N. Shiver,
and Jacob T. Peterson

If you have ever spent the summer in the southeastern region of the United States, you might describe it with two words: hot and humid. Children and adults alike often enjoy jumping in the pool on a scorching summer day. Unfortunately, during summer 2020, this was not a possibility. Throughout the South, and across the country, community swimming pools were forced to close down out of precaution of spreading COVID-19. In Tuscaloosa, Alabama, Freeman swimming pool, a once vibrant indoor/outdoor city pool, remained drained and locked. The Freeman pool is located in Tuscaloosa's West End, one of Tuscaloosa's poorest and underrepresented communities. Just across the street from the Freeman pool is a recreational city park, two city schools, and a local YMCA; all were closed due to COVID-19.

Just three miles up the road is the University of Alabama, a Carnegie-classified higher education institution that values and encourages community engagement. Normally during the summer, the campus and residence halls are buzzing with students taking summer classes and thousands of children and youth from nearby communities participating in summer camps. As you walk through campus you can hear music playing from the residence halls, see students napping on the Quad, and see children playing soccer on the athletic fields. Over a hundred youth programs took place on and off campus during the summer of 2019. Youth from across Alabama, and the country, visit campus to explore areas like football, biology, theater, and every topic in between. However, similar to the Freeman pool, during the summer of 2020, a normally energized campus was lulled by COVID-19.

Across the country, youth programs at the local, state, and national levels had to consider new strategies. Some programs opted for fully virtual operations, some might have had the option to operate using hybrid strategies, while others, unfortunately, were forced to put their programs on hold due to limited resources, funding, or support. In order to remain relevant and meet the needs of the community, the University of Alabama's Division of Community Affairs worked quickly to restructure two of its youth summer programs, Swim to the Top (STTT) and the STEM Entrepreneurship Academy (SEA).

About Swim to the Top and the STEM Entrepreneurship Academy

Before diving into the revamped development of both programs, it is important to recognize the programs in their traditional capacities. Swim to the Top (STTT) is a community-based, out-of-school program for children and youth ages four to fourteen. Partners in West Tuscaloosa include the Benjamin Barnes YMCA and the Tuscaloosa Parks and Recreation Authorities. Through these partnerships, STTT offers free swimming lessons and water safety lessons, physical education, and STEM-based enrichment to YMCA summer camp participants. Children and youth rotate through the three components daily. The program operates with the support of local school teachers and College of Education students who serve as instructors.

The SEA is a week-long overnight camp that typically takes place on the University of Alabama campus. High school sophomores and juniors from the Black Belt region are invited to stay the night, learn from STEM professors in hands-on labs, and meet with facilitators from the Culverhouse College of Business. While high school students are at the SEA, they work with a small group of students from their high school to solve a school community problem using the entrepreneurial and STEM skills they are acquiring during the Academy. At the end of the Academy, the students are encouraged to apply for Divisional seed funding to implement their project once they return to their school community.

Both pre-college programs are sponsored by The University of Alabama's Division of Community Affairs Center for Community-Based Partnerships (CCBP). The CCBP's role is to connect faculty, staff, students and community partners in research-based projects designed to solve critical problems identified collaboratively by community members and the University. Swim to the Top and SEA are two examples of CCBP projects implemented to solve critical problems in West Alabama. The relevance of both programs led to the Division's decision to restructure and implement the programs virtually during summer 2020.

Transition to Virtual Implementation

In order to abide by university and state COVID-19 guidelines and youth protection protocols, transitioning STTT and SEA to fully virtual programming was a required modification. University organizers began by collaborating with community partners, local school districts, and other Universities who had offered similar programs in-person. Three concepts emerged from these early conversations:

1. Access to technology was not as big of a barrier as organizers anticipated.
2. A mix of synchronous and asynchronous learning was preferred for virtual implementation.
3. Community partners expected program implementation.

Once the decision was made to continue with virtual programming, researching different platforms, programs, and resources began. Ultimately both programs utilized a mix of Google Sites and Zoom. These platforms were chosen for two reasons. First, both platforms were used by the school districts during the school year, so the community partners and families were already familiar with them. Second, both platforms were supported by the University, so no additional costs were associated with using them. The next step was modifying the program curriculums to fit within the virtual settings while still focusing on student learning outcomes.

Transitioning STTT to a virtual program required creativity, flexibility, and patience. Through the use of Google Sites, TikTok, and FlipGrid, the swimming, physical education, and academic enrichment components were all delivered virtually to the 4- to 14-year-old YMCA campers. One major curriculum modification took place in the swimming component, unlike past years, student learning outcomes revolved around water safety as opposed to survival and beginning swim skills. Recorded water safety lessons were structured to include a water safety tip and activities students could practice, with adult supervision, using resources like bathtubs, large bowls, small blow-up pools, or sprinklers. For example, during the water safety lesson focused on breath control, students learned about holding their breath under water and blowing bubbles. After learning these skills they were encouraged to practice on their own, either with a bowl and water, bathtub, or swimming pool, and then participate in a TikTok challenge where they could share their skill while engaging virtually with swim counselors and other students. For other lessons, while looking at the STTT Google Site, children first would select their age, and then which component (i.e., swimming, physical education, or academic enrichment) of the program they were participating in. Instructors from each component developed and uploaded weekly content for the children to participate in using blended learning. The YMCA counselors and staff supported the program by promoting the virtual resources and activities.

The transition to virtual for SEA required a special focus on logistics as directors coordinated high school student schedules, volunteer STEM faculty, undergraduate and graduate counselor work schedules, and an online platform. To ensure similar student learning outcomes associated with high school students exploring the STEM disciplines and entrepreneurial components could be reached, the SEA was expanded to be delivered over the course of two weeks. Restructuring the Academy to include two weeks of programming decreased the amount of time high school students and counselors had to be "online" each day. Previous feedback from community stakeholders suggested keeping students engaged by only having them login for short periods of time. Unlike STTT, the SEA primarily utilized Zoom while relying on additional online resources for group work or planning time. Similar to STTT, the SEA counselors were encouraged to support high school teams as they worked on their school projects.

A Theoretical Framework for Community Engaged Scholarship

In order to understand the virtual setting, specifically the impact of the virtual setting on university students working in the community-based programs, a theoretical framework from the literature on community engaged scholarship was used to guide our data collection and analysis. This theoretical framework was chosen because of its intentionality to investigate collaborative university-community programs. Specifically, for university-community collaborative programs to be successful, four interactive elements have to be present. These four interactive elements are known as the four Rs: relevance, reciprocity, research, and resilience.[1]

In order for a university-community intervention to succeed, Pruitt et al. argued that it was crucial that all partners and stakeholders perceived the intervention to be relevant. That is, partners and stakeholders valued the program because they believed there was a need for the program. Pruitt et al. also argued that university-community programs with relatively high levels of reciprocity were more likely to be effective than those with low levels of reciprocity. Pruitt et al. explained when all partners gained from, and equally important, gave to the program, a high level of reciprocity existed which in turn increased their motivation to contribute to a program's success. Paralleling Boyer, Pruitt, et al.

stated that high-quality research of university-community collaborations enabled partners and stakeholders to understand the degree to which a program was successful and reflect on their own contributions, perspectives, and practices. Such reflection, they suggested, should lead to improved programs and contribute to the degree of resilience within the initiative. The degree of resilience within a university-community program determined its longevity, the extent to which it continued to flourish, and its ability to overcome challenges.[2] Programs with a high level of resilience, they suggested, had strong structures and highly competent and committed university personnel and partners who were able to anticipate and overcome challenges.

Design and Participants

Both of the programs shifting to a virtual setting was a novel experience for both the researchers and the participants; therefore we elected to utilize a phenomenological multi-case study qualitative design.[3] Though there were two separate programs with their own unique aspects, they were all bound in their experiences as they progressed through program design and implementation collectively, permitting the multi-case study lens to be applied (Merriam). The participants socially constructed an understanding of their experiences both individually and collectively, therefore utilizing phenomenology was the best fit to engage an understanding of their collective realities.[4] The study was given approval by the university ethics board prior to participant recruitment. Participants included thirteen university students (seven males, six females) with seven identifying as White, five identifying as Black, and one identifying as "other." The participants were all instructors or counselors in one of the case study programs.

Based on data collection[5] and analysis[6] there were four main themes developed from the data analysis that aligned well with the Framework for Community Engagement: relevance, reciprocity, resilience, and research. Pseudonyms were provided for the instructors and counselors that served as participants and who worked the virtual STTT and SEA programs in the summer of 2020.

Relevance
Swim to the Top

The instructors working STTT perceived the program with positive relevance and reflected on the content being taught as something that can make a direct impact on the families in the community. The instructors also understood how programs like STTT were not prevalent in underprivileged communities. Kara, a Swim Instructor, stated, "There are not enough programs like that [STTT] in communities who could benefit from it" (formal interview). The relevance for teaching the promotion of water safety, physical activity, and healthy lifestyle choices is an opportunity provided by the program. Another positive outcome from STTT included how participants could transfer their knowledge to their parents. One instructor expressed, "The students will be able to take what they have learned about water safety and health back to their families. They will be able to educate their families and hopefully start making healthy choices at home and at school" (Kim, formal interview). The transfer of knowledge taught in STTT can provide a positive impact with the entire family, and the participants in our study believe the youth in the program would have a chance to inform their parents on relevant content facilitated by the program.

STEM Entrepreneurship Academy

The counselors working at SEA described the job as a "rewarding experience" (Erica, formal interview) and indicated that it "built student confidence" (Jason, formal interview). The counselors also believed the program was relevant and provided opportunities to the students in the program. An SEA counselor stated, "I think that many students, specifically the population that we offer the program to, probably aren't aware of all the different opportunities. And I think it's relevant because it opens their eyes to different possibilities" (Erica, formal interview). The counselors understood the importance of the students learning about potential educational and career choices at a young age to provide the chance for them to think about and discover what they are passionate about. Knowledge of figuring out career goals may motivate the students to find ways to achieve those goals. The participants in the program can interact with relevant resources and mentors within SEA to help achieve their goals.

Virtual Relevance

The COVID-19 crisis impacted the implementation of community-based programs and provided the opportunity to deliver programs virtually. Instructors and counselors working the programs found delivering the programs "virtually" to be impactful for their professional development. An STTT instructor stated, "it [virtual STTT] opened my eyes to seeing that it can still be done, and you can still make things happen through virtual" (Jack, formal interview). Although the instructors viewed the virtual world as a learning lesson and professional development, there were some negative views on the virtual programs overall impact. A swim instructor explained, "I honestly don't think the program, being delivered virtually, has had much of an impact on the community at this point" (Trey, reflection). Furthermore, an SEA counselor expressed, "I'm concerned about campers that may not be able to focus in a virtual setting" (Kate, reflection). Both statements provide insight on the negative aspect of the virtual programs during the COVID pandemic.

Reciprocity
Swim to the Top

Reciprocity was seen throughout the STTT program in a positive manner. Within the program, instructors received professional development, while the program benefited from having quality instructors. Swim and physical education instructors "benefited a lot" (Julie, formal interview) from the program being virtual. One of the instructors stated, "You can create your own videos and send them out for students to watch and still get them active" (Kim, reflection). Additionally, another instructor stated that, "it [virtual lessons] is something that I could use whenever I'm actually teaching" (Jack, formal interview). The instructors in the quotes are referring to the content they helped create while working in the virtual program. Along with swim instructors benefiting from the resources created, the physical education teacher also perceived the virtual content as positive. She stated, "I have six weeks of content and resources to bring with me wherever I go. I have videos that I can refer to in my future teaching or use in programming" (Julie, reflection). While the instructors benefited from new innovative content, the program (STTT) also benefited by receiving quality content for their participants.

STEM Entrepreneurship Academy

Positive reciprocity was also seen throughout SEA and, like in STTT, the instructors also received professional development. Additionally, the participants in STEM Academy were getting quality counselors invested in their learning. One of the counselors reflected on her experiences working the program and related the experiences to her future career by stating, "I want to be a therapist. So having that interaction and building those skills and on how to communicate with the teenager is going to help me, and also learning skills on how to communicate and lead them through zoom. I'll have to potentially lead clients through therapy sessions over zoom. Well, now I have the skills to know how to handle that" (Sarah, formal interview).

Another aspect that revealed reciprocity in the program was counselors and program participants being similar in age. The counselors felt they were more relatable and excited to work with the participants. An SEA counselor explained, "I really enjoyed hearing the presentations from both the campers and the entrepreneurs. It was nice hearing about things from people similar to my age who are working on" (Erica, formal interview). Additionally, another counselor stated that "I feel like anytime I get the opportunity to see younger people in the same position as me is a good thing" (Kate, formal interview). The SEA having counselors that are relatable to the students, in age and interest, is a strength of the program. The students can see themselves in the counselors and feel confident that they can one day achieve their aspirations.

Resilience
Swim to the Top

Resilience was seen throughout the STTT program. The program going virtual was a challenge for all partners involved. An instructor stated, "We got through the rough patch at the beginning where everyone was confused about the process and we are getting into the sweet spot where positive outcomes may occur" (Julie, reflection). Throughout the program, resilience was seen with everyone involved in the program "in the face of adversity" (Tim, formal interview). Communication and support were the driving factors overcoming many of the obstacles that were in place. The instructors described the communication and support from program leaders and fellow instructors. One instructor stated that "the group of people I was working with, they were great and nice and they made it easier to be here" (Jack, formal interview). Another instructor stated, "I have been supported with these challenges by having constant contact with supporting members of the program. The emails and phone calls make my role in the program a lot clearer" (Trey, reflection). Another factor in demonstrating resilience in virtual STTT was the reflection to improve. When developing component content, the coordinators and instructors were worried about connecting with the students, this prompted instructors to think of ways to engage the students in new ways such as Tik Tok challenges, dance videos, and amusing skits on water safety. Throughout the creation of the new content, instructors were constantly thinking of ways to improve. One instructor stated, "There were fun activities and the challenges were good but maybe we come up with more challenges because that definitely got people [students] to interact with us" (Kara, reflection), while another instructor stated, "I think a lot of things worked well but something we can do better next time is having scripts or just kind of being more scripted on screen" (Tim, reflection). Both instructors are suggesting ways to improve the virtual format. The reflection to improve establishes how invested and committed the instructors were to making the best out of the tough situation.

STEM Entrepreneurship Academy

STEM Entrepreneurship Academy instructors faced adversity throughout the program and had a difficult time with the virtual setting. One of the main issues was the technical and connection problems. In a reflection submission, an SEA counselor stated, "Virtual learning hindered my experience today because I was having issues with WiFi so it kicked me off the Zoom call for a moment. It was also lagging really bad so I didn't hear the speaker and participants clearly" (Kate, reflection). In another reflection an SEA counselor stated, "I experienced some technical issues because of bad weather in my area. Virtual learning sadly makes things like this more likely to happen" (Kim, reflection). The technical issues with the virtual program hindered and made it difficult to interact with the students.

The counselors also voiced that engaging the students with content "virtually" was difficult. A counselor stated, "It's really hard to get them engaged over a screen versus being in person and being able to see them and see what they're thinking and try to get them involved as much as possible" (Erica, formal interview). Engagement with the students was important to the counselors because they wanted to build positive relationships with the participants. A counselor explained, "I am most concerned about forming relationships with all the campers as I won't be able to interact with them in person" (Jason, reflection). The counselors felt the students could "never fully focus" (Kate, reflection) and were missing the "human interactions" (Erica, formal interview). The main difference between SEA and STTT was the Academy was synchronous, in that it took place in real time virtually. The content for STTT was prerecorded and the instructors worked together creating the content, which built a strong bond among them. The SEA counselors were never able to talk in person and were relying on technology to engage with each other.

Research

Swim to the Top and STEM Entrepreneurship Academy

Though not as prevalent as the prior three themes, research did maintain a consistent presence across the data sources. The research component in STTT and SEA served as an important factor for improvement and growth. Both programs received feedback and recommendations from instructors and counselors in the form of reflections and interviews. For example, one swim instructor stated, "One way I think the program can continue to grow is to keep the student reflections for upcoming years. I think these reflections are great ways to see the students' thought process and can help make the lessons better" (Kim, reflection) when describing the reflection process. When researching, it is important to share and promote the programs. An SEA counselor described this process by stating, "Having the opportunity to share what we are teaching with the adults enhances the potential for messages being shared at home, increasing the potential impact and growth" (Kate, formal interview). The previous statement from the counselor is vital for the success of other programs like STTT and SEA. Furthermore, instructors and counselors reflected on specific ways the programs could grow and improve. A swim instructor explained, "I think the program could partner with other organizations to offer more opportunities for students. I think finding a way to partner with local schools to offer this program during the school year would be an awesome opportunity to expand the program" (Trey, formal interview).

The research component can provide a voice to the people working and experiencing the programs. Additionally, having the instructors dedicated to improving the programs is helpful in the data collection process. Both STTT and SEA had instructors and counselors actively participating in providing data to the researchers ultimately leading to a deeper understanding of effective and ineffective strategies in virtual programming that will benefit the program involved in our present work, as well as others.

The Relevance of Virtual Programs

In line with the theoretical framework for community engaged scholarship (i.e., the work of Pruitt et al.), the key findings of this study were that university student instructors and counselors found the virtual programs to be relevant, have a high level of reciprocity, and to be resilient. Overall, despite the quick transition to virtual programming and barriers that accompanied the transition, university students still had a meaningful experience participating in virtual community-based programs. Collectively, these findings suggest that virtual community-based programs provide a valuable experience not only for the community members participating but also for the university students supporting programming. As community-based programs transition back to in-person and hybrid implementation, it is critical to consider university student's roles and the impact student participation can have on their university experience and career.

On the downside, the study indicated that research (e.g., scholarship, assessment, data analysis) did not stimulate a significant amount of reflection by the university students because they were relatively unaware of its existence. In the future this negative finding can be countered by including university students collaboratively in the development of the research plan, data collection, analysis, and dissemination of the results. Including university students in research will not only teach them about community engaged scholarship but will also create new pathways into community engagement in higher education.

In broad reflections, the K–12 learning loss documented to date as a result of COVID-19 raises the stakes for participation in community-based out-of-school time programs. K–12 students in underrepresented communities can significantly benefit from additional out-of-school time resources now more than ever. This chapter presents two programs that remained in operation throughout COVID-19 due to sustainable funding sources, concrete community relationships, and flexible and innovative staff. As programs and initiatives are restructuring post COVID-19, coordinators should prioritize:

1. the needs of their community, and specifically how community needs might have shifted due to the pandemic
2. solidifying foundational relationships with community partners to ensure relevant future programming no matter the circumstance
3. utilizing thoughtful planning and hiring practices to develop programs capable of overcoming challenges

The current study was limited to two community-based programs from one highly supported university. Future research of virtual programming should take place with different organizational structures and in different locations. Additionally, a small sample of university students acted as participants. Examining the perspectives of university students from a variety of programs and institutions would provide additional perspectives. Better understanding the impact of community-based programming on university students has the potential to positively impact not only the university students in the program but also the communities being served. We encourage further work in this field to allow for a deeper knowledge and literature base to be developed, preparing practitioners and researchers for successful future programming.

Programming for the Future

The two programs discussed in this chapter both took place during the summer of 2020. Based on updated university- and state-mandated health expectations, both programs were conducted in person during summer 2021 and summer 2022. Following summer 2020, both programs maintained reciprocal relationships with their respective community partners and were able to operate at the maximum youth capacity deemed safe considering university COVID-19 protocols. The resiliency exhibited by both programs allowed them to successfully operate following the summer of 2020. Since 2020 STTT and SEA have discontinued virtual and hybrid programming; however, two key concepts have been carried into the future. First is the importance of using social media to share content and connect with students, families, and community partners outside of the program. Second, and most important, the steps and the resources have been discovered to respond to a quick online transition, or hybrid, if needed.

NOTES

1. Pruitt, Susnara, and McLean, "Engaged Scholarship Consortium."
2. Pruitt, Susnara, and McLean, "Engaged Scholarship Consortium."
3. Polkinghorne, "Phenomenological Research Methods"; Vagle, *Crafting Phenomenological Research*.
4. Patton, *Qualitative Research & Evaluation Methods*.
5. Data included: weekly journaling, informal interviews, and semi-formal interviews.
6. Two of the authors analyzed the data utilizing a predominantly deductive approach in that the Framework for Community Engagement guided the process (Patton).

BIBLIOGRAPHY

Anthony, Vincent Nanno. "Ensuring the Quality of the Findings of Qualitative Research: Looking at Trustworthiness Criteria." *Journal of Emerging Trends in Educational Research and Policy Studies* 5, no. 2, (2014): 272–81.

Boyer, Ernest L. *Scholarship Reconsidered: Priorities of the Professoriate*. New York: Carnegie Foundation for the Advancement of Teaching, 1990.

Patton, Michael Quinn. *Qualitative Research & Evaluation Methods*. 4th ed. Thousand Oaks, CA: SAGE, 2015.

Polkinghorne, Donald E. "Phenomenological Research Methods." *Existential-Phenomenological Perspectives in Psychology* (1989): 41–60. doi:10.1007/978-1 -4615-6989-3_3.

Pruitt, Samory, Daniela Marie Susnara, and James E. McLean. "Engaged Scholarship Consortium." *Building a Conceptual Framework for Community-Engaged Scholarship*, 2019.

Vagle, Mark D. Crafting *Phenomenological Research*. 2nd ed. New York: Routledge, Taylor & Francis Group, 2016.

7

PROMOTING EQUITY AND INCLUSION THROUGH CRITICAL RESILIENCE PEDAGOGY

Rhian Morgan and Lisa Moody

The journey toward higher education (HE) does not always follow a simple linear trajectory from high school to university. Life happens and, pandemics notwithstanding, there are many reasons why someone's schooling might be interrupted. Systemic issues like poverty and racism can impact children's and particularly teenagers' ability to access and engage in formal learning. Individual circumstances, like illness, learning difficulties, or caring responsibilities can impact school outcomes, and teenagers are not always well placed to make informed decisions about their futures. People also change directions later in life; sometimes the change is in response to unemployment, and other times it is in pursuit of personal fulfilment or the result of a drive to make a bigger impact on the world. Hodges et al. note that "26 percent of young people [in Australia] do not attain a Year 12 or Certificate III equivalent by age 19."[1] Young people in regional and remote areas, along with those from low socioeconomic backgrounds, and Indigenous Australian students have the lowest rates of high school completion in relation to the national average.[2] Despite low school completion rates, many of these students still aspire to careers that require tertiary qualifications.[3]

The Australian government has followed a widening participation agenda in higher education since the 1970s, and in recent years Pathways programs have become a cornerstone of this agenda.[4] In Australia, Pathways programs provide a means of accessing tertiary education for individuals who do not meet the traditional entry requirements for university, either because they did not finish high school or did not get the grades required for their desired course of study.

Even prior to COVID-19, Australian Pathways programs were providing alternate points of entry into HE for many and helping to mediate educational disadvantage by increasing students' preparedness for study.[5]

The COVID-19 pandemic and resulting lockdown was a time of reckoning for many. Increasing unemployment occurred against a backdrop of civil unrest and science denial. Coupled with socioeconomic strains, such as shortages of health workers and IT infrastructure issues, these factors led both individuals and governments to critically examine the role HE could play for people and society in a postpandemic world. HE institutions were recognizing the need for alternate entrance pathways even prior to COVID-19, often in response to government-driven widening participation initiatives. However, the pandemic not only highlighted the necessity of these alternate entry programs but also acted as a catalyst, forcing a reimagining of the ways in which pathways education could be delivered online in short course format.

When compared to international offerings, Australian Pathways programs are akin to Access courses in the United Kingdom. Analogous predegree programs also exist in New Zealand, Canada, Ireland, and South Africa. In the United States there are several options to engage with degree-level, tertiary study. For example, labor market training and credentialing programs, such as certificates, work-based training, and skills-based short courses can facilitate entry into HE. In addition, adult education and college readiness programs offered via massive open online courses (MOOCs), online microcredentials, or competency-based education programs also serve as alternate pathways to HE.[6] Globally, labels such as subdegree, predegree, prebaccalaureate, and HE pathways are common. Funding models also vary widely from country to country. Yet regardless of the structures and labels used, these courses all serve a common purpose of opening up access to higher education to those who do not meet conventional admission requirements.

The enactment of widening participation agendas is a complex undertaking, and participants in predegree courses are often viewed as nontraditional students, which is in itself a contested term.[7] Burke argues that "students associated with non-traditional . . . backgrounds often become characterized by dividing practices that operate to re/classify those students in ways that re/position them as the 'Other.' . . . Students from 'Other' backgrounds are often characterized then through a range of deficit disorders . . . and are positioned by gendered, classed and racialized constructions."[8] Pathways programs can help counteract the othering inherent in institutional conceptualizations of nontraditional students, as these programs rework traditional pathways to higher education. In the Australian context, Pathways programs have a key role to play in facilitating equitable access to HE.

Outside of major metropolitan cities, Pathways programs have been particularly important in supporting the educational needs of individuals in regional, rural, and remote areas and promoting regional economic growth.[9] In 2015 our own regional institution launched a diploma of higher education (DHE), which was designed as an open access pathway to tertiary study. In order to enroll in the DHE, students just needed to be over eighteen years old and meet a minimum English language requirement. The DHE was designed as a twelve-month, on-campus, multidisciplinary preparatory pathway to bachelor-level study in a multitude of fields. The open nature of the program means that it attracts a diverse array of students from varied educational backgrounds and small face-to-face classes, with integrated support services as cornerstones of its success. In any given year, around 35 percent of the commencing cohort do not have high school completion results that facilitate entry into a bachelor's degree program, and more than half will not have finished high school. In this open access context, technical and academic challenges may be further compounded by intersectional disadvantage and negative prior school experiences, resulting in low levels of academic self-efficacy. However, despite these challenges, students who complete a Pathways course are more likely to continue bachelor-level study than those who enter a degree on the basis of high school completion alone.[10] This success is frequently attributed to the specific focus on inclusive pedagogies[11] and engagement, enacted through curriculum design, that is typical of effective Pathways programs.[12] Pathways programs also provide high support environments, characterized by effective integration of support services into curriculum.[13] Through intentional, high support, and inclusive pedagogies these programs seek to open up access to higher education to those who would otherwise not have been able to participate, therefore contributing to increased diversity in a range of degrees, fields, and professions.

Pathways education can be a powerful force for both individual and institutional change. For students, Pathways courses represent a space of transition and becoming, along with all of the messiness and angst that accompanies that. As teachers in this space, we used to joke that we were "crisis immune." Over the years, this phrase helped mediate some of the toll of the emotional labor associated with teaching in the subdegree space.[14] In 2019 as Pathways educators at a regional Australian university, our resolve was tested. The year started with a one-in-one-hundred-year flood that left many of our incoming students unhoused, while other students and staff spent days and weeks cleaning mud and mold from our homes and the homes of friends and family. This crisis was shortly followed by a fire in the students' halls of residence. We managed this as best we could, but no number of calls initiating critical incident response plans, deadline extensions, or trips to counseling services can adequately mediate the trauma experienced by eighteen-year-olds who have just moved out of their home and suddenly find themselves in their first weeks of university with nothing but their pajamas. "Crisis immune" slowly gave way to frequent reassurances that "at least no one got hurt." However, as the year progressed and students were finally able to settle into university life, Pathways staff returned to dealing with the everyday crises of subdegree teaching, such as student homelessness, subject anxieties, and students struggling with social phobia, poverty, bereavement, and other learning difficulties. We did this with a heightened focus on forthcoming legislation surrounding student loans, set to be implemented in 2020. This legislation was going to restrict access to student loans for study if individuals failed 50 percent of their subjects in one year and would have a significant impact on the haphazard nature of open access study. Little did we know that 2020 would actually bring with it a completely different set of challenges.

The Higher Education Relief Package

At the start of 2020, we sat in the "Blessing for the University Year" service (an annual multifaith celebration that attracts even the most agnostic academics through its plentiful offerings of free coffee and muffins) and listened to university dignitaries discuss weathering crises, floods, and fires. We left, joking that all that remained was pestilence. At that stage, the novel coronavirus (later known as SARS-CoV-2) was a peripheral news story happening in China, and we had little idea how unfunny our butchered biblical references were about to become. By March the world was headed into lockdown, and teachers and academics were scrambling to shift years of face-to-face pedagogy online.

Course development rarely takes place in a creative cocoon uninterrupted by deadlines, marking, committees, emails, and the other daily business of academic life. Working through periods of crisis can be emblematic of the experience of educational practitioners; however, this tenet has been brought into sharp relief as a result of the effects of a worldwide pandemic. Despite remaining relatively unscathed by the initial wave of the virus,[15] regional Australian universities still experienced the impacts of a national lockdown that initiated a weeklong closure and pivot to online learning. By April online classes had commenced, and the financial fallout associated with the loss of international students was rippling through the Australian higher education sector, alongside the broader economic impacts of the lockdown. In response, the Australian federal government announced their higher education relief package. The package included funding for a range of short courses aimed at helping unemployed and underemployed Australians gain access to higher education and retrain in the wake of the pandemic. Courses were to be targeted at identified areas of national priority, including health, education, information technology, and science with a focus on expedience, online learning, and fee subsidization.

As a response to the economic downturn caused by COVID-19, these courses point to the role tertiary study can play in community-building initiatives for a postpandemic world. However, without careful course design, the imperative to upskill and reskill in order to mediate workplace precarity and loss of institutional revenue, risked foregrounding neoliberal productivity agendas at the expense of student well-being, during a period of significant societal disruption.[16] From government announcement to enactment, the design and rollout of these courses was to occur in a compressed time frame of five weeks. Only three weeks after the initial shift to online learning, we were now required to design two introductory subjects that could prepare students to enter four distinct disciplines in the space of one eight-week term of study. The timeline was tight, the courses were going to be short, yet as practitioners we were acutely aware that anything we designed must reflect the ideals characteristic of successful Pathways programs (high levels of support, integration of services, and intentional curriculum design) to be effective. The course requirements, determined by the practicalities of teaching during a pandemic and the conditions set by the relief fund, challenged our preconceived notions of what good Pathways education looks like. The development of what came to be known as the "certificate of higher education" consequently occurred at the nexus of emergency remote teaching and intentional online course design. As such, the design process initiated by the pandemic harkens attention to the interplay and dissonance between the varied agendas of practitioners, policy makers, and legislators that shape contemporary higher education.

Actor Network Theory and Action Research

> Technologies, texts, discourses, and notions of pedagogy do not exist by themselves, rather they are assembled from and act in local settings.
>
> —John Hannon, "Breaking Down Online Teaching"

Course design for the certificate was shaped in equal parts by our own teaching philosophies, our institutional culture, hardware and software constraints, and the broader context of the pandemic. Institutional discourses around short courses and understandings of core skills informed decisions regarding structure and the development of learning outcomes. Delivery methods were shaped by global circumstance (as online was the only option) and the institutional platforms available. The design was informed by our own understandings of best practice for Pathways education. The course was equally influenced by a top-down directive to respond to the government's HE relief package. The relief package determined not only funding and fee models for the course but also practicalities, like the course calendar and delivery "streams" (or majors). In order to receive fee reductions students needed to have completed the course by the end of the year and delivery was to feed into the national priority areas of health, education, information technology, and science. Furthermore, our assumptions regarding the cohort were informed by governmental eligibility criteria requiring students to have been "displaced as a result of the COVID-19 crisis and . . . looking to upskill or retrain."[17] The convergence of social, political, and technological factors during the design process meant that the course could be viewed as a "socio-technical assemblage"—an amalgamation of mutually influential human and nonhuman parts (like technologies and policies)—and analyzed using the conceptual lens of Latour's actor network theory.[18]

Actor network theory (ANT) is an approach to the study of the interplay between human and nonhuman actors. Hannon broadly classifies actors as technological, social, or discursive.[19] However, these categories are permeable and the situating of specific actors (in this case, lecturers, learning technologies, and policy) within certain categories is not absolute. For example, the learning management system is a technological actor, constraining teaching practice through functions like quiz formats, but it is equally a discursive actor that shapes the enactment of pedagogical intent through systems like announcements, discussion forums, and content design tools. The flexibility of ANT makes it the perfect tool for analyzing the messy interrelatedness of technologies, experiences, humans, and social contexts that constitute the teaching and learning process. As a result, we made the decision early in the course development to apply this theoretical lens to an analysis of the design process. Viewing curriculum design through the prism of ANT "enables us to trace the ways that things come together, act and become taken for granted, or 'black-boxed.'"[20] Combining this theoretical lens with an action research framework derived from Torbet and Levin, and Greenwood allowed us to reimagine the design process as a reflexive research exercise, rather than just a response to a governmental imperative.[21]

Action research is "inspired by the . . . sense that all our actions . . . are in fact also inquiries" and has been described as a "set of self-consciously collaborative and democratic strategies for generating knowledge and designing action."[22] This method links theory and practice by allowing researchers to analyze while doing. For us, it facilitated reflexive engagement with the assemblage of actors involved in the design process and was particularly suited to the study of remote curriculum development taking place from our makeshift home offices during COVID-19 lockdown. As researchers, we adopted the role of "observant participants in

PROMOTING EQUITY AND INCLUSION   137

TABLE 2. Torbet's action research framework

TERRITORY OF EXPERIENCE	DESCRIPTION	DIMENSION OF PRACTICE
Visioning	The attentional inquiry/witnessing of the interplay between the other areas	Framing: declaring a shared vision or setting an intent
Strategizing	The territory of theory, dreams, and passions—a space of integration	Advocating: setting a goal, aim, or strategy
Performing	Embodied practice, including the experiences of resistance, aesthetic, and time	Illustrating: provision of a visual/concrete picture "based on observed performance"*
Assessing	This territory relates to the external world "wherein performance, its effects, and all things are observed, measured, and evaluated"*	Inquiring: inviting contribution or feedback

* Torbet, "The Practice of Action Inquiry," 208.

[an]ongoing conversation"[23] that was occurring between us, our institution, and broader global circumstances. In a practical sense, this meant paying reflective attention to what Torbet refers to as "territories of experience" and associated "dimensions of practice"[24] (see table 2).

Attending to these areas during the course design process involved a weekly cycle of setting intentions (framing), outlining goals (advocating), recording virtual meetings and developing content (illustrating), and reflecting on progress at an end-of-week meeting (inquiring). This, in turn, kicked off the next week of the development process. The cycle of framing to evaluation also applied at a macro level, where government imperatives and institutional intent informed aims manifesting as course learning outcomes (strategizing). Teaching practice (the performative) was shaped by technological and temporal constraints and ongoing cycles of feedback and reflective evaluation. Stepping back and consciously examining our actions revealed how the course design process itself can be viewed as an assemblage of discourses, experiences, contexts, relationships, and technologies. Intentional curriculum design is about understanding the interplay between these elements. Unpacking the "black box" that is the final curriculum therefore involved tracing the interactions of all these heterogeneous parts that shaped the development of the course.

Designing the Certificate

The discursive foundations for the course predated both the pandemic and announcement of the HE relief package. Broader conversations around flexible delivery prompted explorations of online short courses within our institution earlier in the year, although these had not been intended to be used for delivery of the high-support pedagogy required for Pathways courses. Much of this work was sidelined in response to the initial lockdown and institution-wide pivot to online learning in March, but it was subsequently revived in the context of the certificate in response to the announcement of the HE relief package. In the Pathways department, we had previously been working on a curriculum design framework for use in blended online/face-to-face teaching contexts, where on-campus students engaged with online learning materials using a flipped classroom model. The integrated curriculum alignment framework (ICAF) we developed was intended to promote cross-disciplinary knowledge transfer while also embedding integrated resilience strategies into teaching and learning processes. The requirement to "design a new course now" coupled with the knowledge that the eligibility criteria (and the pandemic) meant students would be experiencing significant personal upheaval, provided a perfect opportunity to implement this framework. Furthermore, the course was intended to provide an open access pathway to higher education, and this necessitated the foregrounding of core academic and digital literacies. As a result, established subjects from the university's diploma pathway were adapted using the ICAF to form the certificate of higher education (CHE); an eight-week online short course that would provide a preparatory pathway into tertiary study. The CHE consisted of two subjects: developing academic skills and learning in a digital environment. Developing academic skills is intended to furnish students with skills relating to reading, research, and writing for academic purposes with a focus on critical literacy. Learning in a digital environment supports students in the development of digital literacies and use of technologies for study, with a focus on core software, such as e-mails, library databases, word processing, data analysis, presentation, and collaboration programs.

The digital literacies and academic skills subjects selected for the certificate course were designed to explicitly support students to interact with technologies for learning and help them develop a sense of self as a scholar. The existing subject shells provided a conceptual foundation for the new subjects. The learning technologies, design tools, and media at hand also played formative roles in shaping the subjects and facilitated translation of assumptions, ideologies, and aims into a cohesive learning experience. We began subject development by deciding how to implement our methodology, which, in and of itself, became part of the assemblage—enacted via technologies, such as cloud storage, online documents, video conferencing, instant messaging, digital calendars, and the collaboration platform Microsoft Teams.

Following Torbet's dimensions of practice model, we structured the design process by creating recurring weekly meetings via Teams. First thing on Monday and last thing on a Friday, we met online to log planning points, set intentions, and later to reflect on the things we had accomplished and learned that week. At the framing/advocating meetings, at the start of the week, we discussed the following points: (1) where we are now, (2) aims for the week, and (3) resources/requirements. We started each week by setting an affirmation. The affirmations often took the form of quotes, memes, or sayings that made us confront aspects of our practice, situations, and self-talk in preparation for the week ahead. Each week ended with a structured reflection where we examined (1) what we did, (2) what we learned, (3) challenges, and (4) successes. These meetings closed with a consolidation—a short statement or quote that captured moments of significance or reflected the weekly zeitgeist. These statements were rarely serious and sometimes ridiculous, but they kept us going through the stresses of the lockdown, remote teaching, and pressure of course design. For example, about four weeks into the course development process, our consolidation statement was, "If you can stay calm while all around you is in chaos, then you probably haven't completely understood the seriousness of the situation." The weekly affirmations and consolidations were written down in our development documents. The processes of resource gathering, technological exploration, and content development that occurred between meetings was also documented, through either shared design documents or recorded meetings. Against the backdrop of lockdown, homeschooling, and ongoing online teaching, this structure provided both respite from the chaos around us and a sense of connection by allowing us to approach the design process as a shared experience, despite the necessity of physical distance. The integration of the socioemotional dimensions of teaching and learning practice inherent in this method is also reflected in the integrated curriculum alignment framework (ICAF) that we developed and refined during this process, albeit from a student, rather than a practitioner standpoint.

As a curriculum design tool, the ICAF seeks to align learning outcomes, assessment items, and teaching episodes across subjects, while concurrently integrating explicit resilience strategies, mapped to the student lifecycle as described by Lizzio and Wilson.[25] As such, the ICAF responds to White and Kern's call for a pedagogy of positive education capable of integrating "learning and teaching for wellbeing and academic mastery."[26] During and in the aftermath of the pandemic, this promotion of connection through pedagogy has been more important than ever. The ideas of horizontal subject alignment behind the framework had been developed and tested within previous iterations of the digital literacies and academic skills subjects that we were adapting. Consequently, its suitability for curriculum work in Pathways subjects and basic structure was already established. However, as we began the initial process of adapting content for an eight-week delivery period, the need for an even more structured approach became apparent. We subsequently created an Excel-based tool that would enable us to map teaching, learning, assessment, and support structures to the pre-liminal, novice, liminal, and post-liminal phases of the student experience.

Readers familiar with the anthropological work of Turner and his conceptions of liminality and "communitas" will note echoes here.[27] Essentially, students in phases of transition are in liminal states, they "are betwixt and between."[28] Students entering higher education find themselves in a space where they are no longer what they were, nor what they will be. During this time, in response to their shared experience transitioning through liminal phases, students form a sense of communitas. For the purposes laid out here, the notion of communitas is seen as a positive that can be harnessed within pedagogical practice to encourage students to work together, support each other, and develop a sense of a shared journey through learning. In part, the intent behind the ICAF is to facilitate this harnessing and allow students and educators to embrace the notion of liminal transition as a foundational component of both curriculum design and the learning experience.

The pre-liminal, novice, liminal, and post-liminal phases of the student experience form the basis of the uppermost horizontal axis of the ICAF tool. The lower horizontal axis maps the resilience strategies to these phases and the vertical axis details the following curriculum design elements:

- subject learning outcomes
- assessment
- topics
- synchronous learning episodes
- asynchronous learning episodes
- feedback
- integrated supports

Filling in the specific curriculum design elements allowed us to align specific learning outcomes, assessments, topics, and classroom activities across subjects. Learning outcomes and supports were also aligned with key aspects of the student life cycle and associated resilience strategies. By providing a space where both the social and technological dimensions of the student experience could be explicitly mapped and aligned across subjects the ICAF became a formative actor in the course design assemblage.

The mapping of resilience strategies to the phases of student transition is outlined in table 3.

TABLE 3. Resilience strategies and student transition

STAGE OF TRANSITION	RESILIENCE STRATEGY	DESCRIPTION	ACTIVITY/EXAMPLE
Pre-liminal	Pre-flection and ways of being	Taking the approach of introspective mindfulness characteristic of reflective practice, but directing it toward that which is yet to come, along with an understanding of self-in-the-moment and self-in-relation-to	Wall activity: Students create anonymous posts describing perceived barriers on a virtual pinboard and then reply to others (or themselves) with messages of support
Novice	Breaking down barriers and forming a community of learners	Ice breakers and group activities, where students begin to form a sense of collective experience	Picture collage: Students create image collages of things that represent them and post on class discussion boards. PASS: Peer-assisted study groups facilitated by past students using online community platforms, such as Discord
Liminal	Chunking	Focusing on one section of work at a time, recognizing that multitasking does not work, and setting aside time for specific tasks to reduce start-up time	Apps for study mega-thread: Students and tutors share productivity and study apps in class discussion threads
	HALT	Hungry, Angry, Lonely, Tired: Mindfully check on your basic needs and emotions	Checking-in activity at the start of class, including brainstorming supports and coping strategies
	The art of objectivity	Developing a sense of assessment as an objective product. Recognizing that we all play multiple roles in multiple contexts—"you are not your grade"	Grading activity: Students use the grading rubric to work in groups to mark exemplars of past students' work
	Internal dialogue	Checking the validity of our own self-talk and working on reframing negative self-talk	Provision of explicit examples of negative self-talk and reframing. From "I can't . . ." of "I'm no good at . . ." to "I'm in the process of learning . . ." (viz. Dweck)
	Maintaining the momentum and stamina	Focusing on well-being and peer support, while being task responsive and keeping each other on track	Peer-review and check-in activities, e.g., post a draft annotation on discussion board for review and provide a review to a peer
Post-liminal integration	Own it!	Integration stage, in which students reflect on their journey and their development of a sense of scholarly identity	Feedforward: Post a piece of advice to future students Create a portfolio of achievements

The pre-liminal stage, which occurred in the week before the start of the course, was aligned to the strategies of pre-flection and ways of being. These strategies engage the same introspective mindfulness characteristic of reflective practice but direct it toward the future and an understanding of self-in-the-moment and self-in-relation-to. This anticipatory practice involves examining one's current situation, context, and direction. At a practical level this played out in the form of an online induction, delivered via the synchronous lecture platform embedded in the learning management system. The induction integrated orientations toward core learning platforms, with information on institutional support services, testimonials from past students, and an outlining of expectations regarding preparation, study, and engagement in academic environments. In addition to allaying concerns regarding the practical dimensions of study, like timetabling and textbook requirements, the session included an interactive wall activity, in which students created anonymous posts detailing any challenges they perceived regarding their capacity to engage in study. Students then responded to either themselves or each other, not necessarily with words of advice or solutions, but with statements of acknowledgment and/or support. In this space, students expressed insecurities regarding their academic abilities, financial worries, and the physical and mental health challenges they faced. Individuals got to see their own concerns and apprehensions reflected in the words of others and began to develop a sense of shared experience. This work in community building continued once the subject delivery started, via the strategies of breaking down barriers and forming a community of learners.

Effective supports during the novice stage, where students start to encounter new learning environments and each other, are fundamental to the development of cohort identity early in the semester. The development of a sense of community within the cohort (via activities such as those in table 3) facilitates peer learning and lays the foundations for the liminal phases of transition where students developed a sense of self as scholar. During this time, synchronous meetings with lecturers oriented around core assessment items were supplemented by asynchronous content made up of video, audio, and interactive tasks, such as quizzes and collaborative annotations of set readings. Peer engagement was maintained via discussion board activities in which students posted content for review and supported each other through collective troubleshooting and informal conversation. Throughout this process we introduced learning strategies, such as chunking (breaking tasks into manageable bites) and associated technologies (like digital calendars). These practical study approaches were supplemented by cognitive strategies, such as the art of objectivity, which impels students to disentangle their "sense of self" from the assessment content they produce. Here, the idea that students are more than the sum of their assessments is drawn out as they are encouraged to view exemplars through the lens of a grading rubric and develop a sense of professional objectivity. This professional detachment further facilitates peer review, reinforcing students' sense of belonging as part of a shared learning community. These processes feed into the final stages of transition, where reflective practices, like the compilation of a portfolio of works, serve to promote post-liminal integration of the newly developed dimensions of self.

During delivery of the certificate these strategies resonated with students, and they formed a noticeable sense of community (despite being physically distanced) within a very short space of time. This development forced us, as practitioners, to confront our preconceived assumptions about the impossibility of emergent peer communities forming in online classrooms. The students, who had never met outside of their online classes, established their own independent "group chat" and took the initiative to meet in the online subject room without their lecturers for collaborative study sessions. There was also a noticeable shift in the in-class dialogue and discussion as students become more familiar with each other; they started joking, sharing references, and anecdotes. These developments demonstrated to us, as practitioners, how community does not necessarily require physical co-presence and can be experienced as a sense of nearness and connection to others.[29] This sense of nearness does not necessarily even require synchronous interactions but can manifest via displays of openness and vulnerability, such as those exhibited during the pre-flection (wall) activity, image collage icebreakers, and peer-review process. Conscious discursive alignment across classroom practice and weekly learning episodes in the two subjects facilitated a cohesive learning experience, further fostering a sense of belonging. This positively influenced students' motivation, engagement, resilience, and persistence, while mitigating the impacts of discontinuities between prior learning and new academic contexts.[30] Instruction in academic and digital literacies, combined with the resilience strategies, prepared students for both the academic and socioemotional realities of tertiary study, while also helping them cope with the professional fallout of the pandemic by allowing them to imagine a new direction. Through technologically mediated engagement with content, curriculum, and each other the students took on their own distinct role in the assemblage of course design, further shaping our own understanding of resilience as practitioners in a tertiary teaching context.

Critical Resilience Pedagogy

The uncritical appropriation of resilience in pedagogical literature and practice is complicated; it can be seen to promote adaptation to conditions of suffering rather than resistance to the structural inequalities that give rise to suffering and oppression in the first place. The 2020 context for teaching courses for the certificate was marked by social and political upheaval. In academia students' struggles with learning during lockdown began to give rise to critical voices drawing attention to the ways in which academic rhetoric can circumvent the naming of oppression, through coded language. In particular, critique was leveraged against phrases like "grit," "under-representation," and "growth mindset."[31] Even more problematic are the assumptions that students are somehow lacking resilience or that individual grit and a growth mindset can override systemic oppression. Resilience and grit, when used in such an uncritical sense, are filtered through a neoliberal lens. This perspective privileges the strength of the individual to overcome adversity rather than framing resilience as a process through which systems that construct, contribute to, or perpetuate adversity are challenged, resisted, and replaced. As Schwartzman notes "within a neoliberalist framework . . . resilience reflects the triumph of the lone hero who single-handedly conquers overwhelming odds. Resilience results from character, reinforcing the meritocracy that accompanies privilege."[32] Rather than promote this conception of resilience, the pedagogy encompassed within the ICAF intends to promote critical understanding of resilience that acknowledges the varied strengths and traumas that lived experiences provide. By encouraging students to draw on their experiences, both as individuals and members of a community, to address the immediate challenges of tertiary study, the framework focuses on how lived experiences equip one to navigate barriers. At the same time, students are encouraged to acknowledge that structures and systems can, and should, be subject to scrutiny and change. As such, the approach to resilience embraced within the ICAF is one that strives to enhance student autonomy and self-efficacy, while fostering collaboration and critical engagement. This approach evolved because, without considering the relations of power, oppression, class conflicts, and hardship that constitute educational and social contexts within which students operate, it is not possible to adequately challenge entrenched disadvantage—the very "thing" to which widening participation purports to do. Ultimately, what we term critical resilience pedagogy draws on both teachers and students to co-construct approaches to teaching and learning that are reflexive, cohesive, and supportive, meanwhile allowing for the transfer of knowledge across disciplines and subjects.

The processes of horizontal subject alignment embedded in the ICAF create a culture of intersubject knowledge transfer from the outset of students' university journey. Conventional notions of alignment in curriculum design tend to be orientated around hierarchical process of "backwards mapping."[33] Policy frameworks serve as top-level organizing devices against which learning outcomes are developed. Learning outcomes then serve as overarching organizational frameworks against which assessment items and individual learning episodes are mapped. Throughout a semester, individual units of study (lessons, modules, and workshops) relate to the knowledge and skills developed during previous learning episodes (or in previous subjects) through processes of integration, subsumption, or segmental aggregation.[34] In the context of HE, degree courses will generally approach the acquisition of knowledge through processes of segmental aggregation or subsumption. Maton associates teaching and learning oriented around such compartmentalized notions of knowledge acquisition with segmented learning and poor intercontextual knowledge transfer. Even in relation to highly authentic tasks, most "students' understandings remain rooted in the context" within which they are asked to apply them, and transfer of knowledge across subjects and disciplines is minimal.[35] In contrast, moving beyond hierarchical knowledge structures and curriculum designs that implicitly promote compartmentalization, segmented learning, and poor knowledge transfer can help promote "cumulative learning, where students are able to transfer knowledge across contexts and through time."[36]

The pandemic and associated imperative to rapidly shift teaching and learning online presented significant challenges, but it also opened our eyes to the powerful potential of a collective working for the betterment of society by overcoming adversity. Encouraging students to see "subject knowledge" as something that is applicable outside of the immediate classroom context opens up the possibility that the critical dispositions developed in every classroom could be applied in extracurricular contexts. As such, a whole-of-course approach[37] to curriculum design that aligns learning and teaching horizontally across subjects creates space for Freirian critical pedagogy by enacting the transference of knowledge within, across, and beyond the classroom.[38] The concurrent integration of critical resilience strategies into teaching practice supports students through the liminal disruptions of self that education entails. When the self is supported, critical engagement with societal structures and processes becomes possible. In this context the students can transcend their roles as neoliberal subjects in a banking model of education theorized by Paolo Freire, or cogs in a pandemic-inspired productivity agenda, to become part of a relational learning community.

Looking Back and Moving Forward

In hindsight, the reflective practice facilitated by an action research framework enabled us to step back and see the assemblage of sociotechnical actors that shaped the development and delivery of the certificate of higher education. The pandemic and associated lockdowns forced us to consider the possibility of providing pathways education online. The government's decision to use university short courses as mechanisms for pandemic recovery served as a creative catalyst, allowing us to reimagine resilience pedagogy in a short course format. The convergence of global circumstances, political discourses, pedagogical practices, and technologies shaped students' learning experiences and enabled the emergence of an enduring sense of community and belonging during this period of significant societal disruption. Pathways programs have always sought to serve marginalized communities and individuals. Students entering these programs generally have interrupted and/or negative experiences of education, frequently compounded by economic circumstances or a sociocultural disconnect with the norms of the academe. A part of our role as educators in this space is to facilitate a shift in perspective from that of being the other, toward a sense of belonging and ownership within the learning spaces students inhabit, whether these be physical or virtual. Moreover, as we move away from those unprecedented times and begin to shape our new normal, there is a need to ensure that academics can engage in reflective teaching practice—practice that resists kneejerk imperatives to develop emergency curriculum, rather than considered, intentional learning experiences.

The capacity of academics to engage in intentional reflective practice was tested by the pandemic. The speed at which face-to-face courses were reconfigured into online formats often meant that pedagogical concerns were subsumed under the necessity of minimizing infection risks in our classrooms. Our experience of teaching the certificate to a cohort of students who *chose* to study online and approached the course with a sense of hope was a positive one. Yet, this positivity was not universally reflected among cohorts who were *forced* into online learning through the circumstances of the pandemic. In a survey conducted by the Australian higher education regulator in late 2020, up to 50 percent of students expressed that they "did not like the experience of online learning and did not wish to ever experience it again."[39] Yet, as Australian infection rates caught up with the rest of the world during 2021 and 2022, it became apparent that some form of online learning is here to stay and as a sector we need to do better.

The students who had used the certificate of higher education as a pathway to further education have since transitioned into various modes of undergraduate study. While the certificate short course was not offered again after the conclusion of the HE relief package funding, the course laid the foundations for a substantive online offering of the diploma of higher education, our main sub-degree pathway. This development may have happened eventually even without the pandemic; however, one of the transformative impacts of COVID-19 on HE was that it forced institutions to engage in agile change. Prior to 2020 the notion of offering the diploma online had met with significant resistance due to a perceived inability to ensure the same levels of high support and peer engagement that were crucial to the success of the on-campus offering. The pandemic forced us to confront our prejudgments and enabled us to demonstrate the possibility of delivering resilience-oriented curriculum online. Good teaching responds to the needs of learners, creates a community in the classroom and fosters resilience, self-reflection, and self-actualization regardless of format, delivery mode, or funding models. An understanding of learning design as a sociotechnical assemblage "performed through dynamic entanglements of both social and material components . . . [that] create multiple, coexisting realities of understanding" can assist in this process. [40] Such an approach allows for resistance to reductive one-size-fits-all orthodoxies of best practices, like the assumption that effective peer engagement requires face-to-face interaction and promotes recognition of teaching and learning as an emergent sociopolitical array "of pedagogies, people, and technology."[41]

Nurturing resilience is necessary, particularly as we seek to reconfigure communities of learning in a postpandemic world. However, critical manifestations of resilience pedagogy are needed to ensure that the realities of systemic oppression and existence of a meritocracy within higher education are not concealed through institutional discourses around alternative pathways and nontraditional students. The processes of horizontal alignment and resilience strategies demonstrated in the ICAF serve as one possible method by which educators can draw together theory and practice to foster critical engagement within and beyond the classroom. By explicitly encouraging students to critically examine academic discourses (such as the conflation of self-worth and grades), the framework destabilizes problematic so-called truths of academia that can negatively impact students' sense of belonging. As educators seek to both respond to, and resist, the imperatives to streamline and cost-cut wrought through the pandemic, we must maintain focus on the fact that education is a relational process and leverage pedagogy to support development of inclusive learning communities.

NOTES

1. Hodges et al., "Enabling Retention.".
2. Lamb et al., *Educational Opportunity*, VI.
3. Gore et al., "Unpacking the Career Aspiration."
4. Gale and Parker, "Navigating Change," 5.
5. See Bennett et al., "'Hard' and 'Soft'"; Bennett et al., "Critical Interventions Framework."
6. Brown and Kurzweil, "Complex Universe," 1.
7. See Moody, "Transition Pedagogy."

8. Burke, "Re/imagining Higher Education Pedagogies," 396–97.

9. See Australian Workforce and Productivity Agency, "Human Capital."

10. See Chesters and Watson, "Staying Power."

11. Within the Australian HE sector, and Australian education more broadly, inclusive pedagogies are understood to be focused on adapting learning materials and strategies to be accessible to all students, rather than creating adjustments for individual student circumstances. For example, using captions for all recorded materials rather than adding these for deaf students only (for elaboration, see Hitch, Macfarlane, and Nihill, 2015)

12. See Shah et al., *Widening Higher Education Participation*.

13. See Andrewartha and Harvey, "Willing and Enabled."

14. Bodenheimer and Shuster, "Emotional Labour, Teaching and Burnout."

15. During the initial wave of the pandemic in 2020 Australia recorded under one thousand deaths nationally. By mid-2021, there had been less than two thousand total cases in Queensland. However, case numbers rose dramatically in 2022 with the arrival of the Delta and Omicron variants and by June 2022 there had been over seven million cases recorded nationally and more than 8000 deaths (Coronavirus Health Alert).

16. Ferguson, "Politics of Productivity Growth."

17. Australian Government, *Foundations for Good Practice*, par. 2.

18. See Latour, *Reassembling the Social*.

19. See Hannon, "Breaking Down Online Teaching."

20. Fenwick and Edwards, *Actor-Network Theory*, 4.

21. Torbet, "Practice of Action Inquiry"; Levin and Greenwood, "Revitalising Universities."

22. Torbet, "Practice of Action Inquiry," 207; Levin and Greenwood, "Revitalising Universities," 29.

23. Torbet, "Practice of Action Inquiry," 211.

24. Torbet, "Practice of Action Inquiry," 208.

25. Lizzio and Wilson, "Engaging Students."

26. White and Kern, "Positive Education," 2.

27. Turner, "Liminality and Communitas," 359.

28. Moody, "Transition Pedagogy," 41.

29. Bayne et al., *Manifesto for Teaching Online*, 142.

30. See Tinto, "Taking Student Retention Seriously"; see Paxton and Frith, "Implications of Academic Literacies Research."

31. "Guide to Coded Language."

32. Schwartzman, "Performing Pandemic Pedagogy," 510.

33. See Biggs and Tang, *Teaching for Quality Learning*.

34. See Maton, "Cumulative and Segmented Learning."

35. Maton, "Cumulative and Segmented Learning," 51.

36. Maton, "Cumulative and Segmented Learning," 45.

37. A "whole-of-course" approach requires collaborative development of subjects within a program of study with a view to assuring course learning outcomes, assessments, criteria, and learning activities are aligned and support student learning. See Lawson, *Curriculum Design for Assuring Learning*.

38. Freire, *Pedagogy of the Oppressed*.

39. Australian Government, TEQSA, *Foundations for Good Practice*, 8.

40. Bayne et al., *Manifesto for Teaching Online*, 8.

41. Bayne et al., *Manifesto for Teaching Online*, 8.

BIBLIOGRAPHY

Andrewartha, Lisa, and Andrew Harvey. "Willing and Enabled: The Academic Outcomes of a Tertiary Enabling Program in Regional Australia." *Australian Journal of Adult Learning* 54, no. 1 (2014): 50–68.

Australian Government. "Information for Students About Government Assistance for Financing Tertiary Study: Higher Education Relief Package" *StudyAssist*. Australian Government. (April 16, 2020). http://studyassist.gov.au/news/higher-education-relief-package.

Australian Government, Tertiary Education Quality and Standards Agency. *Foundations for Good Practice: The Student Experience of Online Learning in Australian Higher Education during the COVID-19 Pandemic—November 2020.* Commonwealth of Australia, 2020. https://www.teqsa.gov.au/sites/default/files/student-experience-of-online-learning-in-australian-he-during-COVID-19.pdf?v=1606953179.

Australian Workforce and Productivity Agency. *Human Capital and Productivity Literature Review: March, 2013.* Department of Industry, Research, Innovation, Science, Research and Tertiary Education, 2013. https://docs.education.gov.au/system/files/doc/other/human-capital-and-productivity-literature-review-march-2013.pdf.

Bayne, Sian, Peter Evans, Rory Ewins, Jeremy Knox, James Lamb, Hamish Macleod, Clara O'Shea, Jen Ross, Philippa Sheail, and Christine Sinclair. *The Manifesto for Teaching Online.* Cambridge, MA: MIT Press, 2020. Kindle.

Bennett, Anna, Ryan Naylor, Kate Mellor, Matt Brett, Jenny Gore, Andrew Harvey, Richard James, Belinda Munn, Max Smith, and Geoff Witty. "The Critical Interventions Framework Part 2: Equity Initiatives in Australian Higher Education: A review of Impact." Australian Government Department of Training. December 18, 2015. https://ncsehe.edu.au/wp-content/uploads/2018/06/23_UoN_AnnaBennett_Accessible_Part1_PDF.pdf.

Bennett, Anna, Barry Hodges, Keryl Kavanagh, Seamus Fagan, Jane Hartley, and Neville Schofield. "'Hard' and 'Soft' Aspects of Learning as Investment: Opening Up the Neo-Liberal View of a Programme with 'High' Levels of Attrition." *Widening Participation and Lifelong Learning* 14, no. 3 (2013): 141–56. doi:10.5456/WPLL.14.3.141.

Biggs, John B. (John Burville), and Catherine So-kum Tang. *Teaching for Quality Learning at University: What the Student Does.* 4th ed. New York: Society for Research into Higher Education, 2011.

Brown, Jessie, and Kurzweil, Martin. "The Complex Universe of Alternative Postsecondary Credentials and Pathways." Cambridge, MA: American Academy of Arts & Sciences, 2017.

Bodenheimer, Grayson, and Stef M. Shuster. "Emotional Labour, Teaching and Burnout: Investigating Complex Relationships." *Educational Research* 62, no. 1 (2020): 63–76. doi:10.1080/00131881.2019.1705868.

Burke, Penny Jane. "Re/imagining Higher Education Pedagogies: Gender, Emotion and Difference." *Teaching in Higher Education* 20, no. 4 (2015): 388–401. doi:10.1080/13562517.2015.1020782.

Chesters, Jenny, and Louise Watson. "Staying Power: The Effect of Pathway into University on Student Achievement and Attrition." *Australian Journal of Adult Learning* 56, no. 2 (2016): 225–49.

Coronavirus (COVID-19) Health Alert. 2021. *Coronavirus (COVID-19) case numbers and statistics.* Accessed July 23, 2021, and June 1, 2022. https://www.health.gov.au/news/health-alerts/novel-coronavirus-2019-ncov-health-alert/coronavirus-COVID-19-case-numbers-and-statistics.

Dweck, Carol S. *Mindset: The New Psychology of Success*. Updated edition. New York: Random House, 2016.

Fenwick, Tara, and Richard Edwards. *Actor-Network Theory in Education*. New York: Routledge Taylor & Francis Group, 2014.

Ferguson, Peter. "The Politics of Productivity Growth in Australia." *Australian Journal of Political Science*, 51, no. 1 (2016): 17–33. doi:10.1080/10361146.2015.1111861.

Freire, Paulo. *Pedagogy of the Oppressed*. New York: Seabury Press, 1970.

Gale, Trevor, and Stephen Parker. "Navigating Change: A Typology of Student Transition in Higher Education." *Studies in Higher Education (Dorchester-on-Thames)* 39, no. 5, (2014): 734–53. doi:10.1080/03075079.2012.721351.

Gore, Jennifer, Kathryn Holmes, Max Smith, Leanne Fray, Patrick McElduff, Natasha Weaver, and Claire Wallington. "Unpacking the Career Aspirations of Australian School Students: Towards an Evidence Base for University Equity Initiatives in Schools." *Higher Education Research & Development* 36, no. 7 (2017): 1383–1400. doi:10.1080/07294360.2017.1325847.

"A Guide to Coded Language in Education Vol. I." *Class Trouble* (February 1, 2020). https://classtrouble.club/blogs/resonance-archives/a-guide-to-coded-language -in-education-vol-i.

Hannon, John. "Breaking Down Online Teaching: Innovation and Resistance." *Australasian Journal of Educational Technology* 25, no. 1 (2009): 14–29, doi:10.14742/ ajet.1178.

Hitch, Danielle, Susie Macfarlane, and Claire Nihill. "Inclusive Pedagogy in Australian Universities: A Review of Current Policies and Professional Development Activities." *The International Journal of the First Year in Higher Education* 6, no. 1 (2015): 135–45. doi:10.5204/intjfyhe.v6i1.254.

Hodges, Barry, Tasman Bedford, Jane Hartley, Chris Klinger, Neil Murray, John O'Rourke, and Neville Schofield. *Enabling retention: processes and strategies for improving student retention in university-based enabling programs: Final report 2013*. Project Report. Australian Government Office for Learning and Teaching, Sydney, Australia, 2013.

Lamb, Stephen, Jen Jackson, Anne Walstab, and Shuyan Huo. *Educational Opportunity in Australia 2015: Who Succeeds and Who Misses Out*, Centre for International Research on Education Systems, Victoria University, for the Mitchell Institute, Melbourne: Mitchell Institute, 2015.

Latour, Bruno. *Reassembling the Social: An Introduction to Actor-Network-Theory*. New York: Oxford University Press, 2005.

Lawson, Romy. *Curriculum Design for Assuring Learning—Leading the Way: Final Report*. Australian Government Office for Learning and Teaching, Sydney, Australia, 2015. http://www.olt.gov.au/resource-curriculumdesign-assuring-learning -leading-way-2015

Levin, Morten, and Greenwood, Davydd. "Revitalising Universities by Reinventing the Social Sciences: Bildung and Action Research." In *The SAGE Handbook of Qualitative Research*, edited by Norman. K. Denzin and Yvonna. S. Lincoln, 27–42. Thousand Oaks, CA: SAGE, 2011.

Lizzio, Alf, and Kieithia Wilson. "*Engaging Students Who Are at Risk of Academic Failure: Frameworks and Strategies*." 15th First Year in Higher Education Conference, June 2012. Brisbane, Australia. Paper Presentation.

Maton, Karl. "Cumulative and Segmented Learning: Exploring the Role of Curriculum Structures in Knowledge-Building." *British Journal of Sociology of Education* 30, no. 1 (2009): 43–57. doi:10.1080/01425690802514342.

PROMOTING EQUITY AND INCLUSION 151

Moody, Lisa. "Transition Pedagogy in the Pre-Degree Space: A process of becoming?" 2018. Research Dissertation, James Cook University, Townsville, Queensland.

National Centre for Education Statistics (NCES). "Percentage of High School Dropouts among Persons 16 to 24 Years Old (Status Dropout Rate) and Percentage Distribution of Status Dropouts, by Labor Force Status and Years of School Completed: Selected Years, 1970 through 2018 [Table 219.75.]." *Digest of Education Statistics.* Institute of Education Sciences. November 2019. https://nces.ed.gov/programs /digest/d19/tables/dt19_219.75.asp.

National Centre for Education Statistics (NCES). "Population Characteristics and Economic Outcomes." *Young Adult Educational and Employment Outcomes by Family Socioeconomic Status.* Institute of Education Sciences. May 2019. https:// nces.ed.gov/programs/coe/indicator_tbe.asp

Paxton, Moragh, and Vera Frith. "Implications of Academic Literacies Research for Knowledge Making and Curriculum Design." *Higher Education* 67, no. 2 (2014): 171–82. doi:10.1007/s10734-013-9675-z.

Schwartzman, Roy. "Performing Pandemic Pedagogy." *Communication Education* 69, no. 4 (2020): 502–17. doi:10.1080/03634523.2020.1804602.

Shah, Mahsood, Anna Bennett, Erica Southgate, and Amer Badarneh. *Widening Higher Education Participation: A Global Perspective.* Amsterdam: Chandos Publishing, 2016.

Tinto, Vincent. "Taking Student Retention Seriously: Rethinking the First Year of University." ALTC FYE Curriculum Design Symposium, February 5, 2009, Queensland University of Technology, Brisbane, Australia.

Torbet, William. "The Practice of Action Inquiry." In *Handbook of Action Research,* edited by Peter Reason and Hilary Bradbury, 207–217. Thousand Oaks, CA: Sage Publications, 2006.

Turner, Victor. "Liminality and Communitas." In *The Ritual Process: Structure and Anti-Structure.* New York: Routledge, 1969.

White, Mathew, and Margaret L. Kern. "Positive Education: Learning and Teaching for Wellbeing and Academic Mastery." *International Journal of Wellbeing* 8, no. 1 (2018): 1–17. doi:10.5502/ijw.v8i1.588.

8

SEARCHING FOR *ŌTIUM* AND FINDING A PEDAGOGY OF ESCAPISM

Alexander Lowe McAdams
with contributions by Nina Cook and Annie Lowe

What does it mean to practice the humanities publicly? Before the pandemic, my answer to this question was pretty straightforward. As civic humanist (CH) program manager in a pre-COVID world at Rice University's Humanities Research Center (HRC), I was responsible for forming and maintaining collegial relationships with secondary school educators in Houston, Texas, for whom I would eventually arrange site visits to the Rice campus. The purpose of this day-long programming was to highlight for urban high school students the excitement and engagement of college-level humanities seminars. This experience was reified with two or three stipend-supported graduate student pedagogy fellows, who would deliver high-quality, accessible educational modules based on their doctoral research.[1] These interactive educational modules emphasized creativity and critical thinking, allowing the high school students we served immersion into an environment not unlike the vibrant humanities seminars one might encounter as an undergraduate.[2] COVID-19, of course, threw a wrench into those plans and changed everything.

In the pages that follow, I discuss my approach as program manager to the unforeseen challenge of running the CH program during pandemic shutdown by outlining what I have come to name a pedagogy of escapism. My contribution here explains the underlying pedagogical philosophies that informed the massive undertaking of transforming an interactive, face-to-face program into a wholly virtual format. To organize this capacious undertaking, this chapter is divided into four sections, each focusing on the theoretical angles that influenced both my managerial decision-making for CH and the pedagogical tenets that continue to inform my work in the Houston community. Most important, this chapter includes crucial reflections of the CH fellows themselves, which appear in three Breakout boxes authored by two of the three CH fellows, Annie Lowe and Nina Cook (our third fellow, De'Anna Daniels, was unfortunately unable to commit to this project).

To illustrate how we collaborated for CH, I first lay out the challenges that both students and teachers faced as they returned to the classroom in the fall 2020 semester in the section "Honoring Living Histories." This section describes the unique stressors that both students and teachers in the Houston Independent School District (HISD) face and contextualizes those challenges against data from both national surveys on student well-being and an open-ended survey that I wrote and developed for our partner educators. These survey data lay the groundwork for a pedagogy of escapism, the contours of which I outline in the second section, called "Finding an Accessible Escape." In this section, I also expand upon the merits of nonevaluative learning experiences that both students and teachers so desperately need but often very rarely receive. To describe what I refer to as "nonevaluative learning experiences," I rely on my background as a researcher of classical reception and borrow the term *ōtium* from ancient Imperial Rome, a principle of relaxed repose that is completely absent of labor. This portion of the chapter drives home my core belief that we as publicly engaged educators owe it to our students to expose them to the joys of learning, not for what it can get them—in the form of accolades, scholarships, and career readiness—but for the sake of learning itself. Here I also lay out the principles of disability studies and how this inquiry continues to inform my understanding of not only facilitating a pedagogy of escapism but also practicing the public humanities in general.

From there, I reflect on how insights in disabilities studies situate my approach both to project management and classroom pedagogy in "Teaching Escapism and Practicing UDL," or universally designed learning. This portion of the chapter also provides a brief historical genealogy of the American education system, its connections to capitalist economic structures, and the detrimental pressures that they place on our students at all levels, from K–12 to university. The fourth section, "Whither Now?", briefly surveys the pedagogical research that grounded our approach and delivery of this unique public-facing program during a most unusual time and reflects not only on our collective experience with CH but also the path forward that this opportunity has created. Last, I conclude with a short call to action for readers who are invested in public-facing scholarship and teaching.

Before diving into the first section of this chapter, it is necessary to explain the CH program's origins, core mission, and how the four of us early-career researchers began stewarding the program. An innovative public humanities initiative operating through the HRC, the CH program began as the brainchild of a Rice alumnus. Working with the Rice administration, the donor envisioned an outreach-based program in which university faculty and/or graduate students visit urban public high schools throughout Houston. The alum was a graduate of Jack Yates High School in the Third Ward neighborhood, where 82 percent of the enrolled student population is considered economically disadvantaged. This campus became CH's first partner. Even though Yates and Rice are fewer than five miles apart, their differences could not be more drastic. Learners from the Yates community rarely venture onto the Rice campus, and historically, a similar claim can be made about the enclave of well-manicured hedges of Rice University. From this vision of closing the gap by opening the gates to Rice's campus to local teens, the CH program was born.

At its core, the CH program is intended to excite high schoolers for whom attending college is not a foregone conclusion. It eventually evolved into a format involving eight to ten high school class visits to the Rice campus, planned by an advanced doctoral candidate, serving as a program manager. The plan includes a budget for transportation and lunch at no cost to the schools, the students, or their chaperones. Once they arrived, the high school students interacted with the grad fellows and their innovative materials and, if time allowed, toured the campus art galleries. In instances where classrooms were unable to travel to the Rice campus, CH offered an abbreviated program, and the fellows found themselves trekking to various high schools across the metro area, as veteran graduate fellow Annie Lowe vividly details in Breakout Box 1.

Breakout Box 1: First Finding *Ōtium*

By Annie Lowe, PhD

When the COVID-19 pandemic abruptly suspended our program in spring 2020, De'Anna Daniels and I had been on a roll. The Civic Humanist program grants fellows a unique kind of independence to collaboratively design and deliver content drawn from our original research. Each cohort channels our individual passions to create interactive modules that uniquely represent the college-level humanities. Leveraging our perspective as teachers, researchers, and graduate students, we advance civic humanism in practice on campus and off. We often traveled to high schools when teachers' classes were not able to come to us at Rice, and we had many opportunities to hone our interactive presentations over the course of several meetings with varying student-and-teacher audiences. During my first year with CH, from fall 2019 to early 2020, I had been able to continually fine-tune my course module, "The Art of Artifice." De'Anna's deft handling of critical context and concepts, inclusion of various contemporary and historical iterations and interpretations of Black mermaids, and way of establishing instant rapport with each classroom were inspiring, and I took notes. Car rides to and from Houston's high school campuses doubled as occasions for casual workshopping, and De'Anna shared her suggestions and encouragement while we rehashed funny moments and students' surprising insights.

As a scholar of not only literary fiction but also hoaxes, cons, tricks, and all manner of cultural artifice, I spend a lot of time thinking and writing about how what is "made up" matters—and when, where, and for whom is it made? How does the artificiality of art relate to its interpretive meanings in a real time and place, in the real world? I study hoaxes as a form of public deception where art and artifice overlap such that presentation is already performance, perception is already interpretation. My studies of artifice as a cultural form include those that evince entertaining and ostensibly harmless effects, such as stage illusions and magic tricks, as well as those that do not. Hoaxes, fake news, and misinformation dramatize and challenge the critical skills and methods in which we hone the academic humanities in civic practice.

The Art of Artifice starts at the common root of both terms, the Latin etymon: *ars*, *artis*, meaning joint or to join. Several English words share this Latinate derivation—the arts both liberal and fine, as well as artificial, articulate, and arthritis. We find that at their root both *art* and *artifice* relate to knowing how to manipulate things and make new ones, which also includes fabricating things from whole cloth. From there, we consider the problem of when and how art extends from manipulating objects to manipulating people, a matter of contention as old as art itself. We spend our remaining time together looking at a series of famous artworks, our discussion centering on the question: How do artworks work on us?

In person, we could physically interact with images of the artworks: experiencing, interpreting, and critiquing how they manipulated us viewers in our shared space from the classroom's projector screen. Hans Holbein's *Ambassadors* had us crouching face-to-face with death to view the distorted skull in the lower foreground. Raphael's *School of Athens* pointed us eye-to-eye with an eternal God via the fresco's conjunction of single-point perspective and heavenly symmetry.

156 MCADAMS, COOK, AND LOWE

Marcel Duchamp's *Fountain* gathered us around a urinal as if it were as ornately sculpted as its namesake. Banksy's *Girl with Balloon* print made us stare and snicker while watching it mechanically shred itself upon fetching $1.4 million at Sotheby's. As we moved through, and around, a variety of art pieces from the last five hundred years, we also reflected on the breadth and depth of scholarly humanistic inquiry and critique, in addition to the relevance of university-level humanities courses to their personal values, creative capabilities, intellectual and civic pursuits—topics that De'Anna's interactive presentation then poignantly exemplified and invited them to practice together.

By spring 2020 we had hit our stride. The students' generous and sophisticated responses to our own research questions and critical concerns made it easy to show them how well prepared they were for higher education. On Tuesday, March 3, 2020, we sat in a large-windowed classroom at Rice's new Moody Center for the Arts, eating catered sandwiches with students and teachers from YES Prep. One of the students scrolled through Instagram photos, showing us the cleverly designed and dexterously decorated cakes his mother, a supposed amateur, made for friends and family. At De'Anna's table, students asked her more about studying genres of Black horror in popular culture and what books she would recommend. As De'Anna explained her work, the students and teachers joined in debating the merits of their favorite scary movies, and new ideas started flowing for her. She handily finished writing a qualifying exam essay while our guests were downstairs in their docent-led tour of the Moody's art galleries. Conversations with students and teachers that morning—and those previous— shaped my dissertation, too, imbuing a richer articulation of how aesthetic artifice enjoins interactive interpretation. That day of programming ended up being the last before pandemic protocols suspended CH visits for the school year. It was a punch in the gut, but nothing compared to the scope of suffering COVID-19 would bring. When we recommenced the next school year, the classrooms, art gallery, and group lunches in which we had found *otium* (*ōtium?*) had become dangerous havens for viral spread. We would have to seek it elsewhere.

When disruption from the pandemic rendered this standard format impossible, this reality did not escape the dean's office, which eyed the program as an easy line-item to cut from the 2020–2021 budget. However, while in-person programming was no longer tenable, the need for CH engagement did not disappear alongside it, as HRC leadership successfully argued to the dean's office. More to the point, the inequities endemic to the urban populations that CH serves were further exacerbated by the pandemic, a chilling observation that the Pew Research Center has recently supported with survey data.[3] Students in these marginalized communities needed the programming now more than ever. Once the program was spared from budget cuts for the 2020–2021 academic year, HRC leadership tasked me, an HRC public humanities postdoctoral fellow and the acting program manager, to reimagine the program while maintaining its ambitious outcomes: to provide compelling, engaging educational content that excited students about participating in college-level studies in the humanities. After some brainstorming and a virtual residency at the National Humanities Center, I called a meeting and the three CH graduate student fellows—Annie, De'Anna, and Nina—got to work.[4]

Honoring Living Histories

Storytelling is powerful agent of change, and our work with Houston-area high schools centers the stories of HISD, both past and present, in addition to the lived experiences of CH partners. Consciously or not, every one of us inhabits complex political and socioeconomic systems, bureaucratic leviathans that often supersede any individual agency and control we may have over our personal lives and relationships. The students in our urban public schools are no different. Therefore, one cannot discuss working with HISD schools during a pandemic without also acknowledging the social injustices that historically haunt US public school systems. As a "relic of the Deep South," HISD's legacy is one of de jure racial segregation and slow desegregation that was precipitously followed by de facto resegregation.[5] HISD's status as this "relic" is evidence of this living history.

If HISD's story sounds familiar, it is because the district's challenges are mirrored in virtually every urban public school system across the United States. After Houston public schools slowly desegregated, white flight drastically reshaped HISD's socioeconomic composition. In 1970, for example, white students accounted for 50 percent of HISD enrollment, yet a mere ten years later, that number decreased by half. In the 1980s, Black student enrollment followed a similar trend, what Houston historian William Henry Kellar describes as "[B]lack flight" to the suburbs.[6] In 2021 the enrollment demographics became even more dramatic. Enrollment of Hispanic/Latinx students has increased to 61.8 percent, while Black and white students make up approximately a third of the total (for a visual of this demographic flux, see figures 3 through 5). HISD's

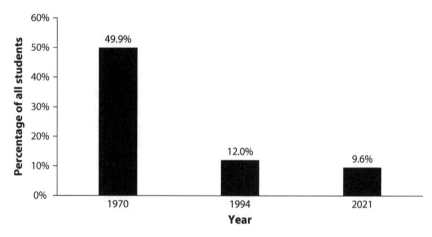

FIGURE 3. HISD K-12 enrollment, white students

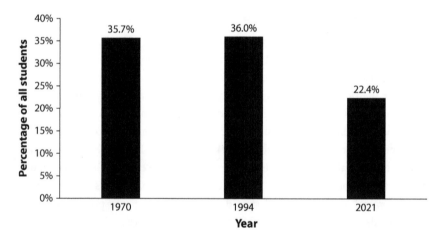

FIGURE 4. HISD K-12 enrollment, black students

living genealogy of racial and sociopolitical inequity and its relationship to white flight and HISD are too complex for this chapter. However, I mention it here because Black and Brown students inhabit these cultural memories daily and have important lived experiences that must be taken into account. These forces informed CH's immersion into classrooms, most especially since three of the four women on our team are white, myself included.

During shutdown, HISD administrators distributed laptops to its 47,785 high schoolers and continued to offer classes online, but the shock of this sudden shift was undeniably palpable.[7] Under the most normal of circumstances, HISD edu-

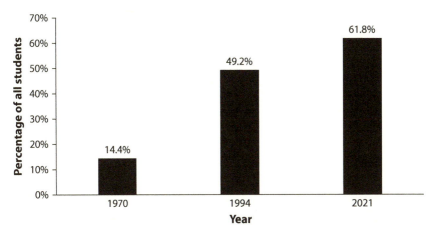

FIGURE 5. HISD K-12 enrollment, Hispanic/Latinx students
Figures 3 through 5 illustrate the vast fluctuation in racial composition throughout Houston Independent School District (HISD). The figures from 1970 and 1994—the fortieth anniversary of the *Brown v. Board* decision—are graphed based on the data provided in William Henry Kellar's *Make Haste Slowly: Moderates, Conservatives, and School Desegregation in Houston*. The 2021 survey data are graphed from HISD's central reporting data. Not reflected in, though inextricable from, these figures are the fact that when affluent white households abandoned Houston's urban center, they took the tax dollars used for school funding with them, leaving the legacy students of HISD without sufficiently funded and resourced public schools in the process.

cators and their students face a unique set of challenges—difficulties that the pandemic only threw into starker relief. Houston is the fourth-largest city in the United States and an incredibly diverse metropolitan area. District-wide, there are two hundred thousand students, a majority of whom are considered either "at risk" (economically disadvantaged) or Title I.[8] The pandemic only exacerbated these inequities.[9] As the largest school district in Texas and the seventh largest in the nation, HISD is a decentralized entity, meaning that even though the district is not subject to the political whims of City Hall, its sprawl across 669 square miles ensures that each school zone operates as its own highly variable, separately functioning enclave. Working with these students demands we acknowledge these complex demographics and variabilities.

The secondary instructors with whom the CH program collaborated hail from diverse personal and educational backgrounds. The four I surveyed for this publication agreed that educating students remotely during a pandemic felt insurmountable. For example, Heights High School English instructor Lucy Seward, who has taught for more than two decades, wrote: "Many remote students were difficult to reach and engage; student attendance in the classroom shifted daily. Many pedagogical strategies were off-limits due to, *inter alia*, social distancing."[10] Emma Burch, an English language arts (ELA) instructor across town at Sharpstown High, a Title I school, expressed similar difficulties, including "finding ways to engage and reach students." In particular, Burch writes, the inability to interact with students in person made both "checking for understanding" and "building personal connections difficult," and she found it challenging to "see how much progress the students were making."[11] Barbara Watkins—a pseudonym for an instructor who wishes to stay anonymous—describes her teaching experience as demoralizing. The teaching faculty at her school, she writes, received "very little training" in virtual teaching. This lack not only made it difficult to distribute resources to students but also contributed to a "sense of hopelessness about how much I, as a teacher, can accomplish." The result, she discloses, made her unsure of "how to be an effective teacher online."[12]

Circumstances were not much different for students. Active Minds, a nonprofit dedicated to mental health awareness, surveyed students during the pandemic. Their data reveal more than 60 percent of high schoolers reported their mental health symptoms worsening. They also detailed an uptick in stress, anxiety, disappointment, sadness, loneliness, and isolation. Despite these pessimistic reports in Active Minds' April 2020 survey, their September 2020 follow-up poll shows that 73.5 percent of high schoolers reported feelings of hope or extreme hope about the future.[13] In an April 2022 post on the Active Minds blog, two college-age students report that while they felt a sense of hope and accomplishment for prevailing in their studies during these unprecedented difficult times, they each admitted that they felt a "lack of support" and "loss of connection."[14] These data reveal the incredible resilience our teen population possesses, but this optimism cannot elide that their mental health continues to suffer. For example, we all understood that HISD high schoolers were victims of an unjustly underfunded system through no fault of their own, and we knew that COVID-19 exacerbated these inequities in vulnerable communities. To address these issues, it was imperative that the CH educational modules reflected our shared pedagogical convictions. To be effective, that pedagogy had to be accessible, equitable, and communally oriented.

From what I have gathered from the qualitative survey data and the informal conversations I have had with educators and high school students, the national data reflect the experiences of both Houston-area students and their teachers. Yates English teacher Rennette Brown—an inspiring educator who has partnered with the CH program for over a decade—describes the "frustration" of teaching during the pandemic "looming" over her: "I often felt defeated and . . .

stuck."[15] Data from Active Minds also reveal that students expressed needing empathy, flexibility, and accommodations from their instructors to help mitigate the communal trauma of daily life amid a global pandemic.[16] Anticipating this need, Brown volunteered that "PATIENCE is a virtue and flexibility was a MUST" for her students in the Third Ward neighborhood of Houston. Patience and flexibility could only go so far for both students and teachers in these remote settings. As Seward discovered, engaging with students needed to extend beyond grading metrics: "I learned (or re-learned) that establishing a relationship with each student is a foundation on which to build learning," she wrote. Watkins' experience reads similarly. "One thing I learned is that numbers do not matter when it comes down to students who may be struggling at home in different ways and for different reasons. . . . It changed my approach in that now I am more interested in going gradeless in my high school class."

Such testimonials have been proof that there is a need for escapism in high school classrooms. The situational stressors that high schoolers must endure daily render a pedagogy for escapism—a practice emphasizing nonevaluative learning—not only a practice of recuperation, but also one of absolute necessity. In practice, a pedagogy of escapism relies on three central truths. Primarily, it supplements everyday classroom activity with learning modules about popular media and entertainment to encourage critical thinking. Second, it is not compulsory: it fundamentally opposes assessment or evaluation, and it does not assign achievement-based tasks. While the CH modules were designed with prompts encouraging creative expression and participation, a pedagogy of escapism grants learners the agency to say no. Last and most pertinent, the pedagogy adheres to the notion that creativity is not only encouraged but also necessary to think critically and vice versa. For CH, our task was to somehow mitigate the imbalance between virtual instruction and the close personal connections that an effective teaching praxis engenders.

Both then and now, the CH team firmly stands by the following premise: the classroom moments that matter most have little to do with Scantron tests or mandated exams. To help create a community, we had to build a program with interactive modules, as well as space for creativity and play. In theoretical terms, a pedagogy of escapism provides students and their teachers an alternative to the rigid structure of state-mandated curricula. Importantly, CH programming during COVID shutdowns reflected this escape from the modern rigors of near-constant testing and assessment because it prioritizes *ōtium*. Social distancing prevented us from reclining *sub arboribus*, under the trees, as the ancients would have, but Annie, De'Anna, and Nina were able to create a metaphorical environment of repose for the students.

Finding an Accessible Escape

To create this new style of programming, we went back to the basics: we consciously integrated Etienne Wenger's magisterial *Communities of Practice* and other writing-center pedagogies to model critical thinking, precipitate deep transfer, and create a vibrant community of learning.[17] Essential to establishing these communities is the notion that Daniel T. Willingham calls "successful thinking" and is the result of what Lauren Bowen and Matt Davis describe as "a sense of belonging and shared purposes that helps to advance collective learning."[18] This "sense of belonging" is crucial to the CH ethos because without community and care, the escapist ideals of our intentions do not come to fruition.

Evidence suggests that this style of nonevaluative teaching not only creates a "sense of belonging" among students but also cascades into "successful thinking." Critically engaged thinking is "successful" in that it prompts deep transfer because it allows students to transfer ideas from one setting and practice those ideas in another. An escapist-based pedagogy therefore functions antithetically to the prescribed educational system that treats learning as "an individual process . . . separated from the rest of our activities," with a "beginning and end."[19] To harness this approach, the graduate fellows designed their presentations around popular media and entertainment with which teens would be familiar—engaging that "sense of belonging" in an academic conversation and allowing students to learn collectively by bouncing ideas off one another.

Crucially, a pedagogy of escapism is founded upon the bedrock of accommodation. We know that learning does not "begin and end" with the *limena* of the formal classroom, and as the etymology of "escapism" suggests, an escapist-oriented curriculum seeks to introduce a "distraction from what normally has to be endured" in an educational setting, primarily the classroom.[20] We focus on the inherent joys of learning and model for students an accessible, equitable, and creative path by sidelining metrics (work) and highlighting joyful learning (*ōtium*). To escape successfully, however, one needs access to an unobstructed path, so our approach to the virtual CH program, as well as our pedagogy, was informed by the massive strides that scholars of disability studies have manifested, most especially through the core principle of accommodation. As scholar-teacher Anne-Marie Womack defines it, accommodation is "the precondition to all learning" and "the most basic act of teaching . . . not the exception" to it.[21] To accommodate in teaching, therefore, is to adapt one's style for another person's understanding. As Womack argues, accommodating students is more than an institution's mandatory compliance with the Americans with Disabilities Act. It adapts to our students' needs, de-hierarchizes the classroom, and impacts how we execute lessons.

By connecting CH's programming to disability studies, I do not suggest that students who attend these schools always-already inhabit disabled bodies. Rather, I use its resonances as social-political theory to highlight the logical gaps in how data report these students' acumen and abilities. My ultimate point is to demonstrate that this issue is not one of education administration, but of historical record. As Douglas C. Baynton writes, by the late nineteenth and early twentieth centuries, assumptions about what is "natural" became suffused with "normality" as a concept. Baynton astutely defines "normality" as "empirical" and "dynamic," a way of making sense of trends and phenomena to meet the needs of a "changing and progressing world," so "human behavior" might align with "the direction of human evolution and progress." This era of American history also saw the origin of the social sciences, statistical science, and industrialization with its need for "interchangeable parts and interchangeable workers"—the very same era that our modern education systems were conceived and founded.[22]

As Baynton writes in his magisterial essay, "Disability and the Justification of Inequality in American History," disability studies' goal is to challenge "the basic assumptions of the hierarchy." We as teacher-scholars can begin to deconstruct the harmful assumptions that metrics-driven data suggest about differently abled and neurodiverse learners. In this viewpoint, disability studies helps to reverse damaging assumptions and "negative connotations of disability" while actively working against ideologies of ableism.[23] This reason is what makes disability studies so formative, and informative, for conceiving an escapist pedagogy. This critical scholarly work offers an opportunity to reframe the learning process for "disadvantaged" students who attend underfunded urban public schools, however those "dis"-abilities or "dis"-assets are defined.

As program manager, I was especially concerned with ensuring that all students received multimodal delivery of the three CH modules because I am neurodivergent myself, and my own education by and large was not an accommodating environment. Womack's point about the nonexistence of normalcy became particularly prophetic during COVID-19 disruption. It is no exaggeration to claim that as our familiar methods of face-to-face synchronous instruction disappeared, so too did our confidence in successfully running a classroom. I experienced this anxiety in my own college classrooms, which served as a prescient reminder: the alienation, and uncertainty I felt attempting to learn new modes of instruction were perhaps parallel to what students feel when they need an accommodated learning environment and never receive it. This UDL-oriented approach came in handy for the CH program participants. Watkins, for example, highlights in her survey responses that our accommodated approach helped her students overall: "Even though I played the [preparatory video presentations] in class, they [the students] were able to watch it afterwards if they weren't present." In addition to providing advanced access to the presentations, we submitted transcripts for all videos, a "helpful" approach that was useful for those students "who required modifications." By precirculating videos and transcripts, we replicated one of accommodated teaching's most central tenets: flexibility and redundancy for those who required accessible tools and resources.

Handwringing over academic rigor is rooted in the very foundations of the modern American educational system, and it has been a part of our thinking about education since the dawn of the twentieth century. The beginning of exclusionary teaching practices can be traced to at least 1905, when F. C. Lewis touted the merits of a teaching method called formal discipline. In the essay "A Study in the Formal Discipline," Lewis reasons that students should experience substantial difficulty in learning to become more "logical" thinkers. Situated in stark contrast to UDL, formal discipline regulates a student's "will" to correct the learner's supposed inherent deficiencies, ensuring students make corrections to better focus on other "virtues."[24] Formal discipline reflects a penalty-based practice; it should not be confused with subject-matter expertise, our contemporary understanding of the term. Here, the word is coded as "punishment or chastisement . . . undertaken as penance."[25] This nomenclature is not a pithy factoid nor a brief history of etymology for the sake of erudition or due diligence. Rather, it is a harmful teaching practice that remains latent in our education systems. By Lewis's metric, embodied difference becomes a sign of errancy, a wayward deficit to be corrected through discipline, often in the form of schoolwork for which students must dutifully pay penance. In my estimation, however, students have paid far too much already. To remove this exclusionary pall from educational spaces, we as educators need to reconsider how we measure successful performance.

Conversations about the intrinsic "value" of education are nothing new. However, I should note that when I offer a critique of our capitalist-informed educational system, I am not suggesting that educators should not be completely unattuned to curricula based on college and career readiness—these are important facets to educating students in an increasingly globalized world. Rather, I intend to show the historical context for why student growth is measured not qualitatively, by evaluating students' growth and competencies, but instead quantitatively, by measuring student performance on the formal discipline of modernity: the multiple-choice standardized test. This overly simplistic evaluation of student performance is what a capitalist-driven system of education not only dictates but also demands of its key players. As Annie, De'Anna, Nina, and I saw it, the CH program that we designed and developed offered more sophisticated alternatives to embrace students' vast multicompetencies beyond what these statistical data are capable of measuring. What we found were invigorated students who asked questions and contributed to discussion, not out of a sense of compulsion or obligation, but genuine curiosity and collaboration. It was impossible for CH to offer a global solution to this commodification of our students, but the hope is that our model may offer a balm to these trends in formal discipline through an *ōtium*-informed pedagogy of escapism. In the next section, I lay out a reproducible means of escape from that system, if only for a momentary reprieve.

Teaching Escapism and Practicing Universally Designed Learning

CH's proposed teaching practice centers three tenets: to encourage learning for the sake of learning, offer nonevaluative creative activities, and stimulate creativity to activate critical thinking by facilitating open-ended questions. To accomplish this task, we instituted a two-step model wherein we precirculated asynchronous video presentations—each aligned with UDL standards and practices—with accompanying handouts, learning aids, and optional activity sheets for students to consult. These presentations and activities functioned as prompts for thought before the live synchronous sessions. In other words, the asynchronous materials for CH programming prepared participating students to apply, or "transfer," skills from videos to the live sessions the CH fellows led via Microsoft Teams. This dual, multimodal approach primed students to internalize what educational psychologists and pedagogy specialists varyingly call deep transfer, deep structure, far transfer, and high-road transfer.

Transfer is crucial. It prepares students for the complex patterns of thinking, thought patterns fundamental to becoming critically engaged citizens and interlocuters. Nina's presentation is a prime example of these principles. To teach comparative analysis, Nina asked her learners to consider two versions of Disney's *Beauty and the Beast* and think about the similarities and departures between them (see figure 6). In her asynchronous module, Nina facilitated deep transfer by summarizing Christopher Booker's seven-plot narrative theory that the teachers then streamed in class. Once Nina joined the classroom for her virtual synchronous sessions, she asked students to consider how many narratives could be applied to each *Beauty and the Beast* rendition. Students thus arrived ready to transfer that knowledge further because Nina's content was intentionally designed to pivot from the asynchronous videos. This instructional design allowed for a larger exploration of entertainment. In turn, the lesson created fodder for analytical thought to which students were able contribute. Consequently, students approached the Disney franchise with a "deep understanding" of the film's "underlying structure," the hallmark of critical thinking

ACTIVITY #2

Material:

Choose at least TWO film stills from any adaptation of *Beauty and the Beast*. You can use the slide deck or do a Google search and locate some new visual interpretations of the Beast.

Assignment:

Compare/contrast the visual depiction of the Beast.
- How does he change visually over time?
- What trends do you see?
- Can we learn anything about how we imagine "beastliness" and how it changes through time from these images?

FIGURE 6. Excerpt from the multimodal asynchronous presentation that Nina Cook compiled for her original module, "The Beauty of the Beast." Two components make this slide particularly exemplary: Nina's commitment, primarily, to open-ended questions that center the learner's perspective, second, her universally designed learning principles in praxis, including a legible sans serif typeface, generous use of white space between each line to prevent overcrowding, and using typography to visually demarcate between content (the "Material") and task (the "Assignment").

(see Breakout Box 2). Rather than treating learning as a game of *Jeopardy*, Nina's practice helped students prepare to answer these questions thoughtfully and with confidence.

Breakout Box 2: A Pedagogical Experiment and Experience

Contribution by Nina Cook

In the 2020–2021 academic year, the COVID-19 disruption presented a series of unprecedented challenges. During the pandemic, my colleagues and I undertook a Herculean feat: we shifted an existing program, based on an interactive, in-person, highly discussion-based model, to a virtual platform. Adapting this material serves as a practical example of the very theory of adaptation I posit in my Civic Humanist presentation, in which we study adaptations to learn about their historical and cultural moment of production. Just as we learn about a specific historical moment through the study of stories and artifacts, an examination of the CH curriculum from last year speaks to its historical moment—this curriculum is a product of a very specific time and pedagogical practice. To stop the spread of COVID-19, in fall 2020 we switched to distance learning, a model that none of the CH fellows had used before. Not only were students' personal lives disrupted by the advent of the virus but also their social and educational environments. The curriculum we produced for the 2020–2021 academic year bears the traces of COVID-19 and our response to it as pedagogues, as well as illustrating the importance of compassion, communication, and creativity in teachers' responses to the pandemic.

Before we entered the virtual classroom, we had to successfully implement the asynchronous portion of the CH program. Each fellow prerecorded a lecture on VoiceThread, a web application that allows users to narrate their slideshows, to prepare our students for synchronous discussions, the lengths of which were highly variable. Due to the complexities of virtual scheduling, I was sometimes allotted an hour to lead discussions on my source material, while at other times I might get only twenty minutes to cover the same material. Because we were given different amounts of time in each class to fill, flexibility was an absolute necessity. Being able to cut material on the fly, respond to students' comments, and go where their interest and discussion led the group was also crucial. Even though the discussion times with students varied greatly from school to school, I used the same prerecorded lecture, roughly thirty minutes in length, to structure a discussion that consciously centered the student's perspective.

To accomplish the task of student-centered virtual learning effectively, I flipped the classroom during my synchronous sessions with the students. This choice was not happenstance. Rather, this pedagogical ideal was consciously implemented and scaffolded in the precirculated asynchronous materials.

My lecture, "The Beauty of the Beast: Archetype and Adaptation in *La Belle et La Bête*," was a short presentation that examined various adaptations of *Beauty and the Beast* across time. Because of its widespread popularity in the Disney franchise, I mostly focused on films to model practices of comparison—what I consider to be a particular way of reading artistic and literary works—that I used as the foundation upon which to build in the live discussion sessions. Specifically, I focused on Disney's 1991 animated classic and the 2017 live-action adaptation of *Beauty and the Beast* to teach students how to compare and contrast. These two distinct versions of the story also conveniently allowed me to shortcut some time with students because the lesson built on students' previous knowledge of the franchise and did not require me to introduce all-new material.

My goal in both the asynchronous and synchronous sessions was to illustrate for students how archetypal stories adapt to cultural and historical frameworks. For example, in our discussions we often looked at Belle's evolution between 1991 and 2017. Rather than being a passive prisoner—as she is portrayed in the 1991 animated classic—Emma Watson's interpretation of the heroine is just that: a heroine. She shows remarkable resilience and intelligence in the film, talking back to her captor, discussing art and literature with ease, and even attempting to escape from confinement.

Students are observant. They almost always picked up on the changes to Belle's character between the 1991 to 2017 versions and the fact that these changes were tied to autonomy and power. Their observations inevitably led to a discussion of gender roles in the 2000s and how feminism within our society affects the depiction of female characters. Usually, this thread would end with a discussion of toxic masculinity and our cultural obsession with the stereotype of the beastly man and the beautiful woman. At this point, I would call up slides with current iterations of this trope and its tendency to adapt the *Beauty and the Beast* source material in similar ways (e.g., with the empowerment of the Beauty character).

Attention to the effect of specific cultural movements on the way we tell stories allowed me to emphasize the importance of studying narratives. The historicist reasoning behind studying art and literature is, after all, contingent upon this contextual layer; we study such disciplines because they teach us about the time period from which these productions emerge. With this perspective, the films become critical objects of study and provide evidence of historically situated ways of being and knowing; these art-objects show that it was possible at a particular time and in a particular place to see and to think in specific ways, ways that often seem entirely foreign to our modern eyes and senses. To make the presentations more interactive, I made sure to include questions that prompted students to engage directly with the content by asking them to consider the differences between the original animated film and its live-action reboot years later.

In the asynchronous lecture, I identified and defined key terms such as "archetype" and "adaptation" and used them as an accessible way to teach literary theory. I found that this approach resulted in an easy-to-digest format because it built on students' knowledge of pop culture and allowed them to transfer it to literary works. Because the lecture was prerecorded, I was able to integrate paintings, GIFs, and other visual material that illustrated for students the ubiquity of the *Beauty and the Beast* trope. I showed the prevalence of a familiar narrative: a misunderstood, "beastly" man finds himself in a romantic relationship with the sweet, innocent "beautiful" girl. I would then follow-up this observation with its ubiquity in modern television, from the CW version of *Beauty and the Beast* (2012–2016) to the television adaptation retold through the story of a detective show on CBS (1987–1990). My intent here was straightforward: it immersed students into the textured history of the story and showed how it reiterates ceaselessly across the ages. Moreover, I emphasized that *Beauty and the Beast* is truly a tale as old as time because our culture cannot seem to escape it.

I continued this thread in the live synchronous sessions, during which I played two clips from the 1991 and 2017 adaptations of *Beauty and the Beast*. Beforehand, I asked students to identify key differences and similarities. I found this approach to be tricky, as students were often uncomfortable engaging vocally over video and could go entire class sessions without turning on their cameras or microphones. To meet students where they were, I leaned heavily on the chat function and began lectures with easy questions to which the students could respond with an emoji or GIF.

I learned that students found answering questions intimidating when I asked them to respond in writing. In contrast, phrasing the question more informally and conversationally—such as "throw it into the chat" or "let me know what you think"—led to more positive outcomes and engagement. I found that if I could get students to start naming television shows or movies that adopt the Beauty and the Beast trope, they were more likely to unmute themselves and engage in vocal discussion.

Recognizing students' multicompetencies was instrumental to the lecture's success here. Many students have a high degree of fluency with nonphonetical language, while responding in writing or extemporaneous speeches leads to profound anxiety. Equally as important, those students who were less interested in "coming on mic" remained engaged in the chat with this exercise. Overall, the asynchronous and synchronous modules worked in tandem: I was able to capitalize on the virtual format by leveraging its flexibility in the digital space and used video clips, GIFs, and emojis (to name only a few) to make the students feel connected to the material.

This online program was a gratifying pedagogical experiment and experience. Though I do not think virtual instruction can truly replace in-person learning, I am beyond grateful for the tools we as teachers have in our digital toolkit. I am equally grateful for the creativity of our CH team, which has prepared me for teaching in a variety of formats. This skill will only grow in value as instructors continue to adapt and remain flexible in the face of a tumultuous, ever-shifting pedagogical landscape. The curriculum we developed is a product of our cultural and historical moment—a testament, however small, to the power and poetry of adaptation, both in theory and in practice.

Annie's synchronous session worked in tandem with Nina's effective implementation of "successful thinking" by recreating Wenger's "communities of practice" model. As she delineates in Breakout Box 3, Annie's "Art of Artifice" presentation focused on the notion that humans do not just create and manipulate art; instead, art also manipulates its viewers. Annie's module carefully walked students through five hundred years of Western art to explain how both Raphael's classical *School of Athens* fresco and Nigerian American artist Doze Kanu's 2018 *Chair [iii]* sculpture, made from spare car parts and concrete, not only are worthy of equal consideration but also function in direct conversation with one another (see figure 7). Annie threaded this needle delicately by showing students how neo-Classical ideals dictated Raphael's approach to the fresco within his own historically confined era. With this context, Annie demonstrated to students how Raphael's art functions as both a visual representation of his artistic practice and an object representative of the era.

But Annie did not stop there. Rather than proclaim that Raphael's fresco is the epitome of Western civilization, she contextualized the fact that the ideals of one generation and culture do not dictate those of another. Consider the visual contrast of Raphael's *School of Athens* to Houston's Slow, Loud, and Bangin' (SLAB) culture, as imagined by Kanu's *Chair [iii]*. Annie included this juxtaposition consciously so that she could practice the central tenet of radical, inclusive pedagogy: to de-hierarchize the role of traditional, Western culture and artistic expression in order to share artworks that more represent the cultural and social backgrounds of the students enrolled in urban schools. Annie's deft framing also included audience input and feedback. She prompted the students to consider several probing questions: "If you were tasked with composing your own *School of Athens*, what figures would you choose? What valued ideals would you want to center? What would you choose *not* to include?" (See figure 8.)

FIGURE 7. Dozie Kanu, *Chair [iii]*, 2018. Poured concrete, steel, rims. 37 × 19 × 16.5 inches. By permission of the artist.

For participating students, the tapestry of responses was inspiring. As a result, Annie's module directly evoked Wenger's radical idea that learning is a "fundamentally social phenomenon," a classroom practice that when exercised becomes a "form of belonging." By asking participants to think about what they would place in their own *School*, Annie activated deep transfer in her audience of eager interlocutors precisely because she encouraged them to create something new, unique, all their own.

FIGURE 8. Raphael, *The School of Athens*, fresco (Stanza della Segnatura, Museo Vaticani). Emerging from conversations with sculpture artist Dozie Kanu and the Civic Humanist fellows, Annie created this optional activity enjoining students to reimagine their own personal version of The School of Athens. This task invites them to reference their own heroes, influences, teachers, and history to represent their own deeply personal values and ideals. Scala/Art Resource, used by permission.

Breakout Box 3: *Ōtium* Regained

Contribution by Annie Lowe, PhD

When we reconvened over Zoom in summer 2020—with Nina Cook joining Alex, De'Anna, and me in the Civic Humanist cohort—our important, if daunting, task was not to reproduce days like our March 3 program in an online medium. Rather, we agreed to reimagine what the programming should become in an intractably different September. Our responsibilities as humanists had changed, and we acknowledged that the format and content of our interactive lectures would change, too.

While workshopping and revising our respective material to complement each other and cohere with our common theme of critical interpretation, two key changes most accounted for the transformation of my part, "The Art of Artifice," for COVID-19 times. Namely, a revised treatment of Raphael's *School of Athens* and a complementary activity option would bookend the recorded lecture, and the work of Houston-born Nigerian-American artist Dozie Kanu would become its centerpiece, replacing the aforementioned madcap assortment of art-historical exemplars.

I used Raphael's canonical *School of Athens* as a classic demonstration of how single-point perspective manipulates viewer reception. Supplementing this spatial emphasis, I overlaid close-up images with graphic markers that allowed us to read the visual text of the fresco together, even if asynchronously. I asked students to critically reflect on how Raphael's visual semantics of divine symmetry, infinite depth, and heavenly transcendence conspire to represent, as a universal ideal, his Greco-Roman assembly of "Great Men."

From Raphael, we would fast-forward five hundred years to investigate how modern and contemporary artworks manipulate and defy art-historical conventions of rarity, radiance, and authority. Holbein's *memento mori* gimmick was not going to work in a socially isolating pandemic, with mortality never far from our collective thoughts. Instead, I found that Dozie Kanu's work could reimagine the site-specificity of the classroom we would have shared by engaging our common context as Houston residents. Kanu's *Chair [iii]* (2018) evokes the general form of a swivel chair, but interpreting it requires a prior knowledge or experience with Houston's slab culture to understand the full context for the visual language it speaks and what it could say. Importantly, for those unfamiliar with Houston slang, "slab" originated as an acronym for customized cars that are "slow, loud, and bangin.'" The base of *Chair [iii]* is a shiny steel car rim, from which a spoked chrome "elbow," or "swanga," extends to hold aloft two concrete slabs forming the seat and back. In the visual language of Kanu's *Chair [iii]*, punning goes beyond parody to become a plastic poetry. Kanu's piece uses a fairly exclusive visual language and addresses a knowledgeable viewer, much as Raphael's *School of Athens* spoke to his intended audience. But this time the art in question spoke to the Houston-area high schoolers as privileged insiders, whose experiences and background knowledge warrant interpretive authority.

As a comparatively new Houston transplant, I had to admit that my own knowledge and experience of slabs was limited to occasional street sightings and pop culture references. I messaged Kanu directly on Instagram for guidance—and to my surprise, he responded! Kanu affirmed a core principle of his artistic practice: art and design have the power to encourage Black people to think otherwise and take creative hold of their circumstances, which include traditional concepts of art and design, function and ideal, as themselves institutional circumstances.[26] As a result, Kanu invites students as fellow insiders to interpret how *Chair [iii]* challenges what institutionally counts as artwork. In turn, the students and I explored how his sculpture contests the common presumption that an artwork has no function except as display—that its uselessness is part of fine art's exclusiveness—and challenges the supposed categorical difference between museum display and other meaningful domains of "ornamental" display familiar to them. When we returned to this artwork in the synchronous meeting, the image of Kanu's *Chair [iii]* furnished the civic scene for our alternative *ōtium*.

Most importantly, Annie's, Nina's, and De'Anna's original modules challenged the notion that learning is adversarial, or, in Wenger's words, that it resembles "one-on-one combat . . . where knowledge must be demonstrated out of context, and where collaborating is considered cheating."[27] In contrast to "combat"-oriented learning, Annie, De'Anna, and Nina created interactive, low-pressure educational modules that taught valuable skills while simultaneously providing both students and their teachers respite from the grind of mandated educational standards. The CH fellows accomplished this task by fostering their audience's creativity—harnessed both actively and concretely—to reinforce the valuable skillsets that standardized evaluation cannot. In other words, Annie, De'Anna, and Nina each created a "sense of belonging" unique to their own pedagogical purposes in that virtual space. By doing so, the CH fellows accomplished what for many was nearly impossible during the pandemic: they brainstormed, and then facilitated, a "shared purpose" for everyone present—a purpose that, when successful according to Bowen and Davis, helps to advance a social environment of collective learning.[28]

Whither Now?

After the 2021–2022 academic year, the future of CH as an innovative public humanities program remains uncertain. Despite the glowing evaluations Annie, De'Anna, Nina, and I received from our partner educators and their students, the Rice University Dean of Humanities decided to erase the innovative involvement of advanced graduate students. This administrative decision does not leave me surprised given my lived experience as both a graduate student and postdoctoral researcher with the institution. Nevertheless, I cannot help but feel dismayed at this turn of events, most especially because the Dean will likely hand over CH to Rice faculty. Particularly upsetting is the Dean's choice to strip the two commodities that advanced graduate students need the most amid a collapsing academic job market: funding to supplement poverty wages and diverse early-career work experience. This decision to give the program to tenured or tenure-track professors, who almost assuredly need neither resource, strikes me as particularly cruel.

Despite these unfortunate developments, CH's programming, as the four of us visualized it, sits at the frontier of the public humanities and offers a model of future programming for forward-thinking deans and administrators at publicly oriented institutions. As we uniquely practiced it, CH modeled useful skills that teenagers need to develop for the adult world. These pathways provided high schoolers with an opportunity to see creativity and critical thinking as enmeshed practices without judgment or negative feedback—avenues that are fruitful for our paths as educators. On a personal level, it gifted me with a newfound sense of community-oriented service that I have been able to replicate, not only in the ōtium-laden civic engagement programming offered to area teenagers with the YMCA Greater Houston, where I work as a civic engagement lead, but also other education-oriented nonprofits around Houston. In these instances, I have taken with me the lessons of my own personal teaching philosophy and the accommodations-oriented approach we practiced for CH.

Students who are taught to solve problems approach the learning process as critical interlocuters. By asking for their input and placing them in the driver's seat, students become contributors to knowledge production, not just passive recipients of it. This approach shows that a community of practice can occur anywhere—from the classroom, to the workplace, to the aspirational ōtium sub arboribus practiced by the ancients. Through communal learning that prioritizes deep transfer, we help prepare students for an inquisitive adult life by teaching them valuable problem-solving skills.

Public school educators already face a litany of challenges, and they by and large do not receive the credit nor resources they and their students deserve. As public-facing scholars, it is imperative that we support our peer educators in secondary schools. We must enhance learning opportunities through that collaboration for intellectually curious, though understandably exhausted students. And, most importantly, we must share with them a pedagogy of escapism, an assessment-free safe house to where both students and their teachers alike can retreat. At this point, we can no longer afford not to. None of us can.

NOTES

This chapter is dedicated to the hard work of all three of the Civic Humanities graduate teaching fellows, but one in particular: De'Anna Daniels, a highly skilled pedagogue and classroom facilitator for CH, who was unable to contribute to this chapter due to extenuating circumstances and competing deadlines. De'Anna currently serves as the program manager for the 2021–2022 CH program, the role that I held from summer 2019 to spring 2021. For an overview of De'Anna's insightful educational modules, see Annie Lowe's reflection in Breakout Box 1.

1. Interested Rice humanities graduate students would apply with a project proposal, CV, and cover letter indicating their interest in the program. Senior-level administrators within Rice's Humanities Research Center (HRC) would then evaluate the proposals and extend offers accordingly.

2. I attribute all credit for the notion that our work encourages both critical and creative thinking to Lowe, one of the teaching fellows who joined the team in 2019 and was invited to remain until she defended her dissertation in June 2021.

3. See Parker, Minkin, and Bennet, "Economic Fallout from COVID-19."

4. I am deeply indebted to the team at the National Humanities Center, particularly NHC Vice President of Education Andy Mink. After an introduction from a mutual colleague, Andy recommended me to attend the NHC's 2020 virtual summer graduate residency "Passionate Teaching in the Research Environment: How to Create Meaningful Online Learning Experiences" (July 13–17, 2020) as I was finishing my post-defense dissertation revisions. The key takeaways from that fruitful week almost entirely informed my contributions to the Civic Humanities 2020–2021 program. For a description of this virtual residency, see the NHC webpage, https://nationalhumanitiescenter .org/education-programs/graduate-students/passionate-teaching-research-environment/.

5. Fuermann, *Reluctant Empire*, 213.

6. Kellar, *Make Haste Slowly*, 166.

7. Houston Independent School District, "HISD At-a-Glance."

8. Title I is a federal entitlement that guarantees additional funding for schools where majority of enrolled students live in low-income households.

9. Houston Independent School District, "2020–2021 Facts and Figures."

10. Lucy Seward, survey response, August 15, 2021. To evaluate the experiences of our partner educators, I circulated a survey that asked four of our most dedicated veteran educators to provide their perspectives on the CH program's effectiveness and contributions. Questions in the survey were either open-ended or asked the educators to rate their comfort and experience with virtual instruction on a scale of one to ten, from least to most comfortable.

11. Emma Burch, survey response, August 15, 2021.

12. Barbara Watkins (pseudonym), survey response, August 15, 2021.

13. Approximately 11 percent of students said they felt neutral about the future, while the remaining 15 percent felt negatively about the future. For the Active Minds data from April 2020 and September 2020, respectively, see: Active Minds, "Impact of COVID-19"; and Active Minds, "Student Mental Health Survey." For a well-researched primer on the systemic disadvantages for students of color in the United States, see Carnevale and Strohl, *Separate and Unequal*.

14. Active Minds, "We Asked Students." For the American Psychological Association's advice on how to support students during these transitions, see "Student Mental Health."

15. Rennette Brown, survey response, August 15, 2021.

16. See Active Minds, "Impact of COVID-19."

17. See Devet, "Writing Center," 119–51.

18. Bowen and Davis, "Teaching for Transfer."

19. Willingham and the State of New South Wales, "How to Teach Critical Thinking," 3.

20. "escapism, n.," *OED Online*.

21. Womack, "Teaching Is Accommodation," 494.

22. Baynton, 35–36.

23. Siebers, *Disability Theory*, 3–4, 5.

24. Willingham, 5; and F. C. Lewis, "Study in the Formal Discipline," 287.

25. "discipline, n.," *OED Online*, www.oed.com/view/Entry/53744.

26. See Markell, Olivares, Kanu, "Dozie Kanu and Jonathan Olivares in Conversation."

27. Wenger, *Communities of Practice*, 3.

28. Wenger, *Communities of Practice*, 49; quoted in Bowen and Davis, "Teaching for Transfer."

BIBLIOGRAPHY

Active Minds. "Impact of COVID-19 on Student Mental Health." April 2020. https://www.activeminds.org/studentsurvey/.

Active Minds. "Student Mental Health Survey." September 2020. https://www.activeminds.org/active-minds-student-mental-health-survey/.

Active Minds. "We Asked Students about Their Mental Health throughout the Pandemic. Here's What We Learned." April 27, 2022. https://www.activeminds.org/blog/we-asked-students-about-their-mental-health-throughout-the-pandemic-heres-what-we-learned.

American Psychological Association. "Student Mental Health during and after COVID-19: How Can Schools Identify Youth Who Need Support?" September 26, 2022. https://www.apa.org/topics/covid-19/student-mental-health.

Baynton, Douglas C. "Disability and the Justification of Inequality in American History." In *The New Disability History*, edited by Paul K. Longmore and Lauri Umanski, 33–57. New York University Press, 2001.

Bowen, Lauren Marshall, and Matthew Davis. "Teaching for Transfer and the Design of a Writing Center Education Program." In *Transfer of Learning in the Writing Center*, edited by Bonnie Devet and Dana Lynn Driscoll. *WLN: A Journal of Writing Center Scholarship*. February 15, 2020. https://wlnjournal.org/digitaleditedcollection2/BowenandDavis.html.

Carnevale, Anthony P., and Jeff Strohl. *Separate and Unequal: How Higher Education Reinforces the Intergenerational Reproduction of White Racial Privilege*. Center on Education and the Workforce—Georgetown Public Policy Institute. July 2013. https://cew.georgetown.edu/cew-reports/separate-unequal/.

Condon, Bill, dir. *Beauty and the Beast*. Disney, 2017. 129 min.

Devet, Bonnie. "The Writing Center and Transfer of Learning." *The Writing Center Journal* 35, no. 1 (Fall/Winter 2015): 119–51.

"discipline, n." OED Online. June 2022. Oxford University Press. https://www.oed.com/view/Entry/53744.

"escapism, n." OED Online. June 2022. Oxford University Press. https://www.oed.com/view/Entry/64246.

Fuermann, George. *Reluctant Empire: The Mind of Texas*. Garden City, NY: Doubleday, 1957.

Houston Independent School District. "2020–2021 Facts and Figures." Accessed July 16, 2022. https://www.houstonisd.org/site/handlers/filedownload.ashx?moduleinstanceid=48525&dataid=317279&FileName=2020-2021_FactsFigures.pdf.

Houston Independent School District. "HISD At-a-Glance." Accessed June 22, 2021. https://www.houstonisd.org/site/handlers/filedownload.ashx?moduleinstanceid=142248&dataid=86735&FileName=HISD_At-a-Glance_102020_ENG.pdf.

Kellar, William Henry. *Make Haste Slowly: Moderates, Conservatives, and School Desegregation in Houston.* College Station: Texas A&M University Press, 1999.

Lewis, F. C. "A Study in the Formal Discipline." *The School Review: A Journal for Secondary Education* 13, no. 4 (April 1905): 281–92.

Markell Ian, Jonathan Olivares, and Dozie Kanu. "Dozie Kanu and Jonathan Olivares in Conversation." *PIN-UP: The Magazine for Architectural Entertainment* (Spring/Summer 2018). https://archive.pinupmagazine.org/articles/furniture-designers-jonathan-olivares-and-dozie-kanu-interview.

Parker, Kim, Rachel Minkin, and Jesse Bennet. "Economic Fallout from COVID-19 Continues to Hit Lower-Income Americans the Hardest." Pew Research Center, September 24, 2020. https://www.pewresearch.org/social-trends/2020/09/24/economic-fallout-from-covid-19-continues-to-hit-lower-income-americans-the-hardest/.

Siebers, Tobin. *Disability Theory.* Ann Arbor: University of Michigan Press, 2008.

Trousdale, Gary, and Kirk Wise, dir. *Beauty and the Beast.* Disney, 1991. 84 min.

Wenger, Etienne. *Communities of Practice: Learning, Meaning, and Identity.* Cambridge: Cambridge University Press, 1998.

Willingham Daniel T., and the State of New South Wales. "How to Teach Critical Thinking." *Education: Future Frontiers.* Parramatta: Department of Education, June 2019. https://apo.org.au/node/244676.

Womack, Anne-Marie. "Teaching Is Accommodation: Universally Designing Composition Classrooms and Syllabi." *CCC* 68, no. 3 (February 2017): 494–525.

9

PERFORMING BLACK LIVES

Elaigwu P. Ameh

Amid the intermingling health and racial pandemics roiling the United States in 2020, the lifeless body of a Black man was found burning in a roadside ditch near Kellogg in central Iowa.[1] The Black man, later identified as Michael Williams, was a forty-four-year-old Grinnell resident who was a father and grandfather. Police investigation and court testimony revealed that he had been clubbed from behind with a baseball bat, strangled by hanging, kept in a basement for days, showed off to friends, wrapped in a blanket, bound with rope and tape, hurled onto the back of a truck, dumped in a ditch by the roadside, and set ablaze.[2] According to the investigation, the murder occurred on or about September 12, 2020, in Grinnell, a small town with a predominantly white population. The 2020 United States Census showed the Grinnell population of 9,564 was 2.5 percent Black or African American and 90.5 percent white.[3]

The gruesome death sparked fears of hate crime in Grinnell and at Grinnell College, an elite liberal arts college in the country with a total undergraduate enrollment of 1,493 in the fall of 2020.[4] I recall talking with some Black students once the news of the burning body got to campus. It was important for me, as a faculty of color at the college, to comfort them, even though I too needed comfort. Deep down, I felt I was as vulnerable as every other Black person at the college, in Grinnell, and in the United States just living their daily lives and troubling nobody. In response, on Sunday, September 20, 2020, Grinnell College cancelled Monday classes, and a statement from the college's president, Anne Harris, and the school's chief diversity officer, Schvalla Rivera, noted that Williams' "stark and brutal murder in the national context of racial justice" had "struck intense fear for the safety of our Black, Indigenous, and People of Color (BIPOC) colleagues, friends, and families. National context [had] become local experience."[5] The statement added: "We live in a predominantly white community and work in a predominantly white college. The murder of Mr. Williams is an incident that is rare in the experience of most Iowans. But for many people of color, this incident is the most recent in an accumulated history of prejudice, mistreatment, and murder."[6]

As a theater scholar and practitioner of color working in higher education, the peak of the pandemic presented challenges on many fronts, including but not limited to what to perform, how to perform, for whom to perform, and with whom to perform. To create performance only about the pandemic was a luxury minoritarian artists, especially artists of color, could not afford. This is partly because, as Harvey Young and Bethany Hughes observe, "marginalized and minoritized communities and the artists that bring to life their stories routinely invoke theater (and performance) as a corrective and a predictive tactic."[7] For us, it was not a question of choosing between the health pandemic and social justice. It was a matter of doing both. Our lived experience as minoritarian populations already dictated that. Since performance, as Stephanie Leigh Batiste attests, "provokes much in the space of the unspoken and unspeakable," and since Black performance, specifically, "carries histories of race onto the stage and performs with, in lieu of, and regardless of its fact," the employment of performance to explore the intersection of Blackness, COVID-19, and racial inequity appealed to me.[8] The ongoing pandemic has, by no means, dismantled generations of systemic injustices against historically marginalized bodies and communities. If anything, it, at worst, has exacerbated them and, at best, has centered them in national and international conversations about race, community, and humanity. To help me streamline my project ideas as I reflected on the converging health and racial pandemics, I asked myself this question: What does it mean to be an arts-based publicly engaged scholar of color in the time of COVID-19? *Project X* emerged as my response to this question.

Project X reminds us of the repellent images of racial inequities that still plague our society. Situated within the nexus of racialized bodies and Black performance, this episodic performance employs the spoken word medium to explore the lived experience of race in the United States, specifically from the standpoint of Black people. Written by me and directed by a final-year student, Malcolm Davis, *Project X* made "history at Grinnell College by being the first mainstage production with an entirely Black cast, Black director, and Black playwright."[9] The cast were Daja Nagra, Elijah Griffin, Obuchi Adikema, Xonzy Gaddis, and Malcolm Davis. The show, which opened on March 19, 2021, was "also the first mainstage production in the known history of the College to be directed by a student."[10] On learning about the project, Malcolm Davis had indicated interest in serving as assistant director, but after having a conversation with him and listening to his interpretation of the work, not to mention his enthusiasm and spoken word savviness, I developed confidence in his ability to direct the show. I stepped down from my role as director and he took over the position. In my capacity as producer for the show, I also served as his mentor, offering guidance occasionally as the need arose, especially as that was going to be his mainstage directorial debut. *Project X* is a series of spoken word pieces, and Davis instinctively connected with the work and tapped into his experience as a poet and a Black person in the United States to direct it (figure 9).

When I was writing the performance, I did not think about who would tell the stories of the Black experience contained in the work. I simply wanted to tell the stories. But, in repeated conversations with the director, it became clear to me that critical to the integrity of the work was having Black people embody

FIGURE 9. The director, Malcolm Davis, giving a preshow talk. Photo credit: S. Benjamin Farrar.

it. In an interview with *The Scarlet and Black*'s Nadia Langley, the director noted: "Being a Black person, and constantly experiencing the trauma of that, and then taking the time out of your day to go to rehearsal and tap into those feelings, into those traumas, and then relive them for the audience is a difficult thing to do."[11] Yet, he believed that Black students would be better positioned to relive those experiences. As part of his artistic vision, he hoped that, in the end, "Black audience members" would "feel heard" and "feel seen," especially as the performance was not "a sort of dressed-up version of the Black experience that [was] going to be funny and positive," but would "not push the audience to think about themselves."[12] His take on audience participation resonates with Tami Spry's performative autoethnography of sexual assault in "Presence and Privacy: Ode to the Absent Phallus," wherein she notes: "the audience not only sees my body as evidence of an assaulted body, they also see my body performing a reflexive critique upon dominant cultural notions of victim and survivor contextualized in that place and in that time."[13] Performance, in this context, transcends mere mirth and demands a critical reflection on the self in relation to a community of selves implicated in the performance on display. It confronts us with the face of the other, its beauty and ugliness, helplessness and aspirations, and challenges us to step into the world of this other, always beseeching, yet continually obliging us to do better—to do right as a community of humanity.

During my reflection on what it means to be an arts-based publicly engaged scholar of color in the time of COVID-19, I considered directing David Feldshuh's *Miss Evers' Boys*, which was nominated for the Pulitzer Prize in Drama and adapted into an HBO movie, which received twelve Emmy nominations, winning in four categories, including Best Picture. The play tells the story of the Tuskegee study, a secret medical experiment in which the United States deliberately withheld treatment from over four hundred poor Black men in a bid for doctors to study the effects of untreated syphilis. I reckoned that the play could serve as a platform for using the art to deepen discussions about medical research, health professionals, and underserved communities in the era of COVID-19. Such a discussion, I thought, would help quell the lingering distrust of medical research and professionals within the Black community—distrust that largely stemmed from the Tuskegee syphilis study. It would expedite candid discussions about past transgressions, while promoting awareness about measures that have been put in place since then to safeguard patients. At the same time, I was also worried that some people might misunderstand the rationale for staging the play during the pandemic and leverage it to spread misinformation and anxiety about COVID-19 vaccination.

Following the gruesome death of Williams, I became determined to create something together with students, which would be research based, engage with the pandemic and social justice, and encourage experimental and experiential learning. I imagined that a devised performance class would be an effective medium for such a creative collaboration among students, and I would only serve as a dramaturg. The course would be a studio where students would create and stage activism-centered performance on the converging health and racial pandemics in the country. Through research, story circles, improvisations, monologues, and script analysis, students would enhance their artistic and analytical skills while working on the project. I was excited about the prospects of the course. Countless times, I envisioned myself working with students on the project in an ensemble-like environment. I anticipated the arguments and counterarguments that would be made about what to be included in the final product. I was curious to see what issues would pique the interest of students after assigning to them a central prompt to guide their research and artistic work. Would we all decide to create one group performance? Or would students decide to each create their own plays in response to the prompt? Would students have enough time to memorize all their lines before opening night? Or would we have to design the performance to allow for reading from scripts? Because of the changing reality of the pandemic, one thing was certain for me ab initio: whatever students needed to create, we would all have to make do with minimal set, costume, and props. Minimalism would be our watchword in the (co-)creation process!

Then the spring I term began. Some students who had skipped the previous term because of the spread of COVID-19 and the transition to online learning and had hoped to enroll in spring I did not enroll. There was a decline in enrollment across the college. This decline was not unique to the college, as many other institutions of higher learning across the world reported the same. I struggled to get students to enroll for my devised course. Only three students enrolled for the course, leaving us with eleven available seats. As if that was not bad enough, one of the three students dropped the course before the first day of class, citing personal reasons that I cannot disclose here. She asked, though, to be part of the mainstage production (without participating in the class). I granted her request, and she proceeded to put on a marvelous show during the mainstage performance. Shortly after she dropped the course, another student signed up for it. The total number was back to three. By this time, we were only a few days away from the commencement of the term. I had a big decision to make about not just the content and the format of the class but also its objectives, learning outcomes, and final creative product. It was clear to me that I had to redesign the course syllabus. In the spirit of the pandemic, I knew I had to be flexible and adaptable. I had already started working on a plan B. I had begun writing parts of *Project X*. By this time, some other students had signaled interest in participating in the mainstage production in varying capacities without being available to take the four-credit course. They would each get two credits instead for their participation in the production alone. The virtual mainstage production I was supposed to direct, I imagined, could take any of the three forms: (a) a student-created devised performance; (b) a performance solely written by me; or (c) a combination of the two. Before the spring I term began, one more student signed up for the class. A few days into the term, the fourth student to enroll sent me an e-mail from his home country, Myanmar, where he had been taking his course online to tell me that a coup had just occurred in the country and that he would be withdrawing from the class to join his friends in protesting against the military dictatorship that had just seized power. I respected his decision, even though I knew the class would miss his brilliance, cheerfulness, and passion for activism.

After a discussion with the three remaining students, we decided that the class be geared toward the creation of short plays about a social justice issue of utmost importance to each of them. In the end, we had three research-centered short plays on three areas of activism: environment, sexuality, and capitalism. In addition to creating their own performances, the students participated in *Project X* as co-dramaturgs. Their dramaturgical work helped provide context and depth to the work of our actors and our guest designer, S. Benjamin Farrar. Since we were all using Microsoft Teams for meetings and as digital reservoir, our dramaturgs uploaded all dramaturgical materials onto Teams. For varying plausible reasons, all the actors for the mainstage production could not enroll for the class originally designed for the production. As a result, we had to set up rehearsals outside of the times allotted for the class. Getting everyone to be in the digital rehearsal room at the same time was challenging primarily because of scheduling conflicts, which partly stemmed from emergent pandemic realities and the changing composition of the ensemble. In response, the director adapted his directing style to the emergent reality, sometimes reorganizing on the go the order for the rehearsal of individual pieces in the performance. When, at the start of rehearsal sessions some actors had not logged in because of internet connectivity challenges, he would switch effortlessly to the next available actor. Such was his dexterity and flexibility. He also set up multiple one-on-one sessions with actors to hone their skills outside the established group rehearsal slots. In the process, he too learned significant life skills, including adaptability, teamwork, people management, time management, and effective interpersonal communication.

As faculty and producer, this virtual production deepened my confidence in the ability of students to direct mainstage productions. Investing a high level of trust in student directors allows them to exercise their creative imagination without inhibition, bringing out the best in them and in the project. Also, this trust rubs off on other students in the production, spurring them to believe in the vision and direction of the student director. No doubt, there were times I needed to make inputs to the rehearsal/directing process, but I made sure to do so in a way that would not undermine the authority of the student director. In our new virtual reality, I relied on private chatrooms to get my message through to the director during rehearsals. At other times, I simply took notes and waited until the end of the rehearsal session to make inputs. There were also times when the director and I were the first to pop up on our Webex screens, so we used those opportunities to cross-fertilize ideas. Occasionally, we set up meetings just for the two of us to discuss salient matters in line with emergent realities in the production process. As producer, I took a backseat in the rehearsal space, paving the way for the director to take the lead.

A Taste of the Product

In line with the overarching theme of Black History Month 2021, *Project X* dissects the intersection of the Black family and the questions of representation, identity, and diversity. It examines the ongoing social construction of corporeal blackness by the other and by blackness itself in our everyday lives. Intentionally, it accentuates often discounted mental health concerns within the Black community. The pandemic, no doubt, has distinctly impacted the mental health of people across the world. Researchers have reported deteriorating symptoms of insomnia, anxiety disorder, depressive disorder, and suicidal ideation among large numbers of people.[14] They have linked some of these symptoms to lockdowns, isolation, job loss, eviction fears, financial troubles, food insecurity, and exposure to COVID-19-related hospitalizations or deaths. However, the pandemic has also affected people disproportionately, with essential workers, low-income individuals, older adults, and communities of color suffering the most, thereby exacerbating often overlooked injustices in society.

At the peak of the pandemic, widespread demonstrations over police killings of unarmed Black people centered racial inequity and the need for reflection, solidarity, and justice across all strata of society. As the pandemic raged, an editorial in the *Journal of Clinical Nursing* warned that "Black people in the United States (U.S.) [were] dying at disproportionate rates from the novel severe acute respiratory syndrome coronavirus 2 (SARS-CoV-2) virus," and that "[a]ge-adjusted COVID-19 mortality rates for Black people [were] 2.8 times higher than White people."[15] The editorial argued that "structural racism and its manifestations including mortgage redlining, employment discrimination, healthcare provider bias, etc., the politicization of COVID-19, and poor access to testing facilities" put Black people at higher risk for the virus.[16] Sandra P. Thomas affirms the editorial's position, noting in *Issues in Mental Health Nursing* that "[m]any Black families were deprived by systemic racism from safe housing that would have allowed physical distancing and other protect strategies" and that racism "had also consigned many Blacks to jobs of high public contact (driving buses, delivering packages, collecting garbage) that elevated their risk of succumbing to the coronavirus."[17] And yet, as Thomas underlines, "Blacks in America are more likely than Hispanics, Asians, or Whites to express concern about the post-pandemic future . . . perhaps because they are also mourning Black deaths perpetrated by racist police throughout the pandemic year."[18] More so, the stigma associated with mental illness "within the Black community" does "present a substantial obstacle to seeking professional help."[19] *Project X* elucidates this stigma and offers an insight into some of the environmental and relational factors that exacerbate the mental health challenges of Black people during the pandemic. This theater project consists of eight distinct but connected performances of Black experience in the United States in the time of COVID-19. Written as choreopoems, these performances include: "Shake It Off," "The Riddle Game: Black History Lesson," "The Inconvenient Talk," "911-Happy Karen," "Black Girl Nurtures," "Ritual Benediction," "I Won't Write My Obituary" (figure 10), and "Strength of Silence."[20]

Specifically, "The Inconvenient Talk" spotlights and interrogates a conversation many Black parents have with their teenagers about race, inequities, and tacit statutes of dealing with the police, white privilege, and societal norms, with a view to protecting their children. The talk takes several forms in the Black com-

FIGURE 10. Obuchi Adikema performing "I Won't Write My Obituary." Photo credit: S. Benjamin Farrar; artist credit: Damon Davis.

PERFORMING BLACK LIVES   187

munity, and its content may vary based on the times, but essentially it represents how parents prepare their children, especially Black boys, for a society in which racism persists and in which they may someday be judged by the color of their skin rather than by the content of their character. It is a heartbreaking but necessary initiation into the world wherein parents, who for so long have sheltered their children, fear what might befall them once they step out of the house as teens. Hence, to avoid setting them up for a rude awakening, Black parents give their children what has been simply called in the Black community "the talk." What follows is an excerpt from "The Inconvenient Talk," showing a Black mother giving "the talk" to her son:

Mama's begotten child
In whom I am well pleased,
Avoid police skirmishes
   like herpes—
Easy to attract, hard to
   banish.

Remember, today and
   always,
To some people, close or
   afar,
You're but a Black boy.
A Black boy you are!
You can never scrape the
   black crust
From your body, Black son.

Do not think me pessimistic
Because I tell the truth
   unfiltered.
I, too, like you, once full of
   optimism
Believed we had seen the
   last
Of Jim Crow and his
   supremacist sharks
When that audacious Black
   prince
Became the 44th custodian
   of this prison.

But, son, I was wrong!
They're still with us, cons among
   humankind.
They're still with us, so unkind,
Craving for the salt in our tears.

If you want to see mama again
When you're in your car, a harmless
   Black boy,
And a blue badge pulls you over, you
   know the type,
Turn off the ignition,
Roll down all windows, even during
   fuming snowfall,
Rest your hands on the steering
   wheel
Or on the dashboard,
Hands visible, face armed with smile,
Even if plastic like an overworked
   flight attendant's.
Tell him where you put your license,
   insurance, registration.
Don't reach for them
Until you get his permission.
If you can, only if you can,
Memorize his badge number
Or his car's license plate
And remain calm
Even if it's hard,
And remain vigilant—

This you must do,
And smile,
And smile even when it
   hurts.

If you must wear your
   hoodie
While you stroll downtown,
Pull your hood down—
Black, white, transparent—it
   doesn't matter.
Just pull it down!
If a siren stops you,
Put your hands up,
Plead: "don't shoot, sir"
Don't forget to add "sir"
Stretch it, hard and long.
It could be the difference
   between
Arrest and rest in peace—
Too many lost sons on the
   nightly news.

Don't try to be a hero, son!
Too many litter our cem-
   eteries already!
Don't play the victim either,
   blue always trumps black,
Blue is always white, always
   right.
Only the might of your
   silence
Or the testimony of your
   phone's camera
Can acquit you
Or at least give me a chance
To hold you in my arms
   again,
Your blood not cold, but
   warm,
Heart beating, not still.

Never reach for your pocket
To fetch your phone
Or even your ID Card
Unless he asks for it.
Remain calm, a lamb!
Remember the magic word "sir"
It's a balm for every sprained ego.
Replying with "sir," you make him
   feel in charge,
With "sir," you also put him on a leash.

Son,
If you've done all I've told you
And "hands up, don't shoot, sir" still
   fails to matter,
Don't think mama lied to you.
Sometimes, even with hands raised,
   grazing the sky,
Black boys still drop
To the ground from the bullets
Of trigger-happy fingers
Who perceive them as a problem
Even before their birth.

Once out of our house, Black son,
You're a moving target for misguided
   hate.
Wherever you head,
You're already in the wrong
   direction—
Sirens lying in wait, waiting to be
   called on you,
Folks lying between white teeth to
   put you in orange suit.
Sometimes I wish you could fly out of
   your skin,
Kaleidoscope of haunting memoirs!
Too bad you're stuck in this choking
   date with melanin—
A blind date your father and I
   imposed on you . . .

Do not think me pessimistic, son,
Because I tell the truth
  unfiltered.
I, too, like you, once full of
  optimism
	Believed we had seen the last
	Of Black boys living life on their
	  knees—
	Silhouettes of lost black sons
	On the nightly news—
	Son, I was wrong![21]

Contrary to instilling fear in Black children or instigating hate within them for the other, the talk aims to build up self-confidence within them, nurturing in them a sense of pride for themselves, their history, and their culture. It also introduces them to the idea that there exist people in society that might perceive them as threats or treat them differently based on their looks. This rather sad introduction is germane because, as Brandi W. Catanese maintains in *The Problem of the Color[blind]: Racial Transgression and the Politics of Black Performance*, "[i]n the theater and in everyday life, knowing how and agreeing to perform your racial role correctly is often a guarantor of personal safety, financial reward, interpersonal respect, and even affection."[22] Rather than raise naïve children, Black parents employ the talk to expose them to the harsh realities of a society in which race matters and racism persists, as demonstrated in the deaths of Black children such as Tamir Rice and Trayvon Martin. In "The Inconvenient Talk," I demonstrate how the talk might be given, especially as it concerns finding the middle ground. In the piece, I suggest that the talk be given such that it does not breed mistrust of other races or law enforcement and discourage interracial interactions or police relations. If anything, as Faedra Chatard Carpenter emphasizes about the work of Black artists in *Coloring Whiteness: Acts of Critique in Black Performance*, "The Inconvenient Talk" seeks to "use whiteness, in both expected and unexpected ways, to complicate readings of both self and other," and by so doing, "evoke a conversation, one that interrogates—rather than simply affirms—the way we interpret and value identity through visual and aural representations."[23] The importance of the police to law and order in society cannot be overestimated; hence, the talk needs to be given in such a way that instills in Black children respect for the police, while also conscientizing the children to be vigilant in their relationships with the police. On the one hand, the talk promotes respect for law enforcement; on the other hand, it advocates caution and de-escalation.

In "911-Happy Karen," I draw attention to the idea that racism is more about a system of privilege than about emotion or skin color. The piece examines whiteness as a privilege many white people take for granted, perhaps because it constitutes a regular part of their lives, regardless of their gender, religion, educational level, or economic status. The white woman who called the police on a Black man

190 ELAIGWU P. AMEH

who was bird watching in Central Park, New York embodies the Karen mentality.[24] His first "offence" was asking her to leash her dog in compliance with park guidelines. His second was that he was Black—a Black man to be precise. The incident, in which the woman, Amy Cooper, exploited her whiteness to summon the police against the African American man, Christian Cooper, who was only asking her to comply with the law demonstrates at once the vulnerability of the Black body in the face of law enforcement and the audacity of white privilege even during the contravention of the law by a white person. It also reveals how racism feeds on two systems: one that grants innocence to some people until they are proven guilty and another that denies the presumption of innocence to some others until they prove otherwise: hence the need for many Black people to resort to using their phones to document racist incidents. Karens such as Amy Cooper leverage both their societal power as white women and the numerous tragic encounters between the police and Black men to achieve their hideous intentions. Here is an excerpt from "911-Happy Karen":

911-happy Karen,
Woke but still asleep,
Eyes wide open but still shut
To the world around you,
To the era in which you live,
Feeling as if God gave you
   the whole world,
You, her majesty the queen
Of privilege.

Dial-happy daughter of
   entitlement,
R-i-n-g, r-i-n-g, r-i-n-g,
Nine One One
At the sight of a darker
   person
Birdwatching while you
   walk your dog,
Selling bottled water while
   you walk,
Causing no harm, just
   having the audacity to
   live.
R-i-n-g, r-i-n-g, r-i-n-g,

Nine One One—
Sirens blare in the distance,
Shrinking what's left of Black
   people's ego
After being bent over
And drained for centuries.

911-happy Karen,
Woke but still asleep,
Ears wide open but still shut—
Tone deaf,
Busybody ref,
Unfiltered tongue—
It mustn't always be about you,
Brittle glass of feelings,
Delicate yet cuts so deeply,
Repressed volcano of bigotry
Bursting open, spewing molten
   magma of hate
On the burdened back of black
   innocence.

Haven't we suffered enough?
Haven't we?[25]

The spoken-word piece also responds to Karens' profound fear of the label "racist," a fear palpable among many white people. This fear does not consider the trauma that a 911 call—or even the threat of such calls—engenders in Black people. The piece reads (figure 11):

You're woke but still asleep,
Mouth wide open but to truth shut!
Ride on! Dial 911!
I too got a phone,
A phone with a video camera—
A Black man's priceless armor
In the concentration camp of bleached privilege . . .

My phone's out,
Your smart mouth now turns into a math genius,
Flipping truth like reciprocals,
Spewing white lies with a straight face,
Giving shame a bad name
Under the scrutiny of live streaming.

Before you play the victim
Or say you didn't mean to threaten me
Or count how many Black friends you have
Or say 'I'm sorry,' the magic words that vanish all iniquities,
Know that life's bigger than your feelings—
Life's not always about you![26]

Whether Karens accept to be identified as racists is inconsequential to the consequences of their actions on Black people—consequences that may include

FIGURE 11. Elijah Griffin performing "911-Happy Karen." Photo credit: S. Benjamin Farrar.

FIGURE 12. Daja Nagra performing "Black Girl Nurtures." Photo credit: S. Benjamin Farrar.

incarceration, anxiety disorder, and even loss of lives. Rather than fret over being caught on camera doing racist things, Karens should undergo critical introspection, accept the shame that comes with being racist, hold themselves accountable, apologize for their actions and, most importantly, desist from doing such again.

In "Black Girl Nurtures," *Project X* recognizes the unappreciated contribution of Black girls and women to the Black family and community (figure 12), describing the Black girl/woman as:

> The burst of light that shames the night,
> The soft glance that quietens the thunder,
> The radiant splendor that dwarfs the diamond,
> The gracious neck that steadies the head,
> The stroke that heals a sickly soul,
> The heart that has no borders . . . [27]

The piece then extols the nurturing spirit of Black girls and women, while simultaneously urging them to:

> Learn to love yourself too
> Again
> And again
> Slow down, pump the breaks sometimes
> On the draining mission to save

> Everyone
> But yourself[28]

Because, after all, they are not:

> A trash bag for everyone's blunders,
> An ashtray for everyone's incinerated hopes,
> A dumpster beneath the dying star,
> Or an unpaid staircase for everyone's wishes.[29]

And they are certainly not:

> An endnote in a novel,
> A baby mama for baby adults—
> Supreme nurturer for all
> Until [they] fall
> Six feet below
> Under the weight of nonstop caring.[30]

In "Ritual Benediction," I present a series of prayers for different groups of Black people, including enslaved Black ancestors, Black people who died during the civil wars, and those who lost their lives during the civil rights/Black power era. The piece also comprises prayers both for victims of police brutality and for the living and the dead in the time of COVID-19 (figure 13). I present only the last two prayers below. The first is a prayer for victims of police brutality:

FIGURE 13. Daja Nagra saying a ritual prayer during the performance of *Project X*. Photo credit: S. Benjamin Farrar.

Great One,
The gentle giant that
inspires self-confidence,
The eye that never blinks,
The ear that understands
every language,
The tongue that secretes no
lies,
Visit us and bring us luck
and joy
In our encounter with the
men in blue.
Watch our steps, protect us!
Hear our cries, defend us!
When words fail us, speak
out for us!

When our breath falters, breathe life
into us!

Help our friends in blue understand
That you created us all
Equally, out of love.
Help us understand that
Before the skin and the badge
You made us all.
But when this understanding fails,
Great One,
Warn us of any danger ahead,
Especially whenever we step out,
And guide us away from its path.
This we pray.
It is well.[31]

The second prayer is for the living and the dead in the time of COVID-19:

Great One,
The protector of the
helpless,
The provider for the
hungry,
The healer of the sick,
The comforter of the
bereaved,

You breathed life into us.
Do not abandon us
As this monster of a virus

Rages, everywhere, every
second!
Save us from its fatal sting!

For those already muted,
Grant them infinite rest in your
abode,
And wipe away the tears
Of loved ones left
behind.
This we pray.
It is well.[32]

Unpacking the Process

The peak of COVID-19 transmission provided opportunities for imagining alternatives to traditional performance forms. Productions no longer must be limited by single sites or even the same time zone, and both actors and audiences must not be in the same location. Audiences also had the option of watching prerecorded shows, just as producers had the choice of streaming their shows live or doing hybrid performances that incorporated both live and prerecorded pieces. In the production of *Project X*, we had to decide whether all the show would be performed live, whether some parts would be prerecorded, or whether everything would be prerecorded. Each modality had its own merits and demerits. We had wanted the hybrid route, with the prayer piece "Ritual Benediction" done live. The plan was to urge the audience to switch off the lights in their homes, light their candles, and join us in reciting a series of prayers. In the end, we settled for the prerecorded format and did not involve the audience as originally planned. For our streaming service, we chose YouTube.

Producing theater at the height of the pandemic required that we unlearn our traditional ways of doing theater and learn new ways, including how to rehearse and perform when the director and actors are not in the same room. In addition to grappling with isolation, internet connectivity, time lags, schedule conflicts, mental health, and family dynamics, we had to ascertain what devices were available to our actors, whether their skills were sufficient to execute the task ahead (at least for the rehearsal stage), and whether we needed to ship professional cameras to them. In cases where we shipped professional cameras and tripods, our stage manager, Anjali Jain, had to set up tech runs for our actors with our tech team, who showed them how to use the equipment for optimal results. Since not every member of our ensemble was on campus, with some living in other states, scheduling became a huge issue. Although every member of the ensemble was living in the United States, not everybody was in Iowa, the location of the college. We had to factor time zones into our scheduling. Shipping equipment to members of our ensemble residing in other states became necessary too. What equipment to send and how soon to send it to our ensemble members to get them to do their part became highly important to the production team.

The decision to produce the mainstage during the pandemic was not at all easy. From the outset, we faced multiple challenges. From enrollment shortfalls to mental health concerns to principal players withdrawing from the production for personal reasons within a few days of opening night, the production was a test not only in the dynamism of performance, but in life generally. It taught us patience, resilience, and gratitude, among many other life lessons. We learned to expect the unexpected, even after doing everything within our power right. We learned to be steadfast in our conviction even in the face of unimpeachable adversity. To be a performance artist, we learned, was not about perfection, but about accepting our humanity, especially our vulnerability and finitude, and about being ready to adapt to unfolding realities on our journey toward our set goals. Ultimately, we learned to live wholesomely, taking care of our mental health and holistic wellness. We turned the unpredictability and adversity that the virtual production process thrust our way into a teaching moment for ourselves as artists and people working within higher education. When we did the first read-through of the script for the performance, I saw excitement etched into the cheeks of every student in the ensemble. The room beamed with enthusiasm and a sense of pride. But, once the tolls of the virtual rehearsals, mounting due dates, and pandemic-related stressors kicked in as we progressed in the production process, the enthusiasm waned, periodically metamorphosing into anxiety. In addition to doing schoolwork, learning their lines, embodying directorial notes, and checking on family members impacted by COVID-19, students had to learn to multitask in the production process.

In our pandemic-constrained production, we asked actors to be more than just actors. We asked them to be dramaturgs, choreographers, videographers, designers, timekeepers, and activists in their own individual performance spaces. We asked them, at different points in the production, to take on roles not traditionally assigned to actors. What we asked them to do was to surmount obstacles, each in their own way and location. Without conceiving it as such at the time of the production, we were asking student performers to live out the creation of great theater, for great theater rests on obstacles, what we make of them, and what they make of us. Our solidarity and collective sense of purpose kept us grounded throughout the process, allaying our anxiety. The idea that we were part of what was bigger than us gave us renewed strength and deepened our relationship to the project and with one another. Each piece in the performance told a story we were all too familiar with, stories that had defined the Black community in the United States for generations and were only aggravated by the pandemic. These were stories that were worth telling and, by telling them, we were doing our own part, at least, in shining the spotlight on a cancer that had debilitated our society for too long—the cancer of racism and racial inequities that continues to afflict us today.

With *Project X*, the theater department's focus was not just on the content of the performance but on the new skills we wanted students to learn. That meant keeping theater alive amid shutdowns and reinventing our ways of creating theater. It involved introducing some students to the use of green screens in the production process. Rehearsals no longer took place in a traditional theater space but in their rooms. Every object in their rooms became a potential prop for their performance. Where to hang the green screen, for instance, and the height and width of the screen, as well as the movement to be made in front of the screens became a factor in the rehearsal process. Flexibility and adaptation became our refrain throughout the process. When I was writing the opening scene, "Shake It Off," I had planned for all the cast to be in the same location and perform a choreographed dance together. We soon discarded that idea after assembling our cast. Some were in Grinnell and others were out of state. We explored having each of the students dance on their own and then have our tech team synchronize the dance using technology. Eventually, we decided to have each student craft and perform their own dance in their respective rooms while playing an Afro dance track specifically recorded by Jerry Alex, a Nigerian music producer, for the performance. Even though actors were to dance freely to the music, they could not wander all over their rooms while dancing. They had to dance in front of the green screen and try not to wander away from the screen. During tech sessions, the show's guest designer and our in-house tech team guided the cast to pay attention to the width and height of the screen and make a mental note of how high and low, or how far right or far left they could go to remain within frame. During rehearsals, we no longer needed to ask students to silence their phones or turn them off; phones had become integral to the production process. Some students used their phones to connect through Webex/Zoom for rehearsals, just as they also used them for recording the first iterations of their performances and sending them to the technical team, who went through the raw files, made suggestions, and readied the students for the final recording session with professional cameras sent to them from the department. Students had varying degrees of technical competence with the equipment, but we worked with every one of them, meeting them at their skill level.

Reflecting on the Project

No doubt, the health pandemic crippled myriad performances across the globe, but it also presented unique opportunities for reinvention and dynamism in performance creation, production, spectatorship, and scholarship. From New York to London, Kolkata to Lagos, performance venues suffered closures, immobilizing the livelihoods of many directors, actors, designers, stage managers, and box office staff. Yet, simultaneously, the pandemic sparked a range of novelties in the production and diffusion of performance. From Broadway to higher institutions, community squares to bare-bones streets, performance artists and scholars explored various ways of engaging with their publics and counter publics across different spatial, temporal, and cultural encumbrances. At the heart of this exploration was the race to acquire appropriate digital technology for one's performance. After the acquisition came the need to learn how to use them to realize an artist's creative vision.

In the production of *Project X*, we used digital technology such as Webex, Zoom, Teams, and YouTube not just to tell our story but to empower our actors and spectators. For instance, spectators who traditionally had to stay within the four walls of the theater to experience a performance could now remain in the confines of their homes and watch it. They could stream it on multiple devices, including television, laptop, and mobile phone. They also had the option of pausing prerecorded performances and watching them at their own pace, rewinding and fast-forwarding them, as they deemed fit. College students, especially those from other countries, whose families rarely could watch them perform on stage pre-COVID-19 had their families watching them, from afar, with only a click of a link, without worrying about visas, flight tickets, or hotel reservations.

However, the pandemic's peak also worsened existing inequities in society. It aggravated generations of systemic injustices against historically marginalized populations, especially Black people. Despite the trauma of the pandemic, police brutality and racism against Black bodies persisted. Through *Project X*, we sought to leverage Black corporeality and Black performance to center overlooked injustices against Black people, with a view to spurring enduring conversations and transformations about race, equity, and solidarity in society.

Our show did not recreate the performance of Williams' death, but it underscored the existential anxiety he shared with other Black people living in the United States. This anxiety continues to grow daily in Black communities amid what appears to be an unchecked indifference to Black deaths in the country. In the case of Williams, law enforcement authorities arrested four white Grinnell residents—Steven Vogel, Julia Cox, Roy Lee Garner, and Cody Johnson—and charged them in his violent death.[33] On December 13, 2021, Vogel was found guilty of first-degree murder and abuse of a corpse and was sentenced to life in prison without the possibility of parole.[34] Prosecutors revealed that Vogel admitted to witnesses that he killed Williams out of jealousy stemming from a "love triangle" between Williams, Vogel, and Vogel's girlfriend.[35] Even though investigators stated that there was no evidence to conclude that the brutal killing was racially motivated, the deceased's family members insisted that it was a hate crime and that it bore the characteristics of a lynching. "If this isn't a lynching, then what is it?" underlined the victim's father, James Williams.[36] His outcry echoes that of many Black parents whose unarmed children have lost their lives to the pandemic of racism and who—instead of receiving empathy—are retraumatized as certain groups or individuals labor painstakingly to disentangle racism from the cause of their children's deaths. It is almost as if hearing the words "it wasn't about race" or "there's no evidence the death was racially motivated" is more rewarding to some people than empathizing with the families of Black victims of white brutality.

Not long after the news broke about the death of Williams, the Grinnell Police Department's chief, Dennis Reilly, wrote to the college community and informed us that he was "keenly aware of the national conversation taking place regarding acts of violence against Black Americans," and added that there was no "continuing threat" to the Grinnell community.[37] To his statement, a BIPOC

PERFORMING BLACK LIVES   199

Instagram account at the college, @gcbipoc, responded: "Chief Reilly's statement is what indifference to Black death looks like. And that is disgusting. . . . Michael Williams deserves real justice, and Black Grinnellians need protection."[38]

As I, an artist of color living through these twin pandemics, reflected on the death of Williams, the trauma it caused within the Black community at the college, and the converging health and racial pandemics, one thing was clear: I could not afford to do a performance about this period without centering how disproportionately the pandemic has impacted Black communities, including the fact that, despite the trauma of the pandemic, police brutality and racism against Black bodies persist. The violent death of Williams, especially the spectacle that the hanging, showing off, and burning created, was a jolting reminder for me.

Nevertheless, performing Black lives during the COVID-19 pandemic draws attention to the constant need to build community across racial lines and intentionally work toward empathy, equity, and healing. It redirects our gaze onto Black lives not as objects of pity or helpless victims of white supremacy but as human beings, with flesh and blood, friends and families, and hopes and dreams like everyone else in society. In its illumination of the deprecation and disappearance of Black bodies, it draws attention to the collective trauma of the Black community, while demanding that we reexamine our priorities and shared values as members of society and the human community. In other words, *Project X* leverages the Black experience in the United States to call for a profound personal and social reflection on the state of our union and the values we hold sacred.

NOTES

1. Iowa Department of Public Safety, "Criminal Charges."
2. Iowa Department of Public Safety, "Criminal Charges," and Dress, "Iowa Man Convicted."
3. United States Census Bureau, "Quick Facts, Grinnell City, Iowa."
4. Institute of Education Sciences, "IPEDS Data."
5. Harris and Rivera, "Classes Cancelled."
6. Harris and Rivera, "Classes Cancelled."
7. Young and Hughes, "Reaffirmation of Life," 84.
8. Batiste, "Introduction," 1.
9. Langley, "'Project X' Makes History."
10. Langley, "'Project X' Makes History."
11. Langley, "'Project X' Makes History."
12. Langley, "'Project X' Makes History."
13. Spry, *Body, Paper, Stage,* 19.
14. Czeisler et al., "Mental Health," 1049–57; Katlyn Nemani et al., "Association of Psychiatric Disorders," 380–86; and Wang, Xu, and Volkow, "Increased Risk of COVID-19," 124–30.
15. Josiah et al., "Intersection," 36.
16. Josiah, "Intersection," 36.

200 ELAIGWU P. AMEH

17. Thomas, "Black Mental Health Matters," 707.
18. Thomas, "Black Mental Health," 707.
19. Thomas, "Black Mental Health,"708.
20. Ameh, "Project X" (unpublished manuscript, July 31, 2022), typescript.
21. Ameh, "Project X."
22. Catanese, *Problem of the Color[blind]*, 19.
23. Carpenter, *Coloring Whiteness*, 237.
24. Vera and Ly, "White Woman Who Called Police."
25. Ameh, "Project X."
26. Ameh, "Project X."
27. Ameh, "Project X."
28. Ameh, "Project X."
29. Ameh, "Project X."
30. Ameh, "Project X."
31. Ameh, "Project X."
32. Ameh, "Project X."
33. Almasy and Hughes, "Four Arrested."
34. Joens, "Iowa Man Sentenced to Life."
35. Dress, "Iowa Man Convicted."
36. Dress, "Iowa Man Convicted."
37. Hill, "Breaking."
38. Hill, "Breaking."

BIBLIOGRAPHY

Almasy, Steve, and Mallory Hughes. "Four Arrested After Black Man's Body Found Burning in A Ditch in Iowa." *CNN*. September 23, 2020. Accessed July 31, 2022. https://www.cnn.com/2020/09/22/us/man-found-dead-iowa-ditch-trnd/index.html.

Ameh, Elaigwu. "Project X." Unpublished manuscript, July 31, 2022.

Batiste, Stephanie Leigh. "Introduction: Black Performance II: Knowing and Being." *The Black Scholar* 49, no. 4, (2019): 1–5.

Carpenter, Faedra Chatard. *Coloring Whiteness: Acts of Critique in Black Performance*. Ann Arbor: University of Michigan Press, 2014.

Catanese, Brandi W. *The Problem of the Color[blind]: Racial Transgression and the Politics of Black Performance*. Ann Arbor: University of Michigan Press, 2011.

Czeisler, Mark É., Rashon I. Lane, Emiko Petrosky, Joshua F. Wiley, Aleta Christensen, Rashid Njai, Mathew D. Weaver, et al. "Mental Health, Substance Use, and Suicidal Ideation During the COVID-19 Pandemic—United States, June 24–30, 2020." *Morbidity Mortality Weekly Report* 69, no. 32 (2020):1049–57. http://dx.doi.org/10.15585/mmwr.mm6932a1external icon.

Dress, Brad. "Iowa Man Convicted of Murdering Black Man Whose Body Was Found Burning in Ditch." *The Hill*, November 17, 2021.

Feldshuh, David. *Miss Evers' Boys*. New York: Dramatists Play Service, 1998.

Harris, Anne, and Schvalla Rivera. "Classes Cancelled on Monday, Sept. 21." Grinnell College. Accessed July 31, 2022. https://www.grinnell.edu/messages/classes-canceled-sept-21.

Hill, Eva. "Breaking: Classes Cancelled Monday, Sept. 21 in Wake of Michael Williams' Killing." *The Scarlet and Black*. Accessed July 31, 2022. http://www.thesandb.com/article/breaking-classes-canceled-monday-sept-21-in-wake-of-michael-williams-death.html?print=print.

Institute of Education Sciences. "IPEDS Data Feedback Report 2021." Accessed July 31, 2022. https://nces.ed.gov/ipeds/dfr/2021/ReportHTML.aspx?unitId=153384.

Iowa Department of Public Safety. "Criminal Charges Announced in Grinnell's Michael Williams Homicide Investigation." Accessed July 31, 2022. https://dps.iowa.gov/criminal-charges-announced-grinnells-michael-williams-homicide-investigation.

Joens, Philip. "Iowa Man Sentenced to Life in Prison for Killing Grinnell Man Whose Body Was Found Burning." *Des Moines Register*, December 15, 2021. https://www.desmoinesregister.com/story/news/crime-and-courts/2021/12/15/iowa-man-sentenced-life-prison-2020-slaying-michael-williams/6493635001/.

Josiah, Nia, Shaquita Starks, Patty R. Wilson, Tamar Rodney, Joyell Arscott, Yvonne Commodore-Mensah, Ruth-Alma Turkson-Ocran, Kynadi Mauney, Oluwabunmi Ogungbe, Janelle Akomah, and Diana-Lyn Baptiste. "The Intersection of Depression, Anxiety, and Cardiovascular Diseases Among Black Populations Amid the COVID-19 Pandemic." *Journal of Clinical Nursing* 30 (2021): 36–40. https://doi.org/10.1111/jocn.15632.

Langley, Nadia. "'Project X' Makes History at Grinnell College." *The Scarlet and Black*, March 18, 2021. http://www.thesandb.com/article/project-x-makes-history-at-grinnell-college.html.

Nemani, Katlyn, Chenxiang Li, Mark Olfson, Esther M. Blessing, Narges Razavian, Ji Chen, Eva Petkova, and Donald C. Goff. "Association of Psychiatric Disorders with Mortality Among Patients with COVID-19." *JAMA Psychiatry* 78, no. 4 (2021): 380–86. http://dx.doi.org/10.1001/jamapsychiatry.2020.4442.

Spry, Tami. *Body, Paper, Stage: Writing and Performing Autoethnography*. New York: Routledge, 2016.

Thomas, Sandra P. "Black Mental Health Matters: Addressing Post-COVID Mental Health Needs of Black Americans." *Issues in Mental Health Nursing* 42, no. 8 (2021): 707–8. https://doi.org/10.1080/01612840.2021.1952017.

United States Census Bureau. "Quick Facts, Grinnell City, Iowa." Accessed June 13, 2022. https://www.census.gov/quickfacts/fact/table/grinnellcityiowa/PST040221.

Vera, Amir, and Laura Ly. "White Woman Who Called Police on a Black Man Birdwatching in Central Park Has Been Fired." *CNN*. May 26, 2020. https://www.cnn.com/2020/05/26/us/central-park-video-dog-video-african-american-trnd/index.html.

Wang, QuanQiu, Rong Xu, and Nora D. Volkow. "Increased Risk of COVID-19 Infection and Mortality in People with Mental Disorders: Analysis from Electronic Health Records in the United States," *World Psychiatry* 20 (2021): 124–30. https://doi.org/10.1002/wps.20806.

Young, Harvey, and Bethany Hughes. "Reaffirmation of Life: Dramatic Theory and Race." *Journal of Dramatic Theory and Criticism* 32, no. 2 (2018): 79–87. Project MUSE.

Part 3

LOSSES AND DISAPPOINTMENTS

10

COMMUNITY ENGAGED MIGRATION RESEARCH

Robert McKee Irwin and Juan Antonio Del Monte

The COVID-19 pandemic has presented unprecedented challenges for the practice of community engaged scholarship, especially with regard to projects aimed at collaborating with vulnerable groups such as migrants. Fundamental public health protocols such as sheltering in place and social distancing indeed present major obstacles to realizing the direct and personalized contact that the concept of engagement generally implies. These obstacles may be more pronounced with vulnerable migrants who are less likely to stay for very long in one place or to have regular internet access and therefore may be difficult to locate or to reach through distanced means. At the same time, the already precarious living conditions of migrants in cities with historically large migrant flows, such as Tijuana, are likely to become even more so in the context of a pandemic, when the delivery of all kinds of cross-border or even local aid is impeded by public health restrictions. Meanwhile, potential migrants themselves weigh a range of threats to their well-being, of which COVID-19 is one of many, in deciding whether to leave their homelands; even as borders officially shut down, migration continues unabated.

We believe that a pandemic is not a time to institute inflexible institutional policies that leave no option but to abandon community engagement but rather one that calls for the development of new strategies to facilitate partnerships with members of vulnerable groups that guarantee their health and promote their welfare. Here we review some of the special difficulties that the pandemic has presented for migrants in Tijuana during its first two years, our attempts to document them, the challenges we have faced in our improvised endeavors in community engaged scholarship during the pandemic, and some of the positive outcomes we have nonetheless obtained.

Community Engagement in Times of COVID-19

We have been working, separately and in collaboration, for numerous years in Tijuana on several different community-based projects with migrants. Del Monte is co-director of the documentary film *Bad Hombres*, filmed mainly in a camp of deported migrants in Tijuana's Matadero Canyon. Irwin has, since 2016, co-ordinated the Humanizing Deportation/Humanizando la Deportación digital storytelling project,[1] in which Del Monte has been a participant. Both projects involve close interactions with migrants, whom we treat not as research subjects but as experts on the human consequences of contemporary migration control regimes, knowledge producers whose stories we help to disseminate. In addition to facilitating the production of nearly 150 audiovisual testimonial narratives of migrants in Tijuana (over three hundred in multiple sites across Mexico and California), the Humanizing Deportation project has also engaged in multiple outreach events in the city, often in collaboration with community organizations such as Dreamers Moms International and the Border Line Crisis Center.[2] We have also participated in projects that foster engagement of university students in Tijuana, including a separate digital storytelling project documenting the contributions of migrants rights defenders coordinated by the legal advocacy group Alma Migrante, with participation of undergraduate students from the Universidad Autónoma de Baja California and the University of San Diego.[3] In early 2020 each had plans to continue community engagement in Tijuana through digital storytelling and outreach projects with students.

We were alarmed by the onset of the COVID-19 pandemic, both the implications of the disease and the measures being implemented to contain it on vulnerable migrant populations in Tijuana, including migrants in transit from Central America and elsewhere and Mexicans arriving from the United States. The former included (1) migrants whose asylum applications to the United States were already being processed under the Migrant Protection Protocols program and whose case reviews were suspended from late March 2020 through late February 2021 and (2) newly arrived migrants who reached Tijuana to find a border that was closed to all but essential crossings in March 2020. The same border remains closed to most asylum seekers over two years later. Meanwhile, deported Mexicans continued to arrive in Tijuana. The United States did not suspend deportations during the pandemic, even when evidence surfaced of COVID-19 outbreaks at the immigrant detention facilities from which migrants were being deported.[4] In addition, both Mexican and Central American migrants, including asylum seekers, caught by Customs and Border Protection officers crossing into the United States without documents have been subject, since March 2020, to immediate expulsions, with tens of thousands arriving in Tijuana over the course of the pandemic.[5]

These expulsions have been carried out under the invocation of section 265 of Title 42 of the US Code, a World War II era health regulation that was never intended to prevent admission to the country. In March 2020 it was implemented by the Donald Trump administration to expeditiously remove unauthorized border crossers including asylum seekers. This measure, put into effect by the Centers for Disease Control, purports to protect public health from the arrival of large numbers of potentially infected migrants. However, critics have argued that Title 42 has, particularly with the widespread availability of vaccines over the course of the pandemic's second year, served less to safeguard public health than to radically obstruct access to the US asylum system.[6] Inconsistent application of the policy further buttresses this argument. For example, in April 2022 Tijuana witnessed the rapid processing of almost fifteen thousand asylum requests from Ukrainian citizens for whom Title 42 was not applied,[7] even as thousands of asylum seekers from places like Central America and Haiti, some waiting two years or more at the border, continued to be turned away. Unfortunately, even as the Biden administration has sought to relax the order, it remains in effect due to an April 2022 federal court ruling blocking its revocation.

Large portions of migrants from both groups (those moving toward the north, and those being expelled from the north) rely heavily on migrant services organizations, including those offering food, shelter, logistical orientation, and legal advice, among others. These institutions were impacted by the measures introduced to control the pandemic. The border shutdown of March 2020 kept volunteers and donations from the United States from arriving in Tijuana. Shelters were forced to limit admissions. Food kitchens accustomed to serving a thousand or more meals a day in large dining halls had to recalibrate. Shelter-in-place orders made it difficult for even locals to help out. These are only a few of the complications service providers faced for the first year or more of the pandemic. Meanwhile, migrants continued moving northward unabated, regardless of shutdowns happening around them.[8] We felt a great urgency to both find out how migrants in Tijuana were being impacted by the pandemic and related public health measures and to devise ways to offer help by deploying university resources.[9]

We were accustomed to working directly and closely with migrants and were deeply concerned that we could not be on the ground interacting with migrants, helping directly to identify problems and find solutions. We felt helpless: the

University of California prohibited nearly all international travel, and stay-at-home orders in Tijuana in the spring of 2020 essentially shut the city down even to local residents. Just as instruction moved to remote formats and researchers reformulated or postponed research projects, we had to reconsider our approaches to community engagement, which at first seemed impossible. But the urgency of the presumably dire ramifications of the pandemic for migrants staying or arriving in Tijuana drove us to begin exploring options.

Approaches to Publicly Engaged Scholarship

Diverse terms name research projects developed from a public interest in transforming the living conditions within the contexts of social realities from which these projects emerge.[10] Here we employ the term "engaged scholarship"[11] to imply linking educational and research processes with direct community collaboration. The methods applied under the rubric of engagement aim to reduce the gap between academic research and applied knowledge that can be used to solve problems in the community.

In engaged scholarship there is a demand for reflexivity regarding the place scholars occupy in the world, our place of enunciation, and the responsibilities of transformation that our practice implies as we study the effects of structural inequalities and systems of oppression. A key element of engaged scholarship in the context of migration is the commitment to the idea that migrants carry a firsthand embodied knowledge, a bottom-up and heterogeneous knowledge that is as important as other kinds of knowledge.[12]

This encourages us to think in terms of collaborative and dialogic knowledge that requires making an effort to horizontalize the relationship between researchers and research communities.[13] We have long recognized that we cannot research migrant communities without their participation in the process. Therefore, we have not been interested in seeking answers through academic theories but rather in finding them through dialogue and encounters with migrants.

On the other hand, some scholarly approaches are helpful in understanding the dynamics of migration from the perspectives of migrants, including those that study "mobile commons," that is, knowledge shared and deployed by migrants along travel routes, political mobilizations among migrants, and the "willfulness" of migrants as they assume that migrants are not mere victims, escaping from one system of oppression to another, but rather autonomous agents.[14] These approaches to migrant knowledge are often clustered together under the rubric of "autonomy of migration."[15]

We should emphasize here that our experience and expertise as engaged scholars is in recording and disseminating migrant stories via various forms of audiovisual production. Our research focuses not on traditional methods of ethnography but rather on deeply collaborative methods, in which rather than try to find answers to specific research questions, we offer platforms for migrants to tell their stories, which then becomes material for analysis. While we recognize that any collaborative process is necessarily co-creative in some ways, our chief concern has always been in "story catching," in recording community stories, while minimizing our role in determining or shaping their content.[16] What we most wanted to do was to collect and learn from stories about the experience of migrants in Tijuana during the pandemic.

Experiments in Direct Community Engagement

Remote Digital Storytelling

Irwin looked to use the Humanizing Deportation platform to record some stories of COVID-19-era Tijuana and was hopeful that a digital storytelling component of a project Del Monte was launching through Universidad Iberoamericana and El Colegio de la Frontera Norte would work out. He also thought about attempting to move Humanizing Deportation forward by remote means, even as working remotely is antithetical to the deeply personal collaborative methodology that the project has employed, with our academic facilitators frequently meeting a half dozen or more times face-to-face with community storytellers during the production process.[17] While with some migrants we have been able to shift part of the process to exchanges via messaging applications, most collaborations entail hours of time spent meeting directly with storytellers.

However, for a few cases prior to the pandemic, we adopted a methodology that was entirely remote, working via an agent. This method came about organically when one of our Tijuana-based community storytellers, Esther Morales, suggested that we produce a digital story with a friend of hers who was living in Durango. While normally face-to-face meetings are key in establishing confidence in the project and in our fieldwork teams, in this case the remote storyteller, Ana María Arroyo, came to trust us because of our strong relationship with Morales, with whom we had first worked in 2017 (producing a three-part story, *Guerrera incansable [Tireless Warrior]*), and who recorded a new story with us in 2018: *Estoy en el lado de los Valientes [On the Side of the Brave].*[18] Arroyo worked with team member Ernesto Zarco Ortiz through an entirely remote process in the production of her digital story *Uniendo a través del corazón lo que la deportación separó [Uniting through the Heart That Deportation Separated].*[19] Just before the pandemic hit, again working with Morales as our field agent, Irwin collaborated with Marcia Yadira Durón, producing her story *Deportación, violencia, discriminación en Honduras* entirely via text messaging between Sacramento and Tegucigalpa, respectively.[20]

We decided to try and apply this method more broadly, and it sometimes worked—but it has been hard to accomplish much. One problem is that this method is not comfortable for everyone. Some migrants who were already familiar with Humanizando la Deportación and had previously been in dialogue with Irwin about publishing their stories balked at working remotely. Some were migrants that already knew Irwin well, so the issue was not one of confidence or trust but rather of discomfort with the depersonalized connection via the screen. Four different storytellers who had already expressed strong interest in contributing to the archive dropped out early in the pandemic when it became evident that there would be no face-to-face meetings with team members in the foreseeable future.

Even among those that were not discouraged by remote collaboration protocols, the additional layer of mediation slowed things down considerably. Although during the first eighteen months of the pandemic, we added some forty new digital stories to our archive, the vast majority of them (thirty-two) were begun prior to the onset of the pandemic through our standard face-to-face collaboration method. Only eight involved a completely remote process carried out fully during the pandemic. And of those, three were stories told by collaborators that members of our fieldwork teams already knew well.

The other five were digital stories created by migrants whom none of our team members had met prior to the pandemic, most of whom signed onto the project thanks to the help of agents in the field in Tijuana. Two feature the stories of a Guatemalan migrant named Ludvin that we met through Esther Morales. With the exception of its recording (realized thanks to Morales and another local agent, journalist Sandra Dibble) his story, *Dos separaciones familiars [Two Family Separations]*, was produced entirely through exchanges of text messages. After the initial contact and recording with Morales and Dibble, Irwin managed all communication with Ludvin (in Tijuana) from northern California, while two team members working remotely, Jesús Galán (in Davis, California) and Yunuen Gómez (in Guaymas, Sonora), created the audiovisual montage and edited it.

Two others are stories of Honduran migrants introduced to us by another agent in Tijuana, Jocelín Mariscal, who recorded their audio, took some photos, and filmed some brief video segments with them. Mariscal managed all direct communication with the migrants with remote assistance from Irwin, while

Ernesto Zarco (living in Davis) carried out the production of the videos, which were published as *Cambio de plan: realizando los sueños en México [Change of Plan: Making Dreams Come True in Mexico]* and *Tijuana tiene muchas oportunidades [Tijuana Has Many Opportunities]*.[21] The fifth case was quite exceptional: Carlos Manuel Ramírez, a deported Mexican who discovered our website on his own and was eager to participate. Experienced in audiovisual production, he was able to produce his digital story almost completely by himself, in dialogue with Irwin and Yunuen Gómez.[22]

Regarding the first four cases mentioned previously, under usual working conditions, our audiovisual production teams would also maintain all contact and communication with community storytellers. Under our remote method, we were adding two additional layers of mediation: the roles of community-based agents, and that of Irwin, who stepped in to coordinate production in order to get an idea of the dynamics and complications that may arise with these remote collaborations. Working in this way felt odd to us, but as these migrants had never worked with us before, it is possible that it all may have seemed all right to them—certainly they never complained, nor did they pull out, as they were free to do at any moment. But the process did take a long time. When we work in the field, the production of a digital story might typically take about a month or maybe six weeks from the first introductory meeting to the final edits and publication of a digital story. Ludvin's story took roughly three months to produce, while the stories of the two Hondurans took five. Without a doubt the added layers of mediation, as well as the mainly remote methods of communication, slowed down our process significantly.

In August 2021 travel restrictions had finally loosened enough for several team members to begin working in the field again in Tijuana. Since that time production has taken off. With thousands of migrants stuck waiting at the border for so long, we found that many were anxious to make their experiences known. While we no longer need to use the remote methods we improvised earlier in the pandemic, we continue to draw from the experience, turning to social messaging media with much greater frequency. We realize that certain applications have become the primary communication means for many migrants, who might prefer, even if only for convenience, to follow most of the production process with us remotely.

INSIGHTS INTO THE COVID-19 PANDEMIC THROUGH DIGITAL STORYTELLING

Even though we did manage to keep the project going during the pandemic, we did not have much success in documenting the experience of migration or deportation during the first year of the pandemic.

It is important to understand that among Humanizando la Deportation's community collaboration protocols is a fundamental practice of avoiding, or at the very least minimizing, interventions into the content of the digital stories by members of our teams.[23] While we recognize that any collaborative process of this kind is necessarily co-creative,[24] and that our particular adaptation of digital storytelling fieldwork methods presents power dynamics that we cannot completely overcome,[25] we seek to minimize our team members' inevitable influence in story content through an intensely personal collaborative process.[26] However, one of our guiding principles, reiterated on multiple occasions in our fieldwork training, is that our role is not to mediate but to facilitate the realization of the vision of community storytellers.

Therefore, in the application of this method, scale is important. If we have a very specific question we would like to explore, we have no way of ensuring that migrants who have experiences relevant to that question will opt to talk about them in their five-minute digital story. Therefore, if we have only a few stories, the question may go unanswered. On the other hand, if we have several dozen or several hundred stories, it is much more likely that the archive will contain some robust data, including possibly some that are generalizable.

In the case of COVID-19, our inability to maintain the scale of our production of previous years (an average of close to a hundred digital stories per year over the first three years of the project[27]) worked against us with regard to learning about the effects of the pandemic on migrants. We made the effort to keep production going during the pandemic because we were concerned about conditions for migrants in Tijuana during the pandemic. However, of the digital stories produced during the first eighteen months of the pandemic, only one refers to it at all, Esther Morales's *Comida calientita en plena pandemia [Nice Hot Food in the Midst of the Pandemic]*. Morales was deported to Tijuana over ten years ago and has become well known for her success with La Antigüita, a small restaurant located in downtown Tijuana specializing in tamales. She is no longer the kind of vulnerable migrant that we worried might be living in perilous conditions during the pandemic. Her digital story does shed some light on the city during the early months of the pandemic, when she was forced to close her restaurant and began offering free food and water to homeless migrants. Eventually she ended up teaming up with Al Otro Lado, a legal services organization that has sponsored a program, managed by Morales, to deliver meals to migrant shelters around the city (the endeavor parallel to Del Monte's project described later).

However, the three Central Americans who offered to record their stories through the Humanizing Deportation project during that period told not of the pandemic conditions but of the reasons for leaving their homelands, the difficulties that they face in trying to migrate legally to the United States, and their decisions to settle, whether short or long term, in Tijuana. *Cambio de plan* and *Tijuana tiene muchas oportunidades* focus very specifically on establishing residency in Tijuana, where their authors have found relative safety and prosperity. The former, Ludvin's *Dos separaciones familiares*, tells of a longer migration history, including a deportation from the United States, and his hopes for reuniting with loved ones in the United States, even as he realizes that he cannot legally enter the United States and must make do temporarily with his options in Tijuana. None refer to difficulties in obtaining food, shelter, or medical care and, even as they appear with mouth coverings in some of their stories' visual materials, there is no reference at all to COVID-19.

The lack of attention to the pandemic raises some interesting questions. Many people chose not to travel internationally prior to the widespread availability of COVID-19 vaccines, whether out of fear of infection or as a civic contribution aimed at containing the spread of COVID-19; the University of California went so far as to forbid nearly all research-related travel for the first 18 months of the pandemic.[28] Travel came to be seen as socially irresponsible: "non-essential travel is now associated in some quarters with a degree of social stigma."[29] Any story of long-distance travel during the pandemic among many in our privileged sector would necessarily include discussions about COVID-19 testing, quarantines, strategies for minimizing risks of infection, feelings of apprehension, and, in many cases, justifications or rationalizations to counter criticisms of interlocutors who themselves cancelled trips and believe that it is everyone's duty to do the same. This was clearly not the thought process of many migrants.

Yet without a doubt, the pandemic altered the living conditions of migrants in Tijuana. Unfortunately, due to institutional restrictions on pandemic travel, we were not able to engage in fieldwork in Tijuana or anywhere else for eighteen months. This required that we try to fill in the blanks to document the difficulties faced by migrants, whether those in transit heading to the United States or those being sent from the United States into Mexico. During that critical period our improvised methods did not permit us to collect enough data to draw meaningful conclusions.

Hot Food for Homeless Migrants

Very early in the pandemic Del Monte began strategizing to carry out community engaged research through a university-based project, working with undergraduates from the Universidad Iberoamericana's Tijuana campus and with graduate students from El Colegio de la Frontera Norte, to deliver food to homeless migrants. Unlike the Humanizing Deportation team at UC Davis, for whom travel to Tijuana was forbidden, Del Monte was able to find student volunteers and obtain university support, applying strict protocols designed to protect both project volunteers and community members, for a program designed to meet immediate and urgent needs of some of the city's most precarious residents. Many of the city's homeless, traumatized after being deported from the United States, suffer from mental illness or addiction to alcohol or drugs and depend greatly on charitable organizations for food, clothing, and hygiene products.

As a working team, two things worried us with the onslaught of the pandemic and the imposed restrictions on movement and mandates to shelter in place. The first was that the shelters and community kitchens (some serving more than a thousand meals to homeless and migrants in Tijuana every day) were having difficulty getting supplies and many were closed; the second thing was that these people were unable to shelter in place because they didn't have a place for sheltering according to the healthy protocols: they were homeless.

We came up with the idea of Comida Calientita (Hot Food) in collaboration with local entrepreneur and activist Esther Morales (mentioned previously). Although she was ultimately unable to work with us at that time, that didn't stop us from launching parallel projects with the same inspiration and under the same name and motivations. Our university-based Comida Calientita sought to meet immediate community needs, while at the same time introducing opportunities for academic team members to carry out qualitative research in the community. This latter research was meant to offer insights regarding the impact of the COVID-19 pandemic and the measures taken to control it on this vulnerable group based on the firsthand experience of these populations.

In a pandemic context, it was imperative for us not only to generate a project with the necessary protocols to ensure the health of all the participants but also to ensure a degree of direct contact sufficient to avoid what local communities have called "academic extractivism,"[30] which consists of extracting information in the study of communities without generating any benefits in return. With this approach, we couldn't merely allude to the social responsibility of scientific research. Responsibility in these matters implies not only the methodological consistency between techniques, data, interpretation, and theory, which would be part of scientific responsibility, but also a commitment to the content of what is analyzed and the construction of a research plan that generates concrete forms of social impact.

In this sense, our first goal was to contribute to alleviating hunger as a way to mitigate, albeit modestly, the vulnerability of homeless migrants in Tijuana. Thus, our top priority was food delivery. But the project also sought to make a longer-term impact. This meant learning more about the characteristics and needs of this community in the context of the pandemic by establishing respectful forms of research with the communities in question to ensure that our project team was not merely thinking about the needs of the community but rather was thinking with the community to strategically use this collaborative knowledge construction to influence or effect social change in ways that would be meaningful for the community.

Therefore, from the start social research methods would not determine the path of our program; on the contrary, it was the food assistance project that was going to determine the steps for social research. Thus, we gave centrality to the general objective of the project—to provide food to the deported population living on the street during the pandemic—and prepared to improvise our research from there.

We initially designed a program to conduct research using collaborative visual methods in which community volunteers would collaborate by offering their vision of the situation. Two lines of highly collaborative research were envisioned: first, these collaborators would document community food practices during the pandemic using photoelicitation, a method in which community participants are given digital cameras and asked to take photos from their daily life practices and encounters.[31] From there, we would work with community collaborators to produce digital stories, following the protocols of the Humanizing Deportation project, with the aim of publishing some of these stories and the photos in the Humanizing Deportation public online archive.[32]

Although the research design initially seemed reasonable (even regarding funding), we soon discovered some flaws during its piloting that forced us to modify our research procedures as we continued with the food delivery. The problems were related to the unstable conditions in which this population lives. It was very difficult to follow up with each person because the same people did not attend every time we offered food, nor were many of them able or willing to follow through with the collaboration as we had expected.

Basically, we had distributed fifteen disposable cameras. Of these, few returned to our hands, either because they were lost, stolen, or sold, or simply because we lost contact with community volunteers, none of whom had a stable address, telephone, or other means of contact. The material from the two cameras that were returned has been developed and reviewed with the community members, with whom we remain in contact.

After a couple of weeks, it was very clear that it was impossible to carry out an investigation of this type in these conditions. We really needed to spend more time working directly with the community storytellers and to realize a much more detailed follow-up than we could without risking becoming a vector of exposure to the virus for these populations—or for our team members, including many students.

We therefore decided to recompose the research component of the project, opting to apply a more conventional (and unfortunately less horizontal) method: a questionnaire that could help us to assess the needs of the homeless migrant community during the pandemic. The survey was focused on four main things: to know who the street dwellers are (sociodemographic data), where they come from (migratory experience), how they live (living conditions), and what they eat (food and health conditions). The application of the questionnaire turned out to be much more practical as we could do it while community members were standing in line, from an adequately healthy distance. Thus, we applied more than one hundred questionnaires during our food deliveries.[33]

INSIGHTS INTO THE COVID-19 PANDEMIC
THROUGH COMMUNITY FOOD DELIVERY

Although we could not consolidate the research project linked to photo elicitation and digital stories, we do not think that this was a failed project. On the contrary, we have learned a lot about working on an engaged research project in the midst of a pandemic with migrant and vulnerable populations. One of the first lessons was the importance of prioritizing the community food assistance project as the guiding principle for our work. On the one hand, this allowed us to meet urgent community needs, and on the other hand, it required us to make our proposal methodologically flexible from the beginning. In the end, our survey on the characteristics of the homeless deported community during the pandemic was highly productive.

The food delivery project was a success. It allowed us to deliver directly to the community between 150 and 200 plates of freshly made food by various local chefs during the months of June to December 2020, as well as two portable sinks where community members could wash their hands before eating the food. These were delivered to a highly visible location near the border, in an area in which an estimated seven hundred people were living in the street. Moreover, our Comida Calientita project served as a vehicle for community organizations looking to devise creative and safe ways to assist vulnerable populations in the city. Tijuana Food Bank, Espacio Migrante, Innova Dental, Menstruación Digna, Distribuidora Zamora, and Eraboy were all eager to help, many donating supplies to prepare the meals or providing urgently needed personal hygiene products that were distributed along with the food. In other words, the project became a mechanism that attracted various entities interested in helping these populations but who had not found a way to do so. Since our return to Tijuana, Humanizing Deportation has partnered ever more frequently with Esther Morales, delivering food to migrant shelters and other similar spaces where we have sought to meet migrants to help document experiences on the migrant trail and at the border over the entire pandemic period.

Finally, the results of the survey allowed us to identify areas in urgent need of attention and were useful to propose a series of lines of advocacy and action. These included carrying out a systematic and consistent statistical registry at national and local level on the homeless population; promoting the documentation of homeless people so that they might access government-sponsored programs for vulnerable populations; implementing COVID-19 vaccination campaigns among these populations; supporting civil society organizations dedicated to the food supply of these populations; promoting human rights campaigns among police forces to reduce the inhumane treatment and arbitrary detentions they carry out. We have promoted these recommendations in both written form and in a well-attended public form that we presented via Zoom in March 2021. While noting that precarious situation of homeless life in Tijuana is the product of a sum of disadvantages that are framed in a structure of criminalizing migration policies and deep social inequalities in Mexico, we believe that these actions could begin the process of breaking the precarious situation in which the homeless of Tijuana have been immersed for many years.

Engaged Scholarship and Essential Research

In retrospect, it is interesting to observe that the United States-Mexico border closure of 2020 inhibited the movement of both migrants and academics alike, with both migrants and US-based academics trapped on one side of the border. Humanizing Deportation was seriously disabled and had to catch up and fill in the blanks. It is sad that communities that might benefit from ongoing collaboration and support from engaged scholars, perhaps even more during a pandemic than at other moments, are kept at a distance because of institutional constraints: universities that won't allow their scholars to travel. Certainly, it is understandable that institutions must take responsibility for supporting public health efforts. However, it is a shame that communities with multiple urgent needs are cut off from some engaged scholars who might be able to safely help them in some way but cannot due to the inflexibility of institutionally imposed travel restrictions.

Notably, both Universidad Iberoamericana and El Colegio de la Frontera Norte permitted carefully designed, community-oriented projects as part of their own institutional commitment to the communities in which their faculty and students have established relationships during the pandemic. They allowed and even funded community aid projects carried out by faculty and students to help groups living in heightened precarity during the pandemic. Many scholars, long encouraged by their home institutions to think globally, felt confident in developing programs and platforms for transnational public engagement. We now find our own ethical commitments to community in conflict with institutions that recoiled in fear, essentially withdrawing their commitments to the global, entertaining no discussion for creative ways of safely realizing transnational projects in the face of COVID-19, and essentially assuming a conservative approach that extended travel restrictions for months beyond the time in which they presented an obvious danger, whether to researchers or to communities abroad. Universities that we thought were committed to global engagement are actually distrustful of it.

For us, engaged scholarship is a form of essential academic labor as far as it is designed to identify, comprehend, and perhaps meet urgent needs of vulnerable populations that are not being otherwise adequately addressed. Ultimately, these are scientific efforts that seek to contribute to the improvement of the living conditions of the population under consideration. Here we envision the need to design institutional protocols for engaged scholarship that are feasible in both ethical and public health terms to deal with community commitments in pandemic emergencies such as this one.

We did carry out some interesting remote research regarding the conditions in Tijuana during the pandemic, including research for two reports and two academic articles. One of the latter, based on interviews with migrants carried out by telephone and social media, identified a range of actions that show migrants to be "a willful social force in Tijuana" in the face of the pandemic, manifestations of what has been called "the autonomy of migration."[34] The will of migrants, we observe here, is ultimately much more robust than the institutional will of academia to assist migrants. Sadly, for academia, engaged transnational scholarship is considered nonessential business.

NOTES

1. Humanizando la Deportación. http://humanizandoladeportacion.ucdavis.edu/en/.
2. See "Diffusion Beyond the Web" in Irwin, "Humanizing Deportation Archive."
3. "Soul of a Migrant," https://almamigrante.org/causes/historia-de-defensores/.
4. Miller et al., "Immigration Policy and Justice."
5. See http://www.politicamigratoria.gob.mx/es/PoliticaMigratoria/Boletines_Estadisticos.
6. Del Monte, "El Título 42."
7. Del Monte, "Contrastes."
8. See Martínez y Quero, *Nuevas dinámicas migratorias*.

COMMUNITY ENGAGED MIGRATION RESEARCH   219

9. See Del Monte and Irwin, "Migrantes en Tijuana."

10. See Doberneck, Glass, and Schweitzer, "From Rhetoric to Reality."

11. See Van de Ven, *Engaged Scholarship*.

12. See Mignolo and Walsh, *On Decoloniality*.

13. See Francés et al, *La investigación,* and Corona Berkin, *Producción horizontal*.

14. See Papadopoulos and Tsianos, "After Citizenship"; Varela Huerta, "Movimientos sociales"; Ahmed, *Strange Encounters*.

15. See Papadopoulos and Tsianos, "After Citizenship"; Scheel, *Autonomy of Migration*; De Genova, *Borders of "Europe."*

16. For "story catching," see Lambert; for minimizing our role, see Román Maldonado, "Reconfiguración metodológica."

17. See Irwin, "Digital Resources"; Román Maldonado, "Reconfiguración metodológica."

18. Morales, *Guerrera incansable [Tireless Warriors]*; Morales, *Estoy en el lado de los Valientes [On the Side of the Brave]*.

19. Arroyo, *Uniendo a través del corazón lo que la deportación separó [Uniting through the Heart That Deportation Separated]*.

20. Durón, *Deportación, violencia, discriminación en Honduras*.

21. Una Migrante Hondureña, *Cambio de plan,* and Fúnez, *Tijuana tiene muchas oportunidades*.

22. Ramírez, *No todo está mal [It's Not All Bad]*.

23. See Irwin, "Digital Resources."

24. See Worcester, "Reframing Digital Storytelling."

25. See Lizarazo, et al, "Ethics, Collaboration, and Knowledge Production."

26. See Román Maldonado, "Reconfiguración metodológica."

27. See "Development of the Archive" in Irwin.

28. See, for example, Zheng, Luo, and Ritchie, "Afraid to Travel"; Neuberger and Egger, "Travel Risk Perception."

29. Flaherty and Nizrull, "Reiseangst."

30. See Pueblos, *Recuento Movilización Estatal*.

31. See Van Auken, Frisvoll, and Stewart, "Visualizing Community."

32. See Irwin, "Digital Resources"; Román Maldonado, "Reconfiguración metodológica."

33. See Del Monte and Bautist, "Persistencia de la precarización."

34. See Irwin and Del Monte, "Migrant Autonomy"; Papadopoulos and Tsianos, "After Citizenship."

BIBLIOGRAPHY

Ahmed, Sarah. *Strange Encounters: Embodied Others in Postcoloniality*. Oxford: Routledge, 2000.

Arroyo, Ana María. *Uniendo a través del corazón lo que la deportación separó*. Humanizando la Deportación #233, 2020. http://humanizandoladeportacion.ucdavis.edu/es/2020/01/08/233-233-uniendo-a-traves-del-corazon-lo-que-la-deportacion-separo/.

Corona Berkin, Sarah. *Producción horizontal del conocimiento*. Bielefeld, Germany: Bielefeld University Press, 2020.

De Genova, Nicholas, ed. *The Borders of "Europe": Autonomy of Migration, Tactics of Bordering*. Durham, NC: Duke University Press, 2017.

Del Monte, Juan Antonio. "Contrastes de lo expedito: el procesamiento de asilo selectivo y diferenciado en la frontera norte," Ciudad de México: Nexos, Observatorio Migrante, 2022. https://migracion.nexos.com.mx/2022/04/contrastes-de-lo-expedito-el-procesamiento-de-asilo-selectivo-y-diferenciado-en-la-frontera-norte/.

Del Monte, Juan Antonio. "El Título 42. Dos años de una política sanitaria al servicio del control migratoria," Tijuana: El Colegio de la Frontera Norte, Observatorio de Legislación y Política Migratoria, 2022. https://observatoriocolef.org/boletin /el-titulo-42-dos-anos-de-una-politica-sanitaria-al-servicio-del-control -migratorio/.

Del Monte, Juan Antonio, and Andrea Bautista. "La persistencia de la precarización en la vida callejera después de la deportación en Tijuana. Un análisis durante la contingencia mundial por COVID-19," *Revista Diarios del Terruño. Reflexiones sobre migración y movilidad*, 12 (July-December 2021): 15–45.

Del Monte, Juan Antonio, and Robert McKee Irwin. "Migrantes en Tijuana frente al COVID-19: impactos y consecuencias de las medidas sanitarias desde la perspectiva de los actores." Óscar Contreras, Coord. *Ciencias sociales en acción: respuestas frente al COVID-19 desde el norte de México*. Tijuana: El Colefio de la Frontera Norte, 2021: 358–75.

Del Monte, Juan Antonio, and Rodrigo Ruiz Patterson. *Bad Hombres*. Mexico City: 1987 Films, 2019.

Doberneck, Diane M., Chris R. Glass, and John Schweitzer. "From Rhetoric to Reality: A Typology of Publicly Engaged Scholarship," *Journal of Higher Education Outreach and Engagement* 14, no. 4 (2010): 5–35.

Durón, Marcia Yadira. *Deportación, violencia, discriminación en Honduras*. Humanizando la Deportación #240, 2020. http://humanizandoladeportacion.ucdavis .edu/es/2020/03/11/240-deportacion-violencia-discriminacion-en-honduras/.

Flaherty, Gerard, and Nasir Nizrull. "Reiseangst: Travel Anxiety and Psychological Resilience During and Beyond the COVID-19 Pandemic." *Journal of Travel Medicine* 27, no. 8 (2020). https://doi.org/10.1093/jtm/taaa150.

Francés, Francisco, Antonio Alaminos, Clemente Penalva, and Óscar Santacreu. *La investigación participativa: Métodos y técnicas*. Cuenca: Pydlos Ediciones, 2015.

Fúnez, Ramón. *Tijuana tiene muchas oportunidades*. Humanizando la Deportación #261, 2021. http://humanizandoladeportacion.ucdavis.edu/es/2021/03/05/261 -tijuana-tiene-muchas-oportunidades/.

Guerrera incansable [Tireless Warrior]. Humanizing Deportation #11a-c. Accessed January 20, 2023. http://humanizandoladeportacion.ucdavis.edu/en/.

Humanizando la Deportación. http://humanizandoladeportacion.ucdavis.edu/en/.

Irwin, Robert McKee. "Digital Resources: The Humanizing Deportation Archive." In *Oxford Research Encyclopedia of Latin American History*, edited by William Beezely. Oxford University Press, 2020. https://doi.org/10.1093/acrefore/9780199366439 .013.855.

Irwin, Robert McKee, and Juan Antonio Del Monte. "Migrant Autonomy and Wilfulness Amidst the Onslaught of the COVID-19 Pandemic at the Tijuana Border." *Crossings: Journal of Migration and Culture* 11, no. 2 (2020):153–68.

Lambert, Joe. *Digital Storytelling: Capturing Lives, Creating Community*. 4th ed. New York: Routledge, 2012.

Lizarazo, Tania, Elisa Oceguera, David Tenorio, Diana Pardo Pedraza, and Robert McKee Irwin. "Ethics, Collaboration, and Knowledge Production: Digital Storytelling with Sexually Diverse Farmworkers in California." *Lateral: Journal of the Cultural Studies Association* 6.1 (2017). http://csalateral.org/issue/6–1/ethics -digital-storytelling-lizarazo-oceguera-tenorio-pedraza-irwin/.

Ludvin. *Dos separaciones familiares* Parts I–II. Humanizando la Deportación #257a-b, 2021. http://humanizandoladeportacion.ucdavis.edu/es/2021/01/25/257a-dos -separaciones-familiares-two-family-separations/.

Martínez, Rosario, and Ulises Quero. *Nuevas dinámicas migratorias en los países norte de Centroamérica y México: caravanas del éxodo centroamericano, COVID-19 y violaciones graves de derechos humanos*. Geneva: Franciscans International, 2021.

Mignolo, Walter, and Catherine Walsh. *On Decoloniality. Concepts, Analytics, Praxis*. Durham, NC: Duke University Press, 2018.

Una Migrante Hondureña. *Cambio de plan: realizando los sueños en México*. Humanizando la Deportación #260, 2021. http://humanizandoladeportacion.ucdavis.edu/es/2021/03/05/260-cambio-de-plan-realizando-los-suenos-en-mexico/.

Miller, Holly Ventura, Melissa Ripepi, Amy Ernstes, and Anthony Peguero. "Immigration Policy and Justice in the Era of COVID-19." *American Journal of Criminal Justice* 45 (2020): 793–809.

Morales, Esther. *Comida calientita en plena pandemia*. Humanizando la Deportación #11e, 2020. http://humanizandoladeportacion.ucdavis.edu/es/2020/10/20/11e-comida-calientita-en-plena-pandemia/.

Morales, Esther. *Estoy en el lado de los valientes*. Humanizando la Deportación #11d, 2018. http://humanizandoladeportacion.ucdavis.edu/es/2018/10/01/87-estoy-en-el-lado-de-los-valientes/.

Morales, Esther. *Guerrera incansable* Parts I–III. Humanizando la Deportación #11 a-c, 2017. http://humanizandoladeportacion.ucdavis.edu/es/2017/07/26/guerrera-incansable-i/.

Neuberger, Larissa, and Roman Egger. "Travel Risk Perception and Travel Behavior During the COVID-19 Pandemic 2020: A Case Study of the DACH Region." *Current Issues in Tourism* 24 (2021): 1003–16.

Papadopoulos, Dimitris, and Vassilis Tsianos. "After Citizenship: Autonomy of Migration, Organisational Ontology, and Mobile Commons." *Citizenship Studies* 17, no. 2 (2013): 178–96.

Pueblos, Comunidades y Organizaciones de Oaxaca que Integran la Campaña Nacional en Defensa de la Madre Tierra y el Territorio. *Recuento Movilización Estatal en Defensa de la Madre Tierra Oaxaca*. Oaxaca: Campaña Nacional en Defensa de la Madre Tierra y el Territorio, 2017. https://educaoaxaca.org/images/Recuento_Defensa_Madre_Tierra_Oaxaca.pdf.

Ramírez, Carlos Manuel. *No todo está mal [It's Not All Bad]*. Humanizando la Deportación #263, 2021. http://humanizandoladeportacion.ucdavis.edu/en/2021/05/19/263-its-not-all-bad-no-todo-esta-mal/.

Román Maldonado, Yairamaren. "Reconfiguración metodológica para las narrativas digitales desde los estudios latinoamericanos y Humanizando la Deportación." In *Humanizando la Deportación: narrativas digitales desde las calles de Tijuana*, edited by Robert McKee Irwin and Guillermo Alonso Meneses. Tijuana: El Colegio de la Frontera Norte, Forthcoming.

Scheel, Stephan. *The Autonomy of Migration? Appropriating Mobility Within Biometric Border Regimes*. Oxford: Routledge, 2019.

"The Soul of a Migrant Defender." *Alma Migrante*. Accessed December 17, 2022. https://almamigrante.org/causes/historia-de-defensores/.

Van Auken, Paul, Svein Frisvoll, and Susan Stewart. "Visualizing Community: Using Participant-Driven Photo-Elicitation for Research and Application." *Local Environment: The International Journal of Justice and Sustainability* 15, no. 4 (2010): 373–88.

Van de Ven, Andrew. *Engaged Scholarship. A Guide for Organizational and Social Research*. Oxford: Oxford University Press, 2007.

Varela Huerta, Amarela. "Movimientos sociales protagonizados por migrantes: cuatro postales desde México, España, Francias y Estados Unidos." *Cuadernos de Estudios*

Transfronterizos /Journal of Transborder Studies, Research and Practice 2015: 1–19.

Worcester, Lara. "Reframing Digital Storytelling as Co-creative." *IDS Bulletin* 43.5 (2012): 91–97.

Zheng, Danni, Qiuju Luo, and Brent Ritchie. "Afraid to Travel after COVID-19? Self-Protection, Coping and Resilience Against Pandemic 'Travel Fear.'" *Tourism Management* 83 (2021). https://doi.org/10.1016/j.tourman.2020.104261.

11

PERFORMING CONNECTEDNESS ACROSS PUBLIC AND DIGITAL SPACES

Debaroti Chakraborty

The pandemic made us come to terms with a moment of sudden pause, a pause that is beyond our control. The first few months for me were wrought with a feeling of being incapacitated, of my inability to cope with the sense of isolation, of helplessly witnessing lives being lost, of fiercely guarding what I call "my family," of an unspeakable fear of losing human touch in times of pain and joy. Robin Dunbar, Emeritus Professor of Psychology at the University of Oxford, said: "Physical contact is a part of the mechanism we use to set up our relationships, friendships and family memberships."[1] He explained that, from a purely physiological perspective, the stroking of hairy skin triggers the endorphin system in our brain, which translates into a feeling of warmth.

Different cultures have been associated with different sets of social behavior, like that of the double air kiss in France, the tight embrace in Italy, or the robust handshake in the Netherlands. Ironically, in India, though the official gesture for greeting is a more physically distant gesture of *namaste* (the palms meet each other by way of showing respect), many rural and urban communities live in physical proximity in tight spaces. While this is due to scarcity of space in relation to the humongous population of the country, it also results from how personal histories and traditional practices shape communities and family systems in the private domain. In large sections of Indian society, community life is predominantly shaped by collective modes of cooking, cleaning, gardening, stitching, learning, leisure, and ritualistic practices. In communities and neighborhoods where the living pattern is still intergenerational, like mine, practices of togetherness and caregiving rely on being physically present with the sick person. It is also usual for strangers to be in close physical contact while traveling by public transport, shopping in crowded marketplaces, walking on narrow pavements, or in the course of any other regular activity. In the initial phase, in urban quarters, the fear of contracting the virus was coupled with the apprehension of hurting people for maintaining physical distance because, in India, the gesture of physical distancing could culturally translate into lack of warmth. The inevitable protocol emphasizing "stay-at-home" deepened an already existing divide within our social fabric. The homeless were made invisible by the protocols. Many, living in temporary houses in crammed localities, were cordoned off from the areas of the "privileged." In the wake of the pandemic, physical contact was drastically curtailed since the transmission of the disease was thought to be based on touch. When we began to experience the loss of community or rather a fear of it, I realized how touch as a sensory experience is replete with multiple meanings and how as a gesture (social and private) it shapes identities and relationships.

As I write this, I am reminded of an incident from the prepandemic world of 2018 when my sister (by way of art) Rosalie Purvis was visiting me in Kolkata. Rosalie and I went to a salon with which I am familiar. While we were inside the salon, Rosalie mentioned to me that she was not feeling well and suffering from a headache. Immediately, the lady who owns the salon invited her to relax and applied lavender oil on her temples and nostrils. I could see that this gesture meant something so profound to Rosalie that she was in tears. Later she shared with me that she couldn't imagine that somebody would touch her after she had mentioned that she had a cold. Though I understood that the generosity of the gesture of care touched her deeply, what I failed to grasp is what the act of touching viscerally meant for her. In the initial phase of the pandemic, when the narrative of touch was transforming and we were experiencing stigma and inhumane attitudes around sick bodies, migrant bodies, and laboring bodies, I reflected on what the power of touch might have meant for Rosalie at that point. I perceived that in the West, a consciousness of fear around contagion already existed, which may have stemmed from prior experiences in collective memory of the influenza and the Spanish flu. Close physical contact with strangers is often deemed to be aggressive, and caregiving necessarily does not translate into lending warmth by being physically present with the sick person. However, the simple act of touching surprised and sheltered Rosalie in an unprecedented manner such that it appeared to her as if she had longed for this sensory experience and sense of community.

More recent studies revealed that COVID-19 is primarily airborne, which shifted the health recommendations as well. In India it is not possible to find less crowded public spaces, and local businesses could no longer sustain the economic loss due to lockdowns. Most sectors gradually opened up with an imposition of masks except for schools and colleges, which continued to function online or were shut until the middle of 2022. The available infrastructure in schools and colleges in rural as well as urban sectors cannot ensure facilities for physical distancing and sustainable hybrid teaching-learning modalities. While official numbers and circulars announced that the education sector is functioning online, in reality, schools and colleges in suburban and rural sectors, could not meet the requirements for smart or spacious classrooms. Large numbers of students who lacked access to internet connection and devices had to drop out. As a community, we helplessly witnessed multiple other borders grow within: borders between schools, between homes, between neighborhoods, between rooms, and between bodies.

A Narrative of Presence in *Postcards from the City—My Home?*

As a professor of performing arts and artist-researcher, I deeply engage with the senses as valuable sites for understanding and articulating experiences that shape my artistic and critical/academic discourses. During the abrupt shift into virtual modes, one of the pressing concerns in my pedagogic processes was about how to reinvent ways of communicating in a world that was ingrained with habits, gestures, and rituals of social sharing and was nourished by physical proximity? Visceral experiences percolate into consciousness, inhabit bodies, and help set up dynamic relationships with public and social spaces, specific to contexts and cultures. In 2019 a couple of months before the grim reality of the pandemic disrupted public spaces across the globe, India witnessed an explosive wave of people's movement against the arbitrary suspension of democratic principles in the Citizenship Amendment Act (CAA) passed by the central government of India.[2] Thousands spontaneously claimed public spaces to protest, perform, sing, dance, paint, and forge solidarities to fight against religious discrimination and for equal right to citizenship. In utter dismay, we witnessed state violence on students inside campuses of public universities for protesting against the CAA as the police played the mute spectator.[3] As much as the abrasive state apparatus attempted to pulverize voices of protest, the experiences of violence bolstered the solidarity between diverse communities: women, Muslims, Hindus, students, liberals, refugees, and others. Exactly around that time, I was trying to direct a student performance that would touch upon the congeniality of megacities. I wanted to engage, as a collective, with lived spaces, with the city as a religious polyglot and the layered sense of belonging that it evokes. I designed a performance walk through the city, with my colleagues and students as cowalkers, to explore a few distinct neighborhoods in the city from the wake of a quiet early hour into the hackneyed rhythms of a busy mundane day. The walk was meant to evoke an intimate relationship with the mapped spaces, a narrative that would prioritize experiences as felt through our senses—sounds we recorded, the objects we found, smells that we registered, people we met, feelings we had, and photographs we captured. The collaborative project attempted to understand how these personal stories relate to identities and inhabited realities of public spaces. We gleaned undocumented narratives of diverse communities that could meaningfully feed into the spirit of the raging protests. This walk led us to the awareness of a cultural history that often overlaps or contradicts with our personal histories to create an undeniably multitoned understanding of "gaze" into public and private spaces, of pluralism and inclusiveness. Some of the layered experiences from this performance walk constituted moments that situated us as an insider as well as an intruder in one's own city, at the same time. The performance walk was followed by a series of workshop over a couple of months, in which the polyphony of experiences was artistically processed to cocreate a multitoned performance titled *Postcards from the City—My Home?*, which we installed in February 2020. The piece primarily focused on the politics of public space, resistance, and conflicting relationships with the city (figure 14).

In the series of workshops, we met in person and shared our experiences through stories, metaphors, sounds, images, and objects, thereby gradually taking steps toward an intimate mode of sharing. I drew upon the method of ethno-mimesis, a practice that exists in the interface of ethnography and arts

FIGURE 14. An interaction with the audience after the installation *Postcards from the City—My Home?* © Debaroti Chakraborty

PERFORMING CONNECTEDNESS ACROSS PUBLIC AND DIGITAL SPACES 227

and prioritizes lived experiences. Ethno-mimesis is described by O'Neill as a "politics of feeling," given that the ethno-mimetic research process involves sensuousness and emotion in tension with reason, rationality, and objectivity. Hubbard and O'Neill draw upon Adorno to explain mimesis as a mode of sensuous knowing, as feeling as opposed to mimicry or imitation: "Mimesis is intended not to mimic or reflect reality, but to encourage a moment of cognition through which we can develop a critical perspective that includes 'empathy' as sensuous knowing. Knowledge is produced, forcing us to abandon instrumental rationality and reach towards a more sensuous understanding that incorporates feeling involvement as well as cognitive reflection."[4]

Ethno-mimesis involves embodied practices (may be collective) like walking, talking, traveling, and eating that allow for reflection on the more-than-rational, a sensory meeting of the inner and outer worlds—for instance, what kinds of moments, sensibilities, and memories are produced or invoked by an incident, a time of the day, a smell, an object, the intensity of a place, and other such elements available to the senses. This participatory praxis method of intimate sharing, of working together through narratives and differences helps in building a sense of community in the process of creative art making. In our creative piece, *Postcards from the City—My Home?*, we recognized sharp contrasts and overlaps in the experience of public and private spaces that, on one hand, articulated the nuanced nature of an inhabited space and, on the other, deepened our relationship with lived spaces in the city.

In an early hour, when the city was waking up, we arrived in Sonagachi, the largest red-light district in South Asia, spread out across obscure alleys tucked away from the heart of the city. Dingy houses leaned on each other, tarpaulin sheets blindfolded the balconies, droopy windows looked out onto the tiny shops outside. An interesting paradox struck me—the neighborhood got its name from a notorious Muslim dacoit-turned-warrior, Sanaullah Gazi (becoming Sona Gachi, which means golden tree in Bengali), though most of the doors and windows are adorned with images of Hindu gods and goddesses. Gazi's *mazaar* (a mausoleum or shrine dedicated to saint or religious leader) was couched at the center of the neighborhood. Amid the rising dissent around the discriminatory CAA, based on religious divides, I recognized a significant history of pluralism that is written into the body of this old neighborhood. As I stood there, I choked with a sense of claustrophobia that sprung from a personal feeling of being an intruder into the private spaces of the community that lived in the closely knit, obscure alleys of that neighborhood (figure 15).

Another strong impression from the walk relates to our interaction with the resolute women who had launched a sit-in demonstration at Park Circus Maidan, a huge playground located in the central part of the city (figure 16). Many women

FIGURE 15. At Sonagachi Lane. Photo credit: Shreya Gupta.

from conservative religious families had stepped out of their houses to join this protest to protect their home, that is, their belongingness to this nation, as they echoed. Some of these women carried their babies to the site of protest, which was marked by practices and objects of daily use like that of broken bangles, bobby pins, torn shoes belonging to a kid, water bottles, empty vials of polio vac-

FIGURE 16. Women's protest against CAA. Photo credit: Glary Ghosh.

cines, and other things. The objects we found spoke to the gendered identities that the women were writing into this movement as mothers, as wives, as teachers, as doctors, as activists, as Hindus, and as Muslims. We collected these objects from the ground of protest to install them in the live performance as objects that embody endurance and resilience that shaped the women's movement. In the course of the workshop, we designed an embodied act based on the objects and oral narratives of the women. I designed and installed all these creative pieces in an intimate space in a way that brought to surface the polyphony of voices and identities that community spaces entail.

A Disease of Absence

A month later, with the outbreak of the pandemic, the resistant bodies and voices were disrupted, and all community spaces disappeared from the city. As a community of teachers and students, our ongoing critical and creative engagement with the city as inhabited public space was disrupted in an unprecedented way. This challenge pushed me to reimagine a model of teaching, research, and arts practice that can validate the former realms of experiences, reinvent ways of engaging with the new social order, and yet find continuities with previous meaning-making processes. I started this pedagogic dialogue with students involving public spaces and community events at a time when all spaces of in-person interaction had to be curbed.

As the spread of the COVID-19 virus exploded in India, the lack of caution and preparedness at the administrative level was substituted by the sudden imposition of a lockdown within a notice of four hours.[5] The new set of protocols, activated as measures to contain the spread of the disease, marked theaters and public spaces of communion as "nonessential" and indefinitely shut them down. The practice and staging of live arts slipped into domains of the "nonessential." Universities, colleges, and schools had to abruptly shift into a remote process of learning, within which the prior sense of community ruptured while teachers and students had to negotiate with newer divides related to accessibility to the internet. The political resistance, which was slowly finding stable ground and involving diverse student communities from across the country, was determinedly scrambled. The theater artist Nicholas Berger wrote in April 2020 that the pandemic has affected the central inspiration of human nature, which is also the bedrock of live performances: the need to assemble.[6] He voiced a deep concern around the pressure on productivity that is prompting a quick shift into the digital, without a serious understanding of the structures and of the modes of communication that might shape this transition.

Communion has been a formative aspect of human societies shaping religious ceremonies, ritualistic practices, social dramas, festivities, rites of passages, mourning, political gathering, and private rituals of sharing. Assembly, characterized by the element of presence, evokes the possibility of building a space of shared consciousness that can validate experiences—simple and nuanced—amplify dissent, give voice to deep-seated anxieties and fear, set up modes of care, and help transcend grief or trauma. Berger quoted Chinua Achebe's novel, *Things Fall Apart*: "A man who calls his kinsmen to a feast does not do so to save them from starving. They all have food in their own homes. When we gather together in the moonlit village ground it is not because of the moon. Every man can see it in his own compound. We come together because it is good for kinsmen to do so."[7] During the first wave, the central powers had already used mechanisms of isolation as tools to rupture communion and dissolve spaces of public dissent. The second wave spelled unspeakable disaster in India, when the government failed to provide security, people were frantically searching for life-saving drugs, oxygen, and hospital beds. There was a dire shortage of vaccines, and the crematoriums and burial grounds were running out of space for the dead. While news of death was systematically buried and bodies disappeared, an obnoxiously expensive parliament building, the Central Vista, was built to stomp authority in the face of history (figure 17).[8]

FIGURE 17.   Public demonstration of discontent. Photo credit: Glary Ghosh

Political theorist Chantal Mouffe observes that democracy envisions a public space that has the ability to foster multiple voices that may not even cohere or reach a consensus (Mouffe 2000). The situation in India reflected an undeniable suspension of democracy in the way voices were gagged, public spaces were emptied out of conflicts, and personal narratives of struggles were made invisible in the face of mathematical models of computation and projection of numbers. This crisis of democracy has a pronounced impact on many institutions like the academy, which normalized uniform parameters for assessing productivity and performance during the pandemic. Virtual platforms have facilitated meaningful academic collaborations and, in many cases, have provided unique opportunities of participation to people with disabilities and other kinds of travel or social inhibitions. It has also been an illuminating experience to see how people across generations and class divides have adapted to the recently formulated online modes of learning.

However, in the remote methods of teaching and learning, made to fit the parameters of a predetermined academic calendar, I experienced an invisibility and inaudibility of stories of human struggle. I teach performing arts in a public university, the pedagogical process of which requires physical presence as intuitive as well as kinesthetic mode of making art. The loss of in-person classes meant a compromised mode of learning—shorter semesters, trimmed modules, crammed online evaluations—fitted to meet the timeline of the academic cycle and the requirements for admission to higher institutes. This modality does not address the knowledge gleaned from methods of teaching and art-making based on the aspect of "presence"—working with material and bodies, relationship to objects and environment, experiences of lived and collective spaces, techniques of listening to human stories. There is a felt need to evolve pedagogic methods that foster the ability to enter into dialogue and to critically work through dissent. The monolithic nature of recent educational policies in India that quantifies teaching-learning processes in the virtual mode defies the very fabric of democracy and experiential aspect of classroom teaching as envisioned by the Radhakrishnan Commission on University Education (1948). I quote sections from the report:

> The institutions of democracy must be flexible, capable of adaptation to the changing needs and conditions of men. We must make modifications whenever we feel that changes are necessary to realise more effectively the ends of individual development and social welfare. Educational systems are built for a time and not for all time. There are no changeless ways of educating human nature.
>
> Freedom of individual development is the basis of democracy. Exclusive control of education by the State has been an important factor in facilitating the maintenance of totalitarian tyrannies. In such States, institutions of higher learning controlled and managed by governmental agencies act like mercenaries, promote the political purposes of the State, make them acceptable to an increasing number of their populations and supply them with the weapons they need. We must resist, in the interests of our own democracy, the trend towards the governmental domination of the educational process. Higher education is, undoubtedly, an obligation of the State but State aid is not to be confused with State control over academic policies and practices.
>
> Equal opportunity does not mean identical opportunity for all. It means the equal availability of education for every qualified person. Our system must provide for every young person education to the extent that he can profit from it and of a character best designed to assure the maximum development of his nature.
>
> The institutions of democracy must be flexible, capable of adaptation to the changing needs and conditions of men. We must make modifications whenever we feel that changes are necessary to realise more effectively the ends of individual development and social welfare. Educational systems are built for a time and not for all time. There are no changeless ways of educating human nature.[9]

The tenets mentioned here are crucial to our times because they seek to ensure freedom in the space of classrooms and lectures such that the teacher and the student can collaboratively focus not only on the cognitive but also on the emotive, artistic, and the reflective faculties of learning to arrive at a holistic understanding. I realized, through conversations with my students, that in the middle of a deluge of online classes and continuous evaluation, there is hardly any possibility to acknowledge the challenges that we were facing due to situations thrown open by the pandemic. My work, *Postcards from the City—My Home?*, reflects that much of what I teach relies heavily on spaces of communion, on dialogue and contemplation, on situations where the personal and the political meet, on locating the body as part of a collective. As these meaning-making tools could not be used as much in my pedagogic practice in the online mode, I was faced with a deeper philosophical question: how can we reimagine a collaborative method of teaching and learning that addresses the experiential realm as a valid site of knowledge?

Toward a Pedagogical Praxis to Understand Absence-Presence

Nicholas Berger urges us to be sensitive to this moment of pause as a kind of an internal preparation to help transcend grief and to foster a renewed approach toward arts. He writes: "We must lean into this pain. We must feel the grief. We must mourn. Mourn the loss of work, the loss of jobs, the loss of money, the loss of life. Mourn the temporary loss of an art form that demands assembly. Lean into the grief. Lean in. Lean in. Lean in. We must remind ourselves that mourning is a human act, not a digital one. It is only in this acknowledgment that we will survive. The internet isn't going to save us, we are."[10]

This idea inspired me to develop an online pedagogical mode that fractures the straitjacketed mode of interaction through black, muted screens. I began to design modules that foreground collective and intimate modes of sharing, multiple perspectives of community participation, social action, and ethics that are shaping lives in drastically new ways during the pandemic. This pedagogic practice encourages setting up a participatory space that helps, on the one hand, to articulate subjectivities, and on the other hand, to critically understand emotional responses, ideas of presence, absence, and silence in the context of affect.

We harnessed ideas from O'Neill's methodology of ethno-mimesis and used them in our virtual workshops. We worked with objects and metaphors, constantly attempting to find personal connections between our virtual and physical spaces. I offered my students prompts to motivate them to bring elements from their physical worlds that add meaning to, contradict with, or interrupt their relationships with the virtual spaces. This collaborative journey opened up vistas into understanding the multiple attitudes and modes of negotiations embedded in the sudden shift from in-person interactions to digital ones. I was surprised to learn about the contradictions in students' responses to virtual classrooms. Some students shared that visually and conceptually the tight boxes and grids of virtual classrooms choke them, while some, who were usually irregular in physical classrooms, began to be more responsive. I realized that the quasi-personal space of a virtual classroom that often gives one the choice to stay shielded from an apparent public gaze helps some to shed inhibitions at various levels.

One of my students shared that she deeply missed the train from her physical world. The train signified mobility for her as she regularly used to take the train from her house in a suburb to the city to attend classes. This journey paved a way for her to connect to a larger community. During the months of lockdown, her life was in stasis as she helped her mother run a local shop through the day while having to simultaneously attend online classes. Another participant spoke of how her connection to the river has transformed as she coped with a deep sense of tragedy. In 2020, during the lockdown, she would cycle down to the river near her house and watch it change color as the sun melted into the river.[11] The shocking image of unidentified corpses surface in the river water, during the second wave, left her in an absolute state of horror. She tried to articulate how she has grown up in a riverine community that attaches a sense of sanctity with the river in the way daily lives and rituals revolve around it. This incident has ruptured her inner faith in the river as a life-giver, a healer, and she is unable to break the silence and speak to the people in her community. This emotional response has an affective quality; it relates to interiority where imprints left by events in history intertwine with subjective consciousness. Kavita Panjabi, in her book *Unclaimed Harvest*, focuses on the relationship between interiority and the actual events in history. She writes:

> I take the term "retroactive forces of interiority" from Benjamin's "Theses on Philosophy of History." Interiority, as used here relates to ones' inner self or mental or emotional being. Its nature is shaped by the rational as well as affective impact of events in intimate, private and public life and in response to them. It involves an ineffable internal processing of layers of experience and desire, and exists virtually as an internal chamber house of echoes, with a selection of them coming into play and interplay in specific circumstances. It is neither absolute nor static, but a continually transforming process. As I see it, the quality of

interiority underlies self-formation and agency—and thereby history making too.[12]

Interiority, as explained by Panjabi, is capable of processing experience in relation to how an event impacts the subject and to how the individual is shaped by other conditions of living. Thus, interiority plays an important role in shaping how one tells their stories, narrates experiences, or acts in a specific circumstance. Many such instances of private experiences point at how layers of human experiences and emotional responses cannot be adequately articulated in or represented by the rational language of social sciences. We need to rely on performative, visual, and qualitative methods that capture ambiguity and complexity. In the virtual classroom, I discussed a set of questions with my students that evoked shared realms of experiences, such as:

> *What, according to you, has been a special space of care?*
> *What does it mean to be proactive during the pandemic?*
> *What makes you feel guilty, in these times?*
> *Let us think of actions, gestures, words, modes of silence through which we*
>   *can share grief as a community.*
> *Build a story of hope from another person's experience.*

This pedagogic process was meant to validate the silent acts of care that were nourished by many besides the more visible political solidarities and contribution of the civil societies and volunteers in fighting the crisis from the front. The simple yet intimate acts of reaching out to loved ones, sharing artwork, playing music, writing poems, knitting, doing one's own dance, or sharing one's moment of joy, are extremely precious ways of telling and listening to stories and experiences shaped by these difficult times. Alessandro Portelli, in his essay "A Dialogical Relationship: An Approach to Oral History," says, "Oral history, however, is not only about the event. It is about the place and meaning of the event within the lives of the tellers."[13]

The understanding of how an event impacts the lives of the tellers requires an approach that entails an attention to how an event is being narrated. This pedagogic practice involved an ethno-mimetic method in conjunction with an intimate model of sharing that facilitated an exchange of experiences such that one person's story inspired another to creatively process and communicate a complex experience. This process of artistic intertwining of consciousness reveals multiple truths and helps transform or transcend complexities of lived experiences by allowing participants to creatively articulate that which was untold or not validated. Adorno alludes to this as the "unsayable," a sharing that enables cognition that can contribute to an alternative meaning making process.[14] Jon

McKenzie, in his seminal book *Perform or Else: From Discipline to Performance* (2000), identifies efficiency, efficacy, and effectiveness to be the three key characteristics of performance that demand a kind of workplace ethos from virtual platforms. However, the windows of virtual platforms present the participants in a private-public space that already contradicts the demands of a more formal, insulated workplace environment. In virtual classrooms we appear on our screens as well as on the screens of our coparticipants, in a headshot view through which glimpses of personal and domestic spaces may be visible. This often threatens to expose vulnerabilities and private spaces that we might not want to foreground.

However, I noted that the platforms have been developed in a way that allows us multiple choices related to our preferences regarding representing ourselves. As teachers and students, while we set up our virtual windows for online classes, we notice the sharp parallels in our engagement with performative elements like that of space setting, choice of background, what we choose to wear, how we negotiate between the domestic and the professional domains, and how we navigate visibility and invisibility. The peculiarities and particularities of these online classes inspired me to focus on how the aesthetic and political representations comment on lived experiences, vulnerabilities, and anxieties. I drew upon Heewon Chang's understanding of auto-ethnography as a methodological practice that engages with an interface of self-narration, ethnography, scientific inquiry, and artistic representation to find possibilities that forge nuanced intimacies between self and others within a shared context.[15]

While I was exploring online teaching and learning processes to forge a deeper sense of connectedness, I came across Troy Anthony and Jerome Ellis's made-for-Zoom performance, *Passing Notes* (Schotzko 2020). They developed this after Ellis's grandfather passed away on April 4, 2020. They empathized with the many people who couldn't hold funerals for departed loved ones due to COVID-19 restrictions. They devised *Passing Notes* as a live, participatory event in which the Zoom platform was intentionally used to share grief and perform a sense of connectedness. The performance touched upon the seven stages of grief, during which participants were welcome to share their own stories of loss. At one point in the performance, participants could change the names on their windows into names of people whom they have lost at some point of time in their lives. I was inspired by the way it evoked a sense of collective sharing and remembering while we were still in isolation. In my online collaborative art-making praxis, I focused, more intently, on a renewed way of looking, sensing, listening, and processing through virtual interfaces where different kinds of subjectivities surface.

In the course of our praxis, we took note of the distinct virtual windows that depict different lives that we live as opposed to the culture of invisibility and inaudibility of virtual platforms. The virtual windows through which we communicate, in this learning and teaching method, became a common motif in all the performative narratives. Participants were invited to write an aspect of the lives that they were living in the depiction of their virtual windows, which emerged as spaces of waiting, spaces of endurance, spaces of resistance, spaces of captivity, spaces of social action. We unmuted our windows to document the starkly different sounds from our lived realities that often seep into our online class sessions such as the ambulance sirens, desperate voices of people being sheltered or queuing up for rations, the coughing of a sick family member in the next room, the clamor of a ceiling fan in the dead silence, the chirping of birds filling up one's isolation, the beep of the oven, the sounds of utensils as one cooks, or the constant interruption of discussions due to the lack of internet access.

Participants were put into groups and encouraged to exchange their worlds, their windows, their stories with their creative partners to create an immersive digital performance series titled *Performing Connectedness*. Ankita Sarkar created a piece using multiple devices in a way that she could not commit to any one screen for a constant length of time. Her overturned screens, broken images, muffled voice, and her presence-absence communicated an increasing sense of fragmentation. Her piece told the story of her creative partner, who had to constantly shift homes and workspaces, while working for volunteer groups and attending classes during the pandemic. She used the chat box to reach out to the audience trying to forge a connection while dealing with an overwhelming sense of mobility.

Koushani Mukherjee, on the other hand, created a piece in which her window was steady, stable, and wrapped in a monotonous white. She had a bag of objects and a story to tell about each of those objects. She would go on to speak about why those mundane objects are precious to her and what kinds of memory of people and places, smell, and sense of touch they carry. This piece spoke to the experience of her coparticipant who tried to hold on to every visceral element as she was stuck in an unknown city, in an unfamiliar room during the pandemic. Pushan Dasgupta set up a virtual window through which he tried to reach out to his fictitious/imagined girlfriend. In a joyous monologue, he shared how they walk through the streets in their hometown, eat signature dishes, sit by the river, and breathe in the silent sky and the cacophony of the city. He used the background setting option on the online platform to project images of these places, positing them to be real. The audience realized the dark irony of how, confined in the inertia of a digital room, virtual experiences have replaced real ones, driving home the compelling question of ultimately what is real! The piece was abruptly stopped with a deliberate disruption of internet services, as the performer struggled to somehow cling on to this virtual-real experience.

In collaboratively archiving the mundane, we notice that a whole new world of perspectives is activated by foregrounding the "performative" being from our daily lives. In the process of making the previously mentioned vignettes, I understood that the virtual platforms used for teaching practices emphatically play out an interesting paradox. They underline the distance/disconnection that we negotiate with but are also informed by an aspect of liveness, choice of representation, and a sense of absent-present dynamic between the participants, which discuss newer forms of intimacies. This thought further motivated my artistic collaborator Rosalie Purvis and me to codirect a multimedia adaptation of Naomi Iizuka's play, *Anon(ymous)*, in 2021 that facilitated a cross-cultural collaboration between students from the Department of Performing Arts, Presidency University (Kolkata), other actors from Kolkata, and students from the University of Maine. The play deals with the estrangement of Anon from their mother because of war and their struggles as they experience discrimination and longing for home. The play, at its core, speaks to the massive exodus of migration, displacement, and the global refugee crisis.

For us in India, it also resonated with horrific experiences of migrant workers, many of whom died on the road and on railway tracks, while walking for miles to reach home during the lockdown in 2021. During this process, one of the incidents that disturbed us was how a teenage boy was laid off from a spice-grinding factory during the lockdown. Like many others, he hung from the back of a truck trying his best to reach his village and ultimately didn't make it. The pandemic made us experience the pain of separation, distance, and loss of lives across borders, even if we have no direct or inherited experience of migration. Rosalie and I wanted to creatively explore methods that can help us work around the distance and the impossibility of having live rehearsals with the ensemble. We designed the scenography so that live actors on stage would interact with actors on screen who would be filmed in India. This deepened the sense of distance between the characters who were separated not only in terms of geographical space but also in the communication medium. The idea of longing and alienation was thus built into the very design of the play.

Actors from across borders were trying to reach out through an imagined idea of connectedness while not really being able to see, touch, or respond to each other in person. The acts were asynchronous, disruptive, fragmented, and surprisingly synchronous at moments when the chorus of refugees from across borders mirrored each other. In the process of our work with the ensemble in refugee scenes, we arrived at renewed meanings of connectedness despite the digital, geographical, and cultural divides. In one of the scenes, which speaks of longing for home, the playwright brings a lot of cultural associations like that of "horchata," "pho," "smell of olives," "joss stick," and others.[16] While these specific cultural references were unfamiliar for actors in Kolkata, in our workshops we tried to imagine a smell, a food, a taste, a flower, a feeling that is close to the warmth of home in situations of distress. The actors responded with words like "panta bhaat" (rice soaked in water overnight), "lebur jol"(lemonade), "aam gachh" (mango trees), and others. The actors articulated personal experiences while connecting through their own inherited memory of displacement. Much later, our thirteen-year-old cast member found a recipe for horchata (a Latin American rice water and cinnamon drink) and made it for the ensemble in Kolkata. To our surprise we realized that although we had never had horchata before, as a primarily rice-eating culture, we are familiar with all its ingredients and the flavors. These inter-cultural explorations through food, smell, taste, objects, and memories facilitated a new kind of connection between the ensemble in Main and that in Kolkata, despite the digital and geographical divides.

Though the story centers around Anon and their mother, the presence of the refugees evokes a sense of connectedness in shared experiences of loss of homes across borders. In the arc of the play as we interpreted it, the refugees, toward the end, shed their individual names, their individual stories, and find solidarity as a unified voice and body of those who are made "anonymous." The ensemble of actors in India and in Maine, in the course of the workshops, embodied similar movements and emotional responses, which emerged from a sense of connectedness through history or an awareness of the contemporary global crisis. The filmed parts were projected on layers of fabric mounted on stage in a way that seemed to flow into the live performance in a disrupted yet tangible form. The malleable and fluid texture of the fabric lent a sense of materiality in the way the actors could go really close, touch, smell, and even wrap the fabric around themselves in moments of desperate longing. Yet the presence of the fabric as a screen emphasized mediation and distance. The staging of this play evoked a liminal space of presence-absence that shapes a new kind of intimacy across digital platforms and cultural and geographical divides (figures 18 and 19).

In my pedagogic and art-making practices, as discussed previously, I have tried to explore the nuances of design that virtual platforms as a performance space offer. I realize that the spread of this pandemic is based on the same gestures that bind a community—the touch, hug, embrace, kiss, participatory rituals, and physical proximity. This poignant moment of pause inspired me to revisit each of these ideas through literature, art forms, experiences, oral narratives such

FIGURE 18. Bell Gellis Morais, Haley Connor, and Koushani Mukherjee in *Anon(ymous)*. Photo Credit: University of Maine & Patrick Wine.

FIGURE 19. Bell Gellis Morais, Bishantak Mukherjee, and Rudrani Guha in *Anon(ymous)*. Photo Credit: University of Maine & Patrick Wine.

that these resources can mobilize new ways of reimagining rituals of mourning, of love, of touch, of care, of connection. This pedagogic process has helped build a new sense of communion and to archive the knowledge and experiences of the everyday from communities of teachers and students, working on collaborative methodologies.

NOTES

1. Quoted in Stokel-Walker, "How Personal Contact Will Change Post-COVID-19."
2. See *The Hindu*'s topic page on the Citizenship Amendment Act: https://www.thehindu.com/topic/citizenship-amendment-act/.
3. Saikia, "Delhi Police."
4. Hubbard and O'Neill, "Walking, Sensing, Belonging," 48.
5. Gettleman and Schultz, "Modi Orders Lockdown."
6. Nicholas Berger, "Forgotten Art of Assembly."
7. Achebe, *Things Fall Apart*, 118.
8. "An Illusion Built on Tragedy," *Economic and Political Weekly*, 7.
9. Radhakrishnan, "Commission Report on Higher Education," 72–76.
10. Berger, "Forgotten Art."
11. Pandey, "COVID-19."
12. Panjabi, *Unclaimed Harvest*, 53.
13. Portelli, "Dialogical Relationship," 1.
14. Hubbard and O'Neill, "Walking, Sensing, Belonging," 48.
15. See Chang, Ngunjiri, and Hernandez, "Living Autoethnography," 2–3.
16. Iizuka, *Anon(ymous)*, 1–2.

BIBLIOGRAPHY

Achebe, Chinua. *Things Fall Apart*. United Kingdom: Penguin, 2013.

Adorno, Theodor. *Aesthetic Theory*. Translated by Robert Hullot-Kento. London: Routledge, 1984.

Bennet, Naomi. P. "Telematic Connections: Sensing, Feeling, Being in Space Together." *International Journal of Performing Arts and Digital Media* 16, no. 3 (2020): 245–68.

Berger, Nicholas. "The Forgotten Art of Assembly." Accessed April 4, 2020. https://medium.com/@nicholasberger/the-forgotten-art-of-assembly-a94e164edf0f.

Chang, Heewon, Faith Wambura Ngunjiri, and Kathy-Ann C. Hernandez. "Living Autoethnography: Connecting Life and Research." *Journal of Research Practice* 6, no. 1 (2010). Accessed July 27, 2022. https://philpapers.org/rec/NGULAC.

Gettleman, Jeffrey, and Kai Schultz, "Modi Orders Three-Week Total Lockdown." *New York Times*, March 24, 2020. https://www.nytimes.com/2020/03/24/world/asia/india-coronavirus-lockdown.html.

Hubbard, Phil, and Maggie O'Neill. "Walking, Sensing, Belonging: Ethno-mimesis as Performative Praxis." *Visual Studies* 25, no. 1 (April 2010): 46–58.

Iizuka, Naomi. *Anon(ymous)*. In *Fierce and True: Plays for Teen Audiences*, edited by Peter Brosius and Elissa Adams. Minneapolis: University of Minnesota Press, 2010.

"An Illusion Built on Tragedy." *Economic and Political Weekly*, 56, no. 22 (May 29, 2021). https://www.epw.in/journal/2021/22/editorials/illusion-built-tragedy.html.

McKenzie, Jon. *Perform Or Else: From Discipline to Performance*. New York: Routledge. 2000.

Mouffe, Chantal. *The Democratic Paradox*. London: Verso, 2000.

Pandey, Geeta. "COVID-19: India's Holiest River Is Swollen with Bodies." *BBC News*. May 19, 2021. https://www.bbc.com/news/world-asia-india-57154564.

Panjabi, Kavita. *Unclaimed Harvest: An Oral History of the Tebhaga Women's Movement*. New Delhi: Zubaan Books, 2016.

Portelli, Alessandro. "A Dialogical Relationship: An Approach to Oral History." Accessed December 23, 2016. http://www.swaraj.org/shikshantar/expressions_portelli.pdf.

Radhakrishnan, Sarvepalli. "Commission Report on Higher Education." *NMIMS Journal of Economy and Public Policy* (2017): 66–76. https://epp-journal.nmims.edu/wp-content/uploads/2017/january/dr-radhakrishnan-commission-report-on-higher-education.pdf.

Saikia, Arunabh. "Delhi Police Did Not Do Their Job." *Scroll.in*. January 31, 2020. https://scroll.in/article/951716/delhi-police-did-not-do-their-job-retired-officials-critical-of-how-jamia-firing-was-handled.

Stokel-Walker, Chris. "How Personal Contact Will Change Post-COVID-19." *BBC News*. April 30, 2020. https://www.bbc.com/future/article/20200429-will-personal-contact-change-due-to-coronavirus.

Svasek, Maruska, ed. *Moving Subjects, Moving Objects: Transnationalism, Cultural Productions and Emotions*. Oxford: Berghahn Books, 2012.

Schotzko, T. Nikki Cesare. "A Year (in Five Months) of Living Dangerously: Hidden Intimacies in Zoom Exigencies." *International Journal of Performance Arts and Digital Media* 16, no. 3 (2020): 269–89. https://doi.org/10.1080/14794713.2020.1827206.

12

NEGOTIATING AND REBUILDING CIVIC ENGAGEMENT THROUGH LOSS

Alicia Muñoz

"What do I do now?" This was a question I repeated to myself again and again over the last year and a half as I struggled to adapt my course's civic engagement component. Like so many people, my work and home blended together; the ground repeatedly shifted underfoot; and grief and pain interjected themselves into daily life. Over a decade ago, I sat in a coffee shop with my department chair to discuss teaching challenges and navigating civic engagement in my Introduction to US Latinx Studies course. Although he encouraged me to write about my experiences, I never did. Now I find myself occupying the role of chair, with an ongoing global pandemic, and lamenting the fact that this person who had encouraged me to write is no longer alive to read the narrative.

Ever since the onset of COVID-19, the buzzword ringing in everyone's ears was "pivot." Classes needed to pivot to online. Work pivoted to telework. Students pivoted to distance learning. Communication and collaboration pivoted to Zoom. Yet, pivot is a facile term, obscuring the substance of loss and extraction left in its wake. In this chapter, I discuss a working community partnership I fostered before COVID-19, my unsuccessful attempts to forge a brand-new relationship with another organization during the pandemic, and the promising new collaboration and work-in-progress that ultimately emerged. I will place these efforts and relationships in the context of pervasive disruption: in student lives, physical space, my own life and work, the priorities of community partners, and the Twin Cities community at large. Undergirding a "pivot" is the necessity of loss, recognizing and accepting this loss, reassessing needs, and valuing possibility. When practicing community-engaged learning and scholarship, we

244 ALICIA MUÑOZ

must consider these elements not just at the level of the individual instructor but also with empathy among all stakeholders.

A Prepandemic Model of Collaboration

In spring 2020 the health concerns and closures brought on by the pandemic forced me to abridge and suspend the civic engagement component I had cultivated over the previous three years. Moreover, it put me in the position of having to identify a new community partner and work toward building a partnership during pandemic times. Every spring semester, my class partnered with Hiawatha Academies, a network of public charter schools in Minneapolis serving students from kindergarten to twelfth grade. The network's mission is to empower its scholars "with knowledge, character, and leadership skills to graduate from college and serve the common good."[1] Incorporating community engagement into a course is a time-consuming endeavor, and multiple studies document the various factors that deter or motivate faculty to do so.[2] I felt compelled to do so because I wanted my students to remember that our class readings and discussions are grounded in the experiences of real people, not static objects of academic study. As Mari Castañeda explains, "The pedagogy of community engagement is very much in line with the principles of Latina/o Studies as well as Chicana/o Studies and Puerto Rican Studies, and courses within these areas of study have historically linked theory with praxis in significant and meaningful ways."[3] When I first introduced this component into the course, I had been a Hiawatha board member for a few months and had become familiar with the schools. According to Margaret Post, Elaine Ward, Nicholas Longo, and John Saltmarsh, "The *engagement* in civic engagement underscores the critical importance of authentic reciprocity in partnerships between those working at colleges and universities and those in the wider community."[4] I worked at a college and my role on the board also made me part of this school community. It was important to me that we collectively create this partnership so that it may be reciprocal rather than extractive. Hiawatha Academies predominantly serves students of color, with 88 percent of students identifying as Latinx. Like many of the Hiawatha students, I too was the child of immigrants, grew up speaking Spanish at home, and came from a working-class background.

The conception and construction of the partnership needed to be a collective effort. Conversations among Hiawatha, myself, and my institution's Civic Engagement Center resulted in a program directed at Latinx fourth graders that exposed them to Latinx history and social themes. One objective was to allow these young scholars to see themselves reflected in class materials and lessons, aligning this effort with one of the goals of the school. My students would visit the school for an orientation session that included an initial meeting with the sixteen fourth graders chosen by the school to participate. What followed were three visits about every two weeks. In the culminating event the fourth graders visited the college campus, which reinforced the school's goal of helping these scholars see college as a viable path.

In designing this program, I tried to keep it small and manageable in terms of time commitment. I am aware that, as the price of tuition continues to increase exponentially, more and more college students are working while attending school, and balancing those obligations makes it more difficult for them to devote themselves fully to civic engagement projects.[5]

In teaching this course and facilitating the community engagement component, I also decided early on to work with a student preceptor (teaching assistant) who had previously taken the course and ideally identified as Latina/o/x. As noted by Christine Cress and Rebecca Duarte, Latinx students who attend an urban university and are involved in community service-learning courses achieve greater gains in leadership development, including their commitment to civic responsibility and desire to become a community leader than similar students not involved.[6] I knew this experience could be impactful for Latinx students taking the course, and having someone with this identity also serve as a preceptor would recognize and validate not just their academic preparation but their intimate knowledge of these communities. Each semester, the preceptor was part of the exchanges with our community partner and took the lead when we visited Hiawatha and during Hiawatha's visit to our campus. As a previous student in the course, the preceptor could also explain the community relationship to newly involved students. This type of collaboration helped shift the service learning from a transaction-based relationship to one grounded in solidarity.[7]

My college students took material from our Latinx Studies course and tailored it for a younger audience in creative and engaging ways. Working in small groups, facilitated by the preceptor, they created mini-lesson plans about topics such as Spanglish, the Young Lords Party, and immigration. The fourth graders also had some input about what they wanted to learn. I shared each prepared lesson with the assistant principal of the Hiawatha school in advance to receive their comments and feedback. Having to "teach" about these topics deepened my students' understanding of the material. Additionally, each student served as a buddy to a fourth grader. This pairing provided the fourth graders with the undivided attention of a young adult, meeting the need for individualized attention expressed by the school. It also further informed my students' experiences with the local Latinx community.

I work at a predominantly white institution; about a quarter of the students enrolled in this course identify as Latina/o/x. I also teach within the context of a Spanish department, so although most of the readings are in English, discussions and written work are in Spanish. The class continually straddles the two languages, and our course material pushes the students to think about their positionality. Though the interactions with the Hiawatha students largely took place in English (the language used at the school), Macalester students also incorporated Spanish at various points. It surprised some of the fourth graders to see that their white buddy spoke Spanish. Nicholas Bowman explains, "the emphatic bonds that occur primarily through interpersonal interaction—as opposed to simply 'engaging' with diversity abstractly through course work or workshops . . . lead to a greater importance placed on social action engagement and, ultimately, to civic action."[8] As one college student commented, conversations with the fourth graders allowed them to "build relationships with the Hiawatha students that allowed for actual reciprocity—each of us learning a bit more about each other's life." Another student felt the most significant educational aspect of this partnership was "thinking about life from their perspective." Fourth graders offer a different view of the world, and this group also brought in stories about language barriers, the challenges of mixed-status families, and conceptions of identity that came up in my students' reflections.

Then in mid-March 2020, Minnesota K–12 schools abruptly shut down, and it wasn't long before the email from the college president's office arrived, informing the campus community that all classes would move to remote learning. The Hiawatha students' visit to Macalester, which included the last lesson, had to be canceled. As Michelle Veyvoda and Thomas Van Cleave recognize, "the most pressing concerns related to teaching and learning during the pandemic involv[e] basic needs" of students and staff.[9] Hiawatha shifted its efforts to providing food and locating hot spots so that students could continue their education remotely. The assistant principal I had worked with was also transitioning to another job that year; this was the second assistant principal we had collaborated with in three years. My students were in the midst of evacuating campus. As the mother of three kids under age six whose school and daycare had closed down, I realized that my aspirations of excellence in teaching dissipated; it became all about getting through the last few weeks of the semester while juggling childcare and teaching obligations. No one had the mental or physical bandwidth to try a virtual gathering, nor the resources and capabilities we have now. Nonetheless, I knew it was important to provide some form of closure to these fourth graders and to my own students. My preceptor and I discussed how best to do so and decided that each college student would prepare a letter/card for their respective buddy that the school could distribute. This allowed them to say goodbye and not just suddenly disappear from the lives of these kids. I share with you an excerpt of a letter written by a fourth grader in response to the card they had received: "I was so mad when the teachers were going to cancel every thing even every fun thing I got very mad. Also I hope I could see every one soon. Also thank you for the note I didn't like it . . . I loved it! Also I liked the latinx classes. . . . right now I am spending more time with my family, I like it this way but the thing that I don't like about this in this way is about the covid-19 it ruined every fun plannings at school. I miss everyone that I now." This fourth grader expressed in their own words what many of us were feeling: frustration, longing, resignation, and hope. Each of the parties involved faced loss and inadequate closure, but this collaboration was just a small part of the disruption and grief we all were to experience in the coming year.

The Thorniness of Forging Brand-New Partnerships

I was disappointed that the Hiawatha partnership I had nurtured for years was no longer feasible, but that would not be the only change forced upon my teaching. As a result of COVID-19, my college also shifted its calendar from two semesters to four modules for the next academic year. In the fall, I would teach a new course, Latinx in the Midwest, and longed to continue bridging the classroom and the community. This new course would be limited to seven and a half weeks. I spent the summer prepping/constructing it for module 2 (October 28–December 15).

Given the topic of the class, I felt I needed to at least try to engage the local Latinx community in some manner, despite the pandemic limiting what was possible. When I learned in mid-July that Hispanic Advocacy and Community Engagement Research (HACER) was working on an East Lake Street Oral History project, sponsored by the Minnesota Historical Society, it seemed like a possible way forward. HACER was established in 1988 and operates as the only advocacy-driven, Latinx-specific research organization in the upper Midwest. Its mission is "to provide the Minnesota Latino community with the ability to create and control information about itself in order to affect institutional decisions and public policy."[10] Several grassroots organizations, service providers, and policymakers seek out their services to inform the work that they do. As such, they have multiple concurrent research projects at a given time.

The East Lake Street Oral History project aimed to record the history of Latinx businesses on East Lake Street and their role in the transformation of this area from being a center of violence and drug trafficking in the 1990s to a more vibrant multicultural area. Back in 1996, a *New York Times* article reported that there had been a record ninety-seven murders the year before and dubbed Minneapolis "Murderapolis."[11] HACER would interview fifteen Latinx business owners and/or community members who played a central role in reshaping this area, with most of the interviewees being between fifty and seventy years old. The pandemic and events that transpired in late May would also need to be acknowledged in the telling of this community's history.

On May 25, 2020, Minneapolis police officers killed George Floyd, sparking several nights of protest and unrest. The community and buildings along a five-mile stretch of East Lake Street were hard hit. The stretch, which runs east-west through Minneapolis' south side, has a long history of being a corridor of immigrant communities. The rioting and arson that occurred, whether by those revolting against injustice or by outsiders striking against communities of color, only exacerbated the economic impact the pandemic had already created on these minority-owned businesses. The *Minneapolis/St. Paul Business Journal* reported the story of one Latinx business. Mauro Madrigal, the owner of the grocery store La Mexicana, woke up to the sound of his security system alerting him that someone had broken into his store. "He checked his security camera feed and saw three people break in through the backdoor. They ransacked the store, breaking cash registers, smashing windows and making off with produce and La Mexicana's safe—which, luckily, had been emptied the day before. He estimates he lost $15,000 in damages that day. After that, Madrigal boarded up windows and doors and spent the next few days defending la Mexicana with a ragtag group including his wife, friends, hired security and neighboring business owners."[12] Directly across the street, shopkeepers at Mercado Central, a Latinx marketplace of thirty-five businesses, similarly picked up the pieces and worked to keep the business safe from rioters for a few nights. In the destruction's wake, my family joined countless others in bringing aid packages to local community organizations. Driving a few blocks north of Macalester along University Avenue, and across the Mississippi River on Lake Street, we saw the eruption of pain and loss made manifest in burned buildings, smashed windows, antipolice graffiti, and artistic remembrances of George Floyd. We also saw the overwhelming outpouring of support, hope, and community as hundreds of people gathered, bearing brooms and dustbins, washcloths and buckets, and bags and bags of food and supplies.

The history of Lake Street, combined with the stresses and tragedies of spring and summer 2020, made HACER's Latinx oral history project timely. The executive director was open to my students assisting with this project in some fashion. The pandemic had delayed the original timeline (January 2020–March 2021) and, though they completed the historical research of East Lake Street, they conducted no interviews prior to everything shutting down in spring 2020. HACER now expected to interview business owners and community members during August/September 2020 so that they could begin the analysis in October. The new projected timeline aligned well with the start date of my course. COVID-19 had scattered my students across the country and, even for those in Saint Paul, restrictions made it difficult to gather, so I felt relief knowing HACER would conduct the interviews as they had the relationships and the expertise. I briefly pondered what my students could do and suggested that perhaps they could help with transcriptions and/or analysis of the interviews. The organization's response was positive. I was excited about the prospect of my students supporting this work. They would not be engaging directly with community members, but through this oral history project, my students would hear these personal accounts and could offer their skills as readers and interpreters of text as the project unfolded.

The executive director connected me with the research associate coordinating the project, and the three of us met via Zoom in September 2020. They had a short list of interviewees to reach out to but had yet to schedule any interviews. I expressed an interest in formally joining the project as a fellow researcher, hoping to deepen my relationship with this organization, and they were excited by that prospect. I needed to be approved by the Minnesota Historical Society so I shared my CV, and like so many things during that year of pandemic and shutdowns, the process was slow and took about six weeks. Simple tasks took longer during COVID-19 as organizations found themselves stretched thin and/or needing to shift their efforts. I regularly reached out to HACER to check in about the project, and at one point was meeting weekly with the research associate on Zoom. What I didn't understand at that time was the degree to which other research projects would take precedence over this one. For example, HACER had partnered with the Minnesota Department of Health to better inform the Latinx community about COVID-19 and worked to assess the needs of the community through polls and video focus groups. Again, HACER understandably pushed back the timeline for the East Lake Street Oral History Project and made little headway on this specific project. As the start date of my Latinx in the Midwest course got closer, it was clear the partnership would not work for this class. Instead, I gambled on being able to connect the next group of students in my Introduction to US Latinx Studies course with the project, since that course did not start until late March 2021. I kept attempting to create a mutually beneficial relationship, yet priorities and timelines were shifting as the oral history project received an extension until December 2021.

During the fall, like so many other mother-scholars, I was feeling the effects of juggling multiple responsibilities. Other essays have reflected on the many challenges faced by women faculty during COVID-19, especially as they relate to caregiving responsibilities.[13] For my part, I was chairing my department for the first time and during the summer had to tear down and rebuild the department course schedule to fit the module system, attended biweekly chair meetings, and sought to prepare myself for online teaching by attending multiple pedagogical workshops. In September, my oldest child started kindergarten remotely and my spouse and I took turns caring for him while working full-time from home, feeling grateful that at least daycare was open for our toddler twins. I was also navigating new terrain with respect to teaching. I had always taught in a semester schedule, and the shift to a module system proved challenging. Instead of fifteen weeks, I had seven and a half weeks to establish rapport with my students and cover course material while also being mindful of major and general education requirements. Additionally, I was continually aware of the risk of overburdening students; it was simply not possible to fit the same amount of material and types of assignments from a full semester course into that compressed time frame, especially with all of the outside stress affecting students. I grappled with the fact that COVID-19 distorted and slowed concepts of time (i.e., days, weeks) and yet, simultaneously the accelerated pace of the module system left little time for contemplation, exploration, and ultimately, the processing of grief. Four days into the Latinx in the Midwest course, I received an e-mail from a department colleague about their "present predicament." As I read their email, tears slid down my face. They were writing to "say goodbye to [their] dearest profession due to the inconvenience of a cancer and its final consequences." And they were apologizing to me for the "whole new set of changes to schedules, duties, and other little details [that] need to be taken care of overnight." Their battle with cancer had been ongoing and had already prompted some changes to the teaching schedule, yet their news still came as a shock. They passed away three weeks later. A cancer death during COVID-19 is still subject to the cruelties of a global pandemic, including having to grieve from a distance and on a screen. I am still processing their absence and imagining what it will be like to roam the halls of my department, knowing they will no longer be there to share their stories, laughter, and wisdom.

Reports have shown the significant impact COVID-19 has had on Latinx communities across the United States.[14] Their overrepresentation in service, construction, and agriculture industries makes them more vulnerable to contracting the virus. Latinx people test positive for COVID-19 at rates higher than would be expected relative to their share of the population. Even though Minnesota's Latinx/Hispanic population is just 5 percent, data from the Minnesota Department of Health in December 2020 showed that 11 percent of those admitted to intensive care units with COVID-19 had identified as Hispanic. According to a study conducted by HACER and University of Minnesota Extension, "43 percent of Latino business owners felt the pandemic is having a significant negative effect on their business revenue, while 35 percent reported a moderate negative effect."[15] These statistics point to the loss of income and the toll the virus has had on these bodies. I include these data as context for the dynamics that I describe later.

When the decision is made to pivot to remote operations, technological capacity comes up against the capacity and priorities of all those involved, including community members. My weekly online meetings with the research associate continued, and the organization conducted the first part of interview number one in mid-November at the Midtown Global Market on East Lake Street, a marketplace with stalls selling food and crafts from cultures around the world. The first interviewees were a brother and sister who own a well-established torta restaurant in this complex. While the interview with the brother was conducted on site, the governor's guidelines quickly became more restrictive as COVID-19 cases continued to climb. HACER tried to offer a virtual platform for the interview with the sister/co-owner, but she was not comfortable with technology and kept pushing for an in-person meeting, despite the higher health risk this posed for her. It is not always simple to pivot to a virtual format and proceed, especially when working with an immigrant population. The foreign-born make up a disproportionately large share of groups with lower levels of digital skills, and US immigrants who speak a language other than English at home are much more likely to have no computer experience.[16] The sister's hesitation to attempt a Zoom interview reflects the digital divide and is familiar to me from personal experiences with my own Spanish-speaking parents. Another factor at play in this interviewee's request to record on site was a desire to showcase their legacy. Since it would be a video interview, they wanted the business they had built to be visible; it was important to respect both their pride in accomplishment and their instinct for promoting their business by grounding their story in that physical space. Between the interviews needing to be in person and the scheduling availability of the interviewees and HACER researchers, the project kept being delayed.

We need to name and make visible the challenges that arise when forging and nurturing a new relationship with a community partner. Darcy Lear and Annie Abbott write, "If we only present the 'pretty' side . . . with the inspiring stories and successful collaborations, we cannot move forward. This is not to say that we are not inspired by all the players in the pedagogy . . . but rather that, like so much work worth doing, it is always a work in progress."[17] I eventually realized that despite everyone's best intentions, the parameters and expectations of my partnership with HACER had not been sufficiently clear. When I first approached HACER, they were receptive to my students and me contributing to this project, and I had tried to name something specific we might tackle. I had also expressed my interest in collaborating as a fellow researcher, and they officially listed me as being part of the project. But, in retrospect, I failed to probe further into how they envisioned us working together. I think the nature of that relationship also changed over time. After seven months of me staying in communication and being flexible to changes in timelines, I needed to confront the reality that the project was not maturing as I had hoped.

In thinking about how to increase my students' engagement with the project, I did contemplate the idea of my students conducting pre- or post-interviews with some of the people on HACER's list. But I was wary of stepping on the organization's toes, and conducting our own interviews in the constricted module timeline seemed impractical. Some of my students did not have much of an understanding of Latinx communities in the United States, nor did I feel that I could adequately prepare them to undertake oral histories with the time I had. Our interviewee pool would further have been constrained to those that could navigate a digital platform since my students were scattered across the country and the campus was closed to outside visitors. Last, there were also other demands on my time that limited what I could do. I was organizing three department faculty searches as chair and serving on the provost search committee for my institution. Meanwhile, my students and I did not have the expertise that HACER possesses in this area, nor the bandwidth to undertake this project; adding this element would not advance HACER's project or our partnership, it would at best enrich only my students' curriculum.

By late February 2021 HACER had managed to complete two full interviews, but there was hesitancy about sharing the raw footage with me. When I sought clarity about this collaboration, the executive director explained that when we first talked, he did see this as an opportunity to have some work done on this project. However, the interviews had not been edited yet, and he felt that sharing the raw footage with my students would have put them in an uncomfortable position of trying to make out something that is still very disconnected. Last, the executive director repeated that they only had two interviews and knew it was best to have a diversity of examples when you are teaching. His words made me realize the extent to which they saw this relationship as a service they were to provide for my students rather than as a mutually beneficial partnership. In response to my question about my role in this project, he invited me to consider working with them as a consultant and noted the role would also be based on how much further I wanted to go with them. He asked if my name was on the record, and when I confirmed that I was officially added to the project back in the fall, they said I would be receiving more communication since they would be advancing a bit more and extended an invitation to join them at an interview if I had the time. I understood their limitations and needs and recognized in hindsight what I had been feeling; HACER was not in a position to invest in fostering a strong relationship nor did they have a real need for us/me. I had strived to develop a new partnership during pandemic times with an organization with which I had no previous history and never met in person, and it had fallen short of what I had hoped for. Instead, I made new contacts and gained a deeper understanding of HACER along with an appreciation for the work that they do.

Leaning on Past Relationships and Building on New Hopes

COVID-19 and all the other stressors had derailed my collaboration with HACER. I pondered how my students could still engage local Latinx history and the revitalization of East Lake Street, but differently: another pivot. After months of giving things up because of the pandemic, it was wrenching to give up on a commitment I had made and let go of this collaboration. My reluctance to pivot earlier and move beyond the HACER project came at a cost in that I had only about two weeks to rethink what my class could do. I hoped we could create something that would be useful to community organizations and strengthen existing relationships. From my conversations with Paul Schadewald, the senior program director of Macalester's Civic Engagement Center, came the idea of creating a story map,[18] and partnering with the Lake Street Council. Founded in 1967, Lake Street Council is a nonprofit organization that engages, serves, and advocates for the Lake Street business community in Minneapolis to ensure the vitality and prosperity of the commercial corridor. Paul knew they were generally open to creative ways of highlighting local Latinx history, heritage, and contributions to Minneapolis. Another hope was that the story map could also be of use as an educational resource. Hence, we began exploratory conversations with the senior strategic initiatives manager at Lake Street Council as well as a teacher at El Colegio, a bilingual and bicultural public high school that serves Latinx students and is located about a mile from the Cub Foods store where Minneapolis police killed George Floyd.

In reaching out to these two people it became obvious how important strong relationships are to these types of civic engagement partnerships, especially in unprecedented times. Established relationships allow for another type of understanding, commitment, and flexibility that is harder to foster with new contacts, something exacerbated when the pandemic overextended everybody. I had previously met our contact at Lake Street Council in person, and my colleague Paul had worked with both him and the teacher at El Colegio. This provided a foundation upon which our virtual interactions were based, something I lacked in my relationship with HACER. It is also important to acknowledge that digital technologies "do not change the need to take deliberate steps to earn community trust, built at the speed of the community. This is an organic process of face-to-face contact, transparency, and open communication, as well as a healthy mixture of structured and informal engagement (regular check-ins and attendance at community functions)."[19] In both cases, I was engaging with Macalester alums, and their knowledge of and relationship to my institution facilitated the clarification of goals and ability to adjust as the project proceeded. The English Language Learner teacher at El Colegio was open to getting his students involved with the story map but knew it could not happen at that moment. Many of his students were working long hours to supplement their family's income, some were recent arrivals to the Twin Cities, and he would need more time to strategize how they could engage with this work. Nonetheless, he agreed to speak with my students about this school and the student body they serve. Lake Street Council was receptive to the story map project and agreed to host it on their website. Their more established relationship with Macalester also allowed them to be up front about the fact that they could not spend extensive time working on the project.

We had a new digital project with achievable goals, but limited time. In presenting the work to my students, I introduced it as the first phase of a project. They would get the ball rolling by doing research and creating an initial story map with the hope that the next group of students taking the course could continue to add to it. My preceptor and I had identified four different subtopics students might engage as they delved into the history of this corridor and the Latinx community: a historical timeline, murals, and cultural celebrations, Latinx nonprofits, and Latinx businesses. I subsequently divided the class into four groups. Of the sixteen students taking the course, only one had previous experience with story maps. We relied on my colleague from Macalester's Digital Resource Center to provide training workshops and serve as a resource throughout the process. Students had to negotiate work with other students, and they had to work toward the larger aim of serving the organization's interests.

Veyvoda and Van Cleave explain that, although indirect service projects can provide value to the community, students engaging in these types of projects are likely to only interact with community leaders and administrators, who tend to be of more privileged backgrounds. Students may miss out on a deeper understanding of community needs and the empathy gained by having direct contact with community members.[20] That proved to be true for my course. My students primarily engaged with our contact at the Lake Street Council. In addition, my exchanges with HACER enabled me to invite Juan Linares, one of the founders of Mercado Central. Linares told the story of how he helped organize the growing Latinx population through an asset-based community organizing model that insisted that all the resources and talents needed to create a healthier community already existed *within* the community. It was this approach that allowed the community to create this permanent entrepreneurial cooperative space. Linares shared this story via Zoom with his camera off. He participated in this virtual conversation, but his black screen still mediated our exchange. We were missing the facial and bodily cues that foster a deeper connection.

This project was also about the mapping of a particular geographic area, yet the limitations of COVID-19 and remote learning made it difficult if not impossible for my students to walk along East Lake Street and ground themselves in the physical place. They could not holistically witness the scars of the pandemic and racial pain, whether healing or still raw, in the remaining destroyed buildings, boarded up windows, newly opened businesses, or murals of remembrance and tribute. In their discussion of the pandemic and our relationship to place, Patrick Devine-Wright et al. observe, "Many people are, at once, more fixed in place, yet more mobile digitally. . . . Residences have become workplaces and schools. . . . At the same time, we are alienated from the places of our daily rounds in some way, and the nature of our future relationships to place are uncertain."[21]

Remote learning enabled my students to work on this local project whether they were physically located in the Twin Cities and familiar with East Lake Street or were piecing together this place they had never visited using websites, stories, and images. My students worked collaboratively with one another, heard from our community partner and guest speakers, and researched local Latinx history and contributions. They were free from geographic constraints, yet, the inability to engage physically with the community limited the depth of their experience. "Sense of place . . . is key to the experience and identity associated with being *of* community."[22] The vast majority of my students were sophomores, who had to pivot to remote learning when their first year of college was dramatically interrupted, and first years, who were new to Minnesota. In either case, they were still familiarizing themselves with the spaces around our college. While technology facilitated certain interactions, these students lost the grounding that comes from sustained presence in a space and begets knowledge, belonging, and commitment.

As the course progressed, the pandemic and the events taking place in the Twin Cities quickly reminded us that we were not operating in a bubble. The Chauvin trial was ongoing, a reminder of the trauma inflicted last summer. Then on April 11, 2021, police killed Daunte Wright in a suburb of Minneapolis. Some of my students were out protesting at night and/or covering what was happening for the college newspaper. One Latina student, in particular, worked with other Black Indigenous People of Color students to provide mutual aid to families living in the apartment complexes across from the Brooklyn Park Police Department. For more than two weeks, she assembled and distributed bags of nonperishable foods and COVID-19 protection items, participated in protests, and visited families to learn more about their needs. She made herself available to this community 24/7, responding to requests at all hours. For example, one mother called at 1 A.M. requesting help to move her children out of the apartment building for a few days to escape the National Guard's traumatizing presence. This work took an emotional and physical toll on my student. Her ongoing community relief efforts consumed her to the point where she could no longer attend class nor work on the story map. We devised a new plan. As a final paper, she wrote a reflective piece about their experiences at Brooklyn Center. I share her voice with you: "Activism is part of who I am. This pandemic has made me realize that my identity is much more intersectional than I had previously thought. My bilingualism connects me to people I have never met. We let down our guard to each other based on the sense that we understand each other's experience because we have lived each other's experience. In communicating with residents of certain apartment buildings, I was glad to practice my Spanish skills and be immersed in a sense of home and community."

I found that despite my best attempts to balance readings, assignments, and the story map project, it still proved to be too much. The announcement that the jury had reached a verdict on the Chauvin trial was another tense moment. I quickly decided to pivot to asynchronous work for the next class session, recognizing how emotionally drained many of us were. With about a week and a half left in the module, Paul, my preceptor, and I met to strategize and adjust once more. The new plan was for my students to continue to create their vision of this story map, grounded in the research they had done, but we no longer expected them to also master the digital skills needed to put it all together. Instead, a summer student employee at the college's Civic Engagement Center would work on pulling together the different parts into a completed story map. The fact that we had been clear from the beginning that this work would be a first step and something to build on rather than a "final" product facilitated this transition. At the last class meeting, my students presented their vision for the story map to our contact at Lake Street Council, providing a touchpoint of how far the project had advanced. They also received feedback from our community partner and made adjustments and notes that I could pass on to the next group. In the end, students submitted to me the text that they had prepared, the images compiled, layout concepts, and personal reflections about why these specific organizations, murals, events, and so on mattered.

Lessons of Letting Go and Valuing the Process in the Return to In-Person Learning

The process of pivoting has necessitated that I also sit with the loss and grief intrinsic to the pivot in order to allow progress. It is farcical to attempt to produce broad conclusions while the twin pandemics of COVID-19 and racism continue to ravage, their scars lingering in the minds, bodies, and homes of so many. The pandemic has not ended, we remain unmoored, and these ongoing crises will require further pivots by academic institutions and community partners. Nevertheless, I carry with me a new understanding of the nature of campus-community partnerships, which includes the importance of gentleness to self, the ability to let go, and resiliency. The work is valuable but can also be an unruly changeling.

In fall 2021 we returned to in-person instruction. I put the story map project aside (for now), since this work is best suited for students in my Latinx in the Midwest course, and reconnected with the ELL teacher from El Colegio. We were both now ready to construct something together, focused on community-building, reciprocal learning, and lived experiences. In the first semester we initiated conversations between Macalester students and his ELL students and hosted the high school students on campus. Knowing that this would be the first time students would be back on campus in over a year, we kept things simple. Students in the course really enjoyed this connection and the way conversations with this community partner intersected with class readings and discussions. In spring 2022 the course continued to work with this same group of El Colegio students, but with a new set of Macalester students enrolled in the course. This time around, Macalester students supported the high school's fundraising efforts by decorating wooden hearts for their auction "Mira mi corazón." Conversations among the high school and college students revolved around four broad themes (choices, journeys, rules, and emotions) that connected to a shared reading. The final product was a book of *testimonios* with original artwork produced by the students during an art workshop led by a local Latinx artist. This compilation allows others to hear these stories and has inspired another generation of El Colegio students who are now looking forward to also forming part of this tapestry of personal narratives. Coming back to teaching in-person, I still utilized the advantages of tools learned during the pandemic, such as the convenience of Zoom for speakers to provide background on their program, and the effectiveness of short FlipGrid videos for students to introduce themselves. It was a great relief, however, to reengage the productive and deeper connective conversations that come out of individuals interacting face-to-face. Through the turbulence, I learned what to let go of, and what is worth making the effort for: to get all partners on the same page to create interactions, whether they produce concrete products, that are meaningful for all.

Joan Clifford makes the argument that we should disrupt the association of service-learning with products and reciprocity and instead shift to talking about service-learning through the concepts of process and solidarity. At the same time, Clifford recognizes the challenge an academic calendar poses to this work: "Because of the limit of time for interactions with the community, it may be difficult to sustain the relationship building that is intrinsic to solidarity."[23] Throughout the year of remote-learning, I endeavored to build an authentic relationship with the community partners I approached. I knew the importance of co-creating projects that are built *with* communities rather than *for* them. Yet, that aspirational model of perfect co-creation assumes a comparable level of prioritization and capacity on both sides of the relationship. The stress and difficulties produced by the pandemic drained both time and energy, making the difficult work of forging new relationships even harder. It also reinforced how critical strong relationships are to being able to advance initiatives in difficult times. My institution's established relationship with Lake Street Council granted us the ability to be vulnerable and flexible and to reimagine what we could do together. Depending on the situation and the nature of the partnership, the work we do might not look like the perfect co-created project we strive for, yet it can nevertheless be mutually beneficial and substantive. By focusing on the process instead of the product, we learn to appreciate each step and the struggles that get us there. In a period fraught with pervasive loss and grief, granting ourselves such grace as scholars, activists, and persons is necessary.

NOTES

1. Hiawatha Academies, "Mission Statement."
2. See Hammond, "Integrating Service and Academic Study," 21–28; Abes, Jackson, and Jones, "Factors That Motivate," 8–13; and KerryAnn O'Meara, "Motivation for Faculty Community Engagement," 14–23.
3. Castañeda, "Transformative Learning," 321.
4. Post et al., "Introducing Next Generation Engagement," 34.
5. Castañeda and Krupczynski, "Introduction," 7–8.
6. Cress and Duarte, "Pedagogía Comunitaria," 54.
7. Joan Clifford, "Talking About Service-Learning," 10.
8. Bowman, "Promoting Participation," 47.
9. Veyvoda and Van Cleave, "Re-imagining Community-Engaged Learning," 1543.
10. HACER, "Our Mission."
11. Johnson, "Nice City's Nasty Distinction."
12. Carlos, "La Mexicana Looks."
13. See Frederickson, "Women Are Getting Less Research"; Kramer, "Virus Moved Female Faculty"; and Willey, "Parenting Policies and Culture in Academia and Beyond," 201–17.

14. Vargas and Sanchez, "COVID-19 Is Having a Devastating Impact," 262–69; and Obinna, "Confronting Disparities," 397–403.

15. Gutierrez, et al., *Impact of COVID-19*.

16. Cherewka, "Digital Divide."

17. Lear and Abbott, "Aligning Expectations," 322.

18. A Story Map presents an online interactive narrative using maps, text, and multimedia to ground information in a geographic context.

19. Wingo, Heppler, and Schadewald, "Introduction."

20. Veyvoda and Van Cleave, "Re-imagining," 1547.

21. Devine-Wright, et al., "Re-placed," 1.

22. Hansen and Patti H. Clayton, "From *for* to *of*," 16.

23. Clifford, "Talking," 10.

BIBLIOGRAPHY

Abes, Elisa S., Golden Jackson, and Susan R. Jones. "Factors that Motivate and Deter the Use of Service-Learning." *Michigan Journal of Community Service Learning* 9, no. 1 (Fall 2002): 5–17.

Bowman, Nicholas A. "Promoting Participation in a Diverse Democracy: A Meta-analysis of College Diversity Experiences and Civic Engagement." *Review of Education Research* 81, no. 1 (March 2011): 29–68.

Carlos, Iain. "La Mexicana Looks to Find Its Footing after Neighborhood Upheaval." *Minneapolis/ St. Paul Business Journal*, June 15, 2020. https://www.bizjournals.com/twincities/news/2020/06/15/la-mexicana-minneapolis-protests-opens.html.

Castañeda, Mari. "Transformative Learning Through Community Engagement." *Latino Studies* 6, no. 3 (2008): 319–26.

Castañeda, Mari, and Joseph Krupczynski. "Introduction: Toward a Latinx Community-Academic Praxis of Civic Engagement." In *Civic Engagement in Diverse Latinx Communities: Learning from Social Justice Partnerships in Action*, edited by Mari Castañeda and Joseph Krupczynski, 1–17. New York: Peter Lang, 2018.

Cherewka, Alexis. "The Digital Divide Hits U.S. Immigrant Households Disproportionally during the COVID-19 Pandemic." *Migration Policy Institute*, September 3, 2020. https://www.migrationpolicy.org/article/digital-divide-hits-us-immigrant-households-during-covid-19.

Clifford, Joan. "Talking About Service-Learning: Product or Process? Reciprocity or Solidarity?" *Journal of Higher Education Outreach and Engagement* 21, no. 4 (2017): 1–13.

Cress, Christine M., and Rebecca Duarte. "Pedagogía Comunitaria: Facilitating Latino Student Civic Engagement Leadership." *AUDEM: The International Journal of Higher Education and Democracy* 4 (2013): 54–78.

Devine-Wright, Patrick, Laís Pinto de Carvalho, Andres Di Masso, Maria Lewicka, Lynne Manzo, and Daniel R. Williams. "'Re-placed': Reconsidering Relationships with Place and Lessons from a Pandemic." *Journal of Environmental Psychology* 72 (2020): 1–8.

Frederickson, Megan. "Women Are Getting Less Research Done than Men." *The Conversation*, May 18, 2020. https://theconversation.com/women-are-getting-less-research-done-than-men-during-this-coronavirus-pandemic-138073

Gutierrez, Rodolfo, Jennifer Hawkins, Juan Pablo Higuera, Neil Linscheid, Brigid Tuck, and Jocelyn Hernandez-Swanson. *Impact of COVID-19 on Latino-Owned Firms in Minnesota*. Minneapolis: HACER and University of Minnesota Extension, 2020, https://hdl.handle.net/11299/218207.

HACER, "Our Mission." Accessed January 19, 2023. https://hacer-mn.org/mission.

Hammond, Chris. "Integrating Service and Academic Study: Faculty Motivation and Satisfaction in Michigan Higher Education." *Michigan Journal of Community Service Learning* 1, no. 1 (1994): 21–28.

Hansen, Faith Beyer, and Patti H. Clayton. "From *for* to *of*: Online Service-Learning as Both Disruption and Doorway to Democratic Partnerships." In *Community Engagement 2.0? Dialogues on the Future of the Civic in the Disrupted University*, edited by Scott L. Crabill and Dan Butin, 12–25. New York: Palgrave Macmillan, 2014.

Hiawatha Academies, "Mission Statement." Accessed January 19, 2023. https://www.hiawathaacademies.org/.

Johnson, Dirk. "Nice City's Nasty Distinction: Murders Soar in Minneapolis." *New York Times*, June 30, 1996. https://www.nytimes.com/1996/06/30/us/nice-city-s-nasty-distinction-murders-soar-in-minneapolis.html

Kramer, Jillian. "The Virus Moved Female Faculty to the Brink: Will Universities Help?" *New York Times*, October 6, 2020. https://www.nytimes.com/2020/10/06/science/covid-universities-women.html

Lear, Darcy, and Annie Abbott. "Aligning Expectations for Mutually Beneficial Community Service-Learning: The Case of Spanish Language Proficiency, Cultural Knowledge, and Professional Skills." *Hispania* 92, no. 2 (May 2009): 312–23.

Obinna, Denise N. "Confronting Disparities: Race, Ethnicity, and Immigrant Status as Intersectional Determinants in the COVID-19 Era." *Health Education & Behavior* 48, no. 4 (2021): 397–403.

O'Meara, KerryAnn. "Motivation for Faculty Community Engagement: Learning from Exemplars." *Journal of Higher Education Outreach and Engagement* 12, no. 1 (2008): 7–29.

Post, Margaret A., Elaine Ward, Nicholas V. Longo, and John Saltmarsh. "Introducing Next Generation Engagement." In *Publicly Engaged Scholars: Next-Generation Engagement and the Future of Higher Education*, edited by Margaret A. Post, Elaine Ward, Nicholas V. Longo, and John Saltmarsh, 1–12. Sterling: Styles Publishing, 2016.

Vargas, Edward D., and Gabriel R. Sanchez. "COVID-19 Is Having a Devastating Impact on the Economic Well-being of Latino Families." *Journal of Economics, Race, and Policy* 3 (2020): 262–69.

Veyvoda, Michell A., and Thomas J. Van Cleave. "Re-imagining Community-Engaged Learning: Service-Learning in Communication Sciences and Disorders Courses During and After COVID-19." *Perspectives of the ASHA Special Interest Groups* 5 (2020): 1542–51.

Willey, Nicole L. "Parenting Policies and Culture in Academia and Beyond: Making It While Mothering (and Fathering) in the Academy, and What COVID-19 Has to Do with It." *Journal of the Motherhood Initiative* 11, no. 1 (2020): 201–17.

Wingo, Rebecca, Jason A. Heppler, and Paul Schadewald. "Introduction." In *Digital Community Engagement: Partnering Communities with the Academy*, edited by Rebecca Wingo, Jason A. Heppler, and Paul Schadewald. Cincinnati: University of Cincinnati Press, 2020. https://ucincinnatipress.manifoldapp.org/projects/digital-community-engagement.

Epilogue

LEARNING FROM OUR GRIEF

Melissa Castillo Planas

I will never forget the endless sirens that passed by my Queens apartment in April 2020. My apartment was on route to Elmhurst Hospital, which became famous as the hardest hit hospital in the nation as COVID-19 cases skyrocketed the hospital to 230-percent capacity in those first months.[1] I will never forget one of my closest students coming to me in March the week before the lockdown, shaking, and telling me she needed to go home. She lived in Rockland County, which was the first area where cases developed in New York State. I gave her a big hug and told her to go, we'd work it out. We still didn't really know what COVID-19 was, other than something that could kill us. I wouldn't hug her again for seventeen months.

Between March and May 2020, New York City was the epicenter of the COVID-19 pandemic in the United States. The city went into lockdown. Restaurants and theaters closed, the wealthy quickly evacuated to rural hideaways, and streets were emptied of people and cars. Governor Andrew Cuomo sent out increasingly desperate pleas for support—for masks, respirators, for medical personnel. Hospitals were overwhelmed with critical care patients; the Centers for Disease Control and Prevention reported that there were over 54,211 hospitalizations and 18,679 deaths during this time, with significantly higher rates in marginalized neighborhoods, where the deadly combination of poverty, essential workers, and Black and Brown ethnicities showed shocking disparities with the white population. While the death rate was 9.2 percent overall during those hectic months, among Black and Latinx communities it was 32.1 percent.[2]

This is exactly the community that Lehman College—the City University of New York's only four-year institution in the Bronx—serves, where the majority of the students are Black and Latinx people from the least affluent borough of New York. They and their families of health care workers, subway conductors, delivery people, grocery store attendants, and nurses' assistants were at the epicenter of the epicenter. While Lehman College, like most of the academic institutions in the state and the nation, scrambled to go virtual, my students were dealing not just with the challenges of accessing online school work but the more immediate existential challenges of tightly packed living quarters in expensive New York apartments, lack of computers and inadequate internet service, struggling to get food, and losing—or even more terrifying in some cases—retaining jobs, while supporting sick and dying family members. I received e-mails regularly about staff and student deaths; CUNY as an institution, not surprisingly, was also hit the hardest among area schools.[3] Any time a student didn't show up to a Zoom meeting, I feared the worst. As a professor, I was helpless. As a poet, I tried to cope by writing, forming a poem-a-day group for National Poetry Month in April with some of my students. The following is one of the poems I wrote.

Self Portrait in the Times of Corona II

After Barbara Jane Reyes

8:23 A.M. Last night I set my alarm at 2:05 A.M. to get groceries. Peapod, Amazon fresh, Instacart all sold out. So I stayed awake until 4 A.M. imagining the mask I would have to wear again.

9:28 A.M. Zoom breakfast as the new normal.

Bacon, muffins, avocado toast, scrambled eggs a veritable feast of everything but hugs, the longing for an embrace palpable amongst the pixels.

11:34 A.M. We cover ourselves desperate for an escape, cramming the car with fur & doggy tongues. They wag along the ride as we imagine a future, try and escape a present, slither among neighborhoods: Yankee stadium, Willis ave, Van Cortland Park, Fordham road. It is desolate outside. It is the closest I have felt to normal in a month.

1:39 P.M. This is when I learned my favorite Mexican restaurant is feeding the South Bronx homeless. I take off my mask. Ask them about their days, wonder about their nights. Leave with mole poblano, tacos al pastor and a cuídate. It's the only word that can escape.

3:02 P.M. I wonder about alcoholics in the time of corona as I watch Ben Affleck play too close to home. It scares me. The precipice is so near.

6:01 P.M. It's the saddest happy hour I've ever been a part of but also the happiest I've been in a long time. Poems lick the tip of a wine bottle, friendship winds around the stem.

8:37 P.M. The table is cleared for the first time in months. I insist on it. It's date night and I have made steaks and mashed potatoes and mushrooms all plated on hope for a little romance. But this stillness is hard to swallow. We choke on the ends.

10:48 P.M. I forget to floss again. Lying in bed I could not close my eyes despite the weight from last night's failures. Every minute too slow, every second too heavy.

2:02 A.M. My words are lost.

Despite the celebration of "pivoting," Alicia Muñoz in this volume reminds us that "Undergirding a 'pivot' is the necessity of loss, recognizing and accepting this loss, reassessing needs, and valuing possibility." Like many, I did pivot. After positive responses to a summer poetry class, I worked with my students and Lehman College alums to create a special chapbook for Lehman's literary and arts magazine, *Obscura*, on "Poetry in the Times of COVID-19."[4] Later that fall 2020, in an effort to keep students engaged, I organized a fully online Hispanic Heritage Month celebration consisting of fourteen events ranging from book talks and panels to comedy, theater, and poetry performances, which garnered 280 individual registrations.

But there were also great losses. As a scholar, my first single-authored academic manuscript was published in March 2020 and resulted in a wave of book talk cancellations. I lost the opportunity to celebrate ten years of research. I lost the ability to conduct new archival research for two years. Still, like professor Ayendy Bonifacio, who reflected on his privilege to work at home unlike all the other members of his family, I was one of the lucky ones:

> There are over two million Latinx people in New York City, many of them members of immigrant families like mine, who work in businesses considered "essential." Grocery store workers, housekeepers,

delivery workers, immigrant owners of small businesses, cabdrivers and undocumented workers worry not only about their immigration status but also a basic income to survive. For them, social distancing is a luxury they simply can't afford. Some 30 percent of Americans have jobs that allow them to work from home. This number shrinks dramatically for black and Latinx people, and, especially, immigrants. Among the U.S. work force, just 16 percent of Latinx workers and 18 percent of black Americans can work from home, while roughly 30 percent of whites and 37 percent of Asian-Americans can.[5]

My students lost learning. My students lost the enjoyment of learning. My students lost family members and jobs. My students lost the ability to pay for their education. My students got lost.

When I returned to in-person teaching in the spring of 2021 after two years away, the classroom felt different. It was the grief we carried; it weighed heavy. I observed their struggle to even make it to the classroom, much less give their full attention to the materials. Writing and motivation was difficult; we were all tired. As I ponder the COVID-19 term "new normal," I wonder why we even used this term at all. Normal means "the usual, average, or typical state or condition,"[6] and what COVID-19 forced us to confront is how elusive normalcy is. My students, like the scholars in this volume, faced vastly different conditions than students just a few miles away at New York City's private institutions. As Black, Latinx, first-generation, immigrant residents of one of the country's poorest counties where the median household income is $36,593, how not "normal" they are was shoved in their faces, daily.[7]

If there is one lesson we take away as publicly engaged scholars in the humanities, I hope it is that we use our privilege for these not-"normal" students and the communities that they come from. I also hope that we don't go back to a system where often our full humanity and lived experiences are not valued; that we don't forget the societal injustice that always existed but that the pandemic forced many to confront more openly; that we give ourselves and each other a little more grace; that, as Rafiana Martinez reflects in her poem, "Self Portrait During Covid," published in the *Obscura* literary and arts magazine special issue, we re-evaluate normal:

> Everyday there's more death. I wonder
>   *If those spirits are at peace. I wonder*
>   *when this will end. I miss*
>   *driving. I miss*
>   *walking in the park. I miss*

> *hearing my kids excitingly tell me about their day at
> school. I miss
> my normal ordinary routine days. The same days
> that used to bore me.*
>
> There's no normalcy and I just want to breathe

Three years post pandemic lockdown, let us take a collective breath and hold it in just a few moments longer. Exhale with our personal, professional, and community losses. Know that with loss is the opportunity to begin again.

NOTES

1. Carrington, "How NY Hospital Faced COVID."
2. Thompson et al., "COVID-19 Outbreak," 1725–29.
3. Valburn, "Lives and Livelihoods," June 23, 2020.
4. Read the issue here: https://obscuramagazine.squarespace.com/projects.
5. Bonifacio, "For Many Immigrants."
6. Definition from "Oxford Languages," https://languages.oup.com/google-dictionary -en/.
7. Stebbins, "Poorest Counties in the US."

BIBLIOGRAPHY

Bonifacio, Ayendy. "For Many Immigrants, an Even Greater Risk." *The New York Times,* April 25, 2020. https://www.nytimes.com/2020/04/25/opinion/immigrants -coronavirus.html.

Carrington, Alexis E. "How NY Hospital Faced COVID Devastation and Came Back from the Brink." *ABC News*, March 28, 2021. https://abcnews.go.com/Health/ny -hospital-faced-covid-devastation-back-brink/story?id=76638912.

Stebbins, Samuel. "Poorest Counties in the US: A State-by-State Look at Where Median Household Income Is Low." *USA Today*, January 25, 2019. https://www.usatoday .com/story/money/2019/01/25/poorest-counties-in-the-us-median-household -income/38870175/.

Thompson, C.N., J. Baumgartner, C. Pichardo, B. Toro, L. Li, R. Arciuolo, P. Y. Chan, J. Chen, G. Culp, A. Davidson, et al. "COVID-19 Outbreak: New York City, February 29–June 1, 2020." *Morbidity and Mortality Weekly Report*, 69 no. 46 (November 20, 2022): 1725–29.

Valburn, Margorie. "Lives and Livelihoods." *Inside Higher Ed*, June 23, 2020. https:// www.insidehighered.com/news/2020/06/23/cuny-system-suffers-more -coronavirus-deaths-any-other-higher-ed-system-us.

Contributors

Elaigwu P. Ameh is an assistant professor in the theater department at St. Olaf College, Northfield, Minnesota. He holds an MA and a PhD in performing and media arts from Cornell University and an MA in development communication from Ahmadu Bello University, Zaria. He is a recipient of the Arrupe College Book Prize for graduating with a First Class in the BA (Hons.) Philosophy program at the University of Zimbabwe, Harare. His many awards/grants include the Public Humanities New York Fellowship, Sage Fellowship, HASTAC Fellowship, and the Bouchet Honors Society Award. His teaching and research interests include performance ethnography, forced migration, postcolonial Africana performances, and race, gender, and inequity. In his work, he underscores the unique priorities and perspectives of sociopolitically excluded people.

Debra A. Castillo is Stephen H. Weiss Presidential Fellow, Emerson Hinchliff Professor of Hispanic Studies, and professor of comparative literature at Cornell University, where she directs the migration studies minor. She is past president of the international Latin American Studies Association. She specializes in contemporary narrative and performance from the Spanish-speaking world (including the United States), gender studies, comparative border studies, and cultural theory. Her most recent books include *South of the Future: Speculative Biotechnologies and Care Markets in South Asia and Latin America* (with Anindita Banerjee), *The Scholar as Human* (with Anna Sims Bartel), and *Transitions in Latin American Literature* (with Mónica Szurmuk).

Debaroti Chakraborty is an assistant professor in the Department of Performing Arts, Presidency University, India. As a researcher her areas of interest focus on oral history, women's narratives, border studies, and on making cross-cultural and intercultural performances based on lived experiences and ethnography. Her doctoral work broadly studies narratives of women in India and Latin America through a comparative perspective in the context of borders. She has been touring, researching, and making performances in collaboration with artist-researchers and communities in India, in the United States, at the United States-Canada border and at the United States-Mexico border. She is the co-editor of two recent volumes, *Centering Borders in Latin American and South Asian Contexts: Aesthetics and Politics of Cultural Production* published with (2022) and *Pandemic of Perspectives: Creative Re-imaginings* (2022).She has been an instructor at the "Bodies at the Borders" collaborative videoconferencing course between Cornell University and Jadavpur University. As an invited lecturer, she teaches Latin American Literatures in other universities. She also writes an invited column for *The Telegraph* as a performance critic.

Nina Cook is a PhD candidate at Rice University. Her dissertation project, tentatively titled "Engaging Frames and Absorbing Names: The Interpolation of the Subject in Visual and Verbal Art," explores the techniques that painters and prose writers invented at the turn of the nineteenth century to absorb an audience into a diegetic world. She continues to be interested in the Public Humanities, following her time with the Civic Humanist Program, and has worked in various ways to translate humanistic knowledge to a wider audience, including serving as dramaturg for the Rice University production of *On the Verge* (2021) and working with a "Big Questions" course entitled "What is Religion?", which sought to expand and elucidate the practice and purpose of religious studies for a variety of fields.

Juan Antonio Del Monte earned a PhD in social science with a specialization in sociology from El Colegio de México, an MA in cultural studies from El Colegio de la Frontera Norte (El Colef), and a BA in cultural sciences from Universidad del Claustro de Sor Juana. He is currently a professor-researcher in the Department of Cultural Studies at El Colef, where he co-coordinates the Observatory of Legislation and Migration Policy of that institution and also, since 2021, is the coordinator of the MA in cultural studies at El Colef. He is a level 1 member of The National Researcher System of the National Council of Science and Technology. His research interests focus on precariousness and cross-border (in)mobilities with emphasis on ethnographic, audiovisual, and collaborative methodologies. His field of work is the northern border of Mexico. In 2019 he codirected the feature documentary *Bad Hombres* about deportees who inhabit the streets of Tijuana.

Maureen O. Gallagher is a lecturer in German studies at Australian National University in Ngunnawal and Ngambri country. She holds a PhD in German studies from the University of Massachusetts Amherst and is currently working on a book manuscript on whiteness in Wilhelmine German youth literature and culture. Her recent publications have focused on inclusive and decolonial pedagogy, race and gender in German colonial literature, and WWI literature.

Robert McKee Irwin holds a PhD in comparative literature from New York University and is professor in the Department of Spanish and Portuguese at the University of California, Davis, where he is also deputy director of the Global Migration Center. He is (co) author or (co)editor of numerous books, including *Hispanisms and Homosexualities, Mexican Masculinities, The Famous 41, Global Mexican Cinema: Its Golden Age, Dictionary of Latin American Cultural Studies, Sports and Nationalism in Latin/o America,* and *Migrant Feelings, Migrant Knowledge: Building a Community Archive,* which brings together research carried out through the Humanizing Deportation digital storytelling project: http://humanizandoladeportacion.ucdavis.edu/en/ that he has coordinated since 2016. His current research focuses on masculinity, affect, and the world-making strategies of migrants in the face of ever more violent and restrictive border control regimes in the context of the Central America-Mexico-United States migration corridor.

Leigh Johnson is associate professor of literature at Marymount University in Arlington, VA. She was a participant in the 2022 NEH Summer Faculty Institute: Transnational Dialogues in Afro-Latin American and Afro-Latinx Studies. Her research on Chicana feminist thinking appeared in *Transnational Chicanx Perspectives on Ana Castillo* (edited by Karen Roybal and Bernadine Hernández, 2021) and *Crossings in Nineteenth Century American Literature* (edited by Edward Sugden, 2022). She teaches classes on gender and sexuality in literature, Latinx literature, and composition. She directs the Summer Humanities Institute, Exploring Latinx DC, for undergraduate students at Marymount University.

Joey S. Kim is assistant professor of English at the University of Toledo. She researches global Anglophone literature with a focus on eighteenth- and nineteenth-century poetics and aesthetics. Her forthcoming book, *Romanticism and the Poetics of Orientation* (2023), highlights the racial and ethnic formation of the poetic subject in terms of Orientalist forms of cultural difference. She has published scholarly and public-facing work in *American Periodicals, Essays in Romanticism, Nineteenth-Century Gender Studies,* *the LA Review of Books, Shondaland*, and elsewhere. A poet as well as a literary critic, her first book of poems, *Body Facts*, was released by Diode Editions in 2021.

Annie Lowe earned her PhD in English at Rice University in 2021. Her doctoral thesis, "Hoax Machina: A Hermeneutics of Hoaxing," received the department's annual Caroline S. and David L. Minter Best Dissertation Prize. She currently runs the local Mirabeau B. Lamar High School's new Writing Lab, which she and Alexander Lowe McAdams helped found in their continuing civic humanist quest for *ōtium* in COVID-19 times. Lowe's practicing interest in writing pedagogy complements her research on avant-garde, modernist, and contemporary literature and theory. Her recent work on ethics and media theory appears in the edited collection *Understanding Flusser, Understanding Modernism* (2021).

Alexander Lowe McAdams received her PhD in early modern literature from Rice University in 2020. Her dissertation, "Theophanic Reasoning: Science, Secrets, and the Stars from Spenser to Milton," reflects her varied interest in a broad range of intersecting topics, from classical reception to the history of astronomy, to the heretical writings of sixteenth-century philosopher-theologian Giordano Bruno. Since then, she served as a public humanities postdoctoral research fellow with Rice's Humanities Research Center and has worked with YMCA Greater Houston's Y Teen L.I.F.E. Civic Engagement division. She teaches part-time at Lone Star College, a community college in Houston, and collaborates with contributing author Annie Lowe to institute and staff the new writing laboratory at Houston's Lamar High School. McAdams has published peer-reviewed essays on both Edmund Spenser and William Shakespeare, the latter of which earned her the Rice English Department's Shirley Bard Rapoport Graduate Essay Prize in 2020.

Lisa Moody is a lecturer and teaching specialist at James Cook University. She worked as a specialist English teacher in high schools between 2005 and 2015 and in tertiary settings since 2011. During this time, she specialized in the fields of literacy and critical literacy. She currently specializes in teaching students in enabling spaces about writing, reading, and researching for the purposes of tertiary study. She recently completed a postgraduate qualification in research methods. This qualification included a research project and dissertation focusing on transition and pedagogy within enabling and sub-bachelor spaces. In 2021 she collaborated with academics and learning advisors at James Cook University to publish an open textbook for new university students titled "Foundations of Academic Success." Her work on curriculum design has also been showcased at the Australian National University's Beyond Year 12 conference, where she led a workshop for high school teachers and careers counselors on developing student resilience through curriculum.

Rhian Morgan is an anthropologist and senior lecturer at James Cook University, specializing in teaching digital literacies in Australian Pathways programs. Her work is orientated around equity in higher education and technology-enabled learning. Her areas of expertise include digital literacies and pedagogical practice, widening participation, and learning design. Her most recent work focused on digital literacies in enabling spaces, curriculum design, and the evaluation of school-based STEM programs for girls in regional Northern Australia. Morgan's work in eLearning design has been featured in the Innovative Research Universities case study collection and she is currently acting in the role of Senior Principal of JCU's Pathways programs providing strategic leadership and coordination of JCU's enabling, bridging and subdegree programs. In 2021 she collaborated with academics and learning advisors at James Cook University to publish an open textbook for new university students titled "Foundations of Academic Success."

270 **CONTRIBUTORS**

The **Motherscholar Collective** was established in 2020 as a means for mothers* with young children to engage in research in innovative ways. The Collective counts nearly one hundred members, a diverse array of motherscholars from every stage along the scholarly path, as well as those who are leaving or have left academia. The work of the Collective supports the intellectual growth of its members and empowers those involved in efforts to dismantle oppressive structures in academia, the workplace, and the home.

Alicia Muñoz is associate professor of Spanish and Latin American studies at Macalester College in Saint Paul, MN. In her teaching and research, she specializes in contemporary Latin American narrative, US Latinx literature, gender studies, and border studies. More specifically, she conducts research on representations of women's violence, articulations of urban space, migration, and women's participation in drug trafficking. Among the courses she teaches regularly are Introduction to US Latinx Studies, Frontera: The US-Mexico Border, and Constructions of a Female Killer. She has published her research in *Arizona Journal of Hispanic Cultural Studies, MELUS, Chasqui, Journal of Latin American Cultural Studies, Revista de Literatura Mexicana Contemporánea*, and *Frontiers: A Journal of Women Studies*.

Jacob T. Peterson is a PhD student in the Kinesiology Department with a specialty in sport pedagogy at the University of Alabama. Peterson works as the program coordinator for community education at the University of Alabama's Division of Community Affairs. His research focuses on the effectiveness of physical activity-based community programs.

Melissa Castillo Planas is an associate professor of English at Lehman College in the Bronx, NY, and the CUNY Graduate Center PhD program in English specializing in Latinx literature and culture. She is the author of the poetry collection *Coatlicue Eats the Apple*, editor of the anthology *¡Manteca!: An Anthology of Afro-Latin@ Poets*, co-editor of *La Verdad: An International Dialogue on Hip Hop Latinidades*, and co-author of the novel, *Pure Bronx*. Her most recent scholarly book project, with Rutgers University Press's new Global Race and Media series (March 2020), *A Mexican State of Mind: New York City and the New Borderlands of Culture*, examines the creative worlds and cultural productions of Mexican migrants in New York City. Her second book of poetry, *Chingona Rules*, was released with Finishing Line Press in September 2021 and was a Gold Medal Winner of the Juan Felipe Herrera Best Poetry Book Award, International Latino Book Awards (2022).

Diana Noreen Rivera is associate professor of literature and cultural studies at the University of Texas Rio Grande Valley. Her research centralizes Mexican American cultural producers via interdisciplinary frameworks, across regional, national, transborder, and global geographies. She was a participant in the 2022 NEH Summer Faculty Institute: Transnational Dialogues in Afro-Latin American and Afro-Latinx Studies. Currently, she is working on a critical edition titled *The Far East Journals and Other Cold War Era Writings of Américo Paredes (1945–1956)* (Michigan State University Press, forthcoming), which recovers Paredes's life writing in the context of the global Cold War. Her essays have appeared in *Aztlán, Journal of South Texas, Recovering the U.S. Hispanic Literary Heritage, Chicana/Latina Studies, Oxford Bibliographies*, and most recently the anthology *Rewriting America: New Essays on the Federal Writers Project* (edited by Sara Rutkowski, forthcoming fall 2022).

Courtney Naum Scuro received her PhD in English from the University of California, Riverside in June 2021. She currently works with Board.org building communities for

CONTRIBUTORS 271

people leading change at the world's largest companies. Through this effort, she begins to explore what impact "publicly engaged scholars" might have on nonacademic professional spaces. She also continues to research intersections between time, embodiment, and politics of difference in early modern England and today. Her publications include "Temporo-Corporeal Politics in Shakespeare's *Henry V* and Other Monster Texts" in *Shakespeare* and "History, Politics, and Spatial Ambiguity in Richard Mulcaster's *The Queen's Majesty's Passage* and Christopher Marlowe's *Edward II*" in *JMMLA*. She has articles in progress on timekeeping in *A Midsummer Night's Dream* and Thomas Middleton's *The Roaring Girl* and is in the early stages of developing a popular press book on troubling relationships to time in Shakespeare's England and today.

Victoria N. Shiver is assistant professor in the Department of Health, Exercise, and Sport Sciences at the University of New Mexico. Her work focuses on out-of-school-time programming with a predominant focus on the development of personal and social responsibility. In tandem, she conducts research on physical education teacher education with a focus on enhanced training in best practice teaching models and culturally responsive pedagogy.

Daniela M. Susnara is the director of planning and assessment for community engagement in the Division of Community Affairs at The University of Alabama in Tuscaloosa, Alabama. She works with students, faculty, and staff across campus to promote community engagement. Her research focuses on out-of-school-time program effectiveness and integrating community engagement within the kinesiology discipline.

Index

Boxes, figures, notes, and tables are indicated by b, f, n, and t following the page numbers.

Abbott, Annie, 251
accommodations: in education-oriented nonprofits, 175; escapism and, 162; flexibility and redundancy as tenets of, 164; students needing during pandemic, 161; in teaching, 163–64; working academic parents in need of, 16
Achebe, Chinua: *Things Fall Apart*, 230
action research, 136–37, 137*t*
Active Minds (mental health nonprofit), 160, 161
actor network theory (ANT), 135–36
Adikema, Obuchi, 180, 186*f*
Adorno, Theodor, 227, 235
Afro-Latinx marginalization, 107
Afghan refugees, 86n30
Ahtone, Tristan, 81
Alex, Jerry, 197
Alma Migrante (legal advocacy group), 206
Al Otro Lado (legal services organization), 212
Al-Youbi, Abdulrahman O: *Perspectives on Higher Education: Impact of the COVID-19 Pandemic* (ed.), 5
Ameh, Elaigwu, 7–8, 179
American Association of Teachers of German, 80
American Psychological Association, 19
American West, mythology of, 97
Anglo-Saxon political traditions, 40
ANT (actor network theory), 135–36
Anthony, Troy: *Passing Notes*, 236
anti-Asian racism, 6–7, 59–73; Asian American as term of exclusion, 60–61; Asian American literature and, 69; Asian and Asian American representation in film and television, 63–64, 65; community engagement and, 63, 66–67, 69; future trends post-pandemic, 70–71; hate crimes and incidents, 59–60, 63, 64, 66, 70; identity-building work and, 63–67; "model minority" stereotype, 64–65, 67, 71n13; oppression and, 62, 77; Orientalism in Western discourse, 7, 60–61, 63, 70;

pandemic effect on, 59–60; perpetual foreigner image of Asian Americans, 64, 67; publicly engaged academic work and, 59, 62–63, 66–67, 69, 70; racialization of virus and, 59, 61–62; teaching experiences during pandemic, 67–70; white supremacy and, 64, 70, 71
anti-Critical Race Theory state legislation, 109
Anzaldúa, Gloria, 95–97, 103, 105
Aoki, Richard, 61
Army National Guard, 256
Arroyo, Ana María, 209; *Uniendo a través del corazón lo que la deportación separó [Uniting through the Heart That Deportation Separate]*, 209–10
Asian American Political Alliance, 61
Asian Americans. *See* anti-Asian racism
Asian American Studies programs, 60
asynchronous social media: Motherscholar Collective using, 28; as traditional live performance alternative, 194–95
asynchronous virtual learning: benefits of, 164; civic humanist (CH) program and, 66, 166–70*b*, 166*f*; digital pen pal exchange and, 94, 100–101, 104–6, 111; Latinx civic engagement course, challenges for, 256; Swim to the Top and STEM Entrepreneurship Academy and, 121, 127
Atlanta spa shooting of Asian women (2021), 60, 62, 64, 71n12
Australia: high school drop out rate in, 131; lockdown in, 75, 134, 146; return to in-person teaching in, 85; teaching in, from US during pandemic, 83–84. *See also* Australian Pathways programs
Australian National University, 75
Australian Pathways programs, 8, 131–51; 2019 crises and, 133–34; actor network theory and action research, 135–37; certificate course design process, 137–43; certificate of higher education (CHE), 135, 138, 145–46; challenges faced by, 133–34; communitas (concept) and, 140; critical

274 **INDEX**

Australian Pathways programs (*continued*)
resilience pedagogy, 143–45, 147; digital
environment learning and, 138; diploma of
higher education (DHE), launch of, 133;
diversity and, 133; higher education relief
package, 134–37, 146; inclusive pedagogies
and, 133, 143–45, 147; integrated curriculum alignment framework (ICAF) of,
138–40, 144; intentional curriculum design
and, 133, 135, 137; international comparison
to, 132; intersubject knowledge transfer
and, 144–45; learning outcomes, 133, 145;
lessons learned and future trends, 145–47;
liminal stage, 140, 141*t*, 143; novice stage,
140, 141*t*, 142; peer communities in online
classrooms, 143, 147; political factors
impacting, 133–36, 146; post-liminal stage,
140, 141*t*, 143; pre-liminal stage, 140, 141*t*,
142; purpose of, 131–34; regional economic
growth and, 133; resilience strategies and,
138–40, 141*t*, 143, 145, 147; student dislike
of online learning, 146; student role in
course design and, 143; supportive nature
of, 133, 144; team planning and meetings,
139; technological factors impacting,
135–36; Torbet's action research framework, 136–37, 137*t*; Torbet's dimensions of
practice model, 139; transition phases of
students in higher education, 140–43, 141*t*,
145; virtual implementation, transition to,
135–36; whole-of-course approach of, 145
auto-ethnography, 236
Azim, Katharina A., 15

Bad Hombres (film), 206
Baraitser, Lisa, 1
Barney, Katelyn, 76
Barreras, Ricardo E., 27
Batiste, Stephanie Leigh, 180
Battiste, Marie, 77–78
Baynton, Douglas C.: "Disability and the
Justification of Inequality in American
History" (essay), 163
Beauty and the Beast (Disney). *See* civic
humanist program
Bell, Lynne, 77–78
belonging, sense of, 162, 174, 227, 255. *See also*
community engagement
Bender, Stacey H., 15
Benjamin Barnes YMCA (West Tuscaloosa,
Alabama), 120. *See also* Swim to the Top
and STEM Entrepreneurship Academy
Beowulf, relevance during pandemic, 40

Berger, Nicholas, 230, 233
Berlant, Lauren, 55n19
Berlin Conference (1884), 86n14
Bismarck, Otto von, 85–86n14
Black, Asian, and minority ethnic (BAME)
perspectives on exclusion, 77
Black, Indigenous, and People of Color
(BIPOC) in academia: Black female
scholars, 17, 22; collaboration between
Black and Latina women, 107; glass cliff
phenomenon and, 65; Grinnell College's
theater arts and, 180. *See also* racism;
specific racial and ethnic groups
Blackboard (educational software), 68
Black Death (1300s), 4
Black Lives Matter, 7–8, 44, 100, 108–9,
179–201. *See also* Grinnell College, *Project
X*
Blacks: Black women in academia, 17;
collaboration between Black and Latina
women in academia, 107; contribution of
Black women to their family and community, 192–93; disproportionate impact of
pandemic on, 185–86, 198, 261; medical
community distrusted by, 182; prayers for
Black ancestors, 193–94; *Project X* meant to
construct Black family life and identity of
blackness, 185–94; "the talk" between Black
parents and teenagers, 186–89. *See also*
Grinnell College, *Project X*; racism
Blackwell, Maylei: *Chicana Movidas: New
Narratives of Activism and Feminism in the
Movement Era* (ed.), 95–96, 102, 106, 108,
110
Blanks Jones, Jasmine L., 15
blended learning: Australian Pathways
programs and, 138; Swim to the Top and,
122
Bonifacio, Ayendy, 263–64
Booker, Christopher, 165
Border Line Crisis Center, 206
borders and borderlands: identities shaped by,
98–99; literature courses, 93–94, 100;
shared experiences of loss of homes across,
239; theory, 103; US-Mexico border, 7, 9,
98–100, 105–6, 217. *See also* Chicana
pedagogy for digital pen pals
boredom, 44–45, 56n30
Bowen, Lauren, 162, 174
Bowman, Nicholas, 246
Boyer, Ernest L., 122–23
Breath of Fire Latina Theater Ensemble, 2
Brooklyn Center, Minnesota, 256

INDEX 275

Brown, Rennette, 160
Bruni, Frank, 3–4
BTS (K-pop group), 63–64
Burch, Emma, 160
Butler, Judith: "The Future of Humanities PhDs," 5

California: reopenings in 2020, 44; stay-at-home order (July 2020), 43
Cambio de plan: realizando los sueños en México [Change of Plan: Making Dreams Come True in Mexico], 211, 213
Campbell-Obaid, Maggie, 15
campus support services for students stressed by COVID-related events, 104
Cantú, Norma E., 95
capitalism, 4, 45, 61, 164, 184
Carpenter, Faedra Chatard: *Coloring Whiteness: Acts of Critique in Black Performance*, 189
Casares, Oscar, 97
Castañeda, Mari, 244
Castellanos, Rosario: "*La única actitud lícita de la feminidad es la espera*," 4
Castillo, Ana, 97
Castillo, Debra A., 1, 95
Castillo Planas, Melissa, 1, 261
Catanese, Brandi W.: *The Problem of the Color[blind]: Racial Transgression and the Politics of Black Performance*, 189
Center for the Study of Hate and Extremism, 60
Centers for Disease Control and Prevention (CDC), 87n48, 207, 261
CFE. *See* Chicana feminist epistemology
The Chair (TV show), 65
Chakraborty, Debaroti, 9, 223
Chang, Heewon, 236
Chauvin trial. *See* Floyd, George, murder of
Chicana feminist epistemology (CFE): activism and activists, 95–96, 102, 107, 108; memory *movidas* and, 110, 111
Chicana/o Studies, 244
Chicana pedagogy for digital pen pals, 7, 93–118; benefits of pen pal pedagogy, 94–95; community engagement and, 93, 97, 111–12, 115; countering right wing rhetoric on border, 99–100, 105; digital pen pal methodology, 99–101; digital spaces and, 96, 102, 103, 110; e-mail etiquette, 100–101; empathy of ethnically diverse digital pen pals, 99, 103, 105; ethnic diversity of pen-pal partners, 99–100, 106–8; goals of, 96, 99;

hallway *movidas* and, 102–6, 111; icebreaker e-mail, 104–5; institutional geographies and demographics, 98–99; learning outcomes, 101; lessons learned and future action, 113–15; pandemic disruption to planned teaching, 93–94; resilience and, 100, 101, 110; resistance of white students, 114; small talk in, 102–3; socialized learning and, 103, 104–5; social politics and, 97–98; solidarity formed among students, 102, 104; storytelling and, 97, 110; *testimonios* (testimonies) and, 95, 96, 110–13; Voces of a Pandemic Oral History Project (2020), 97, 101, 111–13. *See also* Chicana feminist epistemology; *movidas*
Chinese Exclusion Act (1882), 61
Cisneros, Sandra, 97
City University of New York (CUNY). *See* Lehman College
civic engagement in Latinx Studies course. *See* Latinx Studies course, civic engagement's challenges for
civic humanist (CH) program (Rice University), 8, 152–78; accommodation in teaching, 163–64, 174; The Art of Artifice (Western art module), 155–56, 170–72, 172–74*b*, 174; background and mission of, 154–57; communities of practice model in, 162, 170–72, 174, 175; creativity and play in, 161–62, 167, 174, 175; disabilities studies and, 8, 153; Disney's *Beauty and the Beast* (1991 & 2017 versions), used in comparative analysis module, 165–68, 166–70*b*, 166*f*, 174; enrollment demographics, 157–59, 158–59*f*; future action, 153, 175–76; high school visits, 154–56*b*; honoring living histories, 153, 157–62; multimodal instruction using asynchronous and synchronous sessions, 165–66, 166–70*b*, 166*f*; nonevaluative learning experiences, 8, 153, 161–62; *ōtium*, use of term, 8, 153, 156, 161, 165, 174, 175; pandemic disruption and, 152, 156–57; pedagogy of escapism, 8, 152–53, 161–62, 165, 176; publicly engaged scholars and scholarship and, 152–54; revising format and content of interactive lectures, 172–74*b*; sense of belonging and shared purpose and, 162, 174; storytelling and, 157; successful thinking and, 162, 170; teaching escapism and practicing universally designed learning (UDL), 153, 165–74
class divides: in India, 231; mothers of color in academia and, 17

276 **INDEX**

Clifford, Joan, 258
climate change, 2, 5, 30, 54n5, 87n47
Coalition of Women in German, 74–75
Cohen, Robin, 87n45
collaboration and partnerships: migrant research and, 208; Motherscholar Collective and, 21, 23, 24, 28–31; Swim to the Top and STEM Entrepreneurship Academy and, 122–23. *See also* Chicana pedagogy for digital pen pals; Latinx Studies course, civic engagement's challenges for
Collaborative Online International Learning, 95
colonization, 7, 85; academia and, 74–76; anti-Asian racism and, 62; decolonization and, 76–78; decolonizing curricula and, 77; German, 80–82, 85–86n14; land-grant universities and, 81. *See also* decolonization; settler colonialism
Comida Calientita project, 214, 216
community engagement: anti-Asian racism and, 63, 66–67; Chicana pedagogy for digital pen pals and, 93, 97, 111–12, 115; civic humanist (CH) program and, 175; ethno-mimesis and, 227, 233, 235; Minneapolis Latinx community, 244–58; Motherscholar Collective and, 26–27; pandemic increasing need for, 5, 7–9; sense of place and, 255; Swim to the Top and STEM Entrepreneurship Academy and, 120, 129; Tijuana migration research and, 206–8; Turner's concept of "communitas," 140; virtual, 128–29. *See also* India, connectedness across public and digital spaces in; Latinx Studies course, civic engagement's challenges for; migration research in Tijuana
Cook, Nina, 153, 157, 162, 165–70, 172, 174
Cooper, Christian, 190
Cooper, James Fenimore: *Leatherstocking Tales*, 81
Corpi, Lucha, 97
corridos (Mexican folk ballads), 97
Cotera, María E.: *Chicana Movidas: New Narratives of Activism and Feminism in the Movement Era* (ed.), 95–96, 102, 106, 108, 110
Cotera, Martha, 95
COVID-19 pandemic: anti-Asian racist terms used for, 59, 61–62; boredom during, 44–45, 56n30; break-out day from monotony during, 45; convergence with racial pandemic, 180, 183, 190, 257; disproportionate impact on marginalized and vulnerable groups, 85, 157, 185–86, 198, 250–51, 261,

263–64; economic impact of, 94, 134–35, 157, 224–25, 248, 251, 262; higher education business models and, 114, 147; Latinx communities, impact on, 97, 112, 243–47, 250–51, 261–63; morbidity and mortality statistics, 2, 85, 104, 185, 261; New York City as epicenter (2020), 261; personal experiences during, 1–2; politicization of, 185; public health challenges during, 7, 85, 95, 101, 104, 185, 214, 230; socioeconomic strains due to, 132, 185; vaccines/vaccination, 2, 43, 69, 84, 101, 182, 207, 213, 230; WHO declaration of global pandemic, 64. *See also* lockdown; pandemic disruption; temporality
Craig, Geoffrey, 56n33
creativity: in civic humanist (CH) program, 161–62, 167, 174, 175; as common trait of authors, 10; of Grinnell production of *Project X*, 184, 197; in Indian performing arts teaching, 227, 229, 235, 238
Cress, Christine, 245
Criser, Regine, 79
Critical Race Theory, 41–42, 54n3, 106, 109
critical resilience pedagogy in Australian Pathways programs, 143–45, 147
critical thinking, 7, 85, 86, 101, 152, 161–62, 165–66, 175
Cruz, Ted, 40, 52
cultural pluralism, 68, 70. *See also* diversity; interracial/intercultural connections
CUNY. *See* Lehman College
Cuomo, Andrew, 261

Damian Martin, Diana, 17
Daniels, De'Anna, 153, 154–56, 157, 162, 165, 172, 174
Dasgupta, Pushan, 237
Davis, Malcolm, 180–82, 181*f*, 184
Davis, Matt, 162, 174
Decameron Project, 2
decolonization, 7, 75; anti-Asian racism and, 62, 75; defined by context, 76–78, 83; German studies curriculum and, 76, 78–81, 83, 85; immigration and, 79; Indigenous peoples and, 78; metaphorization of, 76–77; migration and, 208n12; university curricula and, 77
Delgado Bernal, Dolores, 95
Del Monte Madrigal, Juan Antonio, 9, 205
deportation from United States during pandemic, 206–7. *See also* migration research in Tijuana
depression, 5, 185

INDEX 277

Derrida, Jacques, 55n16
Devine-Wright, Patrick, 255
Dibble, Sandra, 210
Die Unterrichtspraxis/Teaching German (journal) special issue on diversity, 78–79
digital divide: acquisition of digital technology and learning how to use it, 197; college students without access to internet or suitable technology, 68–69, 225, 262; foreign-born and, 251; rapid transition into digital without fully understanding impact, 230; scholars' collaboration and research, effect of, 27
digital pen pals, 7, 93–118. *See also* Chicana pedagogy for digital pen pals
Digital Resource Center (Macalester College), 254
disabilities. *See* persons with disabilities
disability studies, 8, 39, 153, 163
disadvantaged students. *See* marginalized groups
distance learning. *See* asynchronous virtual learning; virtual classrooms
diversity: in Australian Pathways programs, 133; in Chicana pedagogy for digital pen pals, 99–100, 106–8; decolonization and, 75; German studies and, 78–79; of Houston metropolitan area, 159–60; in Mother-scholar Collective, 18; of protesters against Citizenship Amendment Act in India, 225–29. *See also* inclusion; marginalized groups; persons with disabilities; *specific ethnic and racial groups*
Dragon Lady trope, 64
Dreamers Moms International, 206
Duarte, Rebecca, 245
Dubai brainstorming session (2021), 3, 4
Dunbar, Robin, 223
Durón, Marcia Yadira, 210

Eatman, Timothy K., 28, 66
e-commerce, 4
Edwards, Caroline, 40
Eilert, Meike, 15
El Colegio (Minneapolis bilingual/bicultural high school), 253–54, 257
El Colegio de la Frontera Norte (Tijuana), 209, 213, 217–18
Ellis, Jerome: *Passing Notes*, 236
Ellison, Julie, 66
e-mail pen pals, 7, 93–118. *See also* Chicana pedagogy for digital pen pals
empathy: civic humanist (CH) program and, 160; community-engaged learning and

scholarship and, 243–44; ethnically diverse digital pen pals and, 99, 103, 105; memesis and, 227; Motherscholar Collective and, 18, 24
engaged scholarship. *See* publicly engaged scholars and scholarship
equity. *See* gender inequalities; inclusion; marginalized groups; *specific racial and ethnic groups*
escapism, pedagogy of, 8, 152–78. *See also* civic humanist program
Espinoza, Dionne: *Chicana Movidas: New Narratives of Activism and Feminism in the Movement Era* (ed.), 95–96, 102, 106, 108, 110
ethnography: auto-ethnography, 236; ethno-mimesis, 226–27, 233, 235. *See also* India, connectedness across public and digital spaces in; migration research in Tijuana
Eurocentricism, 76–78, 82, 97, 171. *See also* decolonization; racism; white supremacy and privilege
Excel-based tool, 140

Facebook, Motherscholar Collective's use of, 19–21, 25, 27
false narratives, 54n9
Farrar, S. Benjamin, 184
fascism, 54n9
Feldshuh, David: *Miss Evers' Boys* (play), 182
Fellner, Karlee, 77
feminism: Coalition of Women in German, 74–75; comparative analysis of Disney's *Beauty and the Beast* (1991 & 2017 versions) and, 167; Motherscholar Collective and, 21–22, 23. *See also* Chicana feminist epistemology; radical feminist flexibility
Finch, Charles, 2
Findlay, L. M., 77–78
flexibility: as common trait of authors, 9; failure to complete research project despite, 252; Grinnell course design and, 183–84; learning benefits of, in teaching, 69, 164; motherscholars and, 18, 24, 29, 250; radical feminist flexibility, 6, 17, 18, 22, 24, 25, 27, 30–31; student need for, 69, 161; technological, 184
FlipGrid, 121, 257
flipped classroom, 167
Flores, Francisca, 95
Floyd, George, murder of, 38, 44, 100, 106, 110, 248, 253, 255, 256

278 INDEX

food delivery to homeless migrants, 213–17
formal discipline as teaching method, 164–65
Framework for Community Engagement, 123
Freire, Paulo, 145; *Pedagogy of the Oppressed*, 5
Funaki, Hine, 82

Gaddis, Xonzy, 180
Galán, Jesús, 210
Gallagher, Maureen O., 7, 74
Galloway, Scott: *Post Corona*, 4
Gardiner, Michael, 56n33
Gaspar de Alba, Alicia, 97
Gazi, Sanaullah, 227
Gaztambide-Fernández, Rubén A., 81
Gee, Emma, 61
gender inequalities: comparative analysis of
  Disney's *Beauty and the Beast* (1991 & 2017
  versions) showing, 168; female academics
  with young children facing, 4, 15–18, 20, 28,
  30; glass cliff phenomenon, 65. *See also*
  Motherscholar Collective
genocide in German colonies, 86n14
German Academic Exchange Service, 80
German-American Fulbright Commission, 82
German Embassy funding to academia, 80
Germanistik (German literary studies), 79
German studies, 7; author's pandemic
  experiences and, 74–76, 82–85; Coalition of
  Women in German, 74–75; decolonization
  of curriculum and, 76, 78–81, 83, 85;
  definition of "decolonization," 76–78;
  diversity and, 78–79; funded through
  colonial wealth accumulation, 80–81;
  immigration stories and, 79; lessons
  learned, 84–85; nationalism and, 79–80;
  racism and, 77–79, 82; settler colonial
  studies and, 78–83; visiting academic
  positions in, 80; as whitest modern
  language discipline in US, 78. *See also*
  settler colonialism
German Studies Association, 82
Germany: colonial history of, 80–82,
  85–86n14; foreign policy on cultural
  activities, 80–81; US relationship with, 82
Gesturing Towards Decolonial Futures
  (collective), 84
Goethe Institute, 80, 86n30
Gómez, Yunuen, 210–11
Goodlad, Lauren, 56n27
Google Meet, 1
Google Sites, 121–22
Gosar, Paul, 40
GoToMeeting, 1

Greene, Marjorie Taylor, 40, 52
Greene-Rooks, Jennifer H., 15
Greenwood, Davydd, 136
grief, lessons learned from, 261–65
Griffin, Elijah, 180, 191*f*
Grinnell College, *Project X*, 7–8, 179–201;
  all-Black cast, director, and playwright
  involved in, 180–81, 184; analysis of process,
  194–97; audience participation and critical
  self-reflection, 182; challenges of virtual
  rehearsals and performances, 184–85,
  194–97; converging health and racial
  pandemics, 180, 183, 186, 196, 199;
  enrollment issues, 183–84; examples of
  choreopoems from, 186–94, 186*f*, 191*f*; "The
  Inconvenient Talk" (performance), 186,
  187–89; lessons learned, 195, 197–99;
  "911-Happy Karen" (performance), 186,
  189–92, 191*f*; publicly engaged scholars and
  scholarship and, 180–83; "The Riddle Game:
  Black History Lesson" (performance), 186;
  "Ritual Benediction" (performance), 186,
  193–94, 193*f*, 195; "Shake It Off" (performance), 186; social justice and, 180, 182–84;
  solidarity and collective sense of purpose of,
  185–86, 196; "Strength of Silence" (performance), 186; white supremacy and privilege,
  179–80, 186, 190; Williams murder (2020)
  and, 179–80, 182
Grise, Virginia: *blu* (play), 94
Grosz, Elizabeth, 55–56n22

HACER (Hispanic Advocacy and Community
  Engagement Research), 247–49, 251–54
Haley, Shelley, 54n11
Hannon, John, 136
Häntzschel, Jörg, 80
Harris, Anne, 179
Hass, Kristin Ann: *Being Human during
  COVID*, 4–5
hate crimes and incidents: anti-Asian, 59–60,
  63, 66, 70; anti-Black, 179–80, 198
Heller, N. A., 15
Hernández, Esther, 95
Hernandez-Avila, Ines, 95
Hershfeld, Hal, 56n23
Hesse-Biber, Sharlene Nagy, 21
Hiawatha Academies (Minneapolis charter
  schools), 244–47
Hindus, 227, 229
Hispanic Advocacy and Community Engage-
  ment Research (HACER), 247–49, 251–54
Hispanic-serving institution (HSI), 7, 93, 98

INDEX

Ho, Helen K., 15
Hodges, Barry, 131
Hollywood Foreign Press Association, 64
Holtz, Bree, 19
homelessness: in India, 224; in New York City, 262; students, 134; in Tijuana, 212–14, 216–17
Hong, Cathy Park, 65–66
hooks, bell, 54n13
Houlden, Shandell, 24
Houston Independent School District (HISD), 153, 157–62, 159*f*; inequities within, 159–60; racial composition of, 157–59, 158–59*f*; teaching frustrations during pandemic, 160–61. *See also* civic humanist program
how-to books, 5
HSI (Hispanic-serving institution), 7, 93, 98
Hubbard, Phil, 227
Huen, Floyd, 61
Hughes, Bethany, 180
humanities: higher education in, 5, 152–54, 156; scholarship in, relevance during pandemic, 40
Humanizing Deportation/Humanizando la Deportación, 9, 206, 209–13, 215–17. *See also* migration research in Tijuana
human rights: of Indigenous peoples, 76; promotion for migrants in Tijuana, 217
Hurtado, Aida, 95
hybrid learning, 95, 100, 101

ICAF (integrated curriculum alignment framework), 138–40, 144
Ichioka, Victor, 61
Ichioka, Yuji, 61
Iizuka, Naomi: *Anon(ymous)* (play), 238–39, 240*f*
Imagining America's Tenure Team Initiative Report (2008), 66
immigration and immigrants: Afghan refugees, 86n30; German studies and, 79, 82; German visa regimes, 86n30; Latinx civic engagement course and, 245; migrant workers in India, 238; US-Mexico border, non-Hispanic immigrant understanding of, 98. *See also* migration research in Tijuana
Immigration History Research Center, 62
inclusion: civic humanist (CH) program for high school students, 169–70, 171, 174; crisis compelling, 70; Motherscholar Collective and, 18, 19, 23, 25, 29; through critical resilience pedagogy (Australian Pathways programs),

133, 143–45, 147. *See also* diversity; interracial/intercultural connections
India, connectedness across public and digital spaces in, 9, 223–42; absence-presence understood through pedagogical praxis, 233–41; art-making and "presence," 232; auto-ethnography and, 236; collaborative performance walk through city, 225–27; cross-cultural collaboration in virtual performance of Iizuka's *Anon(ymous)*, 238–39, 240*f*; democracy's requirements to flourish and, 231–32; discontent with government's handling of pandemic, 230, 231*f*; ethno-mimesis and, 226–27, 233, 235; human touch, power of, 224, 239, 241; inter-cultural explorations through senses, objects, and memories, 239; interiority's relationship to historical events, 232–35; lockdown, effect of, 223–25, 229–34, 238; loss of community public spaces, 229–30; mourning of losses during pandemic, 233, 236, 238, 241; pandemic impact, 223–25; *Performing Connectedness* digital performance series, 237–38; *Postcards from the City—My Home?* (performance), 225–29, 226*f*, 233; protesters against Citizenship Amendment Act, 225–29, 229*f*; Radhakrishnan Commission on University Education (1948), 232–33; in Sonagachi, 227–29, 228*f*; spaces of communion and sharing, 230, 233, 235–36; virtual platforms as performative space, 236–39
Indigenous peoples, 7; land acknowledgements and, 7, 70, 74–76, 85n3; language displacement of, 82; low high school completion rates in Australia, 131; pandemic impact, 83, 87n48; pitting against other minorities, 70; settler fantasy of, 81–82. *See also* decolonization
influenza epidemic (1918). *See* Spanish flu epidemic
Institute for Foreign Relations (Institut für Auslandsbeziehungen) report, 80
integrated curriculum alignment framework (ICAF), 138–40, 144
interracial/intercultural connections: community building and, 199; with Latinx community in Twin Cities, 244–46; *movidas* of crossing and, 106–10; in performing of Iizuka's *Anon(ymous)* (play) in India, 238–39, 240*f*; in Sonagachi (India), 227, 228*f*; "the talk" between Black parents and teenagers, 186–89

280 **INDEX**

Irwin, Robert McKee, 9, 205
isolation, 2, 3; collective sharing during, 236; of digital pen pal students in Northern Virginia and Rio Grande Valley, 96, 101, 102, 104; high schoolers experiencing during pandemic, 159–60; inability to cope with, 223; media consumption during, 45–46; mental health issues and, 185; performing arts and, 195; research and writing time afforded by, 63; student contact to counter, 69. *See also* lockdown
Issues in Mental Health Nursing, 186

Jain, Anjali, 195
January 6 Capitol insurrection (2021), 40
Jayaratne, Toby E., 22
Jenkins, Fiona, 83
Johnson, Leigh, 7, 93
Journal of Clinical Nursing, 185

Kanu, Doze: *Chair [iii]* (slab design), 170, 171*f*, 173–74
Karen (slang), 189–92
Keele University's definition of "decolonization," 77
Kellar, William Henry, 157, 159*f*
Kern, Margaret L., 139
Key-DeLyria, Sarah, 15
Kim, Joey S., 6–7, 59
King, Hayden, 74–75
Knott, Suzuko, 79
K-pop bands, 63–64
Kuokkanen, Rauna, 84

land acknowledgments, 7, 74–76, 85n3
Land-Grant College Act (Morill Act, 1862), 81
Langley, Nadia, 182
language courses: enrollments in US higher educational institutions, 81, 82, 87n34; Latinx civic engagement course and Spanish language use, 246. *See also* German studies
Lapayese, Yvette V., 18
Latina/o Studies, 244
Latinx: Afro-Latinx marginalization, 107; disproportionate effect of pandemic on, 97, 112, 243–47, 250–51, 261, 263–64; East Lake Street and oral history project, 247–49, 251, 253–55. *See also* Minneapolis
Latinx Studies course, civic engagement's challenges for, 9, 243–60; benefits of course participation to Latinx students, 245; challenges of oral history project inter-

views, 251–53; community engagement and course design, 244–45; Daunte Wright murder and protests, 255–56; Derek Chauvin, trial of, 255, 256; East Lake Street and oral history project, 247–49, 251, 253–55; El Colegio (Minneapolis bilingual/ bicultural high school), as partner, 253–54, 257; established relationships, building on, 253–56, 258; forging brand-new partnerships, 247–53; George Floyd murder and protests, impact of, 248, 253; Hiawatha Academies (Minneapolis charter schools), as partner, 244–47; Hispanic Advocacy and Community Engagement Research (HACER), as partner, 247–49, 251–54; indirect service projects, limitations of, 254–55; Introduction to US Latinx Studies course, 243, 249; Lake Street Council and, 253–54, 256, 258; Latinx in the Midwest course, 247, 249, 250, 257; lessons learned and future action, 257–58; pivoting in response to pandemic, 243–47, 251, 253, 256, 257; prepandemic model of collaboration, 244–47; reciprocal learning, 246, 257; solidarity in service-learning, 258; story map project and, 253–57, 259n18; student preceptor role, 245; students balancing school, work, and civic engagement projects, 245
Latour, Bruno, 4, 136
Lear, Darcy, 251
Lee, Christina Yuna, 60
Lee, Erica, 62
Lee, Robert, 81
Lehman College (CUNY), pandemic lessons in grief, 261–65; Black and Latinx communities in the Bronx, 262, 264; essential workers and businesses during pandemic, 262–64; Hispanic Heritage Month, 263; "new normal" and, 264; New York City as US epicenter of pandemic, 261–62; *Obscura* (literary and arts magazine) publishing "Poetry in the Times of COVID-19," 263–64; poetry written during pandemic, 262–65
Levin, Morten, 136
Levine, Robert, 55n20
Lewis, F. C.: "A Study in the Formal Discipline" (essay), 164
LGBTQ+ persons in Motherscholar Collective, 18
Lim, Stacey, 15
liminality, 140

INDEX   281

Linares, Juan, 254–55
literature: *Beowulf*, relevance during pandemic, 40; English literature taught in Australia by Asian woman in United States, 68–70; literary theory, teaching to high school students, 169; Mexican American/Borderlands literature courses, 7, 93–94; Shakespearean scholarship, relevance during pandemic, 40–41, 52–53, 54n11, 55n21. *See also* scholarship's relevance and life of the scholar during pandemic
Lizzio, Alf, 139
lockdown, 1, 4; in Australia, 75, 134, 146; California stay-at-home order (July 2020), 43; Chicana pedagogy, changes due to, 94; German studies and, 83; in India, 223–25, 229–34, 238; mental health issues and, 185; motherscholars in, 21; in New York City, 261; repetition and monotony of, 44–45, 50, 56n30; in Tijuana, 208. *See also* losses; pivoting in response to pandemic; remote teaching/learning and scholarship; virtual classrooms
Longo, Nicholas, 244
Lorde, Audre, 54n11
losses: of celebration of book publication, 263; of college students, 264; of community public spaces, 229–30; of human touch, 224, 239, 241; K–12 learning loss, 129, 246–47; mourning of, during pandemic, 9, 233, 236, 238, 241, 250; need to pivot to compensate for, 243; opportunity to begin again from, 265; performing arts and, 231–33; of research time during pandemic, 16–17, 20, 263; of safe social interaction, 44; of significance of time's passage, 39, 43–44, 46–50, 49f, 56n23, 250
Low, Katharine, 17
Lowe, Annie, 153, 154–56, 157, 162, 164, 170–72, 174, 176n2
low-income students. *See* poor and low-income students

Macalester College (St. Paul): Civic Engagement Center, 244, 253, 256. *See also* Latinx Studies course, civic engagement's challenges for
MacDonald, Liana, 82
Mackinlay, Elizabeth, 76
Madrigal, Mauro, 248
Maloret, Thierry (with Klaus Schwab): *The Great Narrative*, 3, 4; *The Great Reset*, 4
manifest destiny, 97

Manthripragada, Ashwin, 79–81, 82
Marchevsky, Alejandra: "Forging a Brown-Black Movement," 107
marginalized groups: Afro-Latinx as, 107; civic humanist (CH) program for high school students, 169–70, 171, 174; disproportionate impact of pandemic on, 85, 157, 185–86, 198, 250–51, 261, 263–64; formal discipline as learning method and, 164; in Houston Independent School District, 157; K–12 students of underrepresented communities, 120–30; lessons learned to pay attention to, 264; migrants as, 205; Motherscholar Collective and, 26–29; students of color and of low-income households, 104, 225, 261–62, 264. *See also* accommodations; anti-Asian racism; Grinnell College, *Project X*; Lehman College, pandemic lessons in grief; migration research in Tijuana; persons with disabilities; racism; Swim to the Top and STEM Entrepreneurship Academy; *specific ethnic and racial groups*
Mariscal, Jocelín, 210
Martin, Trayvon, 189
Martinez, Rafiana: "Self Portrait During Covid" (poem), 264–65
Marymount University. *See* Chicana pedagogy for digital pen pals
masks and masking, 5, 46, 47, 69, 225
Massey, Sean G., 27
massive open online courses (MOOCs), 132
Matias, Cheryl, 18
Maton, Karl, 145
Mawhinney, Janet, 75
May, Karl: *Winnetou*, 81
McAdams, Alexander Lowe, 8, 152
McKenzie, Jon: *Perform or Else: From Discipline to Performance*, 235–36
medical community, Black community's distrust of, 182
memesis, 227
mental health issues: within Black community, 185–86; of deported migrants, 214; of students and faculty, 160, 195
Mercado Central, 248, 254
Merleau-Ponty, Maurice, 71
Mexican American/Borderlands literature courses, 7, 93–94. *See also* Chicana pedagogy for digital pen pals
microaggressions, 101
Microsoft Teams, 138–39, 165, 184, 197
Migrant Protection Protocols program, 206

282   **INDEX**

migration research in Tijuana, 9, 205–22; academic extractivism and, 214; advocacy and action proposed by, 217; autonomy of migration and, 208, 218; *Cambio de plan: realizando los sueños en México [Change of Plan: Making Dreams Come True in Mexico]*, 211, 213; collaborative research design and, 215–17; Comida Calientita (Hot Food) project, 212, 214, 216; community-based agents and, 209–11; community engagement during pandemic, 206–8, 213–15, 217–18; community organization involvement and, 216; data collection affected by travel restrictions, 212–13, 217; deportation of migrants under 42 U.S.C. § 265, 206–7; *Dos separaciones familiares [Two Family Separations]*, 210, 211, 213; embodied knowledge of migrants and, 208; engaged scholarship and essential research, 208–9, 217–18; face-to-face collaboration method and, 209–10; global engagement, institutional distrust of, 217–18; homeless and food delivery as focus of study, 212–17; Humanizing Deportation/Humanizando la Deportación digital storytelling project, 206, 210, 212, 213, 215–17; lessons learned, 216–17; Ludvin (Guatemalan migrant) story (*Dos separaciones familiares [Two Family Separations]*), 210, 211, 213; migrant population in Tijuana, 206–9; overview, 205–6; pandemic impact on asylum applications and, 206–7; photoelicitation, 215–16; power dynamics of, 212; questionnaires used in, 216; remote digital storytelling and, 209–13; social impact of, 213–17; social messaging media and, 209–11; student-engaged projects and, 206, 213–16, 217–18; *Tijuana tiene muchas oportunidades [Tijuana Has Many Opportunities]*, 211, 213; Ukrainian asylum requests granted (2022), 207; unstable living conditions of migrants and, 215–16

Miller, Toby: *A COVID Charter, A Better World*, 4

mimesis, 227; ethno-mimesis, 226–27, 233, 235

Minari (film), 63–64

Minello, Alessandra, 16

Miner, Kathi N., 22

Mink, Andy, 176n4

Minneapolis: East Lake Street and oral history project, 247–49, 251, 253–55; George Floyd murder and reaction in, 248, 253, 255, 256; Lake Street Council, 253–54, 256, 258; Latinx history and culture in. *See* Latinx Studies course, civic engagement's challenges for

Minnesota Department of Health, 249, 250

Minnesota Historical Society, 247, 249

Mok, Jonathan, 59

MOOCs (massive open online courses), 132

Moody, Lisa, 8, 131

Moody Center for the Arts, 156

Moraga, Cherríe, 110

Morales, Esther, 209–10, 212, 214, 216; *Comida calientita en plena pandemia [Nice Hot Food in the Midst of the Pandemic]*, 212

Morgan, Rhian, 8, 131

Morill Act (Land-Grant College Act, 1862), 81

Motherscholar Collective: academic fields of, 31*t*; challenges for mothers in academia and, 15–17; childcare and, 20, 246; collaboration among members of, 21, 23, 24, 28–31; community engagement and, 26–27; conducting research, pandemic effects on, 26–27; decentralized approach to scholarship and, 23, 25, 28; definition of "motherscholar," 15, 18; diversity of members and fields of study, 18, 22, 30, 31*t*; dual identities of mother and scholar, 18, 20, 27, 29; flexibility, importance of to working mothers, 24–25, 29; founding of, 17, 21–23; future action and, 29–31; interdisciplinary knowledge of, 24; lessons learned, 26–29; loss of research time during pandemic, 16–17, 20; marginalized groups and, 21, 26–29; methodology of the study, 22–23; mission of, 20–21, 23; participatory action research and, 21, 27–28; philosophy of, 18, 23–25, 29; publicly engaged scholarship and, 26–27, 31; radical feminist flexibility and, 6, 17, 18, 22, 24, 25, 27, 30–31; sexism faced by academics with young children, 16, 17, 28, 30; social media community networks and, 19–20, 25, 28; videoconferencing use of, 22, 25

Mouffe, Chantal, 231

movidas: Chicana feminist activism and, 95–96; of crossing, 99, 106–10, 111; definition of, 95–96; hallway, 102–6, 111; of memory, 101, 110–13; pedagogical, 96, 98, 100–101, 108, 111, 114–15; students' feedback and, 100

Mukherjee, Koushani, 237, 240*f*

multiethnic/multiracial collaboration. *See* interracial/intercultural connections

INDEX 283

multitasking, 25, 94, 141, 196
Muñoz, Alicia, 9, 243, 263
Mušanović, Emina, 79–81, 82
Muslims, 225, 229
Myles-Baltzly, Colleen C., 15

Nagra, Daja, 180, 192–93*f*
National Humanities Center, 157
nationalism and German literary studies,
  79–80
National Poetry Month, 262
networks of care, 94, 96, 104
New York Times: Decameron Project in, 2;
  Minneapolis dubbed "Murderapolis" in,
  248
Ngambri people, 75
Ngũgĩ wa Thiong'o, 76
Ngunnawal people, 75
Nguyen, An, 59
Nietzsche, Friedrich, 55n18
nonevaluative learning experiences. *See* civic
  humanist program
Norberg, Jakob, 79
normality, pre-COVID, 3–4; disability studies
  offering insight on how to frame loss of, 163;
  elusiveness of normalcy, 264; longing for
  return to, 44, 45, 247; mourning loss of, 10,
  84; "new normal," 264–65; nostalgia of, 53
Novikov, Yakov: "Le Péril Jaune" (essay), 62

Obscura (Lehman College literary and arts
  magazine), 263–64
Oh, Sandra, 65
O'Neill, Maggie, 227, 233
oppression: academics with young children
  facing, 16; anti-Asian racism and, 62, 77;
  Chicana activism against, 95–96, 106–8,
  110; within higher education, 143–44, 147;
  migrants and, 208; university infrastructures and, 85
Orientalism, 7, 60–61, 63, 70
Ortiz, Ernesto Zarco, 209
the Other: German xenophobia and, 82;
  nontraditional students as, 132; performance
  making us confront, 182; shift in perspective
  from that of, 146; social construction of
  blackness by, 185; students of different races
  and cultures viewing each other as, 106;
  Western creation of the Oriental as, 59–62,
  64–65; xenophobia heightened by pandemic,
  6. *See also* anti-Asian racism; Australian
  Pathways programs; Chicana pedagogy for
  digital pen pals

ōtium, 8, 153, 156, 162, 165, 174–75
Otoo, Sharon Dodua, 79
out-of-school program for children (age 4 to
  14), Swim to the Top as. *See* Swim to the Top
  and STEM Entrepreneurship Academy
Özdamar, Emine Sevgi, 79

pandemic disruption: Australian Pathways
  programs and, 133–34, 139; blurring of
  boundaries and, 20, 83–84, 243; community-
  based youth programs and, 119–20, 124;
  community engaged scholarship and, 205–8,
  216–17, 243–44, 249; English literature
  teaching in Australia by teacher in United
  States and, 68–70, 74; enrollment decline due
  to, 183, 225; at Grinnell College in performing arts curriculum, 180, 197; in Indian
  performing arts curriculum, 225, 231–36;
  Latinx civic engagement course and, 243–47;
  migrant services organizations and, 207; of
  partnership between universities, 93–94, 96,
  100–103; reexamination of daily life and
  work practices due to, 6; relationship to place
  and, 255; scholarly mobility and, 207–8, 213,
  217, 263; those who are able to work at home
  vs. those whose essential work or income
  source requires outside-of-home work, 83,
  87n45, 263–64; Tijuana migrant research
  and, 207–8, 213, 217. *See also* lockdown;
  mental health issues; pivoting in response to
  pandemic; virtual classrooms
Panjabi, Kavita: *Unclaimed Harvest*, 234–35
Parasite (film), 63–64
Paredes, Américo: *George Washington
  Gomez*, 94; "The Hammon and the Beans,"
  101
Paris, Django, 68
Parker-Barnes, Lucy C., 15
Parkins, Wendy, 56n33
Pathways programs. *See* Australian Pathways
  programs
patriarchal educational practices, rethinking
  of, 95, 102
Pennell, Summer Melody, 15
pen pal pedagogy, 94–95. *See also* Chicana
  pedagogy for digital pen pals
performing arts. *See* Grinnell College, *Project
  X*; India, connectedness across public and
  digital spaces in
persons with disabilities: disproportionate
  impact of pandemic on, 85; in Motherscholar Collective, 18, 22; opportunities to
  participate virtually, 231

284 **INDEX**

Petersen, William, 71n13
Peterson, Jacob T., 8, 119
Pew Research Center survey on urban education needs, 157
Pilkington, Ed, 40
pivoting in response to pandemic, 93–94, 100–101, 243–47, 251, 253, 256, 257, 263
pluralism. *See* interracial/intercultural connections
Poff, Kimberly, 44–45
police brutality, 193, 199. *See also* Grinnell College, *Project X*; racism
poor and low-income students: Australian legislation on student loan availability, 134; Australian Pathways programs and, 131; graduate students as, 175; at Lehman College, 261–62, 264; pandemic effect on, 94, 104; in Rio Grande Valley, 99. *See also* digital divide
Portelli, Alessandro: "A Dialogical Relationship: An Approach to Oral History" (essay), 232–33
Post, Margaret, 244
privilege: of brown vs. black students, 109; of colonial settlers, 75; of those who can stay home and isolate, 83, 87n45, 263–64. *See also* white supremacy and privilege
Project X. See Grinnell College, *Project X*
Pruitt, Samory, 122–23, 128
publicly engaged scholars and scholarship, 5–7; academia's opinion of, 218; anti-Asian racism and, 59, 62–63, 66–67, 69, 70; Chicana pedagogy for digital pen pals and, 104, 111; civic humanist (CH) program and, 152–54, 175–76; definition of, 39–40, 66, 208; German studies and, 83–85; Grinnell College, *Project X* and, 180–83; marginalized communities, lessons learned to pay attention to, 264; migration research and, 208–9, 217–18; Motherscholar Collective and, 26–27, 31; Texas public school curriculum and ethnic studies, 109–10; theoretical framework for collaborative university-community program, 122–23, 128; time's passage, understanding of, 52. *See also* Voces of a Pandemic Oral History Project
Puerto Rican Studies, 244
Purvis, Rosalie, 224, 238

quarantine, 8, 67. *See also* isolation; lockdown
queer theory, 53n1

racism: education access impacted by, 131; German studies and, 77–79, 82; glass cliff phenomenon and, 65; Grinnell College's *Project X* and, 185–93, 198–99; higher education aimed at combating, 5, 114; Houston Independent School District (HISD), de facto segregation in, 157–59; in literary works, 94; Mexican American/Borderlands literature courses addressing, 93; mothers of color in academia and, 17, 22; pandemic's convergence with racial pandemic, 180, 183, 190, 257; police brutality and murders of unarmed Black men, 179–80, 193, 199, 255–56; as public health issue, 70, 180; racial profiling, 109; student performances exploring lived experience of, 185–94, 196; systemic, 17, 180, 185–86, 198; "the talk" between Black parents and teenagers, 186–89; Tuskegee syphilis study, 182; white indifference to police brutality, 198–99. *See also* anti-Asian racism; colonization; Critical Race Theory; decolonization; Floyd, George, murder of; Grinnell College, *Project X*; white supremacy and privilege
Radhakrishnan Commission on University Education (1948), 232–33
radical feminist flexibility, 6, 17, 18, 22, 24, 25, 27, 30–31
Ramírez, Carlos Manuel, 211
Raphael's *School of Athens* (fresco), 170–73, 172f
Ratanapakdee, Vicha, 59–60
reciprocity: hospitality as, 84; Latinx civic engagement course and, 244, 246; Motherscholar Collective and, 22, 25; STEM Entrepreneurship Academy and, 122, 125–26; Swim to the Top and, 122, 125
Recovering the US Hispanic Literary Heritage (international program), 97, 112
Reilly, Dennis, 198–99
remote teaching/learning and scholarship: at Australian National University, 75; digital storytelling in migration research, 206, 209–13; Hispanic Heritage Month celebration, 263; Latinx civic engagement course and, 255; of Mexican American/Borderlands literature courses offered in partnership between two universities, 94; prepandemic, 114. *See also* asynchronous virtual learning; virtual classrooms
remote work, 5, 83
resilience, 5, 6; Australian Pathways strategies of, 138–40, 141t, 143, 145, 147; Chicana pedagogy for digital pen pals and, 100, 101, 110; of Indian

women protesters against Citizenship Amendment Act, 229; of Latinx civic engagement professor, 257; lived experience and, 144; neoliberal framing of, 144; *Project X* (Grinnell College) production and, 195; STEM Entrepreneurship Academy and, 122, 123, 127; Swim to the Top and, 122, 123, 126–27

Rice, Tamir, 189

Rice University Humanities Research Center, 152, 176n1. *See also* civic humanist program

Richardson, Ivanna, 15

Rio Grande Valley: borderlands culture and identity of, 98–99, 105–6; chronic illness in, 99; pandemic impact, 101, 104, 112, 115; violent stereotypes promoted by right wing, 99–100, 105

Rivas-Rodriguez, Maggie, 97, 101, 111–12

Rivera, Diana Noreen, 7, 93

Rivera, Schvalla, 179–80

Roy, Arundhati: "The Pandemic Is a Portal" (article), 3–4

Ryerson University (Canada), 74

Said, Edward, 62

Saltmarsh, John, 244

Sandoval, Chela, 96

Sarkar, Ankita, 237

Schaberg, Christopher: *Pedagogy of the Depressed*, 4–5

Schadewald, Paul, 253

scholarship's relevance and life of the scholar during pandemic, 6, 39–58; archivization and, 42, 55n16; *Beowulf* and, 40; blending of living life and thinking life, 39, 42, 53n2; historical subjectivity in referring to past cultural greatness, 40–41, 52–53, 54n5, 55nn17–18; lessons learned, 50–51; mask wearing, 46, *47*; monotony and passage of time, 44–46, 51, 54n14; politicization of virus responses, 51; privileged class, loss of safe social interaction for, 44; reflections for readers to bring their personal experiences into the mix, 42, 43, 46, 50; Shakespeare and, 40–41, 52–53, 54n11, 55n21; timesoup (loss of significance of time's passage) and, 39, 43–44, 46–50, *49f*, 56n23. *See also* publicly engaged scholars and scholarship

Schwab, Klaus (with Thierry Maloret): *The Great Narrative*, 3, 4; *The Great Reset*, 4

Schwartzman, Roy, 144

Scuro, Courtney Naum, 6, 39

secondary school programs: Australian high school drop out rate, 131; civic humanist

(CH) program manger's role in, 152; Latinx Studies course in partnership with, 244–47, 253–54, 257; STEM-based enrichment program, 8, 120–30. *See also* Swim to the Top and STEM Entrepreneurship Academy

self-assessment during pandemic, 39–40, 67

self-understanding during pandemic, 4–5

Seminar (journal) special issue on Indigenous studies and German studies, 79

settler colonialism, 7, 85; academia and, 74, 76, 83–84; decolonization and, 77–81; definition of, 81; immigration and, 79–80; land acknowledgments and, 74–76, 85n3; land-grant universities and, 81; languages displacement of Indigenous peoples, 82; replacement mentality of, 81–82; US higher education and, 81–82. *See also* colonization

settler colonial university. *See* German studies; settler colonialism

Seward, Lucy, 159, 161

sexism. *See* gender inequalities

Shakespearean scholarship, relevance during pandemic, 40–41, 52–53, 54n11, 55n21

Shiver, Victoria N., 8, 119

Slow, Loud, and Bangin' (SLAB) culture, 170, 173

Smith, Avery, 82

Smith, Julie, 83

social distancing, 5; of digital pen pal students in Northern Virginia and Rio Grande Valley, 101; of Houston secondary school students, 160, 162; Indian culture's norm of physical closeness and, 224; Indian infrastructure unable to provide for, 225; new mothers and, 19; social greetings and, 223

social justice, 5, 76–77, 114. *See also* Grinnell College, *Project X*

social networking/messaging media: academic use of, 19; conducting participatory research and, 27; critical resilience pedagogy and, 138; migration research and, 209–11; Motherscholar Collective and, 19–20, 25; for new mothers, 15–16; Swim to the Top and STEM Entrepreneurship Academy and, 130. *See also* Facebook; TikTok; *specific social networking sites*

social politics, digital pen pals and, 97–98

solidarity: after police killings of unarmed Blacks, 185–86, 248; among refugees made "anonymous," 239; among students, 102, 104, 196; in Indian protests against Citizenship Amendment Act, 225; service-learning and, 245, 258

286 **INDEX**

Spanish flu epidemic (1918), 4, 224
Spillers, Hortense, 62
Spry, Tami: "Presence and Privacy: Ode to the Absent Phallus" (performance), 182
standardized testing, negative effects of, 161, 162, 165, 174
stay-at-home orders. *See* lockdown
Stein, Sharon, 81
STEM-based enrichment program for youth. *See* Swim to the Top and STEM Entrepreneurship Academy
stereotyping: anti-Asian rhetoric and, 61, 64–65, 67, 71n6, 71n13; Mexican American culture and, 97–98; model minority stereotype, 64–65, 67, 71n13
Stop AAPI Hate, 60
storytelling: Chicana pedagogy for digital pen pals and, 97, 110; civic humanist (CH) program and, 157; Latinx civic engagement course and, 257; migration research, remote digital storytelling in, 206, 209–13; story mapping, 253–57, 259n18
suffering. *See* oppression
Susnara, Daniela M., 8, 119
Swim to the Top (STTT) and STEM Entrepreneurship Academy (SEA), 8, 120–30; age similarity of participants and counselors, 126; community engagement and, 120, 129; components of, 121–22; digital content creation and, 125, 126–27; engaging students, difficulties with, 127; future action, 130; future research needs, 129; impact on families in community and, 124; in-person programs, transition to, 130; lessons learned, 128; opportunities for students and, 124; professional development of instructors and, 125–26; program design and participants, 123, 130n5, 130n6; reciprocity and, 122, 123, 125–26; relevance of, 122, 123–25, 128–29; research component of, 122, 123, 128; resilience and, 122, 123, 126–27; STEM education and, 120, 122; supportive nature of, 126; synchronous SEA vs. asynchronous STTT approach, 127; technical issues and, 127; technology platforms chosen, 121–22, 130; theoretical framework for community engaged scholarship, 122–23; virtual implementation, transition to, 121–22, 130; water safety focus during pandemic, 121
systemic oppression: mothers in academia and, 20; mothers of color in academia and, 17. *See also* racism *at* systemic

Tawada, Yoko, 79
temporality: awareness of, 56n33; Grosz on, 55–56n22; loss of significance of time's passage, 39, 43–44, 46–50, 49f, 56n23, 250; pandemic as time that defines a generation, 45
testimonios (testimonies), 95, 96, 110–13, 257
Texas Department of Public Safety, 99
Thomas, Angie: *The Hate U Give*, 101, 103, 108–9
Thomas, Sandra P., 185–86
Tiger Mother trope, 64
Tijuana migrant research. *See* migration research in Tijuana
Tijuana tiene muchas oportunidades [Tijuana Has Many Opportunities], 211, 213
TikTok, 107, 121, 126
Title I schools, 160, 176n8
Torbet, William, 136–37, 137t, 139
touch/touching, meaning of, 223–24
Treaty of Versailles (1919), 86n14
Trump, Donald, 2, 40, 107, 207
trust: digital technologies and, 254; of Grinnell student director of *Project X*, 184–85; medical community's need to gain Black community's trust, 182; Mother-scholar Collective and, 24, 25, 29
Tuck, Eve, 75, 76–77, 79, 81
Turner, Victor, 140
Tuscaloosa, Alabama, 119–20; Parks and Recreation Authorities, 120. *See also* Swim to the Top and STEM Entrepreneurship Academy
Tuskegee syphilis study, 182

Ukrainian immigrants, asylum granted to, 207
underserved communities. *See* Australian Pathways programs; marginalized groups; Swim to the Top and STEM Entrepreneurship Academy
United States-Mexico border, 7, 9, 98–100, 105–6, 217
universally designed learning (UDL), 153, 163, 165–66, 166f; as opposite of formal discipline as teaching method, 164. *See also* accommodations
Universidad Autónoma de Baja California, 206
Universidad Iberoamericana (Tijuana), 209, 213, 217–18
University of Alabama: campus, 119, 120; Division of Community Affairs Center for Community-Based Partnerships (CCBP), 120. *See also* Swim to the Top and STEM Entrepreneurship Academy

INDEX 287

University of California ban on research-related travel during pandemic, 213–14, 218
University of Maine, 238
University of Minnesota Extension, 251
University of San Diego, 206
University of Texas Rio Grande Valley (UTRGV). *See* Chicana pedagogy for digital pen pals
US Customs and Border Protection, 207
US Department of Education, Office for Civil Rights, 104

vaccines/vaccination: availability of, 2, 43, 84, 207, 213, 230; eligibility for, 101; for migrant homeless population, 217; misinformation about, 182; shortage of, 230; university requirements for, 69
Valenzuela, Angela, 109
Van Cleave, Thomas, 246, 254
Veletsianos, George, 24
Veyvoda, Michelle, 246, 254
videoconferencing in Australian Pathways programs, 138
Vietnam War protests, 61
Villa, Olga, 95
violence: anti-Asian hate crimes and incidents, 59–60, 63, 64, 66, 70; colonialism and, 81; domestic, 2; escalation during pandemic, 2, 93; in India against student protesters, 225; in Minneapolis, 247–48; police brutality and murders of unarmed Black men, 179–80, 193, 199, 255–56; Rio Grande border and, 99, 105; of settler colonialism, 78. *See also* racism
virtual classrooms: benefits of, 83, 164, 184–85, 198, 231, 234; civic humanist (CH) program and, 152, 165–66, 166–70*b*, 166*f*; community and, 143, 146; failure to train teachers for, 160; first-year college teaching and, 63, 68; hospitality of, 82–84; Houston secondary school students, 160–61; intentional curriculum design and, 135, 146; negative aspects of, 125, 146, 160, 231–32, 234; as performative space of person, 236; relevance of, 124–25; Swim to the Top and STEM Entrepreneurship Academy and, 121–22, 127. *See also* asynchronous virtual learning; India, connectedness across public and digital spaces in; Latinx Studies course, civic engagement's challenges for
virtual mutual-support groups. *See* Motherscholar Collective

Voces of a Pandemic Oral History Project (2020), 97, 101, 111–13. *See also* Chicana pedagogy for digital pen pals
Voces Oral History Center, University of Texas at Austin, 97, 112
vulnerable populations. *See* marginalized groups; *specific racial, ethnic, and other at-risk groups*

Wang Yuen, Nancy, 65
Ward, Elaine, 244
Watson, Emma, 168
Weber, Beverly, 78
Weber, Silja, 79
Webex, 185, 197
Weigel, Sigrid, 80
well-being: of migrants, 205; of motherscholars, 19, 20, 249–50; of students, 103–4, 139, 153, 160, 195, 250
Wenger, Etienne: *Communities of Practice*, 162, 170–72, 174
White, Mathew, 139
white supremacy and privilege: in academia, 65, 114; Anglo-Saxon political traditions invoked to support, 40; Blacks in America and, 179–80, 186, 189–92, 198–99; decolonization and, 77; German textbooks showing, 79; hate crimes and, 64, 71n12, 198–99; identity politics and, 70; manifest destiny and, 97; in *Project X* choreopoem on "Karens," 186, 189–92, 191*f*
Williams, James, 198
Williams, Michael, 179–80, 182, 198–99
Willingham, Daniel T., 162
Wilson, Kieithia, 139
Winkie, Luke, 102–3
Wolfe, Patrick, 81
Womack, Anne-Marie, 162
women: Atlanta spa shooting of Asian women (2021), 60, 62, 64, 71n12; Coalition of Women in German, 74–75; collaboration between Black and Latina women in academia, 107; contribution of Black women to their family and community, 192–93; pandemic's effect on feminine sphere, 4, 15–18; as protesters against India's Citizenship Amendment Act, 227–29, 229*f*. *See also* feminism; gender inequalities; Motherscholar Collective
Wong, Vicci, 61
work/life balance in academia, 20, 27, 83, 246, 250
World Health Organization (WHO), 64
Wright, Daunte, 255
Wuhan, China, 59, 61, 62

288   INDEX

xenophobia. *See* the Other

Yang, K. Wayne, 75, 76–77, 81; *Decolonization: Indigeneity, Education, & Society* (with Tuck), 79
Yellow Peril, 59, 62, 71n1, 71n11. *See also* anti-Asian racism
YES Prep Public Schools, 156
Yeun, Steven, 63–64
YMCA Greater Houston, 175
YMCA summer camp (Tuscaloosa, Alabama), 120. *See also* Swim to the Top and STEM Entrepreneurship Academy

Young, Harvey, 180
YouTube, 195, 197

Zarco Ortiz, Ernesto, 209–11
Zoom: Coalition of Women in German conference (2020), 74; as communication/collaboration tool, 1, 100, 126, 172b, 197, 243, 249, 255, 262; convenience of, 257; digital divide and, 251; as familiar digital platform, 1, 121–22, 127; grief shared over, 236; as research tool, 112, 217; technical issues and, 127

Milton Keynes UK
Ingram Content Group UK Ltd.
UKHW012133160823
426985UK00008B/177